Issues in testing business English

The revision of the Cambridge Business English Certificates

Issues in testing business English

The revision of the Cambridge Business English Certificates

Barry O'Sullivan

CAMBRIDGE
UNIVERSITY PRESS

CAMBRIDGE UNIVERSITY PRESS
Cambridge, New York, Melbourne, Madrid, Cape Town, Singapore, São Paulo

Cambridge University Press
The Edinburgh Building, Cambridge CB2 2RU, UK

www.cambridge.org
Information on this title: www.cambridge.org/9780521013307

First published 2006
Reprinted 2006

Printed in the United Kingdom at the University Press, Cambridge

A catalogue record for this publication is available from the British Library

ISBN-13 978-0-521-01330-7 paperback
ISBN-10 0-521-01330-5 paperback

To Maura

Contents

Contents

Acknowledgements

I would like to thank the many people at Cambridge ESOL who contributed to this volume. I was lucky enough to be able to interview many of the individuals who were involved in the development and administration of their tests of English for business purposes, particularly the BULATS and BEC groups. In particular, I am indebted to Hugh Bateman, without whom the book could not have been completed. Others I would like to single out include Mike Milanovic and Nick Saville, who provided historical information and access to internal reports, and Neil Jones, who provided documentation on the grading procedures for BEC. I would also like to thank David Thighe who clarified a number of grading-related issues, and who made valuable comments on the later drafts of this book. Finally, I would like to thank Rowena Akinyemi for all her work in ensuring that this book made it to press.

I would also like to thank the following individuals and institutions for providing information on their tests and for giving their permission for items from the tests to be included in the book:

Certificazione della conoscenza dell'italiano commerciale (Certificate in Italian for Commerce – CIC): Professor Giuliana Grego Bolli and Francesca Parizzi of the Università per Stranieri di Perugia.
JETRO tests: Professor Kiyokata Katoh of Tokyo Gakugei University and Reiko Kimura of the Japan External Trade Organization.
Pitman tests: Glyn Jones of City and Guilds, London.
Cambridge ESOL tests: Dr Mike Milanovic of Cambridge ESOL.
Table on page 101: reproduced by permission of Oxford University Press from Oxford Applied Linguistics: Fundamental Considerations in Language Testing by Lyle F Bachman © Lyle F Bachman 1990.

Finally, I would like to thank Professor Cyril Weir who read various parts of the book and offered invaluable critical comments and advice.

Series Editors' note

The language testing world has flirted with the testing of English for specific purposes for many years. In small scale testing contexts there have been and continue to be numerous specific assessments tailored to particular needs but in the context of large scale international language testing, specific purpose assessments have been far less common.

Cambridge ESOL started testing English in 1913. In some ways you might consider the original Certificate of Proficiency in English (CPE) a specific purpose examination designed to meet the needs of those teaching English although over the years it has become far more general in its emphasis. Cambridge ESOL also collaborated with the British Council on the development of the English Language Testing Service (ELTS) in the 1970s which had six subject specific modules. IELTS, which evolved from ELTS in 1990, saw a reduction in the academic modules to 3 and the 1995 revision of IELTS led to the single academic module alongside a general training variant.

There are many reasons for this retreat by IELTS, both practical and theoretical. Developing numerous multiple modules in the quantities required was a far from easy task. Ensuring that candidates took the right module was difficult. Equating modules proved technically very demanding. Ensuring content appropriateness required access to experts in a number of fields and so on. However, the need to extend the remit of General English assessment remains. The context of Cambridge ESOL English language assessment currently falls into four broad categories. Academic English (IELTS), Business English (BEC and BULATS), Young Learners' English (YLE) and General English (KET, PET, FCE, CAE, CPE and CELS) and in 2006 Cambridge ESOL will launch the International Legal English Certificate. This test seeks to address more specifically English in the legal domain of use.

In *Issues in testing business English*, Barry O'Sullivan provides a framework for classifying and understanding specific purpose language assessment. The first part of the volume provides the reader with a comprehensive review of numerous business English tests as well as business language tests in other languages. Some of the tests described no longer exist so the volume also serves as a useful historical record. This is followed by a detailed look at the revision of the Cambridge Business English Certificates (BEC).

Chapter 1 considers the relationship between general English and English for specific purposes and the definition of a business English construct. O'Sullivan presents a continuum ranging from an unspecified purpose to one that is highly specified. To this he adds construct, test method, skills coverage measurement qualities, degree of specificity/authenticity, non language factors and the reporting of test performance. This provides him with a framework for comparison and he proceeds to evaluate a series of business language tests on this basis. Particular attention is paid to some very widely used tests such as TOEIC, BULATS and BEC although the coverage of less widely known assessments is comprehensive. The text is illustrated with numerous examples of test item types which make interesting reading.

Having provided a detailed context against which to understand BEC, subsequent chapters consider BEC's revision and look in detail at each of the three BEC levels. The discussion of development methodology is interesting as is the focus on test reliability. It is gratifying to note that an examination like BEC, operating on a truncated sample of the test taking population at each of its three levels, demonstrating very good construct and content validity features and using a good variety of realistic material with an authentic orientation, can nonetheless achieve respectably high reliability estimates. Throughout this volume readers are referred to Volume 15 (Weir, Cyril and Milanovic, Michael (Eds) (2003) Continuity and innovation: Revising the Cambridge Proficiency in English Examination 1913 – 2002) in the same series which gives an even more detailed account of the principles that underline the Cambridge approach to test development and validation. The appendix has a comprehensive set of BEC materials but is complemented by a focus on two other tests, the Certificate in English as a Foreign Language for Secretaries and the Certificates in English for International Business and Trade which informed the development of BEC but are no longer available.

The final chapter is particularly important as it discusses in some detail the issue of authenticity and its relationship to the specificity continuum linking the argument in with Weir's validation framework (Cyril J. Weir (2004) *Language Testing and Validation: An Evidence-Based Approach*, Palgrave Macmillan).

O'Sullivan presents a multicomponential view of specificity and is able to clearly distinguish between different tests and tasks using his approach. The volume concludes with a focus on future research suggestions, part of which was arrived at collaboratively with staff at Cambridge ESOL.

Issues in testing business English is the third volume in this series (the other two being volumes 15 and 16) to document both a historical perspective and a study of test revision with a focus on the implications this has. A volume on academic English assessment authored by Alan Davies is forthcoming. This volume documents the history of the assessment of English for academic purposes from the 1950s to the present with a particular focus on the development and validation of IELTS.

Michael Milanovic
Cyril Weir
Cambridge 2005

Abbreviations

ALTE	Association of Language Testers in Europe
APA	American Psychological Association
BEC	Business English Certificate
BULATS	Business Language Testing System
CAE	Certificate in Advanced English
CAL	Center for Applied Linguistics
CAT	Computer Adaptive Test
CBT	Computer-Based Test
CEF	Common European Framework
CEFLS	Certificate in English as a Foreign Language for Secretaries
CEIBT	Certificate in English for International Business and Trade
CIC	Certificate in Italian for Commerce (Certificazione della conoscenza dell'italiano commerciale)
CPE	Certificate of Proficiency in English
DIF	Differential Item Functioning
EAP	English for Academic Purposes
EBC	English for Business Communication
EFL	English as a Foreign Language
ELT	English Language Teaching
EOS	English for Office Skills
ESOL	English for Speakers of Other Languages
ESP	English for Specified Purposes
ETS	Educational Testing Service
FCE	First Certificate in English
GIMS	General Impression Mark Scheme
GQ	General Questionnaire
IATEFL	International Association of Teachers of English as a Foreign Language
IELTS	International English Language Testing System
IRT	Item Response Theory
JETRO	Japan External Trade Organization
JOCT	JETRO Oral Communication Test
JRLT	JETRO Reading and Listening Comprehension Test
KCQ	Key Contacts Questionnaire
KET	Key English Test
LCCIEB	London Chamber of Commerce and Industry Examinations Board

LSP	Language for Specific Purposes
MCQ	Multiple-Choice Question
OET	Occupational English Test
OIBEC	Oxford International Business English Certificate
UODLE	University of Oxford Delegacy of Local Examinations
PET	Preliminary English Test
PLAB	General Medical Council's Professional and Linguistic Assessments Board (test of overseas doctors' language proficiency)
QCA	Qualifications and Curriculum Authority
RITCME	Recruitment, Induction, Training, Co-ordination, Monitoring, Evaluation
RSA	Royal Society of Arts
SAQ	Short Answer Question
TAAS	Texas Assessment of Academic Skills
TEEP	Test of English for Educational Purposes
TFI	Test de français international
TOEFL	Test of English as a Foreign Language
TOEIC	Test of English for International Communication
UCLES	University of Cambridge Local Examinations Syndicate
VRIP	Validity, Reliability, Impact and Practicality

1 Introduction to the testing of language for business purposes

A brief historical introduction

Though there have been formal tests of general proficiency around for many years – see Weir (2003a) for an interesting and informative historical perspective on the Certificate of Proficiency in English (CPE) since its introduction in 1913 – interest in language for specific purposes has a far shorter history, emerging, according to Swales (1984:11) with Barber's (1962) *Some Measurable Characteristics of Modern Scientific Prose*. This is not to say that there has been an awareness of the use of language for specific purposes only in recent times. Schröder reminds us:

> ... when new counting house regulations were issued for the London Salhof in 1554, these stated amongst other things that young apprentices from Germany would have to spend one year with a clothmaker in the country, so that they might get a proper command of everyday English and the more specific technical terms ... (1981:43).

Much of the early work in the area was driven by research which focused on the identification of unique instances of language use in specific contexts (Hüllen 1981a, 1981b, Johns 1980, Lackstrom, Selinker and Trimble 1973, Selinker and Douglas 1985, Swales 1971, to list but a few), the issue of authenticity in the use of materials for teaching (e.g. Carver 1983) and the central place of needs analysis in identifying the specific language needs of learners in given contexts (Alwright and Alwright 1977, Brindley 1984, Gledhill 2000, Hawkey 1978, Hutchinson and Walters 1987, Kennedy and Bolitho 1984, LCCIEB 1972, Robinson 1980, 1985, Thurstun and Candlin 1998, West 1994). As can be seen from the dates of these publications, much of the English for Specific Purposes (ESP) debate was conducted almost twenty years ago, yet many of the same questions continue to be asked today.

Hawkey (2004) outlines the changes in theories of language learning and teaching that lead to the development of a clearly defined ESP methodology, and led to an awareness of the need to establish a set of clearly rationalised testing procedures. In the case of the testing of language for business purposes, the first test to emerge was the Test of English for International Communication (TOEIC). It was developed by Educational Testing Services (ETS) in the USA and introduced in 1979. The test, originally devised for the Japanese market, was based firmly on psychometric–structuralist theory (Spolsky 1995) and represents one of the few remaining (though highly successful from a commercial perspective) examples of a multiple-choice format, standardised, international language test.

While the TOEIC looked backwards for its theoretical underpinning, other tests of business language, particularly those developed in the UK, were beginning to look to a more communicative model. Theorists on communicative competence, particularly Canale and Swain (1980), Hymes (1972) and practitioners like Munby (1978) had a profound influence on the practice of language teaching and testing. One major influence was the facilitation of a movement away from the psychometric–structuralist methodology, based on the teaching and testing of discrete aspects of language, to the psycholinguistic–sociolinguistic era, where language teaching and testing were seen from a holistic or integrated perspective. The shift in emphasis in language teaching from language *knowledge* to language *use* paved the way for a testing methodology which reflected the same ideas. Hawkey (2004) traces the historical development of the theoretical movements of this period and provides a contextualisation for the emerging interest in the teaching and later testing of ESP. With the exception of the TOEIC, the tests described in the following sections have an essentially performance-based orientation in which emphasis is placed on the contextualisation of the tasks and predicted linguistic responses within the business setting.

In the mid-1980s the move to the testing of language for business purposes in the UK began in earnest with the development by the Royal Society of Arts (RSA) of the *Certificate in English as a Foreign Language for Secretaries* (CEFLS) – which was later administered as the *Certificate in English for International Business and Trade* (CEIBT) – and a corresponding move by the London Chamber of Commerce and Industry Examinations Board (LCCIEB) and Pitman (now part of the City and Guilds Examinations Board) to create language tests with a business focus. When the RSA was subsumed into the University of Cambridge Local Examinations Syndicate (UCLES) in 1988 the RSA test was administered by UCLES, establishing its portfolio of language tests for business.

In the early 1990s two new examinations, the Business English Certificate (BEC) and Business Language Testing System (BULATS) were developed by UCLES. It is the former of these tests that forms the basis for the latter part of this book, in which the procedures used by Cambridge ESOL in the Business English Certificate (BEC) suite revision are outlined and exemplified.

During the mid- to late-1990s a number of tests of other languages for business emerged. These included JETRO (Japanese), Test de français international (TFI) from the makers of TOEIC, the Certificate in Italian for Commerce (CIC) and the tests in the BULATS series (French, German and Spanish in addition to the English version).

There is clearly a growing interest in the area of testing language for business purposes, particularly with the internationalisation of business and the need for employees to interact in more than just a single language. The move towards a 'business language' testing genre is reflected in the tests mentioned above and described in the latter part of this chapter.

Theoretical perspectives

In the only serious attempt to date to build a theoretical rationale for the testing of language for specific purposes, Douglas (2000) argues that a theoretical framework can be built around two principal theoretical foundations. The first of these is based on the assumption that language performance varies with the context of that performance. This assumption is supported by a well established literature in the area of sociolinguistics – see for example Labov's (1963) classic study of vowel change on Martha's Vineyard – in addition to research in the areas of second language acquisition (Dickerson 1975, Ellis 1989, Schmidt 1980, Smith 1989, Tarone 1985, 1988) and language testing (Berry, 1996, 1997, Brown 1995, 1998, Brown and Lumley 1997, O'Sullivan 1995, 2000a, 2000b, 2002a, Porter 1991a, 1991b, Porter and Shen, 1991). This fits well with the growing interest in a socio-cognitive approach to language test development where performance conditions are seen to have a symbiotic relationship with the cognitive processing involved in task completion (introduced by O'Sullivan 2000a and discussed in detail by Weir 2004).

In the case of the second foundation, Douglas sees specific purpose language tests as being 'precise' in that they will have lexical, semantic, syntactic and phonological characteristics that distinguish them from the language of more 'general purpose' contexts. This aspect of Douglas's position is also supported by an ever increasing literature, most notably in the area of corpus-based studies of language in specific contexts (Beeching 1997, Biber et al 1998, Dudley-Evans and St John 1996, Gledhill 2000, Thurstun and Candlin 1998).

When it came to an actual definition of specific purpose tests, Douglas places these two foundations within a single overriding concept, that of authenticity, defining a test of specific purposes as:

> One in which test content and methods are derived from an analysis of a specific purpose target language use situation, so that test tasks and content are authentically representative of tasks in the target situation, allowing for an interaction between the test taker's language ability and specific purpose content knowledge, on one hand, and the test tasks on the other. Such a test allows us to make inferences about a test taker's capacity to use language in the specific purpose domain (2000:19).

This definition highlights the core element of Douglas's view of LSP tests; that of *authenticity*. Douglas does not see this as being a simple matter of replicating specific purpose tasks in a testing context, but of addressing authenticity from two perspectives. The first perspective is that of *situational* authenticity, where LSP test tasks are seen as being 'authentic' in that they are derived from an analysis of the language use domain with which they are associated. The second perspective is *interactional* authenticity, which relates to the actual processing that takes place in task performance, what Weir (2004) refers to as theory-based validity.

This definition has not remained unquestioned. In fact, Douglas (2001) himself acknowledges that there are a number of issues left unanswered by his definition, an argument also made by Elder (2001). This criticism focuses on what Elder (2001) sees as the three principal problematic areas identified in the work of Douglas, namely, the distinguishability of distinct 'specific purpose' contexts; authenticity; and the impact (and interaction) of non-language factors.

By non-language factors one of two things is meant. The first relates to the elements of communication not associated with language – in everyday communication, transferral of message is achieved through a combination of language, cues, signals and symbols. There is a broad literature in psychology on this phenomenon (see for example Brown, Palmeta and Moore 2003, Vargo 1994). The second way of looking at this is the impact of background knowledge, in this case of the business domain, on an individual's ability to perform a particular task, in this case related to an aspect of business communication.

The first of these two perspectives is common across all tests of language production, not solely Language for Specific Purposes (LSP) tests. It is not just related to tests of speaking, where variables such as physical appearance, dress, gestures and posture have all been shown to have an effect on interlocutor perceptions of performance (see for example the work in the area of job interviews of Bordeaux 2002, Chia et al 1998, and Straus, Miles and Levesque 2001), but is also to be seen in tests of writing where handwriting and general presentation skills impact on how writing is evaluated by examiners (see for example Sprouse and Webb 1994, Sweedler-Brown 1992). This aspect of performance assessment is certainly a potential threat to test validity, and is typically dealt with in the development of assessment scales or, more likely, through rater/examiner training.

The latter perspective, the extent to which candidates' background knowledge impacts on his/her test performance is again not associated solely with LSP tests. A test of language for specific purposes is situated, by its very nature, in a specific context, and, also by its very nature, expects (if not demands) of its candidates a knowledge of that context. The literature has shown that background knowledge has a significant and apparently systematic effect on LSP test performance (see for example Alderson and Urquhart 1984, 1985, 1988, Clapham 1996, Steffensen and Joag-Dev 1984). It also appears that as a test becomes more highly specific this effect becomes more acute and it would seem that it is at this extreme that the difficulty in teasing apart language performance and task completion occurs – in other words, in a highly specific test, success on a task is dependent on a successful interplay of language and non-language elements. This feature of highly specific tests at one time led to innovations such as in the General Medical Council's Professional and Linguistic Assessments Board (PLAB) oral test where medics assessed the medical content of ESP tasks and the language examiner commented on the language performance (both informal with patients and formal with professional colleagues, on a generic ELT scale) though specialist lexis etc. remained the domain of the subject specialists.

It can be argued that a test of language for a specific purpose should not even try to avoid the background knowledge issue, as it is this that defines the test. How we deal with the situation will depend on the degree of specificity of the test and the inferences we intend to draw from performance on the test.

Turning to the remaining criticisms of an ESP approach to testing, we can see that there are basically two questions that should be addressed. These are:

1. Distinguishing LSP from general language – is it possible and/or feasible?
2. Authenticity – can LSP tests be made both situationally and interactionally authentic?

Distinguishing LSP from general English

There is a considerable body of work over the last thirty years which has quite clearly demonstrated the distinguishability of language use in specific contexts. We can point to the work on the definition of language needs and usage in specific contexts of needs analysis researchers and theorists. Among the influential early work were studies undertaken by Hawkey (1978), who offered a practical demonstration of how needs analysis can lead to a specific purpose curriculum, and Alwright and Alwright's (1977) practical advice on an approach to the teaching of medical English.

In the area of testing language for specific purposes, perhaps the most important undertaking was that of the London Chamber of Commerce and Industry Examinations Board (LCCIEB) in 1972. The LCCIEB had been providing business-related qualifications around the world for almost a hundred years when, in 1972, its language section undertook a major analysis of 'foreign' language use involving over 11,500 employees of almost six hundred international firms. This analysis, and the replications undertaken in the Federal Republic of Germany, France, Greece and Spain between 1982 and 1985, were to prove influential in the development of teaching and testing practice in the UK during the 1970s and 1980s.

In a series of seminal articles in the 1980s, Alderson and Urquhart (1984,

1985, 1988) found that 'academic background can play an important' though not consistent 'role in test performance' (Alderson and Urquhart 1985:201) and that 'particular groups of students may be disadvantaged by being tested on areas outside their academic field' (Alderson and Urquhart 1988:182). They also suggested that their studies 'demonstrated the need to take account of other factors, such as linguistic proficiency' (Alderson and Urquhart 1985:201). At about the same time Steffensen and Joag-Dev (1984) demonstrated the significant impact on comprehension of a reader's cultural background. The picture that is developing here is that background knowledge is a significant factor in specific purpose language testing, a point that was made by Clapham (1996) with reference to highly specific tests.

In fact, Clapham's (1996) study provided quite a few answers, or at least directions in which to look for answers, to many of the questions asked about the impact of background knowledge on performance in LSP tests. While looking at performance on a test of English for academic purposes (International English Language Testing System IELTS), Clapham's interpretation of the results of her in-depth and complex study have direct consequences for the testing of language for any specific purpose. It is therefore worth looking back over Clapham's work. Among other things, Clapham reports that:

- ... students achieved significantly higher scores on the module in their own subject area than on the module outside it (1996:188) ... [though] the results depend on the specificity of the tests (1996:189)
- ... it is possible to identify some of the characteristics which lead to passages being more or less specific, but that these characteristics are not always immediately obvious (1996:191) ... [though] it was the rhetorical function of the passages rather than the sources of the texts which affected their specificity (1996:191)
- it is not always easy to classify candidates into simply defined subgroups, as the evidence from Clapham indicates that her participants were widely read outside of their own area of study (1996:192–3)
- it seems likely that as the modules became more subject specific, background knowledge had a proportionally stronger effect on test scores (1996:193). In addition, subject area familiarity made a significant contribution to test scores, whereas topic familiarity did not ... [this] suggests that knowledge of a subject area might have a greater effect than topic familiarity on the subject specificity of a reading passage (1996:193)
- there seemed to be a threshold below which students did not make use of this [background] knowledge, and above which they did (1996:194).

The implications of the work referred to earlier in the chapter (e.g. Barber 1962, Hüllen 1981a, 1981b, Johns 1980, Lackstrom, Selinker and Trimble 1973, LCCIEB 1972, Schröder 1981, Selinker and Douglas 1985, Swales 1971, 1984, Weir 1983) when seen in light of these findings suggest that there is a clearly definable language of business (and of other areas of specific interest such as science, technology etc.) and that where tests are devised with a deliberately high level of specificity towards an explicit area, then candidates whose background is grounded in that area can be expected to outperform candidates from a different background, given similar linguistic competence.

There is still a problem, however, in defining the boundaries of specific context areas (Cumming 2001, Davies 2001, Elder 2001). It appears to be the case that while we can identify particular aspects of language use as being specific to a given context (such as vocabulary, syntax, rhetorical organisation), we cannot readily identify exact limits to the language that is used in that context. This is because there are no 'exact limits'. Business language, like scientific or medical language is situated within and interacts with the *general language domain*, a domain that cannot, by its very nature, be rigidly defined.

Authenticity

Though Douglas (2000) built his definition of what makes a test 'specific' around the notions of situational and interactional authenticity, he later (Douglas 2001) pointed to some difficulties in operationalising such a definition. The notion of situational authenticity is relatively easy to conceptualise. Situational authenticity refers to the accurate reflection in the test design of the conditions of linguistic performance from the language use domain – Weir's (2004) text and task demands. Tests such as that for air traffic controllers described by Teasdale (1994), where candidates were tested in a situation that closely replicated the specific purpose domain, are as close as we can get to a completely situationally authentic test. The mere fact that the event is being used as a test lessens the authenticity – though I'm sure that few readers would expect that the ability of air traffic controllers to cope linguistically with the demands of their work should be tested in a truly authentic situation! The opposite to this would be the relative situational inauthenticity of the MATHSPEAK test, the specific purpose version of the SPEAK (the institutional form of the Test of Spoken English, the TSE) referred to by Elder (2001), where there is no attempt made to replicate the teaching context it is designed to be generalised to.

However, in the case of interactional authenticity there is a lesser degree of certainty in that, to the present time, it has not been clearly conceptualised, let alone operationalised. Though the common view (that the test should result in an interaction between the task and the relevant language ability) is clear enough, to my knowledge there has not been a significant contribution to its operationalisation – that is, insufficient work has been done to link context-based validity elements to theory-based processing. Test developers and researchers tend to rely on anecdotal evidence or 'expert' judgements to make decisions on the interactional authenticity of a test task – in the review of a range of business language tests that comes later in this chapter, I fall foul of the same tendency.

So, critics of an LSP approach to language testing have raised genuine concerns regarding the distinguishability of distinct 'specific purpose' contexts, authenticity, and the impact on test performance of non-language factors – not just for LSP testing but for language testing in general. I do not believe that these are insurmountable and I will return to the matter in the final chapter of this book.

Assessing performance

While the above issues have focused on the test content and on the theoretical justification for utilising a particular test task, there are other issues in LSP testing that have not really been addressed. Like any test, the reliability (stability, consistency and accuracy) of LSP tests is central to the test's value. In the section devoted to reliability in the context of the BEC suite (Chapter 2) I look in some detail at this issue, so I will not spend time or space here in an extended discussion, except to say that the way we estimate and report the reliability of tests such as the BEC suite is in need of re-appraisal as the statistical approaches taken to date offer us only a limited understanding of the true reliability of these tests.

A related issue is the way in which we evaluate or assess writing and speaking test performances, in that it is associated with the creation of the test score, which is central to any test.

There are a number of issues here:

- the scale criteria
- the level represented by the scale
- the use of the scale (who, how etc.).

The scale criteria

Though the literature abounds with scales that do not seem to have been derived from any particular theoretical or empirical base, the movement in the 1990s towards more supportable scale development means that the current rating scales which reflect best practice in the area tend to have a sound basis (see North 1996, North and Schneider 1998). While the whole area of rating scale development is far too complex to be dealt with adequately in this short section, it is important to point to the need for any rating scale to be based on the same model or perception of language as drives the rest of the test development process. A good example of this are the rating scales used in the Cambridge ESOL Main Suite examinations (Hawkey 2001).

In their response to the criticisms voiced by Foot (1999), Saville and Hargreaves (1999) present a model of communicative ability upon which the Cambridge ESOL Main Suite speaking examinations are based (see Figure 1.1).

This model is based on the earlier work of Canale and Swain (1980) and Bachman (1990), as well as on the Council of Europe specifications for the Waystage and Threshold levels of competence (Saville and Hargreaves 1999:46).

We can see that language competence is described in terms of Bachman (1990:84–98) and Bachman and Palmer's (1996:67) organisational (grammar and discourse), pragmatic and strategic competences.

Figure 1.1 Communicative language ability

Spoken Language Ability		
Language Competence		**Strategic Competence**
Grammatical	**Discourse**	**Pragmatic**	
Syntax Morphology Vocabulary Pronunciation	Rhetorical Organisation Coherence Cohesion	e.g. Sensitivity to illocution	Interaction skills Non-verbal features of interaction

Source: Saville and Hargreaves (1999:45)

The rating scales used in the Cambridge Main Suite Speaking paper examinations consist of four criteria, grammar and vocabulary, discourse management, pronunciation and interactive communication, each of which is awarded a score in the range of 0–5. Though it is not clear from Saville and Hargreaves exactly how the scale is meant to reflect the model of competence they quote, it would appear that it is meant to operate as represented in Figure 1.2.

It is clear from this figure that the notion of pragmatic competence is not explicitly dealt with in the scales (for convenience, only the middle score of 3 is presented in this figure, though the descriptions offered here are similar to the other levels in terms of relevance to model criteria). The notion of pragmatic competence (or knowledge) is seen by Bachman and Palmer as being related to the ability to 'create or interpret discourse by relating utterances or sentences and texts to their meanings' (1996: 69). In other words, pragmatic competence is seen as being comprised of functional and sociolinguistic knowledge and as such has been identified here with the criterion discourse management – which, though the name implies an ability to 'manage' the interaction (in the sense of Bygate 1987), in the context of this scale it is actually concerned with coherence, cohesion and, if this representation is accepted, an ability to demonstrate functional and sociolinguistic competence.

Figure 1.2 Communicative language ability and the Cambridge ESOL FCE analytic scale

Band	Grammar and Vocabulary	Discourse Management	Pronunciation	Interactive Communication
3.0	Grammar is sufficiently accurate. Uses appropriate vocabulary in dealing with the tasks.	Uses adequate range of linguistic resources to deal sufficiently well with the tasks. Contributions may occasionally be limited or lack coherence	Produces individual sounds and prosodic features sufficiently well to be understood. L1 accent may cause occasional difficulty.	Has sufficient interactive ability to carry out the tasks. Maintains flow of language when carrying out the tasks although may occasionally lack sensitivity to turn taking and hesitation may occur while searching for language. Does not require major assistance or prompting to carry out the tasks.

Grammatical   Discourse   Pragmatic

Language Competence   Strategic Competence

When advocating a move towards an integrated language/specific area ability approach, Douglas (2000) suggests using what he refers to as 'indigenous' scales in LSP tests. The argument being that the criteria actually employed in the evaluation of specific purpose performances are specific to the context of that performance – a position which is seen as support for the *inseparability* of language and performance of specific purpose tasks (Douglas 2001, Elder 2001). While the case made by Douglas is strong, there are a number of points which still need further consideration.

The central problem here is one of construct definition, and therefore of the inferences that are to be drawn from a particular test. In the case of the Occupational English Test (OET), for instance, which is criticised by Douglas and by its principle creator, McNamara (in Jacoby and McNamara 1999) for using a 'general purpose' rating scale, rather than one devised from an analysis of the target language use (TLU) situation, the criticism has some basis, in that the scale used was a rather primitive adaptation of the FSI oral proficiency scale (Wilds 1975). However, the test, for whatever reason (the one suggested was bureaucratic expedience) was meant to offer a measure of the ability of overseas health professionals to cope with the English language demands of their particular medical specialisation. The inferences to be drawn from performance on the test were therefore related to their language competence, nothing else. In this respect, the OET appears to have been a successful test. If it were to become a 'true' performance measure (in that it should offer a measure of the test taker's ability to perform the particular medical duties under scrutiny) then clearly a different approach to the evaluation of the performance would be needed. It may be, for instance, that the same role-played performance could be used as a language measure and, when subjected to scrutiny using 'indigenous' criteria (which might include an aspect of language), serve to offer evidence of medical ability (see the reference on page 5 to the PLAB test in the UK).

The level represented by the scale

Scales can be designed to represent a whole range of ability levels, for example see the sample band descriptors for the Test of English for Educational Purposes (TEEP) from the University of Reading – Figure 1.3 (O'Sullivan 1999). As we can see from this figure, this scale ranges from a level of non-language to that of very high competence in the language and is obviously designed to be used across the whole ability range.

When a test is designed to measure language ability on or around a particular proficiency level – for example if we are planning to design a test of writing for candidates at the Common European Framework (CEF) level B2 (Vantage) we are faced with a bit of a conundrum. If we decide to create a scale to describe ability across all levels (see Figure 1.4), with only the portion corresponding to B2 in use for this particular test, we are faced with either making simple trichotomous decisions (the candidate is below this level, at this level or above this level), or describing multiple levels of ability within each of the six ability levels. This would make the scale both extremely difficult to develop and validate and also very difficult if not impossible to use, as raters would be faced with the same problem they met in trying to use the scales devised by Fulcher (1996) where the 'thick' description of typical performance at each scale level was so detailed that the scale became unusable.

Another option is to create a single scale, which is then interpreted at whichever ability level it is to be used at (say C1 or A2). With this type of scale, there is increased pressure on the developer to ensure that the scale is sufficiently clear so as to ensure that users can easily distinguish the different levels of performance within the scale, but sufficiently general to allow the scale to be interpreted at the different levels of ability. While of great practical use, this type of scale is not easy to develop and validate and depends on examiner/rater training and monitoring if it is to be successfully used.

The most commonly used method is to create individual scales for use at each level. In order to ensure that the scales are identifying appropriate levels of achievement at each level they must be linked in some way. This process involves a major investment in resources – and the resulting scale is still

Figure 1.3 The overall impression scale from the Test of English for Educational Purposes (TEEP)

Overall Impression	Score
The writing is completely satisfactory.	9
	8
The writing is satisfactory and generally communicates fluently with only occasional lapses of organisation and structure. Clear well argued position taken.	7
The writing is mainly satisfactory and communicates with some degree of fluency. Although there is occasional strain for the reader, control of organisational patterns and devices is evident. Clear argument, though the writer's point of view is not obvious.	6
The writing sometimes causes strain for the reader. While the reader is aware of an overall lack of fluency, there is a sense of an answer which has an underlying coherence. Somewhat poor control of the language and little evidence of the writer's point of view. May contain occasional direct 'lifting' of the text from the input or inappropriate use of quotations or references.	5
	4
The seriousness of the problems in writing prevents meaning from coming through more than spasmodically. Evidence of systematic plagiarism or excessive use of quotations or referencing.	3
	2
• a virtual non-writer; contains no assessable pieces of English writing • wholly, or almost wholly copied from the source materials • less than approximately 50 words	1
Candidate did not attend or attempt the question in any way.	0

Source: O'Sullivan (1999)

dependent on rater training (though not to the extent of the option suggested above). However, evidence of improvements in inter- and intra-rater reliability suggest that this approach is viable (see Hawkey 2001 and Hawkey and Barker 2004).

The use of the scale (who, how etc.)

The remaining issues associated with the rating scale relate to who should be involved in the development and application of the scale. The first of these issues centres around the content of the scale – to what extent can we define a set of criteria that will offer a valid framework through which a test performance

Figure 1.4 Practicality problem with a single scale across all levels

C2	unused section	1	
C1		2	
B2	'useful' section	3	**'useful' section**
B1		4	
A2	unused section	5	
A1		6	

can be assessed – while the second point refers to the notion of who is qualified to make decisions (based on the scale) in an LSP performance test.

Douglas (2001) argues that the criteria included in a rating scale should emerge from the same needs analysis that is used to define the language use domain, and that these criteria should then be augmented and supported by our currently-used theoretically-based approaches (see Weir 1983). He goes on to suggest a 'weaker' indigenous scale hypothesis:

> . . . in which the indigenous criteria may be used first to supplement linguistically-oriented criteria in line with the construct definition, and, secondly, to help guide our interpretations of language performances in specific purpose tests (Douglas, 2001:183).

What Douglas seems to be saying is that we should attempt to discover the linguistic criteria relevant to making judgements of performance in a particular TLU domain and try to 'square' these with what we know of existing language ability theory. The problem again lies in the area of boundary definition. How can we decide where to draw the line between creating a scale that is very much focused on the task in question and creating a scale that can be used to generalise beyond a specific event? It appears that we cannot easily do this. A scale can allow us to draw one type of inference from our test but not both.

Another problem lies in the fact that in performance tests the rating scale is a link between task performance and test score, so it must be theoretically sound (in that it is tied to our construct definition and allows for meaningful inferences to be drawn from test performance) as well as practically usable. Though there is some evidence to suggest that raters can use rating scales in a similar way irrespective of their background (Lumley 1998, Lumley and McNamara 1995), this is really only an issue where the decision being reached is specific to a particular area and where the test is representative of the 'strong' view of performance testing.

It is important to remember at all times that the purpose of an LSP test is to help us draw inferences on the ability of a candidate to use the language of a specified domain in the context of that domain and in a manner that is appropriate to that domain. Its purpose is not to allow us to draw inferences related to a candidate's ability to perform other than linguistically in the domain itself.

Towards a theoretical conceptualisation of business language tests

The main thrust of this chapter so far is that it is not helpful to take the view that tests can only be seen as being 'specific purpose' (SP) if they are very narrowly focused on a particular 'purpose' area and are representative of, to borrow McNamara's (1996) expression, a 'strong' view of specific purpose testing. Instead there are a number of perspectives related to 'specific purpose' tests that offer a not incompatible expansion to the definition of SP tests offered by Douglas (2000:19).

1. As all tests are in some way 'specific', it is best to think of all language tests as being placed somewhere on a continuum of specificity, from the broad general purpose test such as the Certificate of Proficiency in English (CPE) to the highly specific test (Figure 1.5), such as the test for air traffic controllers described by Teasdale (1994).

Figure 1.5 A view of test specificity

Unspecified   **Highly Specified**
Purpose   **Purpose**

2. Very highly specific tests tend to be very poor in terms of generalisability, while the opposite can be said of non-specific tests. There is not a binary choice in operation here, and if we accept that tests can be developed along a specificity continuum, then it logically follows that a test which appears to be placed somewhere other than the extremes of the continuum will have the potential to be either more or less generalisable.
    We could conceive of a test task that is specific only in that it is placed within the context of an employment/career area (in our case 'business'), and that will be generalisable to the broader 'general language use' context because it is essentially testing non-specific language, or it is not activating the same cognitive processes as a task that is more highly specific does.
3. Where a test is situated closer and closer to the more highly specific end of the continuum, the focus on *situational* authenticity also changes. That is, a highly specific test will most closely reflect the 'real world' situation or context, while a more general, less specific test will be less likely to do so (though it is not impossible that a specific context might be exploited in a

test of general proficiency). In other words, a highly specific test will clearly demonstrate *situational* authenticity.

4. Since we are essentially focused on tests of language, the aim of any specific purpose language test is to attempt to say something about a candidate's language ability within the specific context of interest. Therefore, the extent to which a test task engages a candidate's underlying processing and language resources to the same degree as called for within the specific context domain indicates the degree of *interactional* authenticity of that test task.

5. The degree to which non-language factors impact on a candidate's test performance will reflect the degree of specificity of that test. Therefore, in a highly specific language test it may not be possible to separate the language from the specific event. Where such a test is called for (i.e. a 'strong' form of specific purpose tests) this should be recognised in the definition of the construct and as such the only possible way to assess language performance should be within performance in the event, using, for example, the type of 'indigenous' assessment rubrics or scales suggested by McNamara and Jacoby (1999) and developed by Abdul-Raof (2002).

It is clear from these five points that the notion of 'degree of specificity' is central to any definition of a specific purpose language test – since the impact of other factors will vary, depending on the positioning of a test along a specificity continuum. In the sections that follow, I will review a series of tests of language for business purposes, taking these points into account – though of course no review would be appropriate without some reference being made to other aspects of a test's quality.

Describing tests of business language

In this section, I will review a series of business language tests from the theoretical perspective suggested above. From this review, I hope to find evidence to support such a perspective, leading to a more comprehensive under-standing of the issues involved in the testing of language for business purposes in particular and for specific purpose language testing in general.

Of course, tests should not be evaluated solely on the basis of the theoretical concepts described above. Those qualities that can be seen to offer more comprehensive evidence of the test's usefulness should also be taken into account. Accordingly, the following reviews will be structured using the following framework:

1. A brief introduction to the test.
2. A brief description of the test.
3. An outline of the construct upon which the test focuses.

4. The test method.
5. Skills' coverage.
6. Measurement qualities.
7. Degree of specificity/Authenticity.
8. Impact of non-language factors.
9. Reporting of test performance.

Test of English for International Communication (TOEIC)

1. A brief introduction to the test

The testing of language for the purpose of establishing benchmarks for participants in international business or commerce in the modern era appears to have started with the development of the *Test of English for International Communication* (TOEIC). The test, developed by the Educational Testing Service (ETS) in response to suggestions by the Japanese government (prompted by its large industrial corporations), was first administered in 1979. According to an early test user's guide (ETS 1986:1), the test was designed to test two aspects of learners' language:

- ability to understand a business-related conversation in standard English
- reading English language work manuals, correspondence, technical books and articles.

The TOEIC was designed as a standardised test of reading and listening comprehension, set in the context of international trade and commerce. It consisted of a series of 100 multiple-choice items for each of the two skills tested. While it was originally designed for the Asian (particularly the Japanese) market, its use has now spread to other parts of the world.

2. A brief description of the test

The TOEIC is a 200-item test in which two aspects of a test taker's language are tested, listening and reading comprehension, as mentioned above, there are 100 items for each of the two aspects tested. All items in the TOEIC use a multiple-choice question (MCQ) format.

The Listening section

This section consists of 100 items and takes approximately 45 minutes to complete. Input consists of four parts

1. Statements related to a series of photographs (20 items, 4-option MCQ).
2. Questions, responses required (30 items, 3-option MCQ).

3. Short conversations (30 items, 4-option MCQ).
4. Short talks (20 items, 4-option MCQ).

The Listening section offers a series of activities ranging from very basic level identification of elements related to a set of photographs, through to understanding the content of short conversations and talks. At no time do the test takers listen to extended discourse, nor do they need to actually do anything with the information received (except select either an acceptable reply to a question or a summary of what was heard).

The Reading section

This again consists of 100 items, though here 75 minutes are allowed. There are three parts:

1. Sentence completion (40 items, 4-option MCQ).
2. Error recognition (20 items, 4-option MCQ).
3. Comprehension of short texts (40 items, 4-option MCQ).

The 'comprehension' section has been criticised (Douglas 2000:235) both for the fact that it is non-reciprocal in nature and for the disparate sub-skills that appear to be tested by the different items – which seem to draw on skills such as scanning for detail and making pragmatic as opposed to propositional inferences from a text – in other words, drawing on background knowledge. Another criticism is the decision to use only largely decontextualised short texts, which at best represent fragments of texts, rather than use a variety of text types and lengths. Similar criticisms can be made of the other section; for example, the 'sentence completion' section appears to test grammar and vocabulary, while the 'error recognition' tests sentence level grammatical and lexical awareness – so, while we may be able to say that a test taker can identify errors in a text, we cannot say that that person would be able to identify non-highlighted errors in a longer script, nor can we say that that person would be able to correct any identified errors unless a selection of options is offered. This problem with the length of the texts is also clearly important, with these two sections only dealing with single sentence input.

As mentioned above, this format has not changed since TOEIC was first introduced in 1979.

3. An outline of the construct upon which the test focuses

From the standpoint of the theoretical framework of LSP suggested here, the TOEIC is problematic from a number of perspectives. The description of the test highlights a problem with the way in which the test is specified. It seems that Douglas's (2000:236) criticism that 'it is unlikely that the reading tasks engage the test takers in genuinely communicative behaviour or in genuinely specific purpose language use' suggests that the test should not be considered to be a 'genuine' LSP test at all, and indicates that it should be placed towards the 'general' or 'unspecified' end of the specificity continuum discussed above.

There is also a problem with the inferences that can be drawn from the TOEIC. According to the TOEIC Users Guide, the test:

> ... measures the everyday English skills of people working in an international environment. TOEIC test scores indicate how well people can communicate in English with others in the global workplace. The test does not require specialized knowledge or vocabulary; it only measures the kind of English used in everyday work activities (Chauncey Group 1999:4).

Taking these three assertions separately we can see that there are clear problems.

The test purports to measure everyday skills in an international work environment, yet focuses only on listening and reading – certainly skills useful in such an environment but hardly sufficient to allow us to say anything about the second assertion, i.e. the ability of people to actually *communicate*. The Guide later asserts that speaking and writing are not assessed because they require 'considerable time and expense, both for administering the test and for scoring' (Chauncey Group 1999:8), and are comparatively less reliable than the tests of the receptive skills examined. The assertions concerning the relationship between performance on the TOEIC and on separate indicators of speaking and writing ability appear to have been based, worryingly, on measures of general proficiency in these skills, adding to the confusion as to the 'specific' orientation of the test. This confusion is highlighted again in the final sentence, which suggests that the test writers do not see the language of 'everyday work activities' to be in any way 'specialised' or different from a general language proficiency.

There are other difficulties with the descriptions used by the test developers of the underlying construct, as reflected in the claims (i.e. inferences that can be drawn from test scores). Perhaps the most obvious of these are reflected in statements quoted below from two major TOEIC websites, that for Europe and for the USA. The European site states that the TOEIC measures test takers':

> ... English comprehension, speaking, writing and reading skills in an international environment. The scores indicate how well people can communicate in English with others in business, commerce and industry.

> (source: http://www.toeic-europe.com/pages/eng/the_test_pres.htm accessed January 2004)

On the other hand, the main (USA-based) site for the test claims that:

> ... The TOEIC test measures the everyday English skills of people working in an international environment.

> (source: http://www.toeic.com/2_2tests.htm accessed January 2004)

There is clearly some confusion as to the underlying construct of the TOEIC.

This confusion is manifested in the claims made of what inferences can be drawn from performance on the test (at present there is very limited empirical support for claims regarding language production) and in the very nature of the test – is it a test of general proficiency or a test of language for business-related communication, or both?

4. The test method

The TOEIC has been criticised by Douglas as representing:

> . . . a good example of a well-constructed norm-referenced traditional multiple choice test task, with no doubt high reliability, but extremely limited in the inferences it will allow about language knowledge (2000:236).

This criticism is not particularly surprising given that the TOEIC is a test born of the psychometric–structuralist era (Spolsky 1995), where tests were ratio-nalised by theoretical insights from 'associationist learning theory, structural linguistics, contrastive analysis and psychometrics' and a belief that the 'phono-logical, morphological, syntactic and lexical components of language are isolable as are the four skills of listening, speaking, reading and writing' (Hawkey 1982:124). It is unlikely that any test based on these premises might provide evidence of the kind of communicative behaviour referred to by Douglas (2000). Douglas does have an important point to make. The TOEIC was introduced in 1979, at a time when the theoretical rationalisation upon which it was based had been superseded by what Spolsky (1995) called the psycholinguistic–sociolinguistic era. Possibly the harshest criticism that can therefore be made of the TOEIC is of the failure of its creators to respond to changes in theoretical perspectives of language competence and related changes in language teaching that had already begun to reshape the language testing scene by the mid- to late-1970s, see Hawkey (2004) for a useful historical overview of the period.

The danger of relying on high stakes test instruments based on multiple-choice questions (MCQs) has been highlighted in a number of recent reviews of test evaluation procedures in the United States (see in particular the review of the Texas Assessment of Academic Skills or TAAS by McNeil and Valenzuela 2000). These reviews have highlighted the presence of significant bias in the performance on such tests by minority candidates. When this criticism is coupled with the added problem of test validity (for example independent research indicated that as scores in particular school districts increased on the TAAS test of reading other indicators of the candidates' actual ability to read showed a significant decrease), the danger is even greater. This is not to say that such item types are of no real value; when used in addition to other, more direct measures they can add to our perspectives on the ability of a test candidate (in fact the reality of modern tests means that many batteries, such as the Cambridge

ESOL Main Suite and the proposed new Test of English as a Foreign Language (TOEFL), already employ a variety of item and task types).

5. Skills' coverage

The TOEIC tests reading and listening only, a situation which means that the test is seen by this writer as something of an anomaly. This is because its very existence can only be justified by adapting a theoretical view of language which is in direct contradiction to the test method used. The TOEIC claims to represent a measure of an individual candidate's ability to communicate in a business environment, yet it uses a methodology which pre-dates the communicative era in which language knowledge is tested as opposed to any ability to actually use that language. The only empirical evidence that the inferences drawn from performance on the test can be related to 'communication' comes from Wilson (1989), though there is a serious question mark over the measures he used to compare TOEIC performance with.

6. Measurement qualities

The relationship between the listening, reading and total TOEIC scores are shown below, Table 1.1. The fact that these correlations are really quite high may point to a muddying of the measure and the ability being measured.

Table 1.1 Correlations between TOEIC sub-tests

	Listening	Reading	Total
Listening	1.000	0.822*	0.952*
Reading		1.000	0.957*
Total			1.000

Note: * p ≤ .001

Since the listening and reading scores are included in the total score, it is not at all surprising that there are very high correlations reported between these sections and the overall. What is surprising is the fact that there is such a high correlation between the two sub-tests – in correlation analysis of the reading and listening sub-sections of the Test of English for Educational Purposes (TEEP) (O'Sullivan 1999, Weir 1983) typical correlation coefficients are in the region of 0.5 to 0.6. Very high correlations suggest that the two tests are very strongly related, for example, in one of the few studies to focus on the TOEIC, the reported correlation coefficient between a direct speaking measure and the TOEIC Total score was 0.74. This was seen by the TOEIC developers as evidence that the test can accurately predict candidates' speaking ability (Chauncey Group 1998:1–2), yet the correlation of 0.82 reported here is not seen by the developers as a problem.

The internal consistency estimates reported in the TOEIC Technical Manual (Educational Testing Services 1998:2) for what they refer to as 'the Japanese secure administration' (Woodford 1982:66) are shown in Table 1.2. These figures are not surprising, considering the number of items and the presumably broad range of candidates tested. It should be noted that reliability estimates such as the Kuder Richardson formulae and Cronbach's Alpha are notoriously susceptible to test-taking population variability (so a test can have a reliability of .93 with one population and .63 with another). However, given what we know about the TOEIC population, these numbers appear to be quite acceptable.

Table 1.2 KR-20 Reliability Coefficients for the TOEIC test

Listening Comprehension	0.92
Reading Comprehension	0.93
Total Test	0.96

7. Degree of specificity/authenticity

From the overview offered here, it would appear that the test developers have not attempted to deal with the specificity issue and in terms of the framework suggested by Douglas (2000), it would be very difficult to justify calling this a true specific purposes test. With regard to the concept of situational authenticity, which is reflected in the content of the test in terms of text and task demands, there does not seem to be any evidence that the test reflects the specific language use domain.

Weir (1993, 2004) suggests how the demands of the content domain might be described (see Table 1.3). Here, the limitations of the TOEIC are clearly highlighted. The sample questions from the listening paper that appear in the Examiner's Handbook (ETS 2002:14 and 17 for example) could be from any test of general proficiency. While this is not necessarily a bad thing in itself, the fact that the vast majority of the items (in fact all of the items included in the Examinee Handbook) would be equally comfortable in a general proficiency listening test suggests that there are serious shortcomings across all elements of the text demands' framework – for example, the focus on single word recognition or on listening for detail does not reflect the range of demands of the business context.

Similar limitations can be pointed out for the Reading paper – for example, in the Examinee Handbook, all reading items are based either on sentence-length or short paragraph-length texts and while there are items based on short notices, there is no text longer than approximately seventy words and neither is there anything that resembles any of the more common reading texts from the business context (brochures, e-mails, business letters). Similarly, the task demands on both papers are uniform: a set of equally weighted multiple-choice items, with no consistent purpose attached to task fulfilment (other than achieving a satisfactory grade in the test), a response format that does not reflect that of the target domain and an extremely limited number of operations involved.

Table 1.3 Task and text demands for Listening and Reading

Skill Area	Task Demands	Text Demands
Listening	Purpose	*Linguistic*
	Response format	Mode/channel
	Weighting	Type
	Known criteria	Length
	Order of items	Nature of information
	Time constraints	Topic familiarity
	Intended operations	Lexical range
		Structural range
		Functional range
		Interlocutor
		Speech rate
		Variety of accent
		Acquaintanceship
		Number of speakers
		Gender
Reading	Purpose	*Linguistic*
	Response format	Channel
	Weighting	Text type
	Known criteria	Text length
	Order of items	Nature of information
	Time constraints	Topic familiarity
	Intended operations	Lexical range
		Structural range
		Functional range
		Writer-reader relationship

Source: based on Weir (1993, 2004)

Looking at the issue of interactional authenticity, we can only presume that responding to multiple-choice items alone can never engage the candidate in the kind of cognitive processing evident in listening or reading in a business domain.

In fact this criticism of MCQs is not new. When presenting their model of test task response, Pollitt and Ahmed, suggest that they:

> . . . had found it extremely difficult to model the process of answering multiple choice questions, and are inclined to think that, perhaps for this reason alone, they are of questionable validity for educational assessment (Pollitt and Ahmed 1999:1).

Pollitt and Ahmed were essentially attempting to model the cognitive behaviour of candidates under test conditions, a concept further developed by Weir (2004) in the 'theory-based validity' element of his frameworks. The linking of an understanding of the executive processes and resources available to the test taker is central to the notion of interactional authenticity.

All this suggests that the TOEIC might best be placed close to the 'non-specified purpose' end, calling into question any claim that it might be testing language for a specific 'business' purpose.

8. Impact of non-language factors

There is no evidence that the non-language factors have an unexpected impact on performance on the TOEIC. Since the previous section places the test squarely in the category of 'general proficiency', it is clear that there are no (or certainly very few) elements within the TOEIC that might be affected (negatively or positively) by the business language use domain – for example there are no items in the Examinee Handbook where a background in business would give a candidate an advantage over a fellow candidate without such a background. The fact that there are no business-related texts in the reading part, for example, means that a candidate who has never seen or read a business letter (or has had to respond to such a letter) would be in no way affected by his or her total lack of experience in the business world. While it might be argued that this lack of negative bias is a good thing, it seems counter intuitive that a person without such a background would be seen as capable of communicating 'in English with others in business, commerce, and industry' (Chauncey Group 2002:1).

9. Reporting of test performance

The norm-referencing methodology used in the TOEIC, means that a candidate's test performance is reported in terms of where the candidate might be placed relative to the population who sat for a particular administration of the test. In a situation where a decision is to be made on a candidate's ability to perform (in linguistic terms) in a given context, this is problematic. It might be, in an extreme example, that none of the candidates are actually capable of performing at the level required by an employer. Results of this sort will not tell the employer that this is the case however, only that candidate x is better or worse than candidate y. We can then see that the way in which a test of language for a specific purpose, such as business, is reported is actually a vital characteristic of that test (a similar argument is made by Douglas 2000). If a test is designed to offer an estimation of the ability of a candidate to cope with the linguistic challenges required of a specific business or work environment, then some criterion level must be set below which a candidate should not fall. This criterion should only be set in relation to the specific language use domain and not in relation to the ability of other candidates.

Other tests of language for business purposes

The growing interest in specific purpose testing during the 1990s has resulted in an increased number of tests for business, both for English and other languages. This section looks at a range of such tests, starting out with a representative sample of tests from the UK, Pitman Qualifications and the London Chamber of Commerce and Industry Examinations Board (LCCIEB). There then follow reviews of tests of other languages (French, Italian and Japanese).

Pitman qualifications

The Pitman tests, now administered by the City and Guilds of London, at present offer a pair of tests specifically aimed at business English. These are the English for Business Communication (EBC) and English for Office Skills (EOS).

English for Business Communication

1. A brief introduction to the test

Three levels are available: Elementary, Intermediate and Advanced. According to the test developers, these correspond with the Common European Framework levels A2–Waystage, B2–Vantage and C2 (see Figure 2.4 for a diagrammatic outline of the levels). Unlike the other tests referred to in this chapter, these tests are available both to native speakers and to overseas candidates, provided they have reached a particular level of language ability as measured by other non-business oriented Pitman tests (intermediate standard in the ESOL examination or elementary in the English examinations for the Elementary and Intermediate tests respectively). According to the Pitman website, a 'background knowledge of office practice and organisation is required'.

The tests are integrative in nature, with each of the three levels involving the candidate in writing a range of answers in response to input, often handwritten. Before taking a brief look at the suite, it should be pointed out that it is not at all clear that the developers have considered the language level of candidates who are non-native speakers of English. This is most clearly exemplified by the brief 'Contextualisation' offered at the beginning of each test level. As can be seen from Figure 1.6, the language of these three is almost indistinguishable. This apparent lack of concern with the language of the input undermines the suite, as it is quite conceivable that candidates, particularly at the lower levels, may experience significant difficulties with understanding the input. This will clearly have a negative impact on their test performance.

2. A brief description of the test

The three levels of the test are outlined in the following table (Table 1.4). In this table we can see that the three levels are quite similar in content, but with a greater number of tasks to be completed (in an ever increasing amount of time). It should also be noted that there is no clear substantive difference (apart from the increased number of tasks, which is offset by the increased time allowed) in

Figure 1.6 Contextualisation offered at levels 1–3 of the Pitman EBC suite

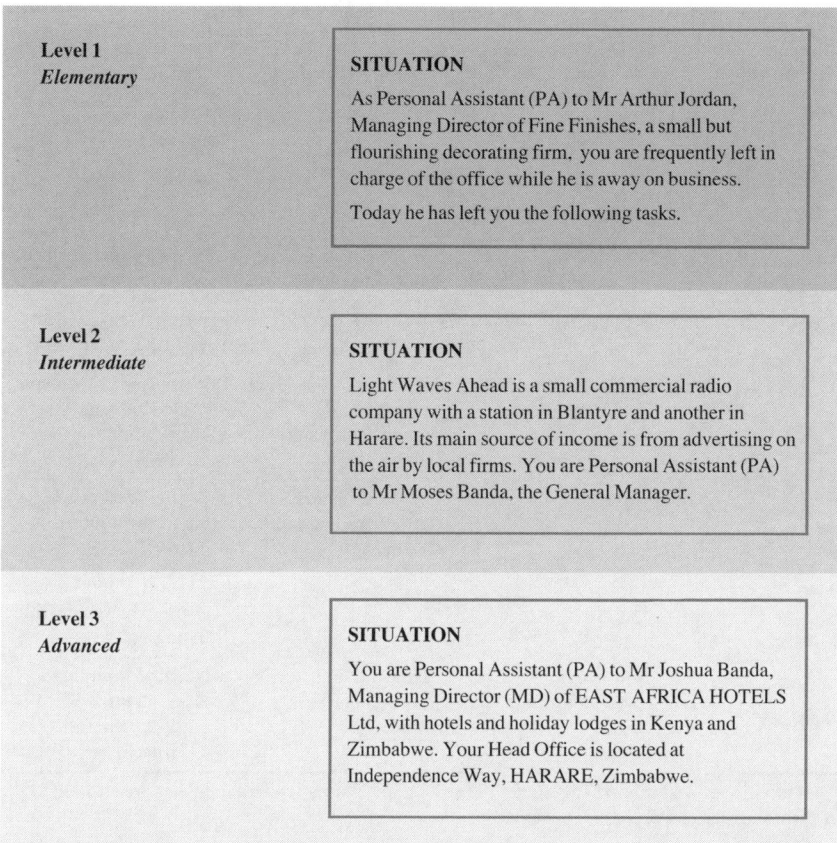

Level 1
Elementary

SITUATION

As Personal Assistant (PA) to Mr Arthur Jordan, Managing Director of Fine Finishes, a small but flourishing decorating firm, you are frequently left in charge of the office while he is away on business.

Today he has left you the following tasks.

Level 2
Intermediate

SITUATION

Light Waves Ahead is a small commercial radio company with a station in Blantyre and another in Harare. Its main source of income is from advertising on the air by local firms. You are Personal Assistant (PA) to Mr Moses Banda, the General Manager.

Level 3
Advanced

SITUATION

You are Personal Assistant (PA) to Mr Joshua Banda, Managing Director (MD) of EAST AFRICA HOTELS Ltd, with hotels and holiday lodges in Kenya and Zimbabwe. Your Head Office is located at Independence Way, HARARE, Zimbabwe.

Level 1 source: Pitman Qualifications English for Business Communication, Past Paper EL–NBC (11:2)
Level 2 source: Pitman Qualifications English for Business Communication, Past Paper EL–NBC (12:2)
Level 3 source: Pitman Qualifications English for Business Communication, Past Paper EL–NBC (13:2)

the output required. It would be interesting to establish, through a latent trait study for instance, what the differences in difficulty of the three levels really are. Unfortunately, there is no publicly available documentation on how difference in level is established or maintained – this criticism can be made of the other test developers referred to in this chapter.

It is not clear from the documentation how the benchmarking to the Common European Framework (CEF) was achieved – whether it was done through a

Table 1.4 English for Business Communications (Pitman)

	Level 1	Level 2	Level 3
Benchmarked	CEF Waystage (B2)	CEF Vantage (C1)	CEF Mastery (C2)
Time Allowed	90 minutes*	120 minutes*	150 minutes*
Contextualisation	Brief (35 words approx)	Brief (35 words approx)	Brief (35 words approx)
Task 1	Writing – guided letter	Writing – guided letter	Writing – guided letter
Task 2	Writing – memo	Writing – fax guided by written instruction	Writing – memo guided by written instruction
Task 3	Writing – fax guided by written instruction	Writing – memo	Writing – fax guided by written instruction
Task 4	Writing – guided letter from written input	Writing – guided short report from charts/tables and written input	Writing – notice/memo guided by written instruction
Task 5		Writing – guided article from written input	Writing – press release guided by written instruction
Task 6			Writing – report from charts/tables and written input
	No word limit set for tasks, all tasks 25 marks	No word limit set for tasks, all tasks 20 marks	No word limit set for tasks, all tasks 20 marks except tasks 3 and 4 (10 each)

* all tests have an additional 15 minutes of reading time during which candidates are allowed to read through the test paper, but not to write.

qualitative comparison between the test specifications and the CEF, or whether evidence was gathered from test candidates (as was done in the ALTE 'Can Do' project).

3. An outline of the construct upon which the test focuses

Taking the test descriptions seen in Table 1.4 as a basis, it is clear that the test levels described are focused primarily on the writing ability of candidates. In fact, the tasks typically involve the candidate reacting to a written prompt, so there is a genuine attempt to mirror the language use domain of the work environment, see Figure 1.7 for an example of how this is conceived in a task from Level 2.

We can therefore say that the construct that seems to underlie the English for Business Communication is that of an integrated reading into writing approach.

Figure 1.7 Example of integrated task (reading into writing) from Level 2 Pitman EBC

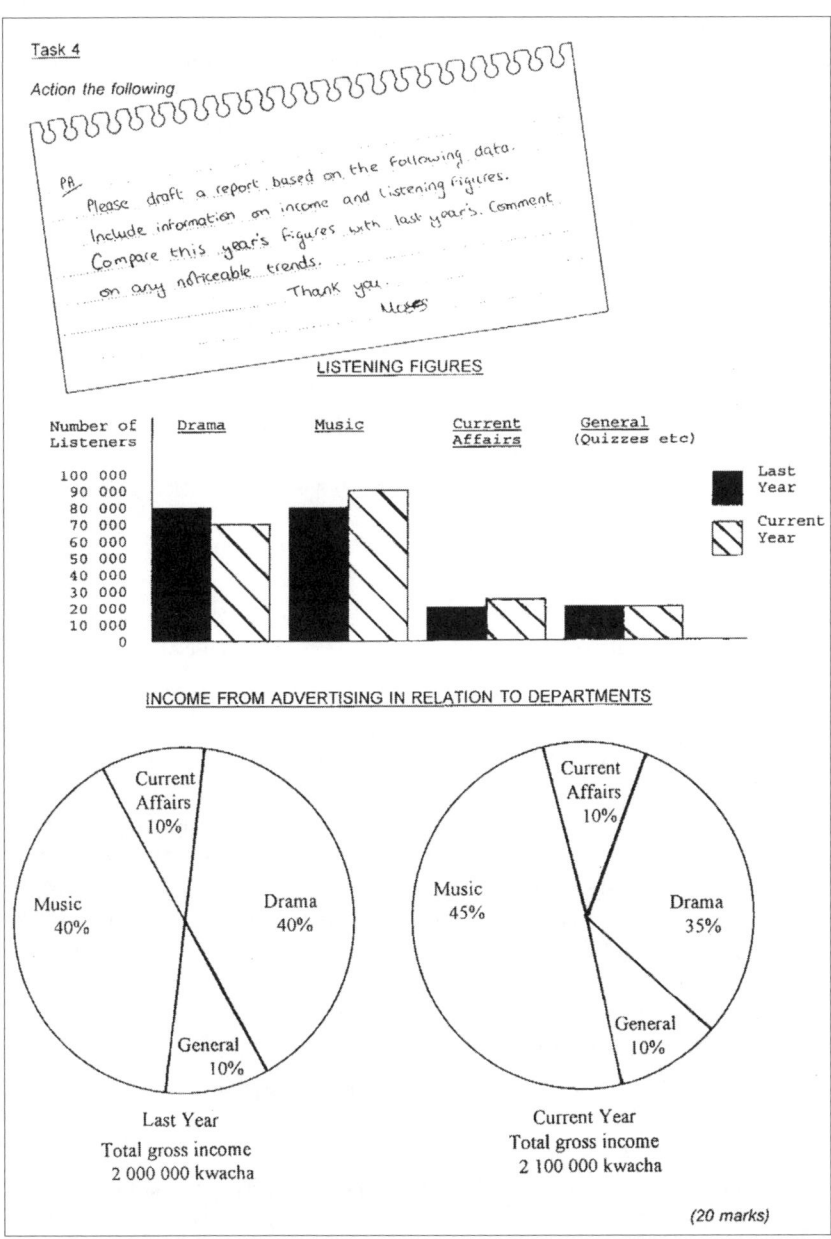

Task 4

Action the following

PA,
Please draft a report based on the following data.
Include information on income and listening figures.
Compare this year's figures with last year's. Comment
on any noticeable trends.
Thank you.
Moses

LISTENING FIGURES

INCOME FROM ADVERTISING IN RELATION TO DEPARTMENTS

Last Year
Total gross income
2 000 000 kwacha

Current Year
Total gross income
2 100 000 kwacha

(20 marks)

Source: Pitman Qualifications English Business Communication, Past Paper EL–NBC (12:6)

4. The test method

As described in the previous section, the test is comprised of a series of written tasks. In the task reproduced above, candidates are told that their work is assessed for quality of layout. Layout is also assessed for one 'memorandum' and one 'letter' task at each of the three levels. The other criteria are 'language' (though exactly what this means is not defined), 'content', 'neatness' and 'legibility'.

5. Skills' coverage

An interesting feature of the tests is the lack of a 'test-like' rubric. Instead, all instructions are included in the input for the tasks. However, it appears that the Pitman series essentially tests only writing – though there is of course a written input to be read in the case of each task, there is no overt examination of the reading skill it is, presumably, tested indirectly through performance on the writing. While this may well represent an accurate picture of the 'real' world, the fact that the skills are integrated in this way means that there is a danger of cross-contamination, in that it will not be clear if a test taker performs poorly due to a lack of reading ability or a lack of writing ability.

This problem is inferred in the [Pitman] Examinations Report when it is stated of Level 2, that

> some candidates lose marks for content because they are so busy inventing information to fit their format that they ignore the real purpose of the report (2000:11).

It could be argued that they may not actually fully understand what the focus is because they have misinterpreted the input. The report goes on to describe the fact that '[Many] candidates fail to read the prompts carefully enough before starting to write' as an 'area of weakness' (2000: 12). It should be pointed out that this is a criticism that could be made of any test using an integrated format. The problem is usually addressed by carefully monitoring the language of the input to ensure that it is written at a level that is below that of the test (so the language of input for a C1 level test is usually aimed at level B2). The worry here is that it is not clear if this monitoring has been adequately done.

6. Measurement qualities

No information is currently available in the public domain.

7. Degree of specificity/authenticity

At first glance, it appears that the test is more 'specific' in nature than the TOEIC. It may therefore be useful to see why this might be the case, so that we can develop a clearer picture of how specificity is manifested in this type of test. So what is more specific about the test?

In order to look at the degree of specificity it is necessary to consider the test from the perspective of situational and interactional authenticity. In the case of the latter there is no actual evidence to support any claims in this respect. However, the evidence from the test descriptions and in particular from the item type described earlier (Figure 1.7) suggests that there is a serious attempt here to recreate a realistic domain-specific task. The above task involves the candidate in the integration of skills (reading and writing) in order to produce a business letter. Clearly, there is a major difference here when we compare the reading tasks in the previously reviewed test, where the candidate was expected to respond at all times to an MCQ item.

In terms of situational authenticity, there is evidence that the developers have tried to recreate a 'business' context through the tasks (often integrating handwritten memos and notes to written output) which all appear to have a very clear business focus.

While all of this is positive, there is some concern over the fact that the tests are only concerned with reading into writing tasks. This very much lessens the true business focus of the tests in that a major element of the business language domain is simply ignored. This has the effect of lessening the strength of any specificity argument we might wish to make for these tests.

8. Impact of non-language factors

Despite the shortcomings associated with testing only a limited aspect of a candidate's language, there is a relatively high degree of specificity in the different levels of this test. With this degree of specificity, comes a potential for non-language factors (such as background variables) to have some impact on test performance. However, before simply accepting that this impact is necessarily negative, let's consider the argument made by Elder (2001) with regard to what she perceived as the negative impact of non-language factors in tests of specific purpose.

Imagine, for example, a test candidate who has had a lot of experience in writing the sort of letter called for in Figure 1.7. It appears only natural that this experience should positively affect that person's performance on the task.

Now imagine a second scenario where another candidate, this time with little business experience, but with a similar level of language ability as the first candidate and a lot of experience in taking MCQ-based tests, is asked to complete an MCQ version of our task. This person too will perform well and again the impact comes primarily from experience of the task type.

When we consider these two situations we see that there are in fact a number of ways of looking at non-language factors. The latter form is clearly problematic as it constitutes a source of context-irrelevant variance. However, the former is quite different, in that it is certainly not 'context-irrelevant', in fact there is a clear argument here for the inclusion of this source of variance in the construct definition of tests in a specific purpose domain.

If we try to dilute our specific purpose tests until there is little or no danger of context-related non-language impact we end up with tests that are basically non-context dependent general proficiency instruments.

9. Reporting of test performance

Test performances are reported using the criterion levels described in Table 1.5.

Table 1.5 Criterion levels for the EBC (Pitman) levels

Criterion	Level 1	Level 2	Level 3
Fail	< 60 marks	< 60 marks	< 60 marks
Pass	60 – 74 marks	60 – 74 marks	60 – 74 marks
First Class Pass	> 74 marks	> 74 marks	> 74 marks

The reported pass rates for the three levels in 2002 are seen in Table 1.6.

Table 1.6 Pass rates for the EBC (Pitman) levels – 2002

Criterion	Level 1	Level 2	Level 3
Fail	21%	32%	41%
Pass	48%	48%	47%
First Class Pass	31%	20%	12%

Source: Pitman (2002).

English for Office Skills

1. A brief introduction to the test

The English for Office Skills' series offers a pair of tests (Levels 1 and 2), the stated aim of which is

> . . . [To] demonstrate accuracy in the use and transcription of English, and the ability to perform office-related tasks to spoken or written instructions (Pitman 2003:40).

Unlike the other tests reviewed in this chapter, the EOS tests are aimed at both native and non-native speakers of English (Pitman 2003:40) and are claimed by its developers to be aimed at '[People] who need to carry out tasks in English where accuracy in writing and following instructions is important' (Pitman 2003:40).

2. A brief description of the test

As with the above Pitman test, the levels of the EOS test are described in Table 1.7.

Section A at each level focuses on spelling and listening comprehension, while Section B focuses on reading comprehension, vocabulary and accuracy. The descriptive table indicates that writing ability is not tested directly, instead it is estimated through a candidate's ability to identify errors in the proof-reading tasks and in the sentence completion task.

Table 1.7 English for Office Skills (Pitman)

		Level 1 Elementary CEF A2 – Waystage [Marks]	Level 2 Intermediate CEF B2 – Vantage [Marks]
Section A	*Spelling*	Sentence read by examiner Target word repeated 20 items – accuracy of spelling [20]	Sentence read by examiner Target word repeated 20 items – accuracy of spelling [20]
	Listening Comp.	Short passage read twice Form completion (written) or message transfer (oral) [10]	Short passage read twice Form completion (written) or message transfer (oral) [10]
Section B	*Reading Comp.*	Read newspaper/magazine article – sentence completion [10]	Read newspaper/magazine article – sentence completion [10]
	Syntax	15 items – proof-reading [15]	20 items – proof-reading
	Vocabulary	10 items – select appropriate word (from two) [10]	10 items – select appropriate word (from two) [10]
	Punctuation	Proof-reading [10]	Proof-reading [10]
	Proof-reading A	Identify error in table of figures [10]	Identify 5 errors in table of figures [5]
	Proof-reading B	Proof-read letter – identify 15 errors (typography, spelling and/or punctuation) [15]	Proof-read letter – identify 10 errors (typography, spelling or punctuation, style) [10]

3. An outline of the construct upon which the test focuses

These tests do not appear to have been designed to offer a measure of a non-native English-speaking test taker's proficiency within a business context, but represent a more vocational measure of practical skills. The underlying construct is somewhat unclear from the test description. The test seems to focus on the form of the language – identifying different aspects of linguistic accuracy as the underlying construct.

4. The test method

The test method is essentially confined to short answer format (SAF) items based either on examiner-read input (tape recordings are, as yet, not used in the Pitman tests), or on written input. The fact that the listening comprehension portion is read by the examiner is quite problematic, as there is a clear possibility of an 'examiner effect' where different people will be more or less clear in their reading aloud (thus introducing an element of construct-irrelevant variance). Apart from this criticism, the test method appears to meet the needs of the test (to test language knowledge rather than language use).

5. Skills' coverage

As was outlined above, the skills covered in the test are limited to the ability to demonstrate knowledge of the language through measures of linguistic accuracy, though as we can see from Figure 1.8 the proof-reading task is more related to identifying differences in the numbers in the tables than it is to identifying language-related differences. The sources of input, therefore, are quite important in this type of test. The listening element of the test consists of two parts, lexical knowledge (listening and spelling) and comprehension (through a short dictation). Here there is no real evidence that the second part measures 'comprehension' (by which I mean understanding) though I acknowledge that this is not an area in which all testers will agree (see for example the arguments of Lado (1961) and Oller (1979) who disagree on what dictation actually tests).

The reading comprehension items are built around a single passage (approximately 350 words at Level 1 and 500 words at Level 2). Items are based on sentence completion, which limits the skill being tested to that of searching for specific information (and possible lexical synonyms). The remainder of both papers contains items related to the display of knowledge of language accuracy.

Both levels contain a proof-reading item as Task 7. In these cases the task is to compare two tables of information, one being accurate and the other said to contain errors (10 at Level 1 and 5 at Level 2). As can be seen from the extract in Figure 1.8, this is not actually a reading task at all – it is a proofing task and is not dependent on language ability.

6. Measurement qualities

No information is currently available in the public domain.

7. Degree of specificity/authenticity

The degree of specificity appears to be quite low. While the tasks have been set in a business context, the tasks that are included are not necessarily related to the business domain. In other words, they are more context-oriented (i.e. they are set in the context of the business domain) than context-focused (i.e. they are designed to test only the language of the business domain). This suggests that the test is more general proficiency focused and should be placed towards the non-specific end of the continuum.

Taking just one task as an example (Figure 1.9, the reading task which begins Section B of each test paper) it is interesting to notice how it measures up with regard to the first items on the list of task demands suggested by Weir (1993),

Figure 1.8 Proof-reading task (#7) from EOS Level 1

---

7 PROOF-READING (A)

In the first table there are no typographical errors. In the second one, however, there are FIVE. Identify each error exactly on the second table putting a circle around it.

EXAMPLE: £1 234   £1 2(43)

Do NOT correct the errors.

CORRECT VERSION

BEST FIXED RATE MORTGAGES				
Lender	Rate	Fixed Until	Maximum Advance	Fee
Hinckley & Rugby BS	1.50%	01/06/98	70%	£250
Melton Mowbray BS	6.95%	30/09/98	90%	£99
Norwich & Peterborough BS	7.99%	01/01/00	85%	£250
Nottingham Imperial BS	8.25%	31/07/00	90%	£350
Royal Bank of Scotland	8.85%	01/07/05	95%	£250

INCORRECT VERSION

BEST FIXED RATE MORtGAGES				
Lender	Rate	Fixed Until	Maximum Advance	Fee
Hinckley & Rugby BS	1.50%	01/06/98	70%	£250
Melton Mowbray BS	6.95%	30/09/99	90%	£99
Norwich & Peterbrough BS	7.99%	01/01/00	85%	£250
Nottingham Imperial BS	8.25%	31/07/00	90%	£530
Royal Bank of Scotland	8.85%	01/07/05	95%	£250

Source: Pitman Qualifications English for Office Skills, Past Paper EL–OFFN (11:9)

Figure 1.9 Reading items from Pitman qualifications EOS Level 2

In the cut and thrust world of stockbroking, a new computerised system is expected to revolutionise the way shares are bought and sold.

Technology is coming to the rescue of private investors who are fed up with the traditional stockbrokers' high prices and discount brokers' poor service. Instead of holding on the telephone for minutes at a time to buy or sell shares, or to ask for a portfolio valuation, private investors can now run their portfolios electronically - through the Internet.

A new company, ShareNet, offers services which range from simple share dealing to sophisticated portfolio management. Launched earlier this year, the service is a joint venture between a software company and a firm of accountants. Its appeal is financial. ShareNet has an attractive scale of charges which dramatically undercut those of traditional stockbroking firms. Fees are as low as 0.5% to 1% per year.

So how does ShareNet work? Customers who wish to buy or sell shares are invited to register

(Extract from approx. 450 word passage)

1 .... and .... have resulted in customer

   dissatisfaction with traditional stockbroking methods.

2 The answer to such dissatisfaction is electronic dealing via ....

(items related to that section of the passage)

Source: Pitman Qualification: English for Office Skills Level 2; Past Paper EL–OFFN (12:4–5) .

purpose and response format. While we would expect to see a clear purpose for reading in any test, within a specific purpose domain this need becomes central to the characterisation of the task. Here, there does not appear to be a clearly specified purpose. As for response format, we would expect in a specific purpose domain task that the response format will replicate that of some element of the domain, again the sentence completion format is not at all relevant to the business domain. This latter criticism is possibly a bit harsh, as it would appear to be very difficult to satisfy the need for business domain-like response formats for all skills – in particular receptive skills.

In terms of task demands, the test can be criticised from the perspective of channel (tape recordings are not used in these tests so the invigilator reads the listening passages aloud), text type (while the reading text shown is based on a magazine-type article it is not typical of business-related reading material, which is more likely to be a letter, e-mail, memo or report), and text length (in this case the text is quite long at about 450 words; however, this is not typical of business texts, which tend to be brief and to the point).

When it becomes clear that the test can be criticised for its context validity (where context validity is seen in terms of task and text demands) the claim of situational authenticity is seen as tenuous.

Unlike the other Pitman test reviewed, there is little evidence here of interactional authenticity. It could, of course, be argued that the test is focusing on a very discrete level of knowledge and that generalisation to the business language use domain is possible. The distance between this micro view of language ability and the macro level of language use is great and such an argument is somewhat difficult to sustain.

8. Impact of non-language factors

From the review to date, it is clear that the inseparability of skills issue is again problematic. This is particularly relevant with regard to Tasks 2 (listening comprehension) and 7 (proof-reading), where there is a real danger of a reader/speaker-related effect in the former and in the latter where the proof-reading skills are focused on identifying numerical rather than lexical or syntactic differences.

9. Reporting of test performance

Test performance is reported in the same way (and with the same cut score boundaries) as the English for Business Communication (EBC) test reviewed above. This means that the Passing level is set at 60% while the First Class Pass level is set at 75%. The pass rates for the 2002 administration are shown in Table 1.8, though no data on the test population are available.

Table 1.8 Pass rates for the EOS (Pitman) levels – 2002

Criterion	Level 1	Level 2
Fail	24%	41%
Pass	34%	33%
First Class Pass	42%	26%

London Chamber of Commerce and Industry Examinations Board (LCCIEB) tests of language for business and commerce

1. A brief introduction to the test

As the name of the organisation suggests, the London Chamber of Commerce and Industry Examinations Board (LCCIEB), has, as its main focus, the provision of specialist examinations in the area of business and commerce. Among the many examinations it offers are a number which are dedicated to the testing of language for business purposes. Since the approach adopted by LCCIEB is rather unique, it will be dealt with somewhat differently to the other examination providers.

The uniqueness of the LCCIEB examinations stems from the adherence to a single framework, which seems to be applied regardless of the language being tested. This effectively means that a single test specification has been used to create what we might call multi-language clones. To illustrate what I mean by this, I will briefly review their '. . . for Business' range of examinations.

2. A brief description of the test

The following table (Table 1.9) is a breakdown of the description of the tests of English and Spanish for Business, as described by the LCCIEB in the extended syllabuses for these examinations.

Table 1.9 LCCIEB tests of language for business and commerce

Test	Skills Tested				Method						CoE Benchmark
	L	S	R	W	MCQ	T/F	SAF	ITr	ExW	Spo	
English for Business											
Preliminary Level			•	•	•	•	•		S		Breakthrough
Level 1			•	•				•	S		Waystage
Level 2			•	•				•	S/L		Threshold
Level 3			•	•			•	•	S/L		Vantage
Level 4			•	•	•		•	•	L		EOP
Spanish for Business											
Preliminary Level			•	•	•	•	•		S		Breakthrough
Level 1			•	•				•	S		Waystage
Level 2			•	•				•	S/L		Threshold
Level 3			•	•			•	•	S/L		Vantage
Level 4			•	•	•		•	•	L		EOP

MCQ – Multiple-Choice questions
T/F – True/false questions
SAF – Short answer format questions
ITr – Information transfer questions
ExW – Extended written output required (S = Short; L = Long)
Spo – Spoken output required
CoE – Council of Europe Framework
EOP – Effective Operational Proficiency
* – Not yet available

3. An outline of the construct upon which the test focuses

Both tests focus on reading and writing skills, and are specified in exactly the same way. While this is not in itself problematic, the fact that the task and item types are essentially identical means that the test developers see no difference between different languages at particular levels of proficiency. While it may seem to be relatively easy to agree that a candidate at a particular level should be capable of performing a particular task or function, the degree of linguistic sophistication needed to achieve this is not exactly the same for all languages. Including the same task regardless of target language is at least potentially problematic.

Alderson (1998) pointed out the danger of adopting such an approach in the context of the DIALANG project in Europe. In this project a test format through which a whole series of official European languages could be tested at equivalent levels was envisaged. The original plans involved devising a set of detailed specifications for the English test and then cloning tests in the other languages from this. The developers found that there were real difficulties in identifying appropriate tasks (as tasks which were seen to be at an acceptable level for one language were found to be more suited to a different level for another language), and in identifying what was considered acceptable performance across different languages for those tasks that were considered appropriate. The solution adopted by the DIALANG group was to allow developers from each language background to interpret the specifications to create an instrument that they considered appropriate. This approach was also taken by the BULATS teams who developed tests in the same four languages as the LCCIEB (these are discussed below).

Not only are the series of tests for each language all based on the same model, in fact, there appears to be no difference in the make-up of the tests in the different languages. For example, the description in the Extended Syllabus documents for a particular task at Level 3 for the German (LCCIEB 2001b:3), Spanish (LCCIEB 2001c:3) and French (LCCIEB 2001d:3) tests is shown in Table 1.10.

Table 1.10 Extract from extended Syllabus for LCCIEB tests of German, Spanish and French

German Level 3 – Task 2	Spanish Level 3 – Task 2	French Level 3 – Task 2
Question 2 involves the drafting of an internal report based on raw data given in the form of graphs, notes, press cuttings, charts, tables, etc. Candidates will have to understand, select, collate and, if necessary, supplement this data in order to write the report in the light of the instructions given.	Question 2 involves the drafting of an internal report based on raw data given in the form of graphs, notes, press cuttings, charts, tables, etc. Candidates will have to understand, select, collate and, if necessary, supplement this data in order to write the report in the light of the instructions given.	Question 2 involves the drafting of an internal report based on raw data given in the form of graphs, notes, press cuttings, charts, tables, etc. Candidates will have to understand, select, collate and, if necessary, supplement this data in order to write the report in the light of the instructions given.

When this is compared to the English for Business documentation (LCCIEB 2001a:3), we find that it is again exactly the same, see Table 1.11. The suspicion

Table 1.11 Extract from extended syllabus for LCCIEB test of English

English Level 3 – Task 2
Question 2 involves the drafting of an internal report based on raw data given in the form of graphs, notes, press cuttings, charts, tables, etc. Candidates will have to understand, select, collate and, if necessary, supplement this data in order to write the report in the light of the instructions given.

that all of the tests are essentially clones of the original English test, which was the first to be introduced, is confirmed when we see the actual tasks.

While the LCCIEB provide details of the syllabuses for each of their examinations, together with specimen papers, sample answers and examiner's report/comments, there is no evidence supplied in support of the approach they adopt in creating these tests in the different languages. The same criticism can be made of the test of Spoken English for Industry and Commerce (SEFIC) and the Foreign Languages for Industry and Commerce (FLIC), with only a single difference between the two sets of examinations (the addition of a translation task at the highest – fourth – level).

4. The test method

From the descriptive table (Table 1.9) we can see that the test includes a range of task and item types, with multiple-choice (MCQ), short answer format (SAF), true/false (T/F) and written production all included in the response options.

5. Skills' coverage

Reading and writing are tested at both levels.

6. Measurement qualities

No information is currently available in the public domain.

7. Degree of specificity/authenticity

These tests appear to be closer to general purpose language tests than to specific purpose instruments, as the following tasks suggest. The reason for this can again be traced to the task and text demands implied in the sample materials provided by the developers (see Figure 1.10).

It is not easy to know what these listening items are testing. The need for 'complete and grammatically correct answers' suggests that the items may be

Figure 1.10 Listening Item – English for Business, Preliminary level (LCCIEB)

Write a sentence to answer these questions. Full marks will only be given for complete and grammatically correct answers.

B12   When does Mr Jones have his lunch?

Answer_____   (3 marks)

B13   Who is speaking on the telephone?

Answer_____   (3 marks)

B14   Who started the telephone conversation?

Source: English for Business, Preliminary, sample paper: 6

focused on grammar (in the Bachman sense – syntax, lexis etc.), though the nature of the task with which they are associated appears to be communicative (information transfer). Other task demands which do not appear to fit with such tasks in the business domain are:

response format – we might expect that the listener would create a message or memo from this type of input, rather than simply respond to a series of discrete items, though it appears that other listening tasks do lead on to a writing task

known criteria – the above example suggests that candidates might have problems responding to the item as the criteria for achieving marks are not related to the apparent communicative nature of the task. For the one piece of writing included in the test the marks are awarded for 'correct titles' (20%), 'the message' (40%) and again 'spelling and presentation' (40%).

In terms of the text demands, it is clear that there are limitations of functional range, nature of information (the items could quite easily be presented as part of a general proficiency test), and text length (only very brief reading and listening extracts used). In addition, the lack of contextualisation means that there is no effort made to establish any meaningful interlocutor-to-listener relationship, so any speaker-related variables remain untapped – again a situation unlikely in the business domain.

The fact that these tests are more focused on the general proficiency domain means that there is some likelihood that the test tasks will not result in the kind of cognitive processing that typifies a business domain task performance. This suggests that it is unlikely that interactional authenticity can be successfully claimed for these tasks. However, it is not at all clear yet if it is possible to effectively identify typical patterns of processing associated with successful task performance in a specific domain.

8. Impact of non-language factors

As we have seen in the other tests reviewed here, the indications are that where a test is situated closer to the general proficiency end of the specificity continuum, there is little danger of non-language factors that may be associated with knowledge of the test context impacting on test performance.

9. Reporting of test performance

Test performances are reported using the criterion levels described in Table 1.12.

Table 1.12 Criterion levels for the English for Business (LCCIEB) levels

	Preliminary	Level 1	Level 2	Level 3	Level 4
Pass	50%	50%	50%	50%	50%
Credit	60%	60%	60%	60%	60%
Distinction	75%	75%	75%	75%	75%

No details are available on pass rates.

Tests for business purposes in languages other than English

Apart from the tests of English for business, and the foreign language tests administered by the LCCIEB, there are a growing number of tests in languages other than English for the purpose of describing candidates' ability to use that language in a business or commercial context. Some of these tests are described now.

Test de français international (TFI)

1. A brief introduction to the test

The TFI is designed to evaluate the level of French of non-native speakers. Like its sister test, the TOEIC, the test is based on a series of MCQ items focusing on reading and listening. Somewhat confusingly, the developers make quite different claims of what the test aims to measure. On the link to the TFI from the main TOEIC website, it is claimed that it can be used to assess 'a candidate's ability to understand, speak, read and write French as it is used in the international workplace and in everyday life' (ETS 2003a). While there is some very limited evidence that this may be the case for the TOEIC, there is no evidence whatsoever to support a similar claim for the TFI. On the TOEIC–Europe website the claim is replaced with a less bold statement that the 'test assesses a candidate's ability to communicate in French as it is used in the international workplace and in everyday life' (ETS 2003b).

Interestingly, the claims made of the TFI and the TOEIC are not always consistent. On the USA-based website the statements made of the TOEIC reflect those more conservative statements made of the TFI on the European site, while the broader claims of generalisability to all four skill areas made on the European site regarding the TFI are reflected on the USA website, but with regard to the TOEIC.

2. A brief description of the test

As mentioned above, the TFI appears to be a clone of the TOEIC – with the same sub-skills tested using the same item types. Table 1.13 offers an overview of the test. At the time of writing, no information was available in the public domain on the make-up of the test, either in the form of a specification or of published support materials.

Table 1.13 Descriptive table of the Test de français international

Section I LISTENING (42 min)	Section II READING (68 min)
I Question-Answer [40 questions]	IV Error Identification [25 questions]
II Short Dialogues [30 questions]	V Incomplete Sentences [25 questions]
III Short Conversations [20 questions]	VI Comprehension [40 questions]

3. An outline of the construct upon which the test focuses

As mentioned before, the TFI focuses on the receptive skills of reading and listening. The claim that it offers a measure of all four skills is neither supported by the multiple-choice-based approach nor by the decision to test only the receptive skills.

4. The test method

The test takes a multiple-choice approach and is solidly based in the same psychometric–structuralist approach as the TOEIC, which, as I mentioned earlier, has long been abandoned as the primary methodology in gathering evidence of a test taker's ability to perform specific language tasks. This is not to say that the approach is incapable of ever providing evidence. On the contrary, when it comes to obtaining estimates of a clearly defined and realised (or realisable) trait the theoretical foundations of the approach are as sound today as they were when they were developed. Among the problems with using the approach as it is manifested in the two tests here (TFI and TOEIC) is that the purported construct, as evidenced by the inferences that developers claim can be drawn from test performance, does not appear to be supportable.

5. Skills' coverage

The TFI consists of two sections, one devoted to listening and the other to reading. As is consistent with the approach taken (see above), the sub-sections present the language in short segments (of reading and listening texts), each designed to test a specific aspect of the language ability of the test taker. However, we can only make assumptions about the test format and content as, at the time of writing, there is no evidence (apart from the outline provided on the TFI website) available in the public domain.

6. Measurement qualities

No information is currently available in the public domain.

7. Degree of specificity/authenticity

Since there is very little information about the test available in the public domain, it is not possible to make any definitive comment on the degree of specificity, though if the TFI really is a clone of the TOEIC, it would appear that it is more a measure of general language proficiency than of proficiency in a specific context, and like the TOEIC, it is unlikely to display evidence of either situational or interactional authenticity.

8. Impact of non-language factors

Again, we do not have the evidence to establish if non-language factors have any impact on test performance.

9. Reporting of test performance

The scores are reported in the same way as the scores for TOEIC, so individual scores are reported for reading (on a scale of 5–495) and listening (on a similar scale) and a total score (on a scale of 10–990). There does not appear to be an attempt to indicate what these scores might mean (for example in terms of a benchmark of ability such as the Common European Framework).

Certificazione della conoscenza dell'italiano commerciale (CIC)

1. A brief introduction to the test

The Certificazione della conoscenza dell'italiano commerciale (*Certificate in Italian for Commerce* – CIC) was developed at the Università per Stranieri di Perugia, Italy during the late 1990s and first administered in June 2000. The test was developed in response to a perceived demand based on the increasing interest at that time in the domain of Italian language for business. The CIC is intended to establish a candidate's ability to use Italian in 'work-related contexts': travel agencies, banks, estate agencies, and industry. To date, the test population has reached the level of approximately six hundred candidates per year – non-native speakers of Italian, working in, or hoping to work in an Italian business context.

At the time of writing, the CIC is the only certificated test of Italian for business.

2. A brief description of the test

The CIC consists of five sub-tests: reading, listening, grammar and lexicon, writing and speaking and is offered at two levels, these are intermedio (Intermediate) which is set at ALTE Level 2 (or CEF Level B1) and avanzado (advanced) set at ALTE Level 4 (CEF Level C1). See Table 1.14 for an outline of the two tests.

As can be seen from this table, the tests offer an extensive assessment of the language level of the candidates. According to the CIC handbook, the tests are designed to certify 'that the holder's knowledge of the Italian language **is adequate for that person to interact and work in business contexts**' [their emphasis] (CIC 2003a:2) and suggests they can be used by:

- people who work or intend to work in international environments and who want to enhance their personal curriculum
- companies and organisations selecting personnel or those who wish to check the qualifications of their employees
- schools/universities with economic and business courses who want to survey or determine the level of knowledge of the Italian language for their own students.

3. An outline of the construct upon which the test focuses

The test appears to have been built around the model of language ability suggested by Bachman (1990) and is similar in design to the Cambridge ESOL model. The test therefore takes the same multi-skills approach as similar Cambridge ESOL tests.

4. The test method

The five components of the CIC are weighted as shown in Table 1.15 and are tested using a variety of item types: MCQ, matching, gap-filling, letters, compositions, and short essays. The method is based, to a large extent, on the use of actual business documentation. These texts are to be found in the reading and listening components, as well as in the writing and speaking papers. Contextualisation of test tasks is evident, particularly in the test papers focused on language production – where there is a very clear description of audience, as well as reference to the required level of formality of the output.

5. Skills' coverage

As mentioned above, the CIC includes measures of five aspects of a test taker's language ability – reading, listening, grammar and vocabulary, writing and speaking.

Table 1.14 Certificate in Italian for Commerce: description

	Intermedio (Level B1)	Avanzado (Level C1)
A. Reading	A1. Careful global reading – 10 MCQ items based on 20 to 120 word passages (business documentation)	A1. Careful global reading – 8 main ideas items (matching – based on business documentation)
	A2. Expeditious global reading (skimming) relate item to passage – 10 items	A2. Careful global reading – passage completion (cloze type, given choice from 13 phrases) – based on business documentation
	A3. Expeditious and careful global reading – finding main ideas in passages 8 items (business documentation – matching and gap-filling)	A3. Careful global – identifying main ideas in passage 5 items (MCQ) – based on business documentation
B. Listening	B1. Careful global – listening for general understanding, 10 items, short monologues – matching)	B1. Careful global – information transformation (note-taking), 11 items (SAF)
	B.2 Careful local – form/memo completion 8 items (phone message – note-taking)	B.2 Careful local – identify speakers and topics (10 items – matching)
	B.3 Careful global – extended text, 4 items based on business-related monologue or conversation (MCQ)	B.3 Careful global – extended text, 4 items (MCQ)
C. Grammar and Vocabulary	C.1 15 item MCQ format	C.1 12 item MCQ cloze format
	C.2 Cloze passage, 10 items (based on business communication)	C.2 Cloze passage, 12 items
D. Writing	D.1 Writing a formal business letter or informal business related email (90–110 words)	D.1 Writing a report based on input from graphs/charts – about 100 words
		D.2 Write an argumentative text to a specific person related to a specific business topic (200 to 250 words)
E. Speaking	E.1 Personal Information Exchange – no preparation	E.1 Personal information exchange – no preparation
	E.2 Interaction – with examiner based on read input (materials given 10 minutes before test)	E.2 Interaction – with examiner based on read input (materials given 15 minutes before test)
	E.3 Long turn – on known work related topic (materials given 10 minutes before test)	E.3 Long turn – monologue on general work related topic (materials given 15 minutes before test)
Total Time	115 minutes	225 minutes

Source: CIC (2003b)

6. Measurement qualities

No information is available in the public domain at the time of writing. However, the test developers are involved in a large scale pan-European project concerning the development and validation of an item bank. This will be used to more accurately define test levels for the CIC (as well as the other tests they currently administer).

7. Degree of specificity/authenticity

From the description of the test presented above we can deduce that there has been an effort on the part of the test developers to include in the CIC tasks that are based on business documentation and that reflect the use of language in the business domain. The degree to which they succeed appears to be mixed, however. As we have seen in the reviews of the other tests, there seems to be a real problem particularly with the receptive tasks. The example shown here (Figure 1.11) is interesting in that the context is clearly that of the business domain and the required output reflects that of the domain, but the degree of scaffolding (in the form of the guides to what to listen for) acts to reduce its situational authenticity. It is difficult to see how this situation can be resolved; after all if we just give the candidate a blank page and tell them to listen to the message we are completely changing the task. In the real world the listeners will bring to the event a great deal of background knowledge related to the particular company they are working for, so a schema for dealing with the call will be in place. The function of the scaffold is to reduce the impact of this lack of schema.

The fact that the tasks are typically based on business documentation and are explicitly benchmarked to the work-related aspect of the CEF and ALTE frameworks (CIC 2003a:5–8) can be seen as evidence of situational authenticity. However, the inclusion of tasks that are clearly not related to the domain (particularly the MCQ responses), and the limitations of tests of receptive skills (implied in the above critique of the listening task) weaken the veracity of this evidence.

From the perspective of interactional authenticity the evidence is also mixed. The variety of task types included at both levels suggests that the interaction between the executive resources available to the candidate and the executive processes (i.e. cognitive and meta-cognitive processing) may well be facilitated at least for some of the tasks (particularly in the tests of production). However, this same variety means that there are tasks that are very unlikely to have the same effect. Here I am referring to those based on the receptive skills, language knowledge display, and in particular those that rely on multiple-choice items.

As for the degree of specificity of the CIC tests, we can see that the test fits into the category of a business-oriented test, with some evidence that at least some of the papers are also business-focused. The writing test is an example of this; there the expected output is in the form of a contextualised business-related text with clearly defined writer/reader relationship and degree of formality.

Figure 1.11 Listening Task B2: CIC Intermediate

B.2
- Ascolterete due telefonate.
- Riempire gli appositi spazi con le informazioni opportune.
- Ascolterete le telefonate due volte.

Prima telefonata

Cliente: *Impresa edile* .... (1)

Articoli ordinati:

n. 1 porta

misure ....(2)

.... (3)

legno .... (4)

Tempi di consegna: .... (5)

Inviare fax al Sig. Mario Bianchi, Direttore .... (6)

numero di fax ....(7)

Even here, there is some question over the tests as the written performances are awarded scores based on language-related criteria – lexical competence, competence in morphology and syntax, sociocultural competence and consistency (CIC 2003a:14). The absence of any task- (and therefore business-domain) focused criterion reduces the likelihood that these are highly specific tests.

8. Impact of non-language factors

The fact that the test consists of a battery of papers, each focusing on a particular skills' area suggests that any non-language impact will be mixed.

9. Reporting of test performance

The criterion level for achieving a passing grade is set at 60% – averaged from the results on all five components through a weighting system described in Table 1.15. This system tells us quite a bit about the interpretation of the construct, with a very clear emphasis on spoken language at both levels (where this component is worth 30% of the total marks available), and the perception that writing becomes more central to business language needs at the higher proficiency level. It goes from being worth just 10% of the total score (the least important sub-skill) at the intermediate level, to 20% at the advanced level, the second most important sub-skill.

Table 1.15 Certificate in Italian for Commerce: weighting system

	Intermedio	Avanzado
A. Reading	40 (20%)	35 (17.5%)
B. Listening	40 (20%)	35 (17.5%)
C. Grammar and vocabulary	40 (20%)	35 (17.5%)
D. Writing	20 (10%)	35 (17.5%)
E. Speaking	60 (30%)	60 (30%)
Total Score	200	200

Candidates are awarded a grade based on a simple addition of the scores achieved on each part of the examination. There are three passing grades and two failing grades – see Table 1.16.

Table 1.16 Certificate in Italian for Commerce: reporting system

Grade A	Excellent	
Grade B	Good	**Pass**
Grade C	Satisfactory	
Grade D	Unsatisfactory	**Fail**
Grade E	Very poor	

There is no information available on the rates of grade achievement for the tests.

Other tests of European languages for business purposes

There are a number of other tests of European language for business (see Table 1.17). While I do not have space here to address these tests individually, it is useful to spend just a little time on them. All of these tests are administered by members of the Association of Language Testers in Europe (ALTE), and all follow similar models – a focus on testing the four skills through a multi-task type approach. For more information on these tests see the section at the end of the book where contact information is given for all currently administered tests referred to in this chapter.

JETRO Reading and Listening Comprehension Test (JRLT)

1. A brief introduction to the test

The Hawaii based Japan-America Institute of Management Science, JAIMS, has been involved in the education (language, business and culture) of Japanese

Table 1.17 Other tests of European languages for business purposes

Levels (ALTE/CEF)	French	German	Spanish
Level 3/B2		ZDf B (Zertifikat Deutsch für den Berut)	CEN (Certificado de Espanol de los Negocios)
Level 4/C1		PWD (Prüfung Wirtschaftsdeutsch International)	
Level 5/C2	DSEC (Diplôme Supérieur d'Etudes Commerciales)		DEN (Diploma de Espanol de los Negocios)

and North American graduates for almost thirty years. The organisation administers a test of Japanese language for business purposes, developed by JETRO (Japan External Trade Organization), with the support of over six hundred companies in Japan. The test was developed during the early 1990s and first administered in 1995. It originally consisted of papers at three levels, though from 2003 there has been a revised format, which consists of a single paper.

2. A brief description of the test

All items in the Reading and Listening Comprehension Test (JRLT) use a four-option MCQ format. The different types of questions are outlined in Table 1.18. From this description, we can see that the test is based on an assessment of the receptive skills of the candidate – the associated oral test is described in the section that follows.

Table 1.18 Item types from the JRLT

	Focus	No. Items	Time
Listening test	Matching written and audio descriptions	10	50 min.
	Matching written expression to context	10	
	Careful global listening	15	
Listening and Reading test	Matching audio description to written text	15	30 min.
	Careful local listening and matching to short written texts	15	
Reading test	Grammar and vocabulary	10	40 min.
	Careful local reading (expressions)	10	
	Careful global listening	15	
Total		100	120

3. An outline of the construct upon which the test focuses

According to JETRO's website:

> 'The JETRO Test is designed to objectively measure and evaluate one's proficiency in using the Japanese language for communication involving a

variety of situations and circumstances, targeting non-native speakers engaged primarily in business' (JETRO:2003a).

The developers also claim that

'The JRLT comprehensively evaluates the examinee's skill in using Japanese to deal with a variety of business-related tasks and problems' (JETRO:2003a).

However, since it is clear that the test is focused only on listening and reading, the construct is actually quite limited. As with other tests, this is not a problem in itself, though making claims that go beyond the definition of the construct upon which the test is based is justifiably seen as problematic, as these claims represent the inferences that the developers believe can be drawn from test performance. The issue is therefore one of validity.

4. The test method

As mentioned previously, the test uses MCQ format items throughout. Most tasks involve matching audio or read input to a visual stimulus. This can be in the form of a photograph (see Figure 1.12 for an example of this task type from the Listening paper), or of a piece of written text (see Figure 1.13 for an example from the Reading and Listening paper).

Figure 1.12 JRLT Listening paper: sample item

1. 部下が上司と打ち合わせをしています。
2. 営業会議を開いています。
3. 商品企画のプレゼンテーションをしています。
4. 転勤のあいさつをしています。

Source: JETRO (2003b)

With the Reading paper, there are three item types. The first of these is actually testing grammar (See Figure 1.14), while the second tests 'forms of speech' using the same MCQ format.

In the final section of the JRLT, the candidate is asked to respond to an item in which they are asked to identify the main point or idea in a text (Figure 1.15).

Figure 1.13 JRLT Reading and Listening paper: sample item

```
リーさんへ

営業課長が、あしたの2時の約束を1時間、
遅くしてほしいとのことです。
4時に、また用事があって出かけるので、
1時間しか時間がないとのことです。
```

質問：社員寮に住んでいるリーさんが、次のようなメモをもらいました。リーさんは、何時に課長に会うことになりますか。

```
1  1時        2  2時

3  3時        4  4時
```

Source: JETRO (2003b)

Figure 1.14 JRLT Reading paper: sample grammar item

質問　需要が供給をうわまわれば、インフレ傾向になることは言う＿＿＿＿＿ね。

```
1  までがない      2  までもない      3  までにない      4  までしかない
```

Source: JETRO (2003b)

5. Skills' coverage

The test includes papers devoted to listening and reading, though there is an integrated listening and reading element (see above).

6. Measurement qualities

Though there are tables of candidature (size and success rate) for each year since the test was introduced, there are no figures available which tell us about the qualities of the test (overall/sub-test reliability, item statistics).

7. Degree of specificity/authenticity

The degree of specificity is not high here, with a clear focus on the language rather than on the context (this can be seen from the items included above where the candidates focus on their knowledge of the language as displayed through their responses to MCQ items). The fact is that the MCQ item format is useful in terms of the testing of aspects of language (or other skills) that lend themselves to being broken down into 'discrete' elements or chunks. However, the very act of decontextualising the language to this degree negates any claims of situational authenticity.

The test appears to be well constructed, though there appears to be a question mark over its situational authenticity. This is because it offers a series of tasks with little effort to create a systematic contextualisation through relating the

Figure 1.15 JLRT Reading paper: identifying overall meaning

```
                                                    平成〇〇年〇月〇〇日

  中村金属株式会社
    製造部長　〇〇〇〇殿

                                        ＫＦエンジニアリング株式会社
                                            技術部長　〇〇〇〇

                    貴社加工工場改修工事に関する件

  拝啓　貴社益々ご清祥のこととお喜び申し上げます。
    さて、この度は掲記の件に関しまして、弊社に発注のご内示を下さいましてあ
  りがたく厚くお礼申し上げます。
    先日お話いたしました通り、細部金額の見積り等は後日お話しさせていただき
  たいと思いますが、取敢えず、弊社技術課長〇〇〇〇、技術主任〇〇〇〇の二名
  を出張させ、事前調査させていただきたく存じます。つきましては、貴社で関係
  者との打合せの日時を早急にお決めいただき、折り返しご回示賜りたくお願い申
  し上げます。
    なお、先般もお願いいたしました、機械の配置図などあらかじめお送りいただ
  ければ幸いです。よろしくお願い申し上げます。
                                                            敬具
```

1 打合せのメンバーを知らせてほしい。

2 見積り金額について検討してほしい。

3 現地調査可能な日時を知らせてほしい。

4 機械配置図を送ってほしい。

Source: JETRO (2003b)

tasks to the sort of demands outlined in the earlier reviews. The interactional authenticity is also questionable as responses to all of the tasks are evaluated using MCQ items, with no reference to the interlocutor/audience for example and little attempt to ensure that the linguistic demands of the texts reflect those of texts in the business domain.

8. Impact of non-language factors

As noted above, the somewhat confused description of the construct tested (as reflected in the levels' ability statements contained on the test website) means that it is not possible to identify what the developers of this test are trying to achieve – though the extent to which the non-language factors actually impact on the test performance is not altogether clear.

9. Reporting of test performance

At the time of writing, the actual reporting mechanism is not available in the public domain, though according to the website there appears to have been a move from a criterion-referenced (i.e. pass/fail) system to a norm-referenced system based on that of the TOEIC and TOEFL. This decision appears to have been made without regard to the basic criticism of this type of system (made here and by Douglas 2000) that the resultant numbers relate to how well the candidate performed compared to other candidates – it does not tell us if the person can survive linguistically in a business environment.

It is required that a score of 530 be reached in order to qualify to sit the JETRO Oral Communication Test, though students who have achieved a passing grade in the final administration of the pre-revision JRLT may also apply.

The JETRO Oral Communication Test (JOCT)

1. A brief introduction to the test

The JETRO Oral Communication Test (JOCT) is an 'add-on' to the JRLT, which can only be taken by candidates who have achieved a score of 530 on the JRLT. Its developers claim that it 'comprehensively measures and evaluates one's proficiency in using Japanese to communicate' (JETRO, 2003c).

2. A brief description of the test

The JOCT is described on the JETRO website as consisting of two parts (see Table 1.19), one involving the test taker and the examiners (there are always two, one specialising in Japanese language and another with a business background) in an interactive dialogue and the other a role-play. Performances are audio and/or video recorded for later evaluation. The holistic assessment scale used in the JOCT is included here as Appendix 1.1.

Table 1.19 Task types from the JOCT

	JOCT Details	Duration
Q & Q	Conversation, led by tester, about the test taker's job and topical subject related to business	15 minutes
Role Playing	Role playing in imaginary business situations, including monologues (short speeches, etc.) to see how the test takers deal with given tasks and situations	15 minutes

Source: JETRO (2003c)

3. An outline of the construct upon which the test focuses

The construct appears to be jointly focused on a candidate's ability to use Japanese in a more social situation (though it should be noted that the notion of a conversation between an examiner and a candidate is probably not sustainable, due to the inequalities inherent in the event) and the candidate's ability to use the language in a typical business setting (as operationalised through a role-play task).

4. The test method

There are two parts. In the first part the candidate interacts with a pair of examiners. Here, the focus appears to be on the candidate (personal information exchange, work experience etc.), while the two available tasks which are meant to exemplify the role-play task in part 2 appear to show the candidate in two different situations, suggesting that this part of the test can vary widely from administration to administration. In one version (a video clip is available on the website) the candidate is engaged in a telephone conversation with an examiner, while in the other the candidate makes a formal speech. The problem here is that the first task involves the candidate in an extended interactive discourse with an examiner while the second involves an extended monologue. We know from experience (O'Sullivan, Weir and Saville 2002, for example) that these different discourse types result in different task output profiles (in terms of the language functions elicited) and may well have an effect on test performance – particularly when we consider the work of Berry (1996, 1997) who has shown that candidates with different personality profiles are affected by task type.

5. Skills' coverage

This test is focused on speaking only, and apart from the input prompts (which are spoken) there is no other skill involved.

6. Measurement qualities

No information is currently available in the public domain.

7. Degree of specificity/authenticity

This seems to be somewhat mixed, with the first (interview) task more focused on general proficiency, while the role-play task is more specific – in that the tasks are very much situated in the context of business.

The example videos of the role-play tasks show a very formal (and not typically business) organisation – for example in the task where the candidate interacts with one of the examiners by telephone, the interaction actually takes place over the phone, but both are sitting at the same desk and are facing each other. This affects the situational authenticity – though a simple manipulation of the setting, to create a physical distance or barrier between the speakers, could to a large extent, negate this criticism. The degree of interactional authenticity is probably higher, with the tasks (particularly in the latter part of the test) more likely to result in the candidates' cognitive processing approaching that of the business language domain.

8. Impact of non-language factors

There does not appear to be a significant impact here of non-language factors, though the 'speech' role-play, the example presented of which is little more than a formal self-introduction, may be more influenced by knowledge of the Japanese business domain. The formality of the language and rhetorical structure of this type of presentation and the non-verbal 'attitude' of the speaker (rigidly standing to attention while speaking) are not for example what a European student might expect. We might therefore find that background knowledge may play a large part in successful performance on this type of task. The question then is whether this is a good or a bad thing. While Elder (2001) argued that this type of non-language impact is negative, we have seen above that it is probably unavoidable where a test is quite specific, and it could well be seen as a positive aspect of this type of test; after all it is part of what makes a test specific.

The other point to make related to this example is that business domains from different cultures may be radically different. So, a learner who is quite proficient in the language but is relatively unfamiliar with the culture may not perform as well as a learner with experience of the business culture but with a lower level of language proficiency.

9. Reporting of test performance

Performance is reported in terms of the evaluation criteria (see Appendix 1.1). No pass/fail criterion is set, so candidates receive a grade only (A+, A, B+, B, C, D). No effort has been made (beyond the brief descriptions offered in the evaluation criteria document) to say what these levels might mean (for example in terms of the CEF).

Summary

The tests reviewed to date differed greatly in the language skills they examined. It is interesting that few of the tests include all four skills, though we shall see below that this is one of the cornerstones of the tests developed by Cambridge ESOL in the UK.

The above tests differed not only in the skills' area, but also in the approach to test and item format, to how productive language was evaluated and to how overall performance was reported. As in any testing situation, there is no best way, though there were examples of decisions that were taken by developers (to use only MCQ; to change from criterion to norm-referencing) that have undermined the validity of the tests. There is also evidence to show that simply saying that a test is 'specific' or not is probably not a good idea: the complexity of the matter means that different parts of a test can be seen to be more or less situationally and interactionally authentic. Clearly a more comprehensive (though practical) system of dealing with this issue is needed.

Before discussing that, it is now time to look at how the UK's most influential developer of both general and specific purpose language tests have come to test language for business purposes.

The development of business English testing at Cambridge

No mention has yet been made of the tests for business with which Cambridge ESOL has been associated over the past decade. I have deliberately refrained from including these tests in a general description of current practice in order to take this opportunity to establish a clearer perspective on the current Cambridge ESOL approach to this aspect of testing. In order to more fully appreciate the approach, we really need to go back to the mid-1980s, before the organisation became involved in business language testing. The tests in the following section are of historical interest, but as they are no longer administered, I will not attempt to offer the same 9-point analysis as was done for the preceding tests, but will instead describe them in terms of their contribution to the historical development of business language testing at Cambridge ESOL.

Certificate in EFL for Secretaries (CEFLS)

In the mid-1980s, the Royal Society of Arts (RSA) in the UK developed a test known as the *Certificate in English as a Foreign Language for Secretaries* (CEFLS). Like the TOEIC, this test was created in response to the perceived need of local clients, and was piloted from 1986 to 1989. Unlike the TOEIC, the format of the test was based on the use of materials supplied by real companies, and was designed as a criterion-referenced test.

The report of the pilot scheme for the CEFLS (RSA 1987:4) indicates that a total of 86 test takers sat the English Oral, Reading and Writing and Listening tests, while six, 11 and 69 test takers sat the French, German and Swedish Translation tests respectively. The high pass rate was indicated by the fact that certificates were awarded to 80 test takers who gained a passing score on all three of the English tests; no mention is made of those who passed the other translation tests.

The Oral test was based on three distinct tasks identified as being representative of 'the type of interactions a secretary would undertake in his/her normal work'.

These were:

1. Initiating a telephone call.

2. Receiving a telephone call.
3. Face-to-face interaction with an unknown participant.

The three parts of the test were linked by a common theme, designed to obviate the necessity for test takers to adopt different personas for each part. Test takers were initially given a role as an employee of a real company (the Parker Pen Company was used for the 1987 pilot). The results of the pilot appear to have been quite satisfactory, though the final task seems to have been problematic, due to the reluctance of test takers to maintain their role (and initiate utterances for example), and the subsequent abandonment by the assessors of the role-play. Unfortunately, no reference is made in the report to the assessment criteria used, though there appears to have been a focus on task fulfilment.

The Listening test consisted of a series of five thematically related tasks (again based around information provided by the Parker Pen Company). The Report tells us that the input was 'recorded at the normal rate of delivery with a range of native speakers and included non-standard speakers' (RSA 1987:8). The tasks are outlined in Table 1.20.

Table 1.20 Listening task types from the Certificate in EFL for Secretaries

Task	Description
1	Respond to customer telephone order (complete sales order form)
2	Respond to oral input with summary (in the form of a telex)
3	Understanding of longer [time not given] input (true/false items)
4	Listen for specific details from two telephone messages (written summary)
5	Three extended messages (answer-phone) MCQ items

These tasks appear to have been well attempted by the pilot group, though the high pass level suggests that there may have been some problem with the level of difficulty of the tasks – the Report (RSA 1987:9) does refer to the relative weakness of responses to Tasks 2 and 4, which required production skills, though no additional information as to why this might have been the case is presented.

The Reading and Writing test (Table 1.21) consisted of a set of seven tasks, each designed to test a particular aspect of the test taker's language ability. These tasks were accompanied by materials taken from sources including the *Financial Times*, the Parker Pen Company's own publicity material, 'and invented tasks made as authentic as possible' (RSA 1987:10).

While the CEFLS can be criticised in hindsight for its relative naivety and lack of professional polish (the pilot test, which is included here as Appendix 1.2 was quite crude in its presentation), there were a number of very interesting and influential aspects of the test that deserve mention. For example, the view of authenticity implied in the use of materials related to real or realistic companies (though adapted or even scripted to suit the test) reflects current thinking to a

Table 1.21 Reading and Writing task types from the Certificate in EFL for Secretaries

Task	Description	Marks available
1	Questionnaire completion	1 mark
2	Proof-reading task (10 discrete items)	5 marks
3a	Formal letter	5 marks
3b	Less formal letter	5 marks
4	Interpreting graphs/graphics (discrete items)	4 marks
5	Formal letter	5 marks
6	Letter and report formal	5 marks
7	Telex	5 marks

great degree and can be seen to satisfy the situational authenticity required of an LSP test (Douglas 2000). This authenticity was maintained in the Speaking test, where a range of tasks were included, while in the Listening test a range of speakers of English were used. The test developers also made efforts to ensure that there was a strong measure of interactional authenticity in the type of tasks chosen, though it is not now possible to establish empirically that actual candidate performances reflected this view.

The fact that this test was very highly specified is not at all surprising, in that it was developed with a particular test taker in mind, and it was never considered a requirement of the test that the results might be generalised to a wider general purpose language context. Of course, the question of a potential impact of non-language ability arises here again and it may well have been the case that familiarity with the domain may have contributed to performance.

When, in 1988, the RSA Examinations Board was amalgamated into what was then the University of Cambridge Local Examinations Syndicate (UCLES), it was decided to broaden the candidate base and CEFLS was redesigned, initially only slightly, and renamed the *Certificate in English for International Business and Trade* (CEIBT).

Certificate in English for International Business and Trade (CEIBT)

The CEIBT consisted of three papers, testing reading and writing, listening and oral interaction. The Reading and Writing paper consisted of an introductory 'Information Page', in which the test taker was introduced to the company and their own position within the company (for the purposes of the test) was contextualised. Among the companies used in the test were Rolls Royce, Japan Airlines, McDonald's and The Body Shop. There followed a series of six tasks where the test taker was expected to respond to a series of authentic stimulae in the form of letters, memos, faxes and reports – though due to the authentic nature of the materials the task formats tended to vary from administration to administration (one of the factors that led to a revision of the test in 1998). Test takers were allowed a total of 150 minutes for completion of the six tasks (this included 10 minutes' reading time).

In the Listening paper, test takers undertook a series of tasks, within the context of the same company. On the basis of what they heard in a series of audio recordings, featuring both native and non-native speakers of English, they were expected to undertake a number of tasks. This paper lasted for approximately 65 minutes including 5 minutes' reading time.

Finally, the Oral Interaction paper consisted of a role-play, where the test taker took the role of a company employee and the examiner took the role of a visitor to the company. The paper lasted for 13–15 minutes, with a total of 15 minutes' preparation time.

While the CEIBT has been praised for its commitment to authenticity of input (see for example Douglas 2000:175), it was this very commitment that had very real practical consequences for the production of the examination. One consequence was the difficulty in implementing full pretesting of the test tasks due to the involvement of real companies. Additional problems identified in a 1994 review document included the large amount of writing required and, perhaps more crucially, the problem of what to do with an item shown by pre-testing not to be operating as predicted – as the test was seen as an integrated unit, a non-performing item could not be replaced with a previously banked example. This latter difficulty also had serious implications for the application of item banking to the test system.

It is interesting to note that what was considered the strongest point of the CEIBT, the authenticity of its input, was also its Achilles heel. Apart from the problems with pretesting referred to above, there were other even more important difficulties. Perhaps the most relevant of these was the extreme view of authenticity illustrated by the insistence on the use of real unedited material. The review document identified the following conditions for the production of the examination:

- 'importance of obtaining genuine materials [emphasis in original] from the company.
- reliance on the materials voluntarily supplied by the context companies, which leads to problems if the company does not oblige [two examples are provided in the review]
- reluctance to edit material obtained from the context company in the belief that this is tampering with 'authenticity' [emphasis in original]
- belief in the importance of ensuring that the tasks on a particular paper would actually be carried out by someone working in a particular department within that company
- unwillingness to consider the use of fictional companies as a setting for CEIBT or to change the names [although this was, in fact, adopted for the revised CEIBT, introduced in 1998]' (UCLES 1994:13–14).

The writer goes on to identify the principal area of concern with this situation: 'it is the materials obtained from the company rather than the existing test specifications which drive the test' (UCLES 1994:14). An additional problem, that of task consistency, was also identified, with examples given of significant variation in reading load and of differences in task format. This latter situation is exemplified by comparing the two CEIBT tests that were administered in 1992 (Table 1.22) where the tasks are not at all similar, either in terms of input or of expected response. See Appendix 1.3 for examples of two CEIBT test papers.

Table 1.22 Comparison of two CEIBT examinations

	June 1992		November 1992	
Task	*Input*	*Output*	*Input*	*Output*
1	Invoice (payment overdue) Brief memo	Letter (complaint)	Report (cover only) Brief note	Letter (informational)
2	Memo Advertising proof (10 errors)	Corrected proof Fax (instructional)	Fax (3 questions) Office files (x 3)	Fax (informational)
3	Graphic design	Letter (request)	Fax (approx. 90 words) Memo (approx. 70 words) Article (approx. 400 words)	Letter (informational)
4	Article (approx. 600 words)	Report (120 words max.)	Memo	Article (informational)
5	Letter (suspending contract) Table + Chart	Letter (argumentation)	Memo (handwritten additions)	Memo (apologies, informational)
6	Application form Memo (x 2) Message Letter	Note (prioritising)		

(Both of these tests are included as Appendices 1.3 and 1.4.)

This table shows how difficult it is to make meaningful comparisons between the different versions of the test. This problem was also reflected in the unpredictability of the difficulty level of the test from year to year, a situation highlighted in the review document (UCLES 1994:16), by the differences in the percentage of candidates achieving a passing grade. It is therefore clear that the commitment to the use of purely authentic materials was compromising the validity and reliability of the test.

Other difficulties with the existing CEIBT included a perceived lack of clarity of definition of the role and purpose of the test – as compared with, for example, the TOEIC. This was seen to affect the marketability of the CEIBT, and to have contributed to its relatively low take up (less than 1500 per year), and the lack of support materials (with no published textbook). As a result of this extensive review, with the addition of feedback from test takers, administrators, and Cambridge ESOL personnel, it was decided to revise the CEIBT. This revision was to take almost three years, with the new version first administered in June 1998.

The main changes to the test were:

- each of the three papers was to become a free-standing certificated test
- each test had a different company context *based on* [my emphasis] an authentic source
- the Reading and Writing test and the Listening test were shortened
- the Oral test now included an additional 'mini presentation' (but overall length did not change).

A comparison of the test outline (Table 1.23) with that of the pre-revision version shows that the changes to the test were actually quite major. The tasks were now less open, in terms of expected response, and while there was definite reduction in specificity, and to some extent in the situational authenticity of the test (mostly in that 'real' companies were no longer used), this does not appear to have been reflected in any way in the potential of the tasks to demonstrate evidence of interactional authenticity. However, the lack of archived data make this impossible to demonstrate empirically.

Table 1.23 Format of the revised CEIBT Reading and Writing test

Task	Main Skill Focus
1	Business correspondence
2	Language systems
3	Business correspondence
4	Reading for detail, global meaning and inference
5	Extended business correspondence

Unfortunately, despite these revisions CEIBT continued to attract very small numbers of candidates.

This situation, when combined with the successful development and introduction of the BEC suite, particularly BEC3, which was aimed at a similar level test taker and was able to build on the success of the earlier BEC examinations, meant that the CEIBT was withdrawn.

Another test that was brought into the UCLES fold in the mid-1990s, and that has had some influence on the Cambridge ESOL approach to the testing of English for business was the Oxford International Business English Certificate (OIBEC).

Oxford International Business English Certificate (OIBEC)

The OIBEC examinations were developed by the University of Oxford Delegacy of Local Examinations (UODLE) during the late 1980s and first introduced in November 1990.

The OIBEC offered tests at two levels, First and Executive. The examinations were designed for people with 'a practical knowledge of English' who were 'learning to use it in a business environment' (UODLE 1990) and were at the pre-intermediate and higher-intermediate levels respectively (or at the levels of 4 and 6 on the English Speaking Union Framework Chart). Both levels were based on case studies, and included papers testing all four skills.

An interesting feature of the OIBEC examinations was the inclusion of an extensive preparation package, which was given to each candidate three days before the day of the examination. This package appears to have been devised to eliminate any individual 'background knowledge' effect on test performance, by giving the candidates three days in which to read through and study the background to the topic for the test they were about to sit.

Also of interest is the fact that the Speaking test used a paired format, the earliest inclusion of this format in a large scale test, though the format seems to have been best exploited only at the Executive level, where the candidates were involved interactively in two tasks (one of which appears to have been seen only as an extension of an earlier task and was not awarded individual marks). See Table 1.24 for an outline of the test.

Commentary

In terms of the criteria referred to in the early stages of the chapter, the three examinations reviewed above can all be said to have been quite clearly specified within a business language domain – and as such are quite 'specific' in that they lie towards that end of the continuum. The changing attitude to situational authenticity can be clearly seen, in that the earlier CEFLS test was devised in such a way as to mirror as closely as possible the target language use domain, a factor which contributed to a high degree of situational authenticity, and 'face' validity, but which meant that the test could not be replicated. The focus on situational authenticity reached its zenith with the CEIBT, a test that was quite popular with certain stakeholders (teachers for example) but less so with others (candidates, test users and test developers).

The contribution of these tests

Apart from the obvious experiential aspects of administering tests of language for business purposes to an international population, these tests appear to have contributed to the current Cambridge ESOL approach to business language testing in a number of ways. The development of the CEFLS through to the

CEIBT in its different versions appears to have demonstrated how the organisation moved from an approach where attention was drawn to the genuineness of the tasks used (in other words the focus was on the situational authenticity of the task) to a perception of the test task which takes into account both its situational and interactional authenticity. The other major change was to understand that different test versions (i.e. different versions of a single test) must be replica-

Table 1.24 Task types from the Oxford International Business English Certificate

	First Level	Executive Level
Preparation package		
Contents	4 pages of written input – range from report to letter to table and graphic.	6/7 pages of written input – consists of a detailed contextualisation, with excerpts from reports, letters, balance sheets, memos etc.
Reading and Writing		
Time allowed	75 minutes	95 minutes
Marks awarded	100	100
Task 1	10 SAF – Reading comprehension, based on preparation materials	Writing – Report completion (based on Prep. Materials) – 2 pages allowed, 20 marks
Task 2	Reading – Inferencing (3 items to be identified, SAF)	Writing – Guided report (based on Prep. Materials) – 2 pages allowed, 15 marks
Task 3	Writing – register (3 items SAF)	Reading – 5 SAF items, based on additional fax input (15 marks)
Task 4	Writing/Reading integrated – table completion/summary	Proof-reading – 10 items in short memo text (10 marks)
Task 5	Guided writing – Memo, no word limit	Writing – briefing paper completion (2 paragraphs) 20 marks
Task 6	Letter writing (scaffolded using additional input) – no word limit	Writing – job application letter (150–200 words) 20 marks
Listening		
Marks awarded	50	50
Time allowed	20 minutes	20 minutes
Task* 1	3 items, based on graph/table (SAF)	10 comprehension items (MCQ) 15 marks
Task* 2	Complete form, based on input (3 pieces of information required – all SAF)	9 comprehension items (SAF) 20 marks
Task* 3	4 items, 1 table completion, 2 additional information, 1 inferencing item * All telephone messages	3 items – corrections to tables [15 marks]

Table 1.24 Task types from the Oxford International Business English Certificate *(continued)*

	First Level	Executive Level
Speaking		
Marks awarded	Not specified	80 marks
Time allowed	20 minutes	20 minutes
Format	2 candidates, 1 examiner	2 candidates, 1 examiner
Task 1 Task 2 Task 3	Each candidate makes a short presentation (2–3 minutes) on the merits of a particular market/strategy. Followed by short discussion. Each given prompt card containing bulleted pros of own point and cons of that of other candidate. Finally, candidates must come to a decision on which to go for.	Presentation – (no time suggested) choice from 5 prompts (5 minutes' preparation time) Decision-making task – from given prompt cards, candidate to candidate interaction (2 minutes' preparation time) Joint summary of findings [not marked]

tions from a clear specification if stakeholders are to make consistent inferences based on test scores.

Both the CEIBT and the OIBEC contributed to the current approach through the move along the specificity continuum, to a situation where the tests which had been based on a high degree of specificity (and low generalisability) were, in their later guises, more centrally located, allowing for a greater degree of generalisability than their predecessors.

Business Language Testing System (BULATS)

First discussed by members of the Association of Language Testers in Europe (ALTE) shortly after the formation of the association in 1990, the main thrust behind the development of BULATS appears to have been the decision to create a series of business language tests with a multilingual dimension. To date, tests have been developed in four languages, English (which will be the main focus of this review), German, French and Spanish. The tests were developed and managed by Cambridge ESOL [English], Alliance Française [French], Goethe-Institut [German] and Universidad de Salamanca [Spanish].

One interesting feature of the BULATS tests is that performance on all of the tests is benchmarked to the ALTE and CEF frameworks, shown in Chapter 2. This allows the test end-user to make informed decisions about performance on tests of proficiency in different languages. While it can be argued that the LCCIEB tests allow for the same cross-language comparisons to be made, there is a big difference in the tests involved. As we could see from the LCCIEB tests, they all follow the same model. The difference with the BULATS tests is that each test is developed and administered independently by experienced test developers who are native speakers of the target language. They may be working from the same basic specifications, but here the developers are more likely to be aware of subtle differences in the language concerned and to take this into account in developing tests that are more likely to represent a valid indication of proficiency in that language for the particular purpose tested.

Another facet of BULATS is the fact that it offers a number of independent tests in each of the four languages currently tested. These tests are:

- the BULATS Standard test – a 110 minute test of listening, reading and grammar/vocabulary
- the BULATS Computer test
- the BULATS Speaking test
- the BULATS Writing test.

Each of these tests will be briefly reviewed in the following parts of this section.

The BULATS Standard test

As mentioned above, this is a 110-minute-long test of reading, listening and grammar/vocabulary. The test is divided into two sections, the listening part lasts for 50 minutes and the reading and language knowledge part lasts for 60 minutes. From the outline of the test in Table 1.25, we can see that it represents a substantial measure of a candidate's proficiency in these areas (BULATS undated/a).

Table 1.25 BULATS Standard test (English): test outline

	Part	Items	Format	Focus
Listening	1	10	MCQ	Matching audio description to visuals or short phrases
	2	12	SAF	Memo/form completion
	3	10	Matching	Identify speaker from list of topics/jobs etc.
	4	18	MCQ	Listen for detail
Reading and Language Knowledge	1	7	MCQ	Reading short memos, signs etc.
		6	MCQ	Selecting appropriate lexical items or chunks
		6	MCQ	Reading for comprehension (300–350 words)
		5	Cloze	
	2	7	Matching	Statements to short texts (up to 60 words)
		5	MC Cloze	Based on 100 word business communication
		5	Cloze	Based on 100 word general text
		6	MCQ	Selecting appropriate lexical items
		6	MCQ	Reading for comprehension (500–600 words)
		7	SAF	Proof-reading – identify and correct errors in text

All of the examples described below are taken from the sample paper available through the BULATS website – the entire sample paper for English is included as part of Appendix 1.4 (see Appendix 1.6 for a copy of the BULATS German paper).

There are four parts to the Listening section. In the first part, candidates are asked to match an audio description to a set of three visuals or short phrases. No writing is expected of the candidates in this section. In total there are 10 items. In the example from the sample item below (Figure 1.16), the candidates are asked to listen to the input and to identify a specific piece of information (here, delivery date).

Figure 1.16 Sample item: Part 1 BULATS Listening (English)

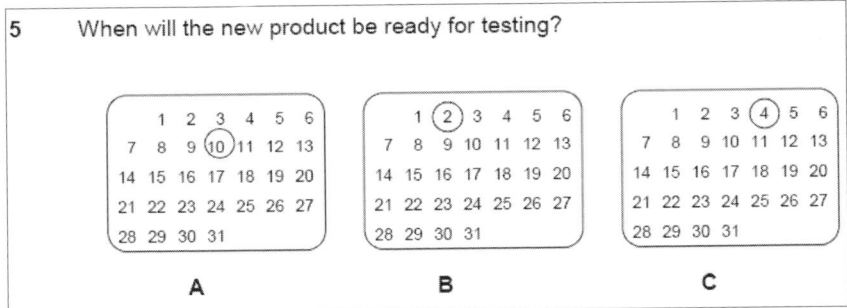

In the second part, candidates listen (just once) to a set of three conversations or telephone messages, and must complete a series of forms, notes or memos, totalling 12 items – all short answer format (SAF). Figure 1.17 shows an example of this task type, where the candidate listens again for specific information and responds using one or two words or numbers.

Figure 1.17 Sample item: Part 2 BULATS Listening (English)

Conversation Two
Questions 15 – 18

- *Look at the form below.*
- *You will hear a woman making a complaint.*

COMPLAINT FORM

Name: Mrs Hector

Address: 31, (15) .... , Rossington.

Tel: 01923 951975

Date: 5 April   Date of Complaint (if different): (16) ....

Branch: (17) ....

Reason for Complaint: Goods damaged due to bad (18) ....

Action: Issue credit note.

In the third part of the test, candidates listen to five people talking about a particular topic – there is no interaction here, all input is in the form of monologic discourse. They should then identify the speaker (from a given list of speakers). In the example shown in Figure 1.18, the speakers are talking about their work. Candidates listen and respond by identifying the views held by each of the five speakers from the list provided.

Figure 1.18 Sample item: Part 3 BULATS Listening (English)

Section One
Questions 23 – 27

- *You will hear five people answer the question 'What do you like about your work?'*
- *As you listen to each one, decide what the person likes most.*
- *Choose your answer from the list **A – I** and write the correct letter in the space provided.*
- *You will hear the five pieces **once** only.*

Example: .... I ....

A	meeting lots of people
B	good salary
C	working on my own
D	variety
E	company has good reputation
F	good office canteen
G	developing useful skills
H	near home
I	foreign travel

23 Person 1 ....

24 Person 2 ....

25 Person 3 ....

26 Person 4 ....

27 Person 5 ....

Finally, candidates listen to a series of three short interactions (see Figure 1.19) and are asked to respond to a set of six MCQ-based items for each listening text, only two of the six items have been included in Figure 1.19. In contrast to the previous section, here the discourse is interactional in nature. It appears that the developers have attempted to avoid, or at least to limit any test method effect by including a range of methods in this part of the test. While there is some reading to be done in order to respond to the items, this is minimal, with the possible exception of Part 3 – where the options range from two to six words in length, though there are only three options.

The Reading and Language Knowledge section of the test is comprised of two parts. Within these parts there are a number of sub-sections (see Table 1.25) which focus on various aspects of reading and language knowledge. This part of the test is not as clearly defined as the first part, with the candidates moving from reading short texts and notices in Section 1 to demonstrating their knowledge of business-related vocabulary in the following section. In the first part, candidates

Figure 1.19 Sample item: Part 4 BULATS Listening (English)

Section Three
Questions 45 – 50

- *You will hear a Personnel Manager interviewing an applicant for a job.*
- *For questions **45 – 50**, circle **one** letter A, B or C for the correct answer.*
- *You will hear the conversation **twice**.*

45   In his current job, David has to

        A   see if certain work has been finished.
        B   assemble parts of a machine.
        C   help people progress in their careers.

46   Most of the time, David works in

        A   the Sales Department.
        B   the main office block.
        C   the production area.

are presented with seven MCQ items all based on short pieces of input (which can be notices, memos, notes, graphics or tables). As with the earlier listening section, the MCQ items all have three options though they are all quite long – up to 10 words (see Figure 1.20). All responses are marked directly on to a computer readable answer sheet.

Figure 1.20 BULATS Reading and Language Knowledge: Section 1

52

> *Here are details of the marketing seminar I told you about. I shan't be able to go myself that day. Let me know if you think it's worthwhile sending someone else from this division.*
>
> *Paul.*

A   Paul doesn't want to send anyone to the seminar.
B   Paul wants you to represent your division at the seminar.
C   Paul wants your opinion about whether someone should go to the seminar.

The following section includes a series of six MCQ items based on knowledge of language use (see the example in Figure 1.21). Here the candidate is asked to identify the most appropriate word or phrase to complete a short sentence. The focus here is on the lexicon (including lexical chunks) of the business domain.

Figure 1.21 BULATS Reading and Language Knowledge: Section 2

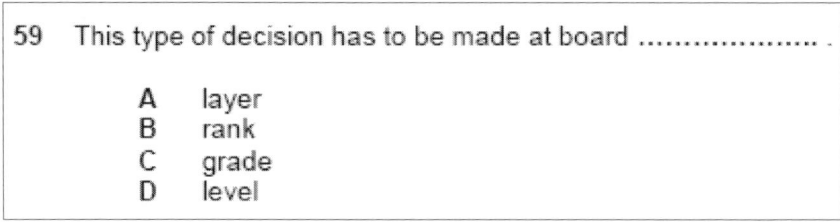

This section then moves on to a series of reading comprehension items which focus on reading for detail from a text of approximately 300–350 words. This section is then followed by a cloze test consisting of five items which appear to be designed to test syntax. While the previous section is quite clearly based on a business-oriented text, the text on which the cloze is based is less obviously business-focused.

Figure 1.22 BULATS Reading and Language Knowledge: Reading item

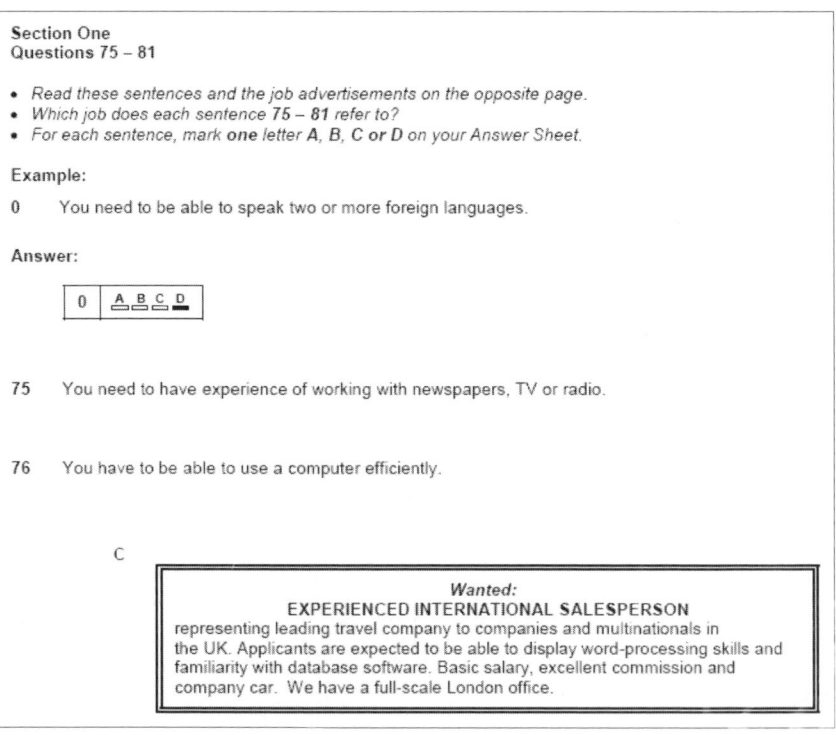

In the second part of the Reading and Language Knowledge paper there are six sub-sections. Here, the focus is on a mixture of reading (Sections 1, 3 and 5), vocabulary (Sections 2 and 4) and grammar (Section 6).

Reading is tested using a variety of item types, matching, cloze and MCQ, with the focus on reading for detail throughout. Figure 1.22 is an example of an item from Section 1 of this part of the test. In this item candidates are expected to match the statements to one of a series of four short texts (I've included only two items and one of the four texts here – for the whole section see Appendix 1.3). Vocabulary is tested using two different formats (cloze and MCQ), an example of the latter is shown here as Figure 1.23.

Figure 1.23 BULATS Reading and Language Knowledge: Vocabulary item

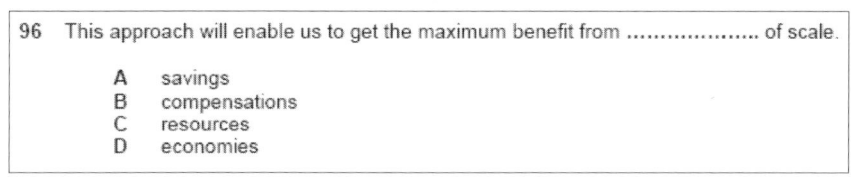

96   This approach will enable us to get the maximum benefit from .... of scale.

      A   savings
      B   compensations
      C   resources
      D   economies

The final part of the test consists of a short letter or memo, on each line of which there may be an error. Test takers are expected to identify which situation applies to each line (correct or including an error) and to indicate what correction is needed where an error has been identified – see Figure 1.24 for an extract from the sample paper supplied by the developers.

Figure 1.24 BULATS Reading and Language Knowledge

- *Your secretary has given you this letter to check.*
- *In some lines there is one wrong word.*
- *If there is a wrong word, write the correct word on your answer sheet.*
- *If there is no mistake, put a tick (✔) on your Answer Sheet.*

Example:

One of the items you ordered from our catalogue | 0 | ✔

is <u>temporary</u> out of stock. | 00 | temporarily

107 | We agreed which my company will act as your agent in northern

108 | Europe. As your agent, we will operate on a commission basis. We will

The BULATS Standard test, therefore, offers a comprehensive measure of a test taker's receptive language proficiency and their knowledge of the structure and lexicon of the language as it is used in a business context. The fact is that the Standard paper is not meant to offer a broad perspective on the language ability of candidates; instead both it and its computer counterpart are supported by additional papers for speaking and writing, so comment should not really be passed on these independent units in terms of approach or construct.

The way in which the test is constructed is interesting: apart from being split along the listening–reading/knowledge divide, within the two parts there appears to have been a deliberate attempt to keep shifting the focus, by moving between different types of item and content – particularly true of the Reading and Language Knowledge paper. This is a situation that might not please all test developers or theorists, as it could be argued that the skills might be more efficiently tested in more compact and homogenous sub-tests. On the other hand, the constant changing may act to maintain interest in this long paper and may actually facilitate more accurate measurement. This is an area on which the test developers might well devise a programme of research in which the impact of the presentation style is investigated.

The BULATS Computer test

The BULATS Computer test is a computer adaptive (CAT) version of the instrument and like the standard version contains sub-tests of listening and reading comprehension, and vocabulary/grammar tasks. The computer version takes advantage of the alternative item types offered by the medium.

The test includes a variety of listening item formats:

- listening to a short monologue to identify the correct response to a written item
- listening to an extended dialogue to answer a series of comprehension items.

The reading items also offer a range of item types:

- reading short texts to identify the correct summary
- reading an extended passage to answer a series of comprehension texts.

Finally, the vocabulary/grammar items tend to use one of two types of cloze item:

- responses from a series of four options
- responses typed directly into text boxes.

We can see, therefore, that the format of the test reflects that of the Standard test, though there are a number of different item types used. Another unique feature of BULATS is the way in which it allows the test user to make a number of decisions which contribute to adapting or customising the test to suit the needs of their situation. A management dialogue box allows the user to indicate which demographic information to include, to decide on the test-supervisor language, the language of instruction (in this case the person might wish that the instructions be given in the candidate's mother tongue – provided it is on the list of options offered – or that they will be in the target language, here English). In addition, this screen also permits the user to decide to allow (or not) the test taker to view their results, to print them or view feedback – depending on the context and purpose of the test all or none of these options might be chosen. As with other CAT tests the results are available immediately upon completion of the test.

Like the Standard version, the Computer test is available in a number of languages, though only the English version is reviewed here due to limitations of space. The test is available on CD in each of the four languages (English, French, German and Spanish).

The BULATS Speaking test

This test is independent from the other BULATS tests. The Speaking test uses the one-to-one format, with a single examiner and test taker (see Appendix 1.5 for a sample paper). All tests are audio recorded and assessed by an independent assessor, as well as by the examiner who participates in the test (BULATS undated/b). Table 1.26 shows how the test is organised.

Table 1.26 Speaking test design – BULATS

Part	Title	Timing	Description	Focus
1	Interview	4 mins	Personal information exchange (answer questions about themselves, their work and interests).	Ability to respond to personal questions in a conversational context.
2	Presentation	4 mins	Talk on topic (choice of three) for one minute – one minute preparation time. Respond to follow-up questions.	Ability to produce extended discourse and to respond to questions on the topic.
3	Information exchange and discussion	4 mins	Simulation – role play from given input (candidate expected to take initiative).	Ability to take a more active part in a conversation.

Performance is assessed on accuracy and appropriacy of grammar and vocabulary, discourse features such as cohesion, fluency, pronunciation, interactiveness, and degree of accommodation required.

Some example tasks for the Speaking test are presented below. The presentation task (Figure 1.25) offers a guided or scaffolded task prompt, where the test taker is given some bulleted points which should be included in the presentation (it is not clear though if there is some penalty for not including these points in the response – in other words, it is not clear if they are suggestions or explicit directions).

71

Figure 1.25 Speaking task types from BULATS (Part 2)

PART 2   Presentation

INSTRUCTIONS

Please read all THREE topics below carefully.

Choose **ONE** which you feel you will be able to talk about for one minute.

You have one minute to read and prepare your talk.
You may take notes.

Topic A

Describe an important business meeting you attended.
You should say:
    where it was;
    what it was about;
    why it was important.

What were the most interesting moments?

Topic B

Describe someone you particularly enjoy working with.
You should say:
    what this person does;
    what sort of work you do with this person;
    why you like working with this person.

Would you change anything about this person? Give reasons for this answer.

Topic C

Describe the best workplace you have ever had.
You should say:
    where the workplace was;
    what you were doing there;
    why you liked to work there.

Would you change anything about it? Give reasons for your answer.

The information exchange task (Figure 1.26) is again scaffolded, though here there is clearly room for the test taker to demonstrate an ability to expand on the topic and to offer their own opinions on aspects of the topic. This has the effect of expanding the range of language functions typically observed in an interview (informational) to include both interactional and discourse management functions, see O'Sullivan, Weir and Saville (2002) for a discussion of this phenomenon.

Figure 1.26 Speaking task types from BULATS (Part 3)

PART 3	Communicative Activity

CONFERENCE ARRANGEMENTS

You have one minute to read through this task.

Information Exchange

You are making the arrangements for a one-day conference at a local hotel. The Examiner is the Conference Organiser for the hotel and is visiting you to discuss the conference.

Find out this information:
  i)   the size of the largest conference room
  ii) the cost for that room
  iii) equipment available

Do you think the hotel is offering you a good service for the price it is charging?

Discussion

Now discuss this topic with the Examiner.

What makes a successful conference?

The inclusion of a variety of tasks, each with a different focus, marks an interesting attempt to extend the range of discourse type. The paper includes informal interactive personal information exchange, formal presentation and information exchange tasks.

The fact that there is a choice of situations offered to the candidates in Part 2 is obviously an effort to ensure that they have an opportunity to perform at their best by selecting a topic on which they feel they can perform well. There is always a danger, of course, that particular topics are either inherently more or less difficult than others, or that the examiner will consider that this may be the case. This opens up the possibility of the examiner compensating the candidate for selecting a 'difficult' topic – even where the topic may not actually be more difficult for the candidate. As with many areas of performance assessment, this is a matter that has received scant attention (though see Lumley and McNamara, 1995).

Though no empirical evidence has been published to date, it would be interesting to see how the final information exchange task works in actual administrations of the test. This format has been found not to work well in a number of tests as the test takers are often reluctant to adapt to a role – this could be due to the difference in power and status between the examiner (the 'expert') and the test taker (the 'novice'). In a test such as BULATS this position is reversed to a large extent, through the creation of a 'work-based' situation, in which the test taker is the 'expert' and the examiner the 'novice'. This is just speculation at this point, though it is certainly worth exploring.

The BULATS Writing test

The BULATS Writing paper consists of a pair of writing tasks, described (Table 1.27) and exemplified below (BULATS undated/c). Performance on the tasks is assessed by two trained and accredited examiners working independently of one another. The criteria used are accuracy and appropriacy of grammar and vocabulary, organisation of ideas, achievement of purpose. As with the other BULATS test papers, the topic and genre of the writing tasks are contextualised in a business setting.

Table 1.27 Writing test design – BULATS

Part	Title	Timing	Focus
1	Short message/letter (50–60 words)	15 mins	Ability to write a short letter, covering (given) relevant points and using appropriate style and tone.
2	Extended letter or report (180–200 words)	30 mins	Ability to write and structure a piece of extended writing, using appropriate style and tone for the intended reader.

As can be seen in Figure 1.27, in the first of the tasks the candidate is given a short text, such as a letter, memo or advert, together with a set of guidelines for writing a reply or follow-up letter. Candidates are expected to cover all of the points in the instructions within about sixty words – though there are no penalties for going over that limit. The task is typical of the business domain in terms of purpose, length, structure and formality of expected output. It can therefore be seen as being appropriate in terms of both the text and task demands of the target domain.

The second task (Figure 1.28) offers candidates a choice of either an extended letter or a report. The same can be said of this choice as was said of the choice offered in the speaking test, and the developers would be well advised to monitor these options for any unintended bias. On the other hand, both tasks are very definitely focused on the business domain, and like the first task, the developers can claim that the options represent tasks that are very strong in terms of situational authenticity. The tasks are also quite likely to result in interactionally authentic performances as they again reflect the task and text demands of the business domain.

Figure 1.27 Writing task from BULATS (Part 1)

PART 1

You have received this letter from a local hotel.

Dear Miss Jones

Further to our phone conversation this morning, I am writing to say our Conference Centre will be available all day on 17th November. Could you confirm the booking and let us know what arrangements you require for meals?

Yours sincerely

John Williams
John Williams

Write a reply:

- confirming the booking;
- saying how many people will attend;
- explaining what lunch arrangements you require.

Write **50 – 60** words on the opposite page.

Commentary

The BULATS tests offer an interesting insight into the way language testing in general and specific purpose language testing in particular began to change in the early 1990s.

Before this period, the traditional Cambridge ESOL approach (which typified the 'British' approach) had been to focus primarily on performance-based assessment. By this I mean that the tests had been shaped over the years to reflect a current view of the learning process, see Weir's history of the growth of the CPE (2003a), while the need to reflect contemporary thinking on psychometric aspects of language testing seemed to take second place. The BULATS tests were designed at a time when the influence of psychometrics was still quite strong, with, for example, the TOEFL/First Certificate in English (FCE) comparability study (Bachman et al 1995) suggesting quite strongly that the latter test lacked adequate psychometric quality and issuing dire warnings of the consequences of this apparently fatal flaw. The tests, far from abandoning the existing philosophy can be seen to have moved to embrace the two, often conflicting, movements, by combining a variety of item and task types as well as a variety of response types. BULATS also includes papers on all four skills in addition to a

Figure 1.28 Writing task from BULATS (Part 2)

PART 2

EITHER

Task A

Your company wants to set up some training courses for staff. You have been asked to write a report recommending the type of training people in your department need most.

Write the report, describing the training you most recommend.

Write about:

- the type of courses;
- why these courses are necessary;
- which staff should attend them

  and any other points which you think are important.

Write **180 – 200** words on the following pages.

OR

Task B

Due to recent growth, your company offices are no longer large enough and the company directors have decided to move to bigger premises. You have been asked to report on an office building that you have visited for the company

Write the report, explaining why you think the building would be suitable.

Refer to relevant factors such as:

- size and layout;
- cost;
- facilities

  and any other points which you think are important.

Write **180 – 200** words on the following pages.

---

separate grammar/vocabulary paper – as we will see later, this reflects the type of test associated with one of the main BULATS partners (Cambridge ESOL).

Of interest here is the way in which BULATS can be interpreted in terms of the degree of specificity issue. It is clear from the examples shown previously that the different papers seem to be taking somewhat different perspectives on the candidates' ability, with some being quite specific in their content and contextualisation (suggesting a high degree of situational authenticity), while others are apparently deliberately less focused on the business context. This range supports the notion that specificity is not as straightforward as we once thought. When a test is as complex as the one described here, there will be a range of degrees of specificity within the test (see Table 1.28).

Table 1.28 BULATS – degree of specificity in the different papers

Paper	Degree of specificity	Comment
Listening	Medium/High	Quite a large emphasis on social language, though with clear business-oriented contextualisation
Reading	Low/Medium	Some focus on business-related text types
Grammar/ Vocabulary	Low/Medium	Some focus on business-related text types
Speaking	Medium	Essentially based on more social aspects of spoken language use (though again set in a business context)
Writing	High	Very much focused on writing in a business context

In a similar way, we can discuss the related issues of authenticity and the impact of non-language features on performance. The variation throughout this test is highly likely to be reflected in tests in which a similarly complex design is used, and is equally likely to result in a broader perspective on the candidate's language ability within the business, or other specific, context and hence to the drawing of more valid inferences from performance on the test as a whole.

The development of the BEC suite

The origins of the Business English Certificates (BEC) can be traced to a series of meetings during 1991–1992 between UCLES representatives and the National Education Examinations Authority (NEEA) in China. At these meetings, the area of business English was identified by the Chinese partners as being in urgent need of a new, fresh approach, one designed specifically for a Chinese population.

By the end of 1992, the decision to develop such a test had been made, along with the decision that the test should be certificated at a low level. With this in mind, a prototype was developed using the Key English Test (KET)/Preliminary English Test (PET) model – these represent the lowest levels of the Cambridge ESOL Main Suite general proficiency tests. This prototype included a detailed specification and sample paper.

The partners agreed that the prototype represented an appropriate design and a decision was made in early 1993 to proceed with the development of the test as a joint venture. This led to a detailed exploration of the practical issues involved in operationalising such a project, issues such as marking, processing, cost, printing, etc. At this early stage it became apparent that the proposed speaking paper would be problematic from the perspective of examiner recruitment (it should be remembered that, at that time, there was a serious shortage of qualified and experienced English language teachers in China). For this reason, it was decided that only those students who had successfully completed the other test papers would be offered a speaking component.

The first administration of the BEC took place in China in the autumn of 1993. Table 1.29 gives some idea of the scale of that first administration.

Table 1.29 Details of the first BEC administration (China)

Number of candidates	3212
% of candidates achieving a passing grade	97%

Even before the first administration of the BEC, it was decided that the existing test should be supplemented with another, higher level test, envisaged as being linked to the existing test in terms of design model, though aimed at a higher level. This meant that the Business English Certificates (as the suite was now called) was to consist of a pair of related examinations, called BEC1 and BEC2.

The design and planning phases of the new test were completed by late 1993, and an operational test was developed during the summer of 1994. This new test was first administered, again in China, in the autumn of 1994. Table 1.30 outlines the scope of the 1994 administration.

Table 1.30 The 1994 BEC administration (China)

	BEC1	BEC2
Number of candidates	4974	3121
% of candidates achieving a passing grade	93%	72%

Following the early burst of development, there followed a hiatus in which the existing tests became well established in the 'base' market of China. During this time interest in the test in other Asian countries, particularly in India, began to grow. This growth into other markets was not seen as being problematic, as there was nothing in the test design that might cause it to be of use only in a Chinese context.

Meanwhile, changes in the demographics of the test population, both in China and in the newer markets, resulted in an increased demand for a test at a higher level to the existing pair, an idea that had been in existence at the time of the CEIBT review in 1994. Extended discussions at this time into the feasibility or need for an addition to the BEC suite, were influenced by the existence of the CEIBT (see the discussion of its development and administration above), which had been designed to test language at a level comparable with the proposed test. Eventually, however, operational difficulties with the CEIBT (again see above), and the expressed preferences of BEC stakeholders for any new test to have a design similar to that of the existing BEC examinations, led to the decision to develop what was to become known as BEC3.

Work on the new test began, with the test going live in 1996. This new test was planned to extend the range of the BEC suite upwards, and was bench-marked to the Certificate in Advanced English (CAE), ALTE level C1. The design of the test was again based on the other BEC examinations, offering the same range of papers. This design is summarised in Table 1.31.

Table 1.31 The BEC suite design

	BEC1	BEC2	BEC3
Paper 1 – Reading and Writing	•	•	•
Paper 2 – Listening	•	•	•
Paper 3 – Speaking	•	•	•

During the period 1998–2000, the BEC suite spread to other parts of the world and by the end of this time the overall candidature had grown to over 45,000. Changing demographics within the BEC population, related again to changes in the original market, and changes related to the expanding candidature set the context for the revision with which the next part of this book is concerned. The following chapters outline the Cambridge test development cycle in relation to the revision of the BEC suite (Chapter 2) and the actual changes to the test papers (Chapter 3).

Issues resulting from this review

It would appear from this review that there are a number of different approaches to the testing of language for business purposes. The tests reviewed appear to be less than highly specific, in that they are more likely to focus on language use in a particular context, than on the performance of very specific context-related tasks. The fact that there is a range appears to support the argument made above, that the specificity continuum exists and that tests placed at different points along the continuum will differ not only in terms of specificity, but also in terms of situational and interactional authenticity, and in terms of the impact of non-language factors on the abilities being tested.

There is also evidence here of a difference in rationale for including tasks in a specific language test. In general purpose testing, the primary reason for including particular tasks is to elicit samples of language which can then be evaluated by a trained rater. On those occasions when task completion may be relevant, we can usually trace the relevance to the specific purpose of that portion of the test – an example of this in a performance test of writing would be where the test taker must complete a job application form, a task that goes beyond the bounds of general language use. In tests of language for specific purposes, the notion of task completion becomes more central.

Here, the test taker is often explicitly judged, along with other predetermined language-related criteria, on whether a particular task has been adequately, or sufficiently completed – this is where Elder's (2001) inseparability argument is most clearly seen. It can be argued that relevance and adequacy of response is a feature of all tests. However, the primary purpose of a task in general language tests is to elicit a sample of language which will be judged on its linguistic merits (where relevance and adequacy are features of sociolinguistic and pragmatic competence). The issue in LSP tests is to decide to what extent the relevance and adequacy of task performance should be judged in relation to the language use context in addition to its linguistic merits.

Considering these issues again, together with the suggestions made in relation to degree of specificity and generalisability above, it might be useful to re-conceptualise specific purpose tests in general, and business language tests in particular. In order to do this, it is necessary to revisit the three core areas of concern suggested by Elder and Douglas.

1. Degree of specificity

If we take the continuum suggested earlier and extend it to its natural conclusion, that is infinity (represented by the symbol ∞) in both directions (Figure 1.29), it becomes obvious that while a theoretical conceptualisation of the extremes is possible, a practical application of these extremes is not. This can be seen even in the test described by Teasdale (1994) where within the language of air traffic controllers there will of course be unique or *precise* aspects of the language, but there will always be a proportion of non-precise language.

Figure 1.29 The degree of test specificity continuum

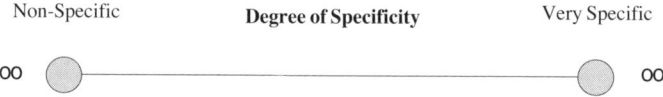

Since there is a clear link between the degree of specificity and the definition of the construct – in that changes to one will affect the other – the obvious implication will be that the inferences that can be drawn from performance on a test task will be related to the degree of specificity of that task.

2. Authenticity

In addition to the notion of specificity, the other principal concern with business language and other LSP tests is that of authenticity. It appears from the brief review of current practice offered previously, that a task, and in particular a task related to the receptive skills, can normally be shown to have only a measure of situational authenticity – though for an example of a truly situationally authentic task see Abdul-Raof (2002) whose participants actually performed real conference presentations that were video recorded and later evaluated by colleagues from the same profession, as well as by language specialists.

As for interactional authenticity, task performance is clearly affected by the participants in that performance, and since its presence (or absence) is therefore subject to factors outside of the control of the task writer/test developer it appears to be a somewhat unrealistic expectation that all administrations of a test will be found to demonstrate interactional authenticity. Instead, it seems more reasonable to suggest that tasks can be shown to demonstrate this aspect of authenticity under particular operational conditions, but not necessarily under all operational conditions. In other words, if it can be shown that a typical successful test taker will be prompted by the task to demonstrate an interaction between their communicative competence and features of the specific target language use domain, then interactional authenticity can be claimed of the task. While this operationalisation may not be precise enough for some readers, it does represent a practical and measured solution to the problem.

3. Impact of non-language factors

The interesting thing about this feature of tests of specific purpose is the fact that the impact appears to be most obvious where the test is more highly specific, in other words, where it is more difficult to separate the different elements of the ability being tested. This was exemplified in the tests reviewed above where a greater effort had been made to situate the test more clearly in the specific purpose domain. Here, there seems to have been a greater likelihood that the performance might be influenced by non-language factors.

The point of interest here is that there are a number of potential sources of impact, and that these are not only related to business ability or knowledge. In fact, the sources are related to the task itself and to the way in which the task is assessed. The implication is that the more specific a test the more likely the impact of non-language factors.

The more complex tests reviewed above demonstrate that 'degree of specificity' is not necessarily a notion that can be applied to a test as a whole. Instead, it is certain that these complex tests will contain papers, and even sections of papers, that have been deliberately manipulated so as to be more or less specific in focus. This suggests that the impact of non-language factors will also vary within a test.

2 The revision of BEC

The Cambridge ESOL test development/revision methodology

The Cambridge ESOL approach to test development and revision is essentially cyclical and iterative in nature (as can be seen from the summary presented in Figure 2.1). Like all other Cambridge ESOL tests, the original BEC tests were developed using this methodology, and again like other tests, in time a number of elements combined to create a perceived need for a revision. Among these elements were advances in test production methodology (many linked to the various projects described below), and changes to the test candidature. The original BEC examinations were designed primarily for the Asia–Pacific region, particularly China, and as the candidature grew in size over the years, it also changed with the growing international interest in the suite. The decision was therefore made in 1998 that any revision of the test should be undertaken with this wider candidature in mind. Other factors which influenced the perception of the developers included an expansion of our knowledge of how language is used in the specific context of business (through developments in corpus linguistics for example), to a general broadening of our understanding of the whole area of language testing. All of these combined to impact on the decision to instigate a revision in 1999.

The Cambridge ESOL framework

The following review of the Cambridge ESOL framework will begin by re-stating the general approach to testing language that informs the framework (see Saville 2003). This approach is the main driving force behind all Cambridge ESOL test development projects.

The Cambridge approach

Saville identifies 'five main factors' which underpin the Cambridge ESOL approach.
These are:

Figure 2.1 The Cambridge ESOL test development model

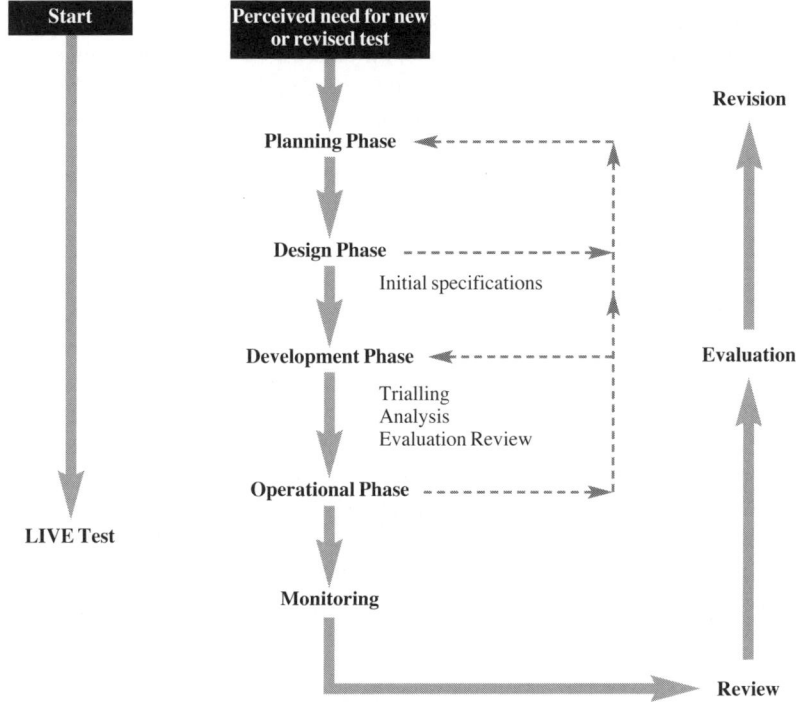

Source: Saville (2003:79)

1. To assess language skills at a range of levels, each of them having a clearly defined relevance to the needs of language learners.
2. To assess skills which are directly relevant to the range of uses to which learners will need to apply the language they have learnt, and cover the four language skills – listening, speaking, reading and writing.
3. To provide accurate and consistent assessment of each language skill at the appropriate level.
4. To relate the examinations to the teaching curriculum in such a way that they encourage positive learning experiences and to seek to achieve a positive impact wherever possible.
5. To endeavour to be fair to all candidates, whatever their national, ethnic and linguistic background, gender or disability (Saville 2003:62).

Assessment of a wide variety of language skills

The BEC suite examinations, like the other Cambridge examinations, include the full range of language skills in their design. That is, all three levels of the BEC suite consist of papers devoted to the assessment of proficiency in the four skills of listening, speaking, reading and writing. In addition, the different papers offer a wide range of response formats through the inclusion of a variety of tasks and item types within each skills' paper. The benefit of including a variety of task types in the Speaking paper, for example, has been demonstrated by the recent work of O'Sullivan, Weir and Saville (2002) who, when developing a set of observation checklists for monitoring test task responses (in terms of language functions elicited) were able to show that the different task types resulted in strikingly different function profiles.

A system of criterion levels

The BEC suite consists of a set of three examinations, each of which has been devised to target a distinct level of ability. Like the Cambridge ESOL Main Suite examinations these have been linked to the Common European and ALTE frameworks through a process of benchmarking candidate responses to 'can do' questionnaires (essentially a series of self-assessment instruments developed to elicit from test candidates estimates of what they 'can do' within the four skills' areas in different performance contexts – social, study and work). The impact of this project on the BEC revision is described below, but also see Jones (2000, 2001b) for a clear outline of the project.

This whole approach allows us to view the three examinations not simply as unique measures, or even as a set of linked measures covering a broad spectrum of language ability within a business context, but essentially as a single unit, with individual elements focused on particular criterion levels of proficiency. The greatest benefit of such a system is that it allows us to make comparisons of tests both vertically (in that they can be shown to measure distinct levels of language proficiency) and horizontally (so that each distinct examination can be shown to represent an empirically described level of ability).

Another advantage of this criterion levels' approach is that it permits us to view an estimate of attainment within any single test in terms of a broad multilevel range of language ability, rather than within the confines of a single level. The implications of this will be discussed in the relevant section below.

The ALTE *Can Do* scales were developed to provide a series of criterion-related statements at each of the levels covered by the BEC suite in relation to the specific domains which are covered in these examinations (situated language use for social and work purposes). Together with the criterion scale, the *Can Do* scale provides an external benchmark through which stakeholders can establish a meaning for reported performance levels.

Assessment for a variety of purposes

The BEC suite of tests are a good example of how Cambridge ESOL has concentrated on the creation of a range of tests and examinations which are designed for *a variety of purposes* rather than relying on a single test to address many purposes. Even within these tests there is a recognition that specific purpose language tests are *context-oriented* rather than *context-focused*. By context-oriented we mean that the tests are set in the context of business and will include language that is socially-oriented as well as business-oriented, in recognition of the fact that much specific purpose language combines these two areas. Context-focused refers to tests that are designed to test only business language. In fact, the LCCIEB needs analysis project (LCCIEB 1972) quite clearly demonstrated that a context oriented approach is most likely to reflect actual practice in the business language domain. The tests reviewed in Chapter 1 demonstrate that the context-oriented approach is typical of current practice in the area.

A commitment to quality and fairness

The traditional conceptualisation of fairness focuses on technical aspects of tests, such as the reliability of sub-tests. However, the view of fairness that is now more commonly accepted incorporates more wide-ranging considerations such as the production and validation of test materials and assessment procedures. Recent events in national testing systems in the UK (failures in test data management systems – Scottish Qualifications Authority 2000; test security – Edexcel 2001; and in test editing Edexcel 2002) demonstrate that these aspects of a test's development are as relevant to test fairness as the technical aspects referred to above. Cambridge ESOL ensures test quality through a system of total quality management, where a series of quality checks are put in place at all points of the development and administration process, see Weir and Milanovic (2003).

An ongoing programme of test revision

One of the great advantages of the Cambridge ESOL commitment to research (both qualitative and quantitative) throughout its different suites of examinations and test systems, is the way in which research findings in one area routinely feed into other apparently unconnected examinations. Examples of this include the work in the early 1990s on the development and validation of the use of interlocutor frames in tests of speaking (first envisaged as a methodology for controlling input in the Main Suite Speaking papers, but now used throughout the Cambridge ESOL examinations); the development of the observation checklists (originally developed as part of the CPE revision project but now used – in different guises – across the Cambridge ESOL range of tests); and not least in the development of quantitative analysis tools for equating tests in particular examination suites – a development of particular interest when it came to the revision of the BEC suite.

The title of a presentation made by Weir (2002) at the annual IATEFL conference in York sums up the commitment of Cambridge ESOL to an ongoing programme of review and revision. The title (The History of the CPE,

1913–2013) demonstrates that that particular test, which had just undergone a major revision, was already being reviewed, at the item, sub-test, and paper level, so that any future revision is based on an accurate longitudinal picture of both how it performs and how it is perceived throughout the life of this current version. In the same way, the BEC suite is also under constant scrutiny. This process of ongoing revision is also to be found in a number of the tests described in Chapter 1 – indeed a number were revised during the writing of this book. Sadly, there are still tests out there that have not changed since their introduction (e.g. the TOEIC is still essentially the same test as was introduced a quarter of a century ago – even though the way in which we understand and engage with language and communication has changed radically in the intervening period).

Some of the five elements are related to what we might call 'core' values of the Cambridge ESOL organisation – the testing of multiple skills has been a defining feature of Cambridge ESOL examinations since the introduction of the CPE in 1913 (Weir 2002, 2003a), while the commitment to the creation of test instruments and systems for use in a variety of contexts and for a variety of purposes is also long established. Since this book is meant to focus primarily on the BEC revision, it would be more interesting to look at the process in terms of how things like criterion levels and ongoing validation/revision are dealt with and how the developers ensure that the reported grades are accurate and consistent.

A system of criterion levels

As mentioned above, the individual tests in the Cambridge ESOL examinations and test systems are designed to be seen not in the context of a single level, but within a wider multi-level context. This concept was realised through the Cambridge ESOL Framework Project (see Jones 2000, 2001b) which resulted in a practical and useful instrument which has been used by the organisation to classify its examinations within a common system of levels.

With the formation of the Association of Language Testers in Europe (ALTE) in 1990, the work on the framework project expanded to involve collaboration with other international organisations (such as the Council of Europe and the European Association for Quality Language Services or EAQUALS) and fellow ALTE members. This expansion also broadened the aims to include some of the following key areas of activity:

- ALTE and Common European Framework
- ALTE CAN DO project
  - Development of CAN DO scales
  - Validation of the scales
    - Linking learner-responses to their performance on examinations
    - Linking ALTE Can Do Statements to the CEF
- production of Multilingual Glossary of Testing Terms in 10 languages

- production of guidelines for training item writers, including the Council of Europe Users Guide for Examiners as supplement to the Common European Framework
- development of Content analysis checklists for analysing and comparing examinations
- an evaluation of the Council of Europe's Vantage Level (UCLES 2000:2).

One aim of this expanded view of the project was to promote what Jones referred to as 'the transnational recognition of certification in Europe' (2000:11). The project also identifies a series of distinct levels of language ability and as such is ideal as a benchmark against which individual tests are measured. This facilitated the other aim of the project, which was to link levels of language ability across European national boundaries to a common proficiency scale.

While a complete description of the project is clearly beyond the scope of this book, it may be useful at this juncture to briefly overview its central elements. Figure 2.2 outlines the project, though does not do justice to the complexity or to the range of different sub-projects that contributed to the overall design.

Figure 2.2 The Cambridge ESOL/ALTE framework project (outline)

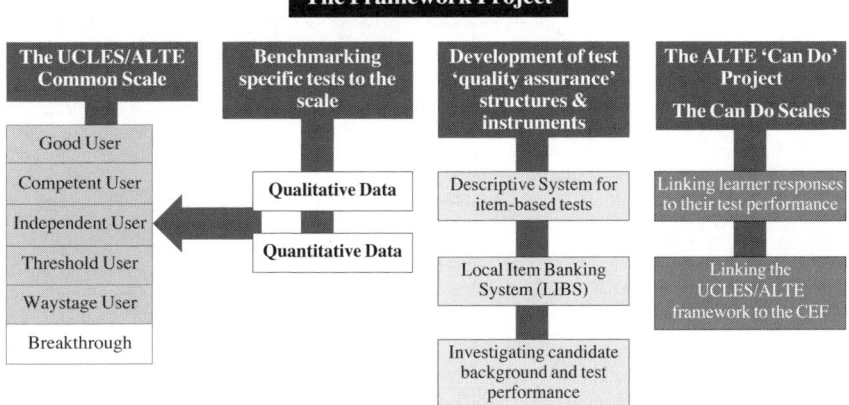

Though this volume is dedicated to the BEC revision, and not to the framework project, it is clear that all parts of the project have had a direct impact on the BEC revision process.

The impact of the 5-level system/Common European Framework

The 'Can Do' project – see Jones (2000, 2001b) for an introduction – was devised with the principal aim of providing a comprehensive description of what language users can typically do with the language at a number of distinct levels, in the various language skills and in a range of contexts. The project was created with the purposes of:

- helping end users to understand the meaning of exam certificates at particular levels, and
- contributing to the development of the Framework itself by providing a cross-language frame of reference.

Basically, the 'Can Do' project was meant to offer a practical guide to the application of the framework in test development. This is summarised neatly in the following figure (Figure 2.3) from Jones (2001a). Here, we can see that the project aimed to provide a framework through which examinations for different languages and contexts could be compared.

Figure 2.3 The aims of the 'Can Do' project

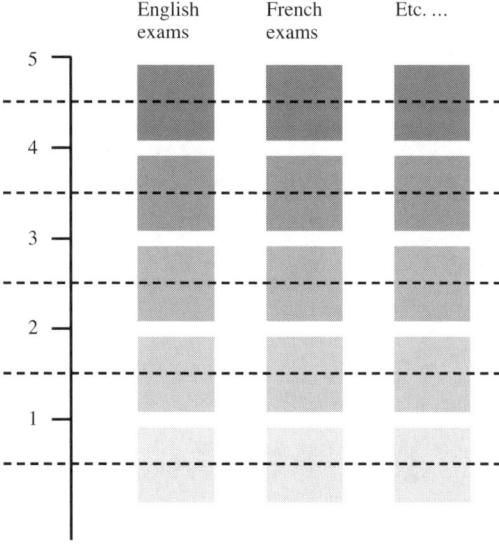

Figure 2.4 shows where the three BEC examinations are designed to fit within this system of criterion definition. In order to ensure that this relationship is more than just at a superficial level, a series of research studies was carried out. These focused on the exploration of the nature of the relationship from a qualitative perspective by using expert judgements to establish links between each of the three BEC tests and a relevant ALTE level. In addition to this qualitative data, quantitative data generated by the ALTE 'Can Do' project provided additional support for the equivalence claims implicit in Figure 2.4.

Figure 2.4 Benchmarking the BEC suite to the CEF and ALTE framework

A Common European Framework of Reference Council of Europe						
	C	C2	Mastery	ALTE Level 5 Good User	CPE	
		C1	Effective Proficiency	ALTE Level 4 Competent User	CAE	BEC Higher
	B	B2	Vantage	ALTE Level 3 Independent User	FCE	BEC Vantage
		B1	Threshold	ALTE Level 2 Threshold User	PET	BEC Preliminary
	A	A2	Waystage	ALTE Waystage User	KET	
		A1	Breakthrough	ALTE Breakthrough Level		

This process was made somewhat more complex due to the fact that the original BEC tests were not benchmarked to individual levels within the ALTE framework. One design feature of the original BEC suite was that BEC1 (the lowest of the three levels) was created to straddle the Waystage and Threshold levels – accounting for at least some of the perceived difficulties with the test. Since the decision to address this represents one of the major changes to the BEC suite it will be dealt with in Chapter 3.

The 'Can Do' scales currently consist of approximately four hundred statements (translated into thirteen languages – Catalan, French, Portuguese, Danish, German, Spanish, Dutch, Greek, Swedish, English, Italian, Finnish, Norwegian) which are organised into three general areas (social and tourist, work and study). Obviously, for this validation project the work-related scales were used. Each of the three areas are further sub-divided into a series of more specific areas, each of which in turn includes up to three scales (listening/ speaking, reading, writing). Figure 2.5 is a graphical representation of the organisation of the 'work-related' statements. As can be seen in Figure 2.5, each of the three areas has been sub-divided into a number of more specific situations; these are seen as being related to a particular aspect of the work environment and as drawing from a range of language skills. In the example shown, only the listening/speaking and writing language skills are identified as being required for the meetings and seminars situation. The 'Can Do' statements for the work-related section are therefore built around each element of Figure 2.5, so there will be statements at up to five levels related to the two language skills' areas identified here within the context of meetings and seminars. The reason that

Figure 2.5 The ALTE 'Can Do' work-related statements

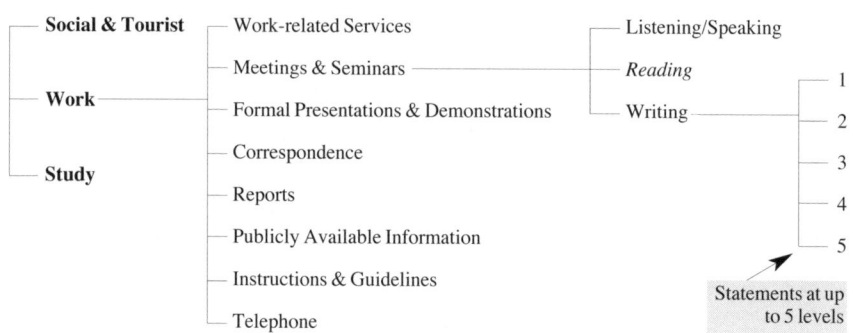

there are 'up to' five levels is in recognition of the fact that in some instances even a relatively basic level of proficiency is sufficient to successfully deal with a situation.

Another advantage to the linking of each test in the BEC suite to a single scale is related to the way in which we think about the reliability of the judgements made in score/grade awarding. While the area of reliability as it relates to the BEC tests (and potentially to all tests which are designed to work only at a limited range of ability) will be discussed in the following section when the qualities of test usefulness are examined, it is useful to make a connection at this point between the ALTE framework and the notion of reliability.

Figure 2.6 shows how results on one examination can be situated in relation to the much wider continuum of ability – so the proficiency level of a candidate who achieves a Grade C for BEC Vantage can be seen beyond the specific test to the whole range of proficiency as described in the ALTE/CEF framework. In this example a Grade C on BEC Vantage can be seen in terms of BEC Vantage (1), the BEC suite as a unit (2), and the whole range of ability as described by the CEF/ALTE frameworks (3). Reliability, therefore, becomes a matter of the accuracy of level assignment within the overall continuum, and implies a very different perspective on how evidence of this 'reliability' should be reported.

Defining the construct of business English

The construct of business English as operationalised in the BEC suite of tests is based on the clear specification of the concept from a number of perspectives:

- test taker
- theory-based validity
- context-based validity
- scoring validity.

Defining the construct of business English

Figure 2.6 Viewing an estimate of attainment at one level in terms of all levels

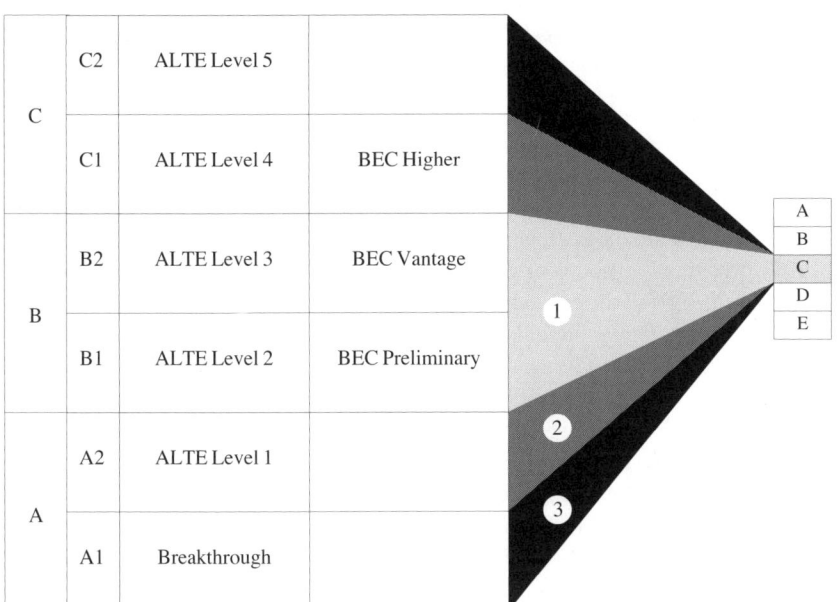

The test taker

Cambridge ESOL routinely collects information about test takers by asking them to complete a Candidate Information Sheet (CIS). This is done primarily to ensure that there are no tasks or items that result in uncharacteristically low test performance from a particular sub-group of the population. Another reason for gathering this information is to better understand the population so that appropriate tasks and items are included in the test.

The candidate information collected reflects two of the three groups of test taker characteristics' categories suggested by O'Sullivan (2000a), namely, physical and experiential characteristics – the third group of characteristics is psychological, which is seen as more of a research issue related to test design, see for example O'Sullivan (2000a), who investigated among other variables, the effect on performance of candidate perceptions of the personality of peer candidates in the FCE test of speaking. By collecting data on the physical characteristics of the candidates, validation officers can carry out bias studies (to ensure that there is no gender bias for example, or no bias that may be related in some way to the age of the candidate), while developers can ensure that accommodations are set in place which can allow students with special needs an equal

91

opportunity to sit for their tests, see Gutteridge (2003) and Taylor and Gutteridge (2003) for a description of the approach taken by Cambridge ESOL.

By knowing more about the background of each candidate, the test developer can also investigate the degree to which particular background variables might impact on test performance, a particularly relevant area of research in a specific purpose test.

Theory-based validity

In their response to the criticisms voiced by Foot (1999), Saville and Hargreaves (1999) presented a model of communicative ability, grounded in the work of Bachman (1990) and upon which the UCLES Main Suite Speaking examinations are based. This model also forms the basis of the BEC suite tests. It takes account of the executive resources available to the candidate in terms of their communicative language ability and also the metacognitive strategies they will need to deploy for effective communication in the spoken mode.

The model, see Figure 1.1, is itself based on the earlier models of Bachman (1990) and Canale and Swain (1980), as well as on the Council of Europe specifications for the Waystage and Threshold levels of competence (Saville and Hargreaves 1999:46). Though this model deals adequately with the cognitive aspects of language as communication, or what Weir (2004) refers to as theory-based validity, it does not satisfactorily address the importance of the context of language use on performance (Weir's context validity). Recent developments in the socio-cognitive approach to defining language proficiency for testing purposes (Chalhoub-Deville 2003, McNamara 1996, O'Sullivan 2000a, Weir 2004) stress the necessity of looking at both the context- and theory-based validity of tests and the interaction between these. In other words, defining the construct involves at its core a description of the test taker (in which theory-based validity is embedded) in the context of a particular language domain as mirrored in a test. In order to complete the definition, some evidence of the scoring validity of the test is required, so that decisions or inferences based on test scores can be shown to share the same theoretical rationale as the other elements of the construct.

In line with this socio-cognitive development, Cambridge ESOL defines the construct from these multiple-validity perspectives of which communicative language ability is only one aspect. These are discussed briefly below and then in more detail in Chapter 5.

Context-based validity

The handbooks for the BEC suite provide sets of specifications for the tests that are freely available in the public domain. These specifications outline

Figure 2.7 Defining the construct

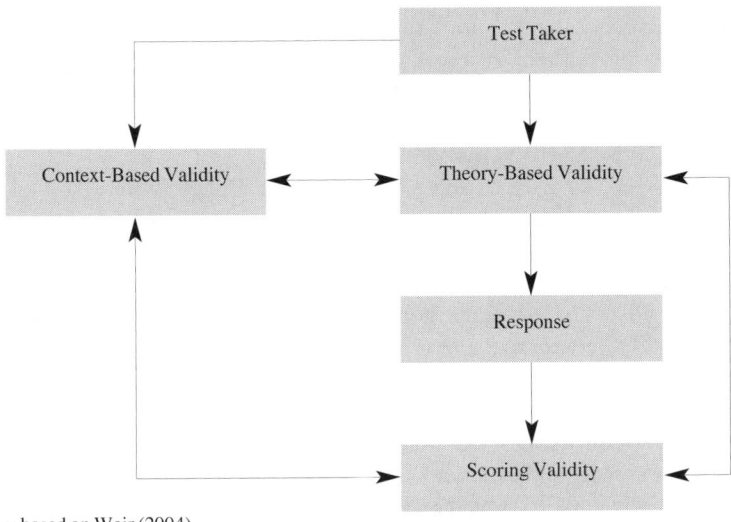

Source: based on Weir (2004)

the language demands of the tasks and items included in the test, while also identifying the conditions under which the tests are administered. More detailed specifications are prepared for use by test writers within Cambridge ESOL in order to ensure the compatibility of different versions of the same test in terms of what is being tested, how it is to be tested, and how the tests are to be administered.

As can be seen from the earlier sections in this chapter, the language of the BEC suite of tests has been closely linked (or benchmarked) to the Common European Framework (CEF). This ensures that the content and levels of each test version can be seen in terms not only of the BEC suite, but also of the range of ability as defined by the CEF. In addition, Ball (2002) described how the wordlists for the three BEC levels were revised based on extensive corpus-based research further grounding the context validity of these tests.

In addition to looking at the language of the tasks (input and expected output), the performance conditions are designed, as far as is practicable, to reflect those of the business language domain – both in terms of the physical replication of the domain and of the replication of the conditions in which aspects of language ability which can be used to define the domain are potentially present (in the linguistic responses of successful candidates). In order to complement these areas, Cambridge ESOL also ensures that all tests are administered in a systematic and fair way according to pre-set guidelines. These guidelines – which again attempt to reflect the business domain where possible – add to the situational authenticity of the test event, while setting the foundations for fair and reliable scoring and interpretation of scores.

Scoring validity

The final element of the definition relates to the transformation of the candidate response into a meaningful score. In the past, test developers (and users) were most interested in the area of reliability in all its guises (stability, consistency etc.). However, it is now believed that this represents just one aspect of what Weir (2004) calls scoring validity.

While this area is discussed in greater detail in Chapter 5 of this book, it is useful at this juncture, to look at the relevance of scoring validity in the definition of the construct.

Since scoring validity is concerned with all aspects of the score awarding procedures, all decisions made here should reflect the developer's view of language ability and approach to testing. In the BEC suite, this means that the model of language ability should be reflected in both theory- and context-based validity evidences as well as in the scoring procedures. This can be shown for the BEC suite Speaking tests for example, by linking the tasks and the rating scale to the Saville and Hargreaves model (Figure 2.8). Each element of the model is reflected initially in the expected response by a test taker to a particular speaking task (context-based) and in the predicted language knowledge of the test taker (theory-based). The elements are then reflected in the rating scale used to make judgements related to the actual response on the task. This triangulation is a basic requirement for meaningful scoring of any test event.

Figure 2.8 Linking the Model to the Rating Scale

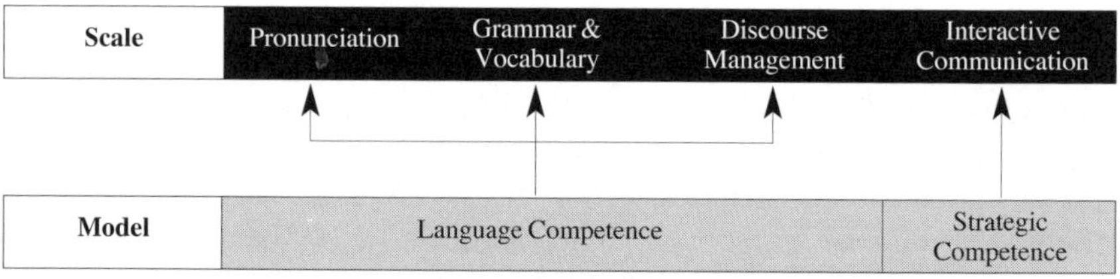

In the very brief overview offered in this section, I have attempted to give the reader some idea of the complexity of construct definition. While suggesting a model of language ability on which tests are based is an important element of this definition, on its own it is clearly not enough. The approach taken by Cambridge ESOL described above marks an attempt to ensure that the construct is defined from the multiple perspectives suggested by Weir (2004) which are described in more detail in the final chapter of this book.

An ongoing programme of validation and test revision

This section will focus on a number of issues central to the Cambridge ESOL test development methodology. These are related to the qualities of test usefulness as identified in the Validity, Reliability, Impact and Practicality (VRIP) system.

Examination qualities VRIP

As mentioned by Saville (2003: 65) all Cambridge ESOL examinations are built around four 'essential' qualities:

- validity
- reliability
- impact
- practicality.

These four qualities were abbreviated by Saville to VRIP, a convention I will also follow here. Also similar to the approach of Weir (2004) will be my consideration of the four qualities as being of central importance to the overall usefulness of any test. I would argue, however, that the former pair, validity and reliability, are actually two aspects of the unitary concept of validity – and that this view may provide us with a more useful model of test development than a model in which the pair are separated, but more of that later.

Before discussing the impact of VRIP on the BEC revision process, I will first briefly summarise the concept of VRIP as outlined by Saville (2003), and summarised in Figure 2.9.

Validity

The view of validity, as seen by Saville (2003), is best described as 'mainstream' in that it propounds the by now widely supported 'unitary' model suggested by Messick, which sees multiple sources of evidence as adding different levels of support to the central issue of validity. This view places construct-related validity at the core of validation. For this reason, it is considered imperative that a test should be based on a model of communicative language ability that can be empirically supported. According to Saville and Hargreaves (1999), the model which drives the Cambridge ESOL test development and revision practice (see Figure 1.1) has been influenced by the work of Bachman (1990) and the Council of Europe, among others.

The rationale behind collecting evidence of content-related validity has to do with the need to demonstrate 'the degree to which the sample of items, tasks, or questions on an examination are representative of a defined domain of content.

Figure 2.9 The four qualities of test usefulness

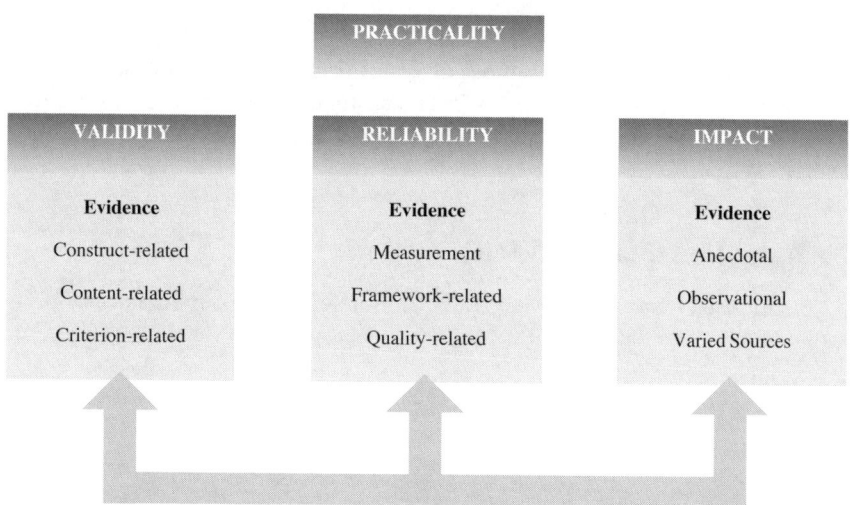

It is concerned with both relevance and coverage' Saville (2003:67). This representativeness can be specified through a model (as the model suggested by Saville and Hargreaves 1999 is used to specify the Cambridge ESOL tests) in addition to judgements made by experts in the field. Expert judgements may also be used when making decisions on the relative importance of various samples.

The relevance of content validation becomes apparent when we consider one particular feature of a test – a feature often associated with Cambridge ESOL Main Suite examinations and of particular relevance in the BEC series – that of authenticity. Weir (2002) argues that 'the relationship between the "input" and the expected response or "output" is an important feature of content validation'. He goes on to suggest that:

> The examination content must be designed to provide sufficient evidence of the underlying abilities (i.e. construct) through the way the test taker responds to this input. The responses to the test input (tasks, items, etc.) occur as a result of an interaction between the test taker and the test content. The authenticity of test content and the authenticity of the candidate's interaction with that content are important considerations for the examination developer in achieving high validity (ibid).

This can be seen as offering evidence in support of Messick's view of validity, in that it is difficult, if not impossible, to draw a clear distinction between the concepts of construct- and content-related evidence of a test's validity.

More evidence in support of Messick can be found in the way in which the BEC series (in the same way as the other Cambridge ESOL examinations) are benchmarked to an external criterion – in this case the ALTE framework. This benchmarking is an important aspect of the design of the tests, and also has implications for test content. We can therefore see that all three aspects of validity are interlinked to form a 'unitary' conceptualisation of validity.

Reliability

The view of reliability within the Cambridge ESOL test development framework is that it 'concerns the extent to which test results are *stable, consistent, and free from bias and random error*' (Saville 2003:69). The need to develop instruments that conform to this view is, of course, paramount. However, the fact that no practical consideration of how reliability decisions impact on a test can be made without also considering the implications that these decisions might have on the validity of the inferences we can draw from performances on that test means that there is a limit to the lengths to which it is possible to go in order to achieve maximum reliability. This last statement, apparently obvious though it is, actually highlights a real concern with the way in which we estimate the reliability of our tests.

Problems with the existing measures

The most critical error in the perception of reliability of many test developers and test users is the assumption that estimates of internal consistency that are based on item variance are measures of test reliability. I would argue that these estimates are particularly useful for certain types of test (e.g. multi-item standardised tests where there is clear evidence that the items are deliberately chosen because they test a single construct) but are not suitable for a criterion-referenced test, particularly where there is a truncated test population (i.e. a limited range of proficiency is represented in the population).

The attenuation paradox, first identified by Loevinger (1954), identifies a critical deficiency in the way we measure reliability. While writers such as Brown (1996:192) and Hughes (1989:31) suggest that 1.0 represents a 'perfect' reliability coefficient, the attenuation paradox means that, for a test to achieve this 'perfection' the only possible response patterns are a perfect full score or a perfect zero score. So the data set represented in Table 2.1, will result in a 'perfectly' reliable test (i.e. it will have a reliability coefficient of 1.0).

Table 2.1 Example of the response patterns in a 'perfectly' reliable test

Cand IDs	Item 1	Item 2	Item 3	Item 4	Item 5	Item 6	Item 7	Item 8	Item 9	Item 10
1	1	1	1	1	1	1	1	1	1	1
2	0	0	0	0	0	0	0	0	0	0
3	1	1	1	1	1	1	1	1	1	1
4	0	0	0	0	0	0	0	0	0	0

The other difficulty with the way in which we estimate reliability lies in the fact that it is not even necessary that the response patterns should be neatly divided into two equal groups of candidates. In fact, if only a single candidate achieves a perfect full score while all others score zero, the test will still appear to have a 'perfect' reliability.

One problem with this feature of how 'reliability' has come to be seen is that it is very much dependent on the test population. Where a population contains examples of extreme behaviour the likelihood is that the 'reliability' estimate will be high. The implications for any test that is benchmarked to a particular level of performance, as is the case with the BEC suite (as well as the Cambridge ESOL Main Suite examination and the Pitman and LCCIEB tests referred to in Chapter 1), is quite clear. Where a test is drawing on a truncated population, in that the ability range of the test takers is confined to a relatively narrow range of ability, the estimates of internal consistency will always be low. This type of measure is therefore unsuitable for analysing the type of tests referred to here, that is level-based tests (though it may be used as a practical measure of comparing the internal consistency of different administrations of the same test which have been proven to have similar truncated candidate populations). To put it another way, and perhaps more accurately, it is not reasonable to expect that these tests will result in the very high measures of variance-based internal consistency that can be achieved by tests which test across a wide range of ability.

The real difficulty lies in the fact that we have come to accept that estimates based on internal consistency (KR20, Chronbach's alpha) are accurate indicators of the reliability of a test. They are not.

Saville also argues that 'in the case of the Cambridge ESOL examinations, which employ a wide variety of task-based materials and item types . . . very high internal consistency may not be an appropriate aim' (2003:70). He goes on to suggest that the replacement of discrete point multiple-choice items by task-based exercises (which provide far greater context and authenticity, both situational and interactional) means a reduction in the number of items and also of the estimated reliability using an internal consistency estimate.

Cronbach's alpha does not divide the test according to tasks, but items, so that both halves of the test may contain items from one task. Items from one task are not independent of each other to the same degree as discrete items. That is to say, if a candidate has correctly answered the first item of a multi-item task they are more likely to answer the next item correctly because of their response to the first item. In this case Cronbach's alpha would exaggerate the reliability of such a test in much the same way as if the candidate's response to the same item was placed in both halves of the split test (Anastasi 1988).

A solution to the above would appear to be if the internal consistency of a test is calculated by splitting the test according to task, not item. However, as we can expect candidates to perform differently according to task type, the reliability coefficient calculated in this way would be lower than for a discrete item test even if the discrete item test contained a variety of (single item) tasks and is therefore not, strictly, comparable.

The problem is compounded for tests such as BEC. Not only is the test population truncated, but also the task types tend to result in reliability measurements that are not comparable to those values calculated on a fully discrete item test. What is clear from the above is that these estimates do not tell the whole story about a test's reliability.

However, internal measurements of reliability, such as Cronbach's alpha, are useful in the test development process in providing convenient conventionalised measurements of reliability between different parallel forms of the same test. This occurs in different administrations of the same test at different sessions throughout the year. Here the error noted above in what may be termed the 'absolute' reliability is not as important as the insight the measurements give in maintaining standards across different administrations.

Estimates have been systematically calculated for BEC suite tests over the years. Based on the information contained in Tables 2.2–2.4, it is possible to make reference to the kind of cross-administration comparisons mentioned above. It is possible to see, for example, that the internal consistency of the Reading and Listening papers varies very little over the different sessions reported in a 2-year period. It is interesting to note also that the estimates are high enough to be considered acceptable in a norm referenced test for a population where there is a full range of ability.

Table 2.2 Reliability (Cronbach's alpha) for BEC Preliminary, Reading and Listening components, selected sessions 2002–2003

Session	Reliability Reading	Reliability Listening	Sample Size
May–02	0.85	0.84	1087
Nov–02	0.85	0.82	905
May–03	0.86	0.87	1064
Dec–03	0.86	0.83	1873

Table 2.3 Reliability (Cronbach's alpha) for BEC Vantage, Reading and Listening components, selected sessions 2002–2003

Session	Reliability Reading	Reliability Listening	Sample Size
May–02	0.82	0.83	1458
Nov–02	0.86	0.78	754
May–03	0.84	0.80	1084
Nov–03	0.85	0.81	998

Table 2.4 Reliability (Cronbach's alpha) for BEC Higher, Reading and Listening components, selected sessions 2002–2003

Session	Reliability Reading	Reliability Listening	Sample Size
Mar–02	0.85	0.85	511
Nov–02	0.85	0.86	271
May–03	0.81	0.78	581
Nov–03	0.85	0.80	359

As with the Cambridge ESOL Main Suite examinations, reliability of the BEC suite tests of Speaking and Writing should be seen from the perspectives of the accuracy and consistency of the ratings which are awarded, as dictated by the current American Psychological Association Standards (APA 1999).

Cambridge ESOL tests have included the pair format as the standard format for all Main Suite speaking papers since the early 1990s and all BEC levels are based on the format (with two candidates and two examiners, one in the role of interlocutor/assessor and the other in the role of observer/assessor). Since both examiners use slightly different scales (the interlocutor uses a holistic scale which is derived from the four criteria analytic scale used by the observer), there are some problems with any simple correlations between the scores they award. However, there are similar difficulties with any correlation procedure, as the outcomes are affected by the nature of the scale used and by the range of ability of the test population

In addition to calculating the correlation of scores awarded by raters, it may also be fruitful to compare the grades each individual examiner's score might lead to – in other words, an examination of classification accuracy. Multi-faceted Rasch (MFR) analysis has been suggested as a possible solution to the inter-rater reliability problem. This process produces output tables for the different variables (or facets) included in the analysis. Each output table includes a 'separation reliability' estimate. Where the output table for candidates is concerned we would hope that the separation reliability is high (indicating that the candidates have a range of significantly different ability). As far as raters are concerned, we want the separation reliability to be low (indicating that they have the same severity).

Since Rasch is a probabilistic model, the expectation is that the raters will be locally independent (they will demonstrate some amount of disagreement). This suggests that MFR offers an interesting solution, though the different scales will represent a practical (though not insurmountable) concern in designing a study. The other difficulty with MFR is that it is ideal for experimental studies, whereas little work has been done to date in expanding the method into a large-scale 'real world' test, mainly due to the problem of establishing connectivity issues among the raters – though initial groundwork has been undertaken by Myford and Wolfe (2000) in their study of minimal connectivity requirements for a large-scale test administration. Weir (2004) also suggests that generalisability theory may offer another direction of exploration. It would appear that for any performance test (of writing or speaking) it would be safer to report reliability from a number of perspectives rather than rely on any single estimate.

The above discussion essentially argues that the notion of 'reliability' as it exists is not useful for the type of tests I am writing about here, except as a convenient and conventionalised means of comparing similar tests with similar truncated populations (e.g. in different administrations of the same test) as noted by Saville (2003:71). Instead, it would be more beneficial to see the true relia- bility of a test as being centred on the degree to which, to repeat Saville 'the results are *stable, consistent,* and *free from bias and random error*' (2003:69). This definition essentially brings us back to the perspective suggested by Bachman who sees reliability as being associated with 'sources of error in a given measure of communicative language ability' (1990:160). The sources of threat to reliability are suggested in Figure 2.10.

Figure 2.10 Factors that affect language test scores

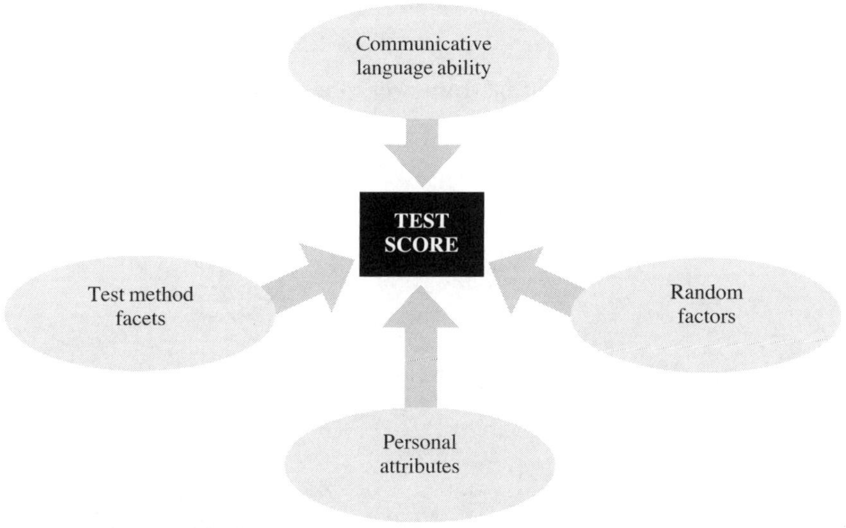

Source: Bachman (1990:165)

Bachman (1990) argues that test method facets should be seen as being related to the *testing environment,* the *test rubric, input* and *expected response,* and the *relationship between input and respons*e (1990:118–152) and as being '*systematic* to the extent that they are uniform from one test administration to another' (1990:164). This notion of systematicity is also applied to the definition of 'personal attributes' (1990:164); random factors are seen by Bachman (1990:164–5) as being unsystematic variables associated with:

- the candidates (such as mental alertness, emotional state)
- the test facets (such as changes in test performance conditions)
- the test administrators ('idiosyncratic differences in the way different test administrators carry out their responsibilities')
- incomplete language sample
- scale imprecision.

When this view of reliability is considered, we can really see the limitations in the 'reliability as internal consistency' perspective that currently dominates language testing – certainly if we are to take what we read in journal articles and test reports as reflecting current practice. We can also include among these 'random' factors sources of variance implied in the Milanovic and Saville (1996) framework, see Figure 2.11. When we consider the likelihood that the variables included in this framework are potential sources of systematic and/or unsystematic or random variance, we get some notion of the difficulties involved in establishing the conditions for truly reliable testing to take place, and of the necessity of seeing *true reliability* as being a function of what I would call *test quality*.

Figure 2.11 A conceptual framework for performance testing

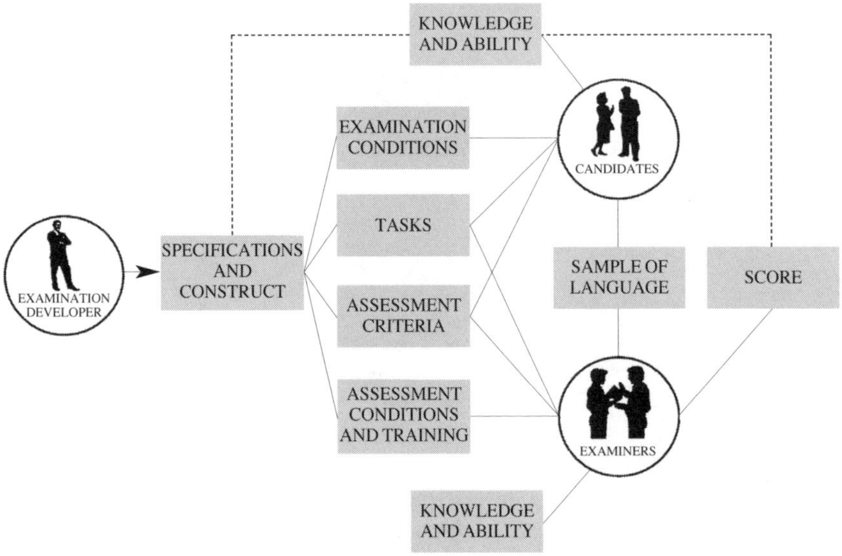

Source: Milanovic and Saville (1996)

102

This then raises the question of how we demonstrate true reliability. I would argue that the true reliability of any test is a unitary concept, much like the way we look at test validity, but with multiple perspectives, again much like with validity. Therefore, to demonstrate it we need to provide evidence of test quality across a whole range of perspectives, and as far as the BEC suite is concerned, one major source of evidence is the way in which the overall approach to test development, construction and administration outlined above is applied to the suite.

Impact

Saville suggests that:

> 'From a validation perspective, it is important to be able to monitor and investigate the educational impact that examinations have within the contexts they are used. As a point of principle, examination developers like Cambridge ESOL should operate with the aim that their examinations will not have a negative impact and, as far as possible, strive to achieve positive impact' (2003:74).

He identifies the following issues as central to any test organisation's validation procedures, this in reference to an *a priori* perspective on Messick's notion of Consequential Validity:

- the development and presentation of examination specifications and detailed syllabus designs;
- provision of professional support programmes for institutions and individual teachers/students who use the examinations
- the identification of suitable experts within the field to work on all aspects of examination development
- the training and employment of suitable experts within the field to act as question/item writers in examination production
- the training and employment of suitable experts within the field to act as examiners' (op. cit.).

Within the context of the BEC revision, these issues have been approached in a number of ways (Table 2.5).

In addition to the above issues, Saville argues for a similar concern with an *a posteriori* perspective on test impact when he suggests that procedures also need to be put into place after an examination becomes operational to collect information which allows impact to be estimated. This should involve collecting data on the following:

- who is taking the examination (i.e. a profile of the candidates)
- who is using the examination results and for what purpose
- who is teaching towards the examination and under what circumstances
- what kinds of courses and materials are being designed and used to prepare candidates

Table 2.5 Impact issues in the BEC tests (a priori)

Issue	Action
development and presentation of examination specifications and detailed syllabus designs	through the dissemination of information through the BEC website (www.cambridge-efl.org/exam/business/bg_bec.htm) and the latest BEC handbooks (downloadable from the website)
provision of professional support programmes for institutions and individual teachers/students who use the examinations	through the professional seminar programme
identification of suitable experts within the field to work on all aspects of examination development	through the appointment of leading researchers and academics to act as consultants in all aspects of the revision process
training and employment of suitable experts within the field to act as question/item writers in examination production	through the provision of detailed training manuals (e.g. CAMBRIDGE ESOL's involvement in the ALTE Item Writers Guidelines' Project) and the recognition of expertise within the organisation
training and employment of suitable experts within the field to act as examiners	through detailed Minimum Professional Requirements' (MPR) documents, and the setting of rigorous selection and accreditation standards

- what effect the examination has on public perceptions generally (e.g. regarding educational standards)
- how the examination is viewed by those directly involved in educational processes (e.g. by students, examination takers, teachers, parents, etc.)
- how the examination is viewed by members of society outside education (e.g. by politicians, businessmen etc.) (Saville 2003:75).

These issues have been addressed in the BEC suite examinations as outlined in Table 2.6.

Practicality

Though its importance is often neglected in the language testing literature, practicality is 'an integral part of the concept of test usefulness and affects many different aspects of an examination' (Saville 2003:76).

The section above, in which the project structure was described, is particularly important here as we can see that it includes many of the aspects of practicality suggested by Saville as being of relevance to any test:

- 'the management structure for the development project
- a clear and integrated assignment of roles and responsibilities
- a means of monitoring progress in terms of development schedules and resources
- a methodology for managing the examination production process when

Table 2.6 Impact issues in the BEC tests (a posteriori)

Issue	Action
who is taking the examination	data related to the candidates is routinely collected through the Candidate Information Sheet (CIS) and used in test, task and item level analyses
who is using the examination results and for what purpose	These are monitored through routine surveys of stakeholders (both formally and informally). The data collected are used in all major decisions regarding the tests in question – particularly in making decisions related to review and revision.
who is teaching towards the examination and under what circumstance	
what kinds of courses and materials are being designed and used to prepare candidates	
what effect the examination has on public perceptions generally	
how the examination is viewed by those directly involved in educational processes	In the BEC revision two revision questionnaires were developed: • general (primarily aimed at teachers)
how the examination is viewed by members of society outside education	• key contacts (for principal stakeholders).

the examination becomes operational (item writing, vetting, moderation, pre-testing, item banking, question paper construction)' (Saville 2003:77).

For the BEC examinations (as with other Cambridge ESOL tests), practicality is a major concern, impacting on a whole range of areas of test production, administration and evaluation. The areas concerned have been identified in Weir and Milanovic's work on the CPE revision, though clearly the list is equally valid for the BEC examination:

- design features related to format and content of the four skills approach
  e.g. length of papers – number of items and time allowed, type of tasks
- test production features
  e.g. number of items required, replicability of tasks
- availability of the examination in terms of:
  examinations dates and the frequency of administration
  location and number of centres
- level of fees to be paid by test takers
- central costs in terms of:
  production of question papers
  marking and scoring
  validation
- local costs in relation to administration at centres
  e.g. hire of venues, training and deployment of oral examiners, etc.

- central administration
  entry procedures – exchange of data with centres
  collection of fees
  despatch of materials
  marking and grading procedures
  issue of results
- local administration at centres
- security
- special circumstances
  e.g. arrangements for candidates with special needs.

Recruitment, Induction, Training, Co-ordination, Monitoring, Evaluation (RITCME)

One aspect of 'test usefulness' that has an impact on a number of the above areas of concern is that of the structure and maintenance of what is known as the Team Leader system for examiners (this is particularly relevant to the examiners who are involved with the assessment of the productive skills).

As the reader can imagine, the logistics of administering a test on an international level are beyond the experience of most organisations, let alone individuals. In tests of speaking, for example, there is evidence of an 'interlocutor effect' (Lumley and O'Sullivan 2001, O'Sullivan 1995, 2000a, 2000b, 2002a), an 'observer/assessor effect' (McNamara and Lumley, 1997 – where the assessors were apparently systematic in taking into account what they perceived as the adequacy of the performance of the examiner in awarding a score to the individual candidates), and a 'candidate by task effect', for example Berry (1997) demonstrated how candidates of different psychological make up performed more or less well depending on the task. While the latter effect is more related to test design (suggesting that any performance test would benefit from a variety of tasks), the former pair of effects highlight the need for the careful recruitment, induction, training, co-ordination, monitoring, and evaluation of all examiners.

As with the other Cambridge ESOL examinations (in which over 10,000 examiners participate on a regular basis worldwide), there are a number of levels of professional responsibility within the BEC examiner system, in addition to the Cambridge ESOL staff. These levels are summarised in Figure 2.12.

At the operational level are the Examiners (both oral and written). In countries where there are sufficient numbers of examiners to merit it, there are Team Leaders who have responsibility for the professional supervision of examiners. Team Leaders typically work with anywhere from 5–30 examiners. Where there is an ample number of Team Leaders in a country, they will be supervised by a Senior Team Leader, the average ratio being 15:1. It should be noted that all of the above are actually practising examiners, so while there is a

Figure 2.12 The Team Leader system

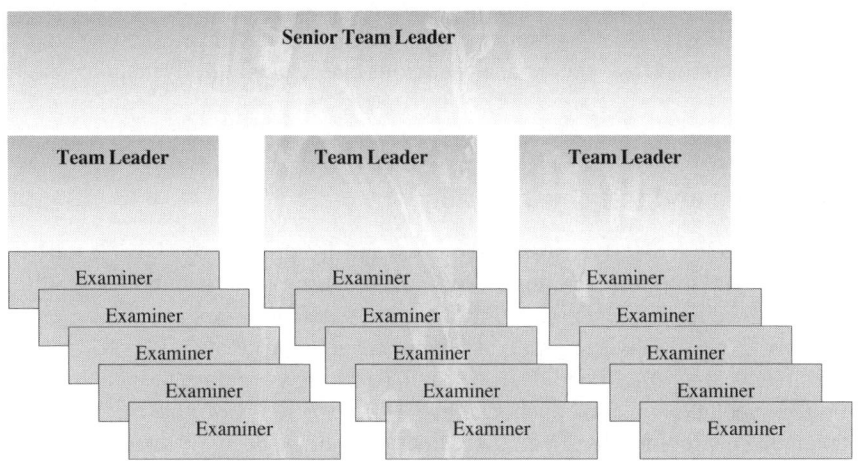

hierarchical structure, its principal rationale is to ensure that there is a clear two-way channel of communication through the test administration system.

The set of procedures which regulates the activities of these three professional levels is summarised by the acronym RITCME – Recruitment, Induction, Training, Co-ordination, Monitoring, Evaluation. Each procedure is defined by a list of minimum professional requirements, which sets down the minimum levels and standards (for recruitment, induction, training programmes, etc.) that must be achieved in order to meet the professional requirements of administering the Speaking tests and sustain a fully effective Team Leader System (Taylor 2000).

The great advantage to this set of guidelines is that it allows local examination secretaries outside of the UK to ensure that their practices mirror that of the UK-based parent group. Cambridge ESOL itself 'has the primary responsibility for the supervision and deployment' of examiners in the UK (UCLES 1999:1).

Ensuring accuracy and consistency of grades

An important aspect of the Cambridge ESOL approach is the concern with ensuring that the final grades awarded to candidates are a consistent, accurate and a fair reflection of the levels defined in the ALTE/CEF frameworks and that scores and grades reflect a consistent language ability over time.

A number of key areas, related to the work of the research and validation unit within Cambridge ESOL, are briefly discussed below but the process of ensuring construct and content validity permeates the test construction process at each stage. For example, items are commissioned from experienced ESOL professionals who receive ongoing training. Similarly, at the pre-editing stage items are examined by experts for any obvious biased or culturally inappropriate material.

Pretesting and test construction

The construction of tests to specified content and difficulty targets is achieved by the item-banking process employed for BEC as for other Cambridge ESOL exams. Reading and Listening items are pretested under exam conditions, on a suitably large and diverse group of learners at an appropriate level. Wherever possible these are BEC candidates who will be taking an exam in the near future. Pretests include so-called anchor items. These are items of known difficulty taken from previous live administrations that have been selected for their adequate facility, discrimination and difficulty and perceived lack of bias towards or against one or more groups of test takers.

Writing and Speaking tasks are trialled on a smaller but representative group of candidates to ensure that they elicit the desired responses and that the tasks do not contain lexical items or phrases within the instructions that would be problematic to candidates at that level.

When the response data are analysed the anchor enables the difficulties of the pretested tasks to be located on the measurement scale which underlies the Cambridge/ALTE levels' system.

Item banking

The calibrated tasks are then stored in a sophisticated item bank: LIBS (Local Item Banking System). This is a computer-based management and analysis tool developed by UCLES, not only to store calibrated items but to handle the entire production process. LIBS contains a large bank of materials for use in the examinations, which have been fully edited and pretested according to the procedures described in some detail by Saville (2003:90–95). LIBS enables complete test versions to be constructed to quite precise targets in terms of content and difficulty. However, versions may still vary slightly in mean difficulty, because most items are embedded within tasks and thus cannot individually be juggled to achieve an exact mean difficulty.

Item banking exploits latent trait (item response theory) techniques. The particular latent trait model used by Cambridge ESOL is the Rasch model, which has proved to be well-suited to the construction of a broad measurement framework capable of accommodating a suite of communicative language proficiency exams at different levels and covering a range of skills.

Administration

The conditions under which the exam is administered are also important for ensuring that all candidates are given an equal chance to perform to their best. The assessment of the Speaking component is particularly important in this regard, and depends on the professional skills of the oral examiners, so that the training, standardisation and monitoring of this cadre can be seen as a vital element in the achievement of a common standard.

Marking, scaling, weighting

Following the administration and before grading can take place, candidates' responses must be captured and marked.

Three kinds of marking are employed:

1. Automatic, in the case of Reading and Listening multiple-choice tasks, where the candidate indicates a choice on an optically markable answer sheet.
2. Clerical, in the case of short free-text responses which allow a strictly limited set of correct answers, and which can be marked to a high degree of reliability by clerical staff under the supervision of a co-ordinating examiner who has analysed live responses to ensure that the key is complete and understood by clerical markers.
3. Examiner marking, as in the case of Writing, where trained and standardised examiners apply a mark scheme and their knowledge of the level to assign a mark.

The next step is scaling, where the distribution of marks for the Writing component is adjusted to compensate for differences in the marking patterns of Writing examiners. Scaling is designed to ensure that markers who are more lenient or severe compared to all other markers have their individual marks for candidates adjusted to compensate for these tendencies. In scaling the distribution of marks for all candidates in writing is compared to the distribution of marks for candidates of a particular marker. Adjustments are made to the marks of candidates at a number of points on the markers' candidate writing score distribution to bring this in line with all candidates' writing score distribution. Allowances are made for the difference in mean and standard deviation of the markers and all candidates as observed in the Reading and Listening components.

Next marks for each component are weighted. For BEC as for other Cambridge ESOL exams the general principle is adopted that each component should contribute an equal proportion of marks to the total available for the exam. Thus in the case of BEC each of the four components contributes 30 marks to the exam total of 120. In fact the number of raw marks in the Reading paper is greater than 30. A candidate's Reading mark is thus weighted by multiplying it by 30/45 (for Preliminary and Vantage) or 30/52 (for Higher).

A candidate's total mark in the exam is a simple sum of the marks gained in each component, after the processes described above.

Grading

A passing grade at BEC locates a candidate within a broad proficiency framework: Passes at BEC Preliminary, Vantage and Higher correspond to ALTE Levels 2, 3 and 4, or to Council of Europe Levels B1, B2 and C1 respectively. Thus BEC can be broadly compared with other exams at the same level.

For such interpretations to be valid it is of course necessary that BEC be graded to a consistent standard. Every stage of the exam administration cycle, from test design through exam conduct to marking and grading, is relevant to ensuring this consistency.

The grade thresholds should reflect a constant standard across sessions, but the precise number of marks needed to achieve each grade will vary within a narrow range, reflecting a judgement about the difficulty of the components in a particular session. This judgement is based on several types of quantitative and qualitative information:

1. The difficulty of each objective component. The estimate of this depends on the calibration of items at pretesting and another, independent, calibration given by live anchor tests. These are short tests of items with known difficulty and suitable facility and discrimination levels, administered to a proportion of candidates at the same time or shortly before the administration of the exam itself. In BEC all candidates are requested to complete anchor tests. This ensures that a representative sample of candidates sits the anchor tests and that the estimate of difficulty for items and components calculated using anchor tests can be checked for the effect of first language and ability on performance in the anchor tests. The difficulty of Reading and Listening components are arrived at then by examining and weighing three, independent, sources; pretest statistics, live anchor statistics, and comparisons with performance of live candidates in the criteria-based components Speaking and Writing.

2. The performance of particular 'cohorts' i.e. major groups of candidates, compared with their historical trends. While it is clear that cohorts may follow upward or downward trends, reflecting changes in the size or make-

up of the group, it is expected that these trends will be steady, and that grading should not result in abrupt shifts in the pass rate for many cohorts.
3. A judgement about the standard applied to the performance components (Speaking and Writing). The mark schemes for these are criterion referenced, and thus the marks awarded should directly reflect the standard. Mean scores at task level and feedback from chief examiners are noted to indicate whether individual tasks in writing have proved difficult. If so some correction will be made for this in the grading.

Estimating the internal consistency of each administration

While acknowledging the potential difficulties associated with reporting internal consistency estimates for each BEC examination, Cambridge ESOL reports the estimates for each BEC level for Reading and Listening (see Tables 2.2 to 2.4). The overall consistency of an exam such as BEC, i.e. it is comprised of several component papers, is known as its composite reliability.

Using the Feldt and Brennan (1989) approach, the composite reliability for the BEC suite tests has been reported by Cambridge ESOL as lying in the range of 0.88 to 0.91 for all sessions in 2003 (see Table 2.7). When viewed with all of the other procedures that are in place to ensure the accuracy of the final grades awarded to candidates, these figures can be seen as adding significantly to the overall reliability evidence.

Table 2.7 Composite reliability and SEM for all BEC Levels 2003

Level	Session	Mar 03	May 03	June 03	July 03	Nov 03	Dec 03
BEC P	Comp R*	0.90	0.90	0.90	0.90	0.89	0.90
	Comp SEM**	4.89	5.33	4.99	5.30	5.06	5.28
	Sample Size	2008	1064	1956	885	982	1873
BEC V	Comp R	0.90	0.89	0.89	0.91	0.90	0.89
	Comp SEM	4.92	4.84	4.89	4.31	4.85	4.61
	Sample Size	1819	1084	2926	791	998	1760
BEC H	Comp R	0.90	0.88	0.88	***	0.89	0.89
	Comp SEM	3.83	4.08	3.94		4.20	4.01
	Sample Size	482	581	1565		359	952

*R= Reliability
**SEM= Standard Error of Measurement
*** No administration

Additional procedures

Several additional procedures are followed to ensure that as far as possible candidates' final grades reflect their true ability.

Grade review is a process which follows grading in which the Writing scripts of candidates just below the passing grade are reviewed, and if necessary the Writing mark is amended.

Examination centres may ask for 'special consideration' on behalf of candidates because of personal circumstances surrounding the exam, or because they believe the administration of the exam was such as to disadvantage them – for example, that the Listening component was disrupted by noise outside the exam room. Where appropriate these cases are evaluated by a panel which follows guidelines and is informed by relevant statistical information on the performance of the candidates. This statistical information examines the discrepancy between the marks achieved in the administration of the component under question and the performance of the candidates in their other components (allowing for differences in mean score and standard deviation between components) to observe if there is a significant difference between the two.

Cases of alleged malpractice are also investigated, and where proven results are withheld.

All the procedures outlined above are not specific to BEC but rather are standard practice across Cambridge ESOL examinations, and are dealt with in more detail in Weir and Milanovic (2003:88–109).

The context for the revision of BEC

Since the early 1990s there have been major documented revisions to a number of the Cambridge ESOL Main Suite examinations, most notably the Certificate of Proficiency in English (CPE), see Weir (2003a). In this excellent overview of the (CPE) revision project, Weir outlines in great detail the development cycle devised by the organisation for these revision/development projects that informs the Cambridge ESOL language testing systems. In his review, Weir looks not only at the latest revision to the CPE and the methodology that supported that process, but demonstrates the connections between the revision practice and its outcomes over the long history of the CPE (it was first administered in 1913). While such a historical perspective is clearly beyond this book, after all the testing of language for business purposes is a very new phenomenon, as can be seen in the previous chapter, it is worthwhile revisiting the revision methodology in order to better understand how the present BEC suite has come to reflect the Cambridge ESOL language testing philosophy both of test quality and content.

The development cycle has been outlined in detail by Saville (2003) and will be summarised in the remainder of this chapter only in relation to the impact it has had on the BEC revision project.

The revision process

The Planning and Design phases for the BEC revision project took place between 1999 and 2000 and included the production of preliminary revised specifications, consultation with stakeholder groups as well as some experimental trialling – though the lessons learned from the recent FCE and CPE revision projects were also influential.

The development phase, which included trialling and analysis of proposed changes took place in 2000. The specifications for internal use were approved in 2000 and a revised specifications' booklet was published in early 2001.

Groups involved in the revision process

The review/revision process was, as in other Cambridge ESOL revision projects, initiated within a project review group at one of its regular meetings. For a very detailed and informative overview of how this process was applied in a formal revision project, see the chapters by Ashton (Chapter 3); Weighill and Shaw (Chapter 4); Barratt (Chapter 5); Boroughs (Chapter 6) and ffrench (Chapter 7) in Weir and Milanovic (2003). The rationale for the BEC revision was less related to actual or perceived dissatisfaction with the tests, but to an awareness of the various changes (detailed above) which resulted in an expanded and more culturally diverse candidature.

As with the CPE revision, the first stage was to set up the necessary management structures to oversee the review or revision project. This meant the creation of a **Management Steering Group** chaired by the Director or Deputy Director EFL and consisting of Cambridge ESOL senior management (e.g. group managers and the project co-ordinator). This group was empowered with the oversight of the whole process and the management of resource allocation. Among the specific duties of the group were:

* to define parameters
* to initiate research and development
* to make judgements
* to ratify the revised specification
* to allocate appropriate level of staff time for co-ordination of the project and participation in an **Internal Working Group**
* to create a number of **Consultants' Working Groups** (one group per skill area, each group was headed by a member of the internal working group).

The internal working groups were made up of Cambridge ESOL specialist staff (including research and validation staff).

These groups were asked to:

- co-ordinate external groups
- act on recommendations from the steering group
- trial revised specifications
- develop and propose final specifications to the steering group
- report on the revision project to the steering group.

Finally, the Consultant Working Groups, which consisted of Cambridge ESOL consultants (typically senior researchers and academics at key British universities), specialist internal staff and research and validation staff were charged with devising revised specifications for each component of the tests.

The plan for the revision project was similar to that designed for the CPE project, in that it focused on the main areas shown in Table 2.8.

Table 2.8 BEC revision project plan

Number	Item	Focus
1	Consultation exercise	Consultation exercises
2	Identify areas for revision	Identify priority areas for revision
3	Redraft specifications and item writer guidelines	Draft specifications
4	Trialling	Trialling
5	Wordlists	Validation projects
6	Validation work	
7	Information seminars	
8	Publication of revised specifications	Finalised specifications
9	Item writer guidelines and training	Release of information
10	Sample materials	
11	Release information to the public and centres	
12	Live test material production	Training
13	Training of oral examiners	
14	Live administration	

While many of these areas are of little interest to the reader in that they are relatively mundane and an 'everyday' part of any test development project, the first area is of particular interest in the BEC revision process as it was clearly influential in all later decisions. It is therefore to this aspect of the process that we now turn.

The consultative exercises

The internal working group first established a **Project Plan**, starting with a

Situational Analysis. The key aim of this phase of the project was to establish a project timeline with an anticipated end point.

The situational analysis began with a review of validation evidence, which had been routinely gathered since the earliest administration of the BEC tests. This evidence was related to the qualities of test usefulness identified in the Cambridge ESOL approach, and discussed in the relevant section above (i.e. validity, reliability, impact and practicality).

In order to gain insights into the impact of the existing BEC tests, a survey of the views and attitudes of major stakeholders was conducted. There also existed an amount of formal and informal feedback collected over the years, though this was not considered sufficient on its own to allow for major decisions to be made. The stakeholders consulted included:

• Local Secretaries who administer the exam
• the language schools/teachers preparing candidates
• the senior consultants and other professionals who are employed to work on the materials and assessment procedures (Senior Team Leaders, Team Leaders, chairs of item writing teams, Principal Examiners etc.).

Two main groups were surveyed using a pair of questionnaires designed by the working groups for the project. These groups were BEC centres (the questionnaires were expected to be completed with teachers involved in preparing candidates for the existing BEC tests) and people with detailed knowledge of the BEC tests (who were also experts in language testing). These two questionnaires are outlined briefly below, while the results are reported in the relevant chapters related to the different skills.

One of the questionnaires was called the Key Contacts Questionnaire (KCQ), and was designed to elicit information from major stakeholders around the world, including local secretaries of major markets. The KCQ consisted of a total of 60 statements in a series of sub-sections which looked at overall or general comments as well as at the papers within each level (see Table 2.9).

All items offered a 5-point scale ranging from 'strongly agree' to 'strongly disagree', with an additional 'no knowledge' option.

A total of 40 KCQs were distributed in early 1999 of which 21 were returned. In the resulting interim report, presented in May 1999, a number of points were highlighted as being problematic. These were:

• the speaking paper in general
• the reporting of the speaking paper (as a separate mark)
• the level of BEC1
• one section of the BEC1 Reading and Writing (Part 5).

At the same time as the KCQ, a second instrument, called the General Questionnaire (GQ), was distributed to 300 test centres around the world, of which a total of 67 responded. The GQ consisted of a set of seven items related

Table 2.9 Key Contacts Questionnaire – design

Focus		Number of Items
General Comments		7
BEC1	Reading and Writing	10
	Listening	6
	Speaking	4
	General	3
BEC2	Reading and Writing	6
	Listening	5
	Speaking	4
BEC3	Reading and Writing	9
	Listening	4
	Speaking	2

to BEC1, seven more for BEC2, eight for BEC3 and three items devoted to overall impressions of the suite. The results of the GQ are summarised in Table 2.10.

As can be seen from this table, there was a clearly positive feeling for the tests though there was a suggestion that the Speaking paper at each level (with the possible exception of BEC3) was less than satisfactory – with over 13% expressing a high degree of dissatisfaction with the paper in BEC1 and BEC2 (just short of 8% expressed a similar level of dissatisfaction with the speaking paper in BEC3).

Table 2.10 General Questionnaire – results summary

Test	Paper	% Satisfaction
BEC1	Reading	95% positive
	Writing	95%
	Listening	90%
	Speaking	59%
	General	86%
BEC2	Reading	92%
	Writing	85%
	Listening	89%
	Speaking	65%
	General	85%
BEC3	Reading	93%
	Writing	85%
	Listening	100%
	Speaking	85%
	General	88%

In addition to the questions about the BEC papers, respondents were asked to comment on the proposal to amalgamate the CEIBT (see Chapter 1) with BEC3 – as both tests were essentially aimed at the same candidature. The response to this item indicated that a clear majority (76%) of the respondents believed it was a good idea.

The various consultative exercises resulted in the identification of a number of areas which were potentially in need of revision. These were:

1. Changes to the overall structure of the tests:
   - more transparent names
   - BEC Preliminary to be refocused to the Main Suite PET level
   - speaking to have a stronger business focus
   - one overall grade (this included the issue of weighting of component papers)
   - more explicit benchmarking for each level.
2. Other changes to specific test papers:
   - more time for Reading and Writing
   - Reading and Writing separate in Vantage and Higher
   - choice of tasks in Higher Writing (Part 2)
   - more attractive presentation
   - Speaking tests improved to generate greater range of language.

Summary

In this chapter I reviewed the context for the revision of BEC, focusing on the test development and revision methodology currently employed by Cambridge ESOL. The revision was seen to have taken place through the setting up of task specific groups who were initially guided by the outcomes of an extensive consultative exercise – in which the impressions and observations of a range of stakeholders were elicited.

The actual approach taken was guided by Cambridge ESOL's five pronged approach, which is designed to show a commitment to the assessment of a wide variety of language skills; assessment for a variety of purposes; a system of criterion levels; quality and fairness; and finally to an ongoing programme of validation and test revision.

Another key element in the Cambridge ESOL approach is the focus on the VRIP (Validity, Reliability, Impact and Practicality) system of identifying examination qualities. While all of these were discussed, the focus on how reliability of language tests is viewed and reported was highlighted – with the suggestion that what was called true reliability is not simply a measurement issue, but is related to all aspects of test and test system quality.

The design of the revision project was highlighted through the impact on the decision-making process of the consultation exercises. The main findings of these exercises were described in terms of the changes suggested both within the different levels and within each test. In the following chapter, these changes will be described.

3 Major changes to the suite

Before looking at the changes to the individual papers in the BEC suite, it would be useful to first identify and briefly describe some of the more significant changes that have been made. Copies of sample papers at all three levels for the original BEC suite can be found in Appendices 3.1 to 3.3, while past examination papers for all three levels of the revised suits are included as Appendices 4.1 to 4.3, and are published by Cambridge ESOL (2002a, 2002b, 2002c).

Reporting of results as one overall grade

In the original BEC design, performance on the Speaking paper was reported as a separate grade. This was because the original construct design did not include a speaking component, partially due to the perception in the market for which the test was originally designed that speaking was not as relevant to business needs as the other skills, and partially to practical constraints. The main constraint was the lack of the considerable resources required to effectively operate a Team Leader (TL) system (see Chapter 2). However, a Speaking paper was made available to those candidates who had successfully completed the other papers as it was felt that the inclusion of a separate grade for these candidates gave a useful indication of the candidate's language profile in the days before graphical profiling was introduced.

By 1996, the TL system was in place in China and from that time all candidates were offered a Speaking paper. When the BEC suite came up for review in 1999 graphical profiling was an established part of the Cambridge ESOL approach to test performance reporting (i.e. in the Main Suite tests). This meant that the conditions were in place for these innovations to be introduced.

The original system of reporting meant that each candidate received an overall grade for performance on the three skills (Reading, Writing and Listening). In addition, for those candidates who had passed at this point, a Speaking paper was offered, performance on which was reported as:

- 1 – Higher
- 2 – Minimum satisfactory
- No Grade – less than satisfactory or absent.

Since the revised BEC suite examinations are designed to mirror the Main Suite tests at similar levels (see Figure 2.4), the reporting procedures reflect this. For BEC Preliminary, results are reported as two passing grades (Pass with Merit and Pass) and two failing grades (Narrow Fail and Fail). This follows the model used by the Cambridge ESOL Main Suite test at the equivalent level (PET).

Again following the model of the equivalent level Main Suite tests (FCE and CAE), in the BEC Vantage and BEC Higher, results are reported as three passing grades (A, B and C) and two failing grades (D and E).

For all levels of BEC, candidates receive statements of results which, in addition to their grades, show a graphical profile of their performance in each skill. These are shown against the scale Exceptional – Good – Borderline – Weak, and indicate the candidate's performance in each skill (see Figure 3.1). This scale takes account of relative differences in candidates' performances across components and also if candidates have met fixed criteria in the Speaking and Writing components. It is solely designed to provide feedback to candidates to allow them to make considered judgements on their strengths and weaknesses and so to allow them to adjust the focus of their language learning in the future.

Figure 3.1 The BEC statement of results

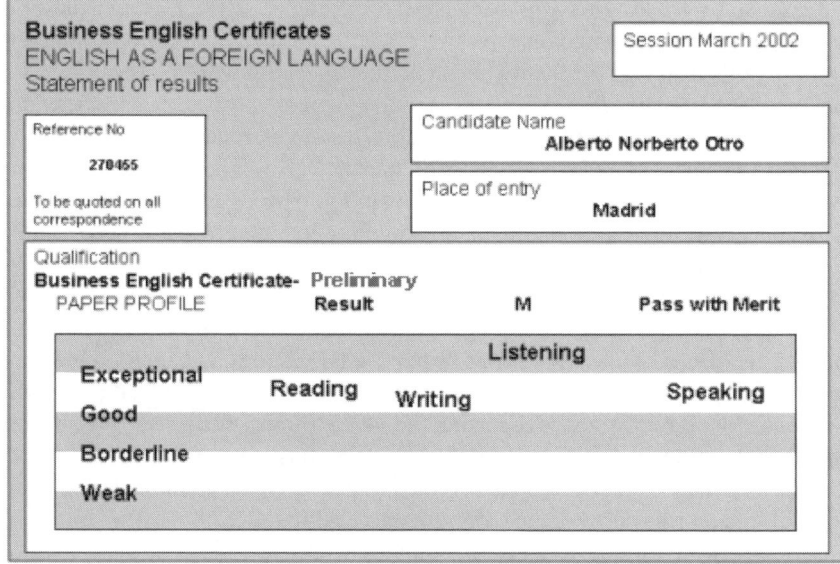

An additional impact of reporting performance as a single overall grade was the notion of how the individual components were to be weighted.

Weighting of components

One change that has been made is the weighting of the different components of the tests, both within each paper, and within each BEC level. This weighting system was designed both for improved measurement characteristics and to encourage a positive washback effect.

Within each paper

The system of scoring within each of the Reading papers is outlined in Tables 3.1 – 3.3. As can be seen from these tables, there have been very minor changes to the internal weighting of the papers. The greatest single changes are to be found at the initial level, where there are an additional five items in the general comprehension and grammar sections.

Table 3.1 Internal weighting – Reading BEC1/BEC Preliminary

Main Skill Focus	BEC1	BEC Preliminary
Reading and vocabulary	10	10
Reading interpreting visual information	5	5
Reading comprehension	15	18
Grammar	10	12
	40	45

Table 3.2 Internal weighting – Reading BEC2/BEC Vantage

Main Skill Focus	BEC2	BEC Vantage
Reading (scanning and gist)	7	7
Reading comprehension	5	5
Reading (gist and scanning for detail)	8	6
Vocabulary	15	15
Reading and grammar	10	12
	45	45

Table 3.3 Internal weighting – Reading BEC3/BEC Higher

Main Skill Focus	BEC3	BEC Higher
Reading (gist and main idea)	8	8
Reading (details and structure)	6	6
Reading (gist and scanning for detail)	6	6
Vocabulary	10	10
Reading and grammar	10	10
Grammar	10	12
	50	52

Within the Writing paper the changes in weighting are to be found in Tables 3.4 – 3.6. From these tables, we can see that it is at the initial level that the most significant change has been made. These have the effect of making the three levels more similar in terms of how the tasks are presented and weighted – with each level now consisting of a pair of tasks, the first of which is worth one-third of the available marks and the other worth the remaining two-thirds.

Table 3.4 Internal weighting – Writing BEC1/BEC Preliminary

Main Skill Focus	BEC1	BEC Preliminary
Reading of written input	5	Now a reading task
Note, message, memo or e-mail writing	5	10
Letter writing	10	20
	20	30

Table 3.5 Internal weighting – BEC2/BEC Vantage

Main Skill Focus	BEC2	BEC Vantage
Note, message or memo writing	10	10
Correspondence, report or proposal writing	15	20
	25	30

Table 3.6 Internal weighting – Writing BEC3/BEC Higher

Main Skill Focus	BEC3	BEC Higher
Report writing – describing, comparing, inferring	10	10
Report or proposal or correspondence writing	20	20
	30	30

Tables 3.7 – 3.9 indicate that the changes in internal weighting within the Listening papers are again quite small. It is only at the earliest level that there is any change to be found. Here, there is an increase in the number of items in the initial set of tasks – where the focus is on listening for detail, with the emphasis on the second set of items reduced.

Table 3.7 Internal weighting – Listening BEC1/BEC Preliminary

Main Skill Focus	BEC1	BEC Preliminary	Main Skill Focus
Listening for detail	8	8	Listening for specific information
Listening for detail (numbers)	4	7	Listening for specific information
Listening for specific information	10	7	Listening for specific information
Listening for detail	8	8	Listening for gist/specific information
	30	30	

Table 3.8 Internal weighting – Listening BEC2/BEC Vantage

Main Skill Focus	BEC2	BEC Vantage
Listening for detail	12	12
Listening to identify topic, context, function etc.	10	10
Listening for specific information	8	8
	30	30

Table 3.9 Internal Weighting – BEC3/BEC Higher

Main Skill Focus	BEC3	BEC Higher
Listening for detail	10	10
Listening to identify topic, context, function, opinion etc.	20	20
Listening for specific information		
	30	30

Finally, while there have been major changes within the Speaking paper there has been no change in the internal weighting. This is because the Speaking paper, like other Cambridge ESOL Speaking papers, is scored by the awarding of a single score or set of scores (by the interlocutor and observer respectively) at the end of the test event – i.e. no distinction is made of performance on the different tasks.

Within each level

In the original BEC suite, the Reading paper was seen by the developers as being the most relevant skill for the candidates likely to sit the tests. For this reason the Reading paper was the most heavily weighted. However, changes in the test population, both within the original market and in the emerging BEC markets, meant that this situation could no longer be supported. Each paper in the revised BEC tests is equally weighted, meaning that each skill now contributes 25% of the total marks available to the candidate. The effect of this is very clear. In the original tests, there was a very heavy weighting on the receptive skills (over 70% of the available marks not including the Speaking test). The new weighting means that there is a far greater emphasis on the productive skills, even at the lowest level. This change in emphasis is designed to bring the BEC tests into line with the Cambridge ESOL approach (outlined in Chapter 2) and to promote what is perceived as positive washback. There was a slight difference in the weighting profile of the BEC2 papers when these are compared with BEC1. Again, the more heavily weighted components were related to the receptive skills, with 45% of the available marks awarded for reading. A similar picture was found in BEC3.

Table 3.10 Weighting at BEC1/BEC Preliminary

Level 1	Reading	Writing	Listening	Speaking
Old system	40 (45%)	20 (22%)	30 (33%)	Optional – reported on different scale
New system	45 (25%)	30 (25%)	30 (25%)	40 (25%)

Table 3.11 Weighting at BEC2/BEC Vantage

Level 2	Reading	Writing	Listening	Speaking
Old system	45 (45%)	25 (25%)	30 (30%)	Optional – reported on different scale
New system	45 (25%)	30 (25%)	30 (25%)	40 (25%)

Table 3.12 Weighting at BEC3/BEC Higher

Level	Reading	Writing	Listening	Speaking
Old system	50 (45%)	30 (27%)	30 (27%)	Optional – reported on different scale
New system	52 (25%)	30 (25%)	30 (25%)	40 (25%)

These tables show how the weighting process has been used to radically alter the overall distribution of focus within the BEC suite. In the original versions, the Reading paper was apparently seen as the most important, with 45% of the available marks available at each of the three levels. The Writing paper was least heavily weighted at BEC1 with a systematic increase in weighting as the level of the test increased. This system was designed to show the greater importance of writing as overall proficiency level increased.

Speaking to have a stronger business focus

The original BEC Speaking papers were criticised during the consultation exercises for being too general in nature and for not really having a strong 'business' orientation. The example of Task 2 from BEC1 (Task 1 was based on personal information exchange during a one-to-one interview) highlights the perceived problem, see Figure 4.16 in the next chapter. While we can see from the task that the topic of the information exchange task is business-related, the expected output is at a very basic level (with little meaningful interaction or even language required to complete the task).

The revised test at this level (BEC Preliminary) has been radically changed. While the opening task remains focused on personal information exchange, the time allowed has been much reduced. The old Task 2 has now been replaced with a pair of tasks designed to elicit a broader range of language (see the section on the Speaking papers in the next chapter). In the new Task 2, candidates make a mini-presentation on a business-related topic (see the example in Figure 4.17 in the next chapter). In this task, there is clearly a greater emphasis on production of language (the candidates may choose one of the two options, take one minute for preparation, and then speak for a further minute on the topic).

In Task 3, the examiner outlines a scenario (see Figure 3.2), which the candidates discuss for two minutes before being asked further questions.

These examples from BEC Preliminary demonstrate how the paper at this level has changed, with a broader range of language potentially elicited, and more relevantly for this section, a clearer focus on the business context. The tasks shown here can claim a far greater degree of specificity (in terms of task content and focus) and authenticity (both situational and interactional) than the original BEC speaking task at the same level.

Figure 3.2 Discussion task – BEC Preliminary

EXAMINER FRAME (excerpt)
Now, in this part of the test you are going to talk about something together.
Scenario:
I'm going to describe a situation.
A company has decided to introduce a general training programme for new staff. Talk together about the topics the company could include in the programme and decide which 3 you think are the most important.
Here are some ideas to help you.
CANDIDATES' PROMPT SHEET
General training programme for new staff
<ul><li>Equipment</li><li>Computer skills</li><li>Company organisation</li><li>Company rules</li><li>Customer service</li><li>Product training</li><li>Health and safety</li><li>Foreign languages</li></ul>

Source: Cambridge ESOL BEC Handbook (2001:40)

Other major changes

In addition to the changes described above, there are a number of related changes to the BEC suite which at first sight appear cosmetic, but upon further inspection reveal something of how the benchmarking process (mentioned before in Chapter 2) impacted on the way in which the three individual tests were situated in terms of the Common European Framework.

Names

One criticism of the original BEC suite was the suggestion that the names of the tests were less than helpful to the stakeholders who either had to decide at which level the tests were aimed or what performance they were based on, for example what BEC2 might mean in terms of language ability.

The revised BEC exams have been renamed, partly in order to answer this criticism, but also to comply with the accreditation requirements of the Qualifications and Curriculum Authority (QCA) in the United Kingdom – all tests in all subjects must submit documentation to the QCA in order to be accredited for use in the UK. The exams were also renamed in order to reflect the growing influence of the Common European Framework (CEF) and Association of Language Testers in Europe (ALTE) framework.

Table 3.13 Changes to the BEC names

Original name	Name after revision process
BEC3	BEC Higher
BEC2	BEC Vantage
BEC1	BEC Preliminary

As can be seen in Table 3.13, the names of the revised exams have been changed from the original numbered system to one that more clearly reflects the level of each of the three. The most obvious of the names is BEC Vantage, named after the CEF level at which it is benchmarked (B2 or Vantage). The others are possibly more obvious to the stakeholder who may be unfamiliar with the CEF/ALTE frameworks.

Another area of potential confusion with the original system was the fact that the numbers of the BEC tests did not correspond with the ALTE or CEF levels they were designed to reflect, i.e. BEC1 was benchmarked to ALTE Levels 1 and 2, BEC2 was benchmarked to ALTE Level 3 and BEC3 to ALTE Level 4.

The renamed exams were, with the exception of BEC1/BEC Preliminary, designed to replace the existing levels with an exam at the same level – though as we shall see in the coming chapter, there were changes in the papers making up the tests. Therefore we can say that the new BEC Preliminary represents the more challenging end of BEC1 (see the following section where this is explored in more detail).

Level of BEC1/Preliminary

The results of the consultative exercise (see Chapter 2) indicated that, with the exception of the Speaking tests, the most noticeable area of concern was with BEC1. This concern was based on the fact that it essentially straddled two levels of the CEF/ALTE framework and was dealt with in the original test by giving four passing grades (with two each designed to reflect performance at each of the two levels tested within the test). Though this system was accepted and used by the BEC stakeholders, the difficulty of adequately sampling from the broad language domain covered by the test, given the constraints of test time and administration, made the system difficult to operationalise in the longer term.

Table 3.14 Level of BEC1 and BEC Preliminary

Original Business English Certificates	National Qualifications Framework Level	Council of Europe (ALTE) Level	Revised Business English Certificates
BEC1	Entry 3	B1 (ALTE Level 2)	BEC Preliminary
	Entry 2	A2 (ALTE Level 1)	

The re-focusing of this level was achieved through the dual process of a detailed reference to the CEF/ALTE frameworks, and by making cross-comparisons with the Main Suite tests which were representative of the same level CEF/ALTE levels.

An outline of the perceived level criteria for the revised examinations was presented at a revision group meeting in October 1999. This document contained the data from which Table 3.15 has been created. In the table we can see again that all three of the revised exams have been more deliberately benchmarked, with level descriptions, outlines of both formal language knowledge and language use that more clearly identify the level at which each exam has been aimed.

Summary

In this short chapter I have outlined the major changes to the BEC suite. These changes have been in the areas of:

- how results are reported – with a graphical representation of a performance profile, designed to have a diagnostic use for the candidate
- the weighting of the components both within papers and levels – this has the

Table 3.15 Revised BEC level criteria

	BEC Preliminary	BEC Vantage	BEC Higher
Level Description	This is a test for candidates at Cambridge/ALTE Level 2 [CEF B1]	This is a test for candidates at Cambridge/ALTE Level 3 [CEF B2]	This is a test for candidates at Cambridge/ALTE Level 4 [CEF C1]
Formal Language Knowledge	Learners at this level are expected to deal with a specified grammatical inventory and understand and produce a restricted variety of structures. They should demonstrate knowledge of certain vocabulary items.	Learners at this level are expected to be able to handle the main structures of the language and demonstrate knowledge of a wide range of vocabulary.	Learners at this level are expected to be able to handle complex structures and demonstrate knowledge of a wide range of vocabulary.
Language Use	Learners at this level can: • extract specific information from short spoken exchanges without necessarily understanding every word • give and receive personal information in a conversational context • take down information in order to complete a form or memo • read and understand a variety of business-related texts • interpret charts and diagrams • produce a variety of written texts in order to convey specific information or feeling.	Learners at this level can: • understand the overall meaning and key points of a non-specialist presentation or discussion • participate in a conversation giving personal information, exchanging information and expressing opinions • take down information from phone conversations and public announcements • read and understand general business letters, reports, articles and leaflets • produce letters, memos and simple reports.	Learners at this level can: • engage in extended conversation • contribute effectively to meetings and seminars • take accurate notes during meetings • write reports and draft instructions • understand most correspondence, articles and reports where information is overtly stated • use the telephone for most purposes • negotiate successfully in most situations.

advantage of ensuring that the different elements of the papers and sub-skills within levels are seen as contributing equally to the candidate's competence

• a stronger business focus for the Speaking papers – this will be seen more clearly in the coming chapter in which the changes to the individual papers are exemplified, and where it is clear that the major changes have come in the BEC Speaking papers

• the naming of the papers – while these name changes are in one way superficial, they do have a role to play in the way the different levels are seen both within the British education system, and in the way they are seen within the context of the ALTE/CEF levels

- the level of BEC1/Preliminary – where the original paper was not clearly benchmarked to any definite level; the revised BEC Preliminary is now more obviously representative of the ALTE/CEF B1 level, where the original attempted to straddle the A2 and B1 levels.

4 Changes in the BEC papers

In Chapter 4, I will describe the way in which the revision process has led to changes in the BEC suite of examination, and since the four skills of Reading, Writing, Listening and Speaking are tested in the suite (in that order) this will be reflected in the organisation of the chapter. Sample copies of the three tests in the revised BEC Suite can be found in Appendices 4.1 to 4.3.

Changes in the Reading papers

In the following section of the BEC revision overview the changes made to the Reading papers at the three levels are presented. The changes are described in terms of the outline of the Cambridge ESOL approach outlined in the previous

Table 4.1 BEC1 Reading paper outline

Part	Items	Main Skill Focus	Focus	Format	Marks
1	1–5	Reading and vocabulary	Understanding intended meaning (short texts, e.g. signs)	3 option MCQ	5
2	6–10	Reading and vocabulary	Understanding basic vocabulary (from business signs, adverts)	Matching (5 from 8)	5
3	11–15	Reading interpreting visual information	Interpreting information from input (e.g. charts)	Matching (5 from 8)	5
4	16–22	Reading comprehension	Comprehension of written input (e.g. report)	T/F/not included	7
5	23–26	Reading comprehension	Comprehension of written input (e.g. information sheet)	3 option MCQ and matching	4
	27–30	Reading comprehension	Same input	Select correct options (4 from 7)	4
6	31–40	Grammar	Grammar use in context (rational deletion cloze)	3 option MCQ	10
				Total marks	40

Total time allowed 70 minutes (40 Reading items + 3 Writing tasks)

chapter. As will be seen throughout the chapter, there are occasions when no major changes were made to individual papers; this is particularly true of the Reading papers, where the review process suggested that there were no major changes needed.

BEC1 and BEC Preliminary

At BEC level 1, the Reading paper was originally designed to test a range of reading-related skills including both vocabulary and grammar in context, general comprehension and scanning for detail (see Table 4.1).

As can be seen from the outline of the revised paper at this level the construct remains very much the same. The changes that have been made include the addition of five items in the latter half of the test and the provision of additional time. However, as the Reading and Writing papers are presented as a single unit at this level it is not clear exactly how the candidates will use this additional time, see the chapter relating to the changes in the Writing paper for some additional comments on this. The additional items have had the effect of adding to the internal consistency of the paper.

The single most important change in the BEC1/BEC Preliminary Reading

Table 4.2 BEC Preliminary Reading paper outline

Part	Items	Main Skill Focus	Focus	Format	Marks
1	1–5	Reading and vocabulary	Understanding intended meaning (short texts, e.g. signs)	3 option MCQ	5
2	6–10	Reading and vocabulary	Understanding basic vocabulary (from short input)	Matching (5 from 8)	5
3	11–15	Reading interpreting visual information	Interpreting information from input (e.g. charts)	Matching statements to chart data	5
4	16–22	Reading comprehension	Comprehension of report	T/F/not included	7
5	23–28	Reading comprehension	Comprehension of written text	3 option MCQ	6
6	29–40	Grammar (in context of reading text)	Grammar use in context (rational deletion cloze)	Cloze (3 option MCQ)	12
7	41–45	Reading and information transfer	Reading for specific detail from two written inputs	Form completion	5
				Total marks	45

Total time allowed 90 minutes (45 Reading items + 2 Writing tasks)

paper was a tightening up of Part 5, and the introduction of a new form completion task as Part 7 – actually, it was originally part of the Writing paper but was moved here to reflect more accurately the construct being tested in both papers. Other important changes to this paper included the addition of alternative input sources to Part 2 – where the candidate now identifies specific elements within more 'realistic' sources.

In the original version of Part 5 (Figure 4.1), we can see that there is a single text (either divided into four paragraphs or presented as four sub-texts). Based

Figure 4.1 BEC1 Part 5 Reading

PART FIVE

Questions 23–30

- Read the information sheet below about conference centres.
- Answer questions **23–30** on the opposite page.

> **EASTBY COMMERCIAL DEVELOPMENT OFFICE**
> **Conference Centre Information**
>
> Conference organisers often have difficulty finding a suitable place to hold a conference. We would like to suggest four conference centres in our area where you are certain to find good service and value.
>
> THE CORNWELL CONFERENCE CENTRE
> The Cornwell is twenty kilometres from Eastby and is most easily reached by car or coach. It has two conference rooms, each holding up to three hundred people, and three seminar rooms, each designed for a maximum of forty. There is also a first-class restaurant. There are excellent telephone, fax and e-mail facilities. The price per head also covers bed and breakfast in a nearby hotel.
>
> THE EASTBY BUSINESS CENTRE
> Companies needing a good social programme as well as meeting rooms are well looked after at the EBC. The management can arrange concerts and discos on request. The EBC is located opposite the main entrance to the City Museum on Bateman Street. As parking space is not available at the Centre, the management recommends that guests leave their cars in the Eastby Railway Station car park, which is free.
>
> THE GREENHILL CENTRE
> The Greenhill, only five kilometres from Eastby, is a good choice for small conferences and meetings. It is popular with many companies based in the area and its highly-trained reception staff speak a number of foreign languages. There are three comfortable meeting rooms, seating ninety people in total, all well equipped with audio-visual aids. The Centre offers a special price if all three rooms are hired together. Guests can stay overnight in the nearby Greenhill Hotel, which has outdoor tennis courts.
>
> THE METRO REGENT
> The Metro Regent is a large, modern hotel in beautiful gardens, with a conference hall suitable for up to two hundred people. It is only ten minutes by train from Eastby city centre, which has many tourist attractions. Cars and minibuses can be rented from the hotel. There is a busy programme of conferences at the Metro Regent, especially in the summer, so early booking is advisable. The hotel is closed for the whole of November and for the New Year.

- For questions **23–26**, choose the correct answer.
- For each question, mark **one** letter (**A**, **B** or **C**) on your Answer Sheet.

23 The cost per person at the Cornwell includes

    A   telephone calls.

    B   all meals.

    C   hotel accommodation.

24 The Eastby Business Centre advises conference guests to park

    A   outside the main entrance.

    B   at Eastby Railway Station.

    C   opposite the City Museum.

25 The Greenhill Centre is frequently used by

    A   local companies.

    B   foreign companies.

    C   television companies.

26 The most popular time for holding conferences at the Metro Regent is

    A   New Year.

    B   Summer.

    C   November.

- For questions **27–30**, use the information in the text to match each conference centre with the service it offers **(A–G)**.
- For each question, mark the correct letter **(A–G) on your Answer Sheet**.
- Do not use any letter more than once.

27 The Cornwell Conference Centre	**A** discounts
	B secretarial support
28 The Eastby Business Centre	**C** excellent food
	D games room
29 The Greenhill Centre	**E** organised entertainment
30 The Metro Regent	**F** sightseeing trips
	G vehicle hire

Source: Cambridge ESOL BEC Handbook (2000:21)

on this reading input there are four comprehension items (three option, MCQ format) that ask the reader to read for specific details from individual sub-texts, and a further four items focusing on reading for detail, but this time using a matching format. The task seems to have been intended to provide the reader

Figure 4.2 BEC Preliminary Task 5 Reading

PART FIVE
Questions 23 – 28

- Read the article below about a businessman's plans for developing a shopping centre.

- For each question **23 – 28**, on the opposite page, choose the correct answer.

- Mark one letter (**A**, **B** or **C**) on your Answer Sheet.

Shaking Up the Business

Since becoming Chief Executive of the Star City shopping centre and exhibition halls, Peter Maurice feels he has done a lot. Now, though, he wants to change the whole feeling of the business. 'Visitors should feel we are looking after them,' he says. 'Very often the public go into a shop and find so much there that they can't decide what to buy, so they don't buy anything. Keep it simple, that's the key to retailing.'

At Star City, staff are encouraged to tell managers, including Maurice himself, what they think of them. 'The things they say about me are what I expect, because I'm fairly self-aware – I know what I'm like and that I can make people a little angry. But I'm very much in favour of change, and everyone knows that a lot needs to be done.'

He learnt his management techniques the hard way. 'At 23 I went into business and lost money. I had to learn fast. Then, at 32, I won an export contract to Hong Kong. I admire the strength of character and the ambition of the people there, and brought back two very significant words: "No problem". Then I took a course at Harvard Business School. It was very hard work, but worth it.'

As well as running Star City, Peter Maurice controls Big Events, which organises exhibitions. At the moment, Big Events is working on plans for a boat show to rival the Capital Boat Show, which in 2004 is moving from its traditional site at Star City to a new venue.

Maurice has created an unusual company structure. 'The

financial director and commercial director are responsible to me directly, but in my first week here, the head of Marketing resigned. Then the same happened with Human Resources. I said to both teams: "Do you want to self-manage?" That's what they decided to do – it can work if you have people who work well together and can report to you as a team,' he explains.

For the immediate future, Maurice will continue with the essential work of updating the centre. After that, he plans to look at ways of expanding Star City beyond the present conferences and exhibitions, to include major shows and concerts. 'I want a lively centre full of exciting events, where my well-trained staff are ambassadors for the company.'

SAMPLE QUESTIONS

26 What is Maurice's exhibitions company, Big Events, planning to do in 2004?

    A   take control of the Capital Boat Show

    B   move the Capital Boat Show to a larger venue

    C   hold an event to compete with the Capital Boat Show

27 Which of these departments has a director who reports to Peter Maurice?

    A   Finance

    B   Marketing

    C   Human Resources

Source: Cambridge ESOL BEC Preliminary, Examination Report and Past Examination Papers (2002:28–29)

with a dual focus (reading for comprehension and detail), but ultimately appears to test the same thing within both parts – task developers also reported that it was very difficult to find suitable texts, a problem which ultimately led to the failure of the task as the text requirements of the different formats in the two parts were different – comprehension items can quite successfully be based on short cohesive texts while items that focus on reading for detail require longer relatively 'shapeless' texts.

In the revised version of Part 5, this problem has been addressed through the decision to create a task with a single focus (see Figure 4.2). Here we can see that there is a single reading text of approximately 350 words. This input is accompanied by a series of six comprehension items, each related to a separate paragraph in the input text.

The effect of this change is to simplify the section, giving a single clear focus on how the text is to be exploited. This is in marked contrast to the original design, in which the task purpose was not really made clear to the candidate or the test observer/evaluator.

BEC2 and BEC Vantage

At BEC2, the Reading paper was again designed to test a range of reading-related skills. At this level, the reading and writing skills were, as with BEC1, tested using a single paper. The situation was changed with the revision and two separate papers were offered. This complicates any comparisons of the Reading papers, though really only in that it was never clear how candidates used the time allowed for the Reading and Writing papers at BEC2 while with the BEC Vantage (the revised title for the examination) the time for each paper is set. It was also a concern that candidates could take information from the Reading and use it in their Writing in an inappropriate manner.

In the same way that Task 5 on BEC1 was found to be problematic, the fact that Task 5 in BEC2 (See Figure 4.3) was based on two sets of items related to two different texts meant that it too was in need of change – more related to simplifying the task writing process than to changing the actual content of the task. The actual change to the overall task is small, as the activity engaged in for both the original version and the revised version (Figure 4.4) is the same – both involve identifying problematic or non-problematic lines in a short text. In BEC2 the task had two parts, with the first focusing on a possible extra word in any line and Part 2 on a possible incorrect word which had to be corrected (it was possible in both cases that there was no error in a line).

Another problem with the task was related to the format of the second section. Here the candidate was first meant to identify a possible error and then write the correct word in the response boxes in their answer book. The difficulty is that the candidate might see a problem where none exists and offer a correction, missing the real problem. Where the correction offered actually matched the expected

Table 4.3 BEC 2 Reading paper outline

Part	Items	Main Skill Focus	Focus	Format	Marks
1	1–7	Reading (scanning and gist)	Understanding overall meaning (short texts)	Matching (7 sentences to 4 texts)	7
2	8–12	Reading	Understanding text structure	Text completion (5 gaps with 9 options)	5
3	13–20	Reading (gist and scanning for detail)	Interpreting overall meaning and identifying specific details	Matching (each part 4 from 7)	4 4
4	21–35	Vocabulary	Recognising vocabulary use in context	MCQ cloze	15
5	36–40	Reading and grammar	Proof-reading task	Identify and correct error	5
	41–45	Reading and grammar	Proof-reading task	Identify and correct error	5
				Total marks	45

Total time allowed 90 minutes (45 Reading items + 2 Writing tasks)

Table 4.4 BEC Vantage Reading paper outline

Part	Items	Main Skill Focus	Focus	Format	Marks
1	1–7	Reading (scanning and gist)	Understanding intended meaning (short texts, e.g. signs)	Matching (7 sentences to 4 texts)	7
2	8–12	Reading	Understanding text structure	Matching (sentence level gaps)	5
3	13–20	Reading (gist and scanning for detail)	Interpreting overall meaning and identifying specific details	MCQ (4 option)	6
4	21–35	Vocabulary	Recognising vocabulary use in context	MCQ cloze (4 option)	15
5	36–45	Reading and grammar	Proof-reading task	Identify additional unnecessary words	12
				Total marks	45

Total time allowed 60 minutes (45 Reading items)

response the candidate would be seen by the examiner to have answered correctly – this is because the candidate did not have to identify the position of the error. This meant that the task was very difficult to write and it was not always certain that the candidates' responses matched the expectations of the task writer.

The BEC Vantage version of the task has a single text of 14 lines (the first two of which are examples) in which the offending word is said to be 'either grammatically incorrect or does not fit in with the meaning of the text'. While this version may not mimic a genuine proof-reading task, it does offer the tester more control over the output, making for a potentially more reliable set of items, while at the same time offering a somewhat more viable proof-reading task where the candidates are required to access a wider range of linguistic knowledge in order to respond. There is, of course some question as to whether a proof-reading task represents a test of reading ability, or a test of linguistic knowledge set in a reading context.

Figure 4.3 BEC2 Task 5 Reading

PART FIVE

Section A

Questions 36 – 40

- Read the memo below about a health and safety matter.
- In most of the lines **36 – 40** there is **one extra word** which does not fit. One or two lines, however, are correct.
- If a line is correct, write **CORRECT on your Answer Sheet**.
- If there is an extra word in the line, write the **extra word in CAPITAL LETTERS on your Answer Sheet**.

Examples:

0   Before signing up the delivery note, could you please check

      `0` `U` `P` ☐ ☐ ☐ ☐ ☐ ☐

00 that the consignment is complete and undamaged.

      `00` `C` `O` `R` `R` `E` `C` `T` ☐ ☐

        We recently had a health and safety incident at one of our sites

36 which was not properly recorded. The accident did not involve with

37 any member of the permanent staff, but which happened to an

38 electrical contractor working at the new site. Will you please ensure in

39 future that Central Administration are informed immediately of any

40 accident occurring on company property and that all of details are

        recorded in the Accident Book kept in Central Administration.

Source: Cambridge ESOL BEC Handbook (2000:49)

Figure 4.4 BEC Vantage Task 5 Reading

PART FIVE
Questions 34 – 45

- Read the article below about market research.

- In most of the lines **34 – 45** there is one extra word. It is either grammatically incorrect or does not fit in with the meaning of the text. Some lines, however, are correct.

- If a line is correct, write **CORRECT** on your Answer Sheet.

- If there is an extra word in the line, write **the extra word** in CAPITAL LETTERS on your Answer Sheet.

- The exercise begins with two examples, (**0**) and (**00**).

Examples:

| 0 | I | N | | | | | | | |
| 00 | C | O | R | R | E | C | T | | |

Market Research

0	Market research involves in collecting and sorting facts and opinions from specific groups
00	of people. The purpose of research can vary from discovering the popularity of a political
34	party to assessing whether is a product needs changing or replacing. Most work in
35	consumer research involves interviewers employed by market research agencies, but
36	certain industrial and social research is carried out by any specialist agencies. Interviews
*	
44	Market research agencies which frequently organise training, where trainees learn how to
45	recognise socio-economic groups and practise approaching to the public. For information
	on market research training and qualifications, contact the Market Research Association.

---

*Note: some questions have not been included here

Source: Cambridge ESOL BEC Vantage, Examination Report and Past Examination Papers (2002:28)

It is clear from the two tables (Tables 4.3 and 4.4) and the two figures (Figures 4.3 and 4.4) that there are no other major changes to the Reading paper. Both the number of items and the general focus of the items remain the same. A review of the actual tasks shows that the setting of tasks in a business context remains the same in the two versions, with the only change being that to Task 5, described above. (See Appendix 4.1 for examples of the Reading papers from the three examinations on the revised BEC suite.)

BEC3 and BEC Higher

Tables 4.5 and 4.6 contain the outlines of the Reading papers at the highest of the three BEC levels (BEC3 and BEC Higher respectively). There are no real changes here, with the exception of a slight increase in the number of items for the proof-reading section. Like the change to BEC2, BEC Higher splits the Reading and Writing papers.

Table 4.5 BEC3 Reading paper outline

Part	Items	Main Skill Focus	Focus	Format	Marks
1	1–8	Reading (gist and main idea)	Understanding intended meaning (short texts, e.g. signs)	Matching (8 sentences to 5 texts)	8
2	9–14	Reading (details and structure)	Understanding of specific details and structure of 'authentic' business text	Text completion (6 gaps with 8 options)	6
3	15–20	Reading (gist and scanning for detail)	Interpreting overall meaning and identifying specific details	MCQ (4 options)	6
4	21–30	Vocabulary	Recognising vocabulary use in context	MCQ cloze (4 option)	10
5	31–40	Reading and grammar	Rational deletion cloze completion	Cloze	10
6	41–50	Reading and grammar	Proof-reading task	Identify additional unnecessary words	10
				Total marks	50

Total time allowed 100 minutes (50 Reading items + Writing tasks)

From this brief review of the Reading papers at the three BEC levels, we can see that there were very few substantial changes made in the revision process. The feedback from the consultation exercise (reported in Chapter 2) suggested that the only real area of concern with the BEC papers lay in Part 5 of BEC1. This problem was dealt with by eliminating the double-focus of the part so that there was a single clear area of interest. In general, the changes, though slight, appear to have made the construct clearer. The papers are more consistent in the way they approach the testing of reading, with the emphasis on careful reading for gist and for detail, with an additional focus on testing vocabulary and grammar in the context of reading.

Changes in the Writing papers

As we saw in the review of the changes to the Reading papers, there were changes to the way in which the Reading and Writing papers are presented. In

Table 4.6 BEC Higher Reading paper outline

Items	Main Skill Focus	Focus	Format	Marks
1–8	Reading (gist and main idea)	Understanding based on 'authentic' business text	Matching (8 sentences to 5 texts)	8
9–14	Reading (details and structure)	Understanding of specific details and structure of 'authentic' business text	Text completion (6 gaps with 8 options)	6
15–20	Reading (gist and scanning for detail)	Interpreting overall meaning and identifying specific details	MCQ (4 options)	6
21–30	Vocabulary	Recognising vocabulary use in context	MCQ cloze (4 option)	10
31–40	Reading and grammar	Rational deletion cloze completion	Cloze	10
41–52	Reading and grammar	Proof-reading task	Identify additional unnecessary words	10
			Total marks	52

Total time allowed 60 minutes (52 Reading items)

the original format, the two papers were presented as a single unit, with a total time given to the candidates. This may have had an unintended negative effect in terms of time management (and a potentially negative washback effect, where writing is seen as being of lesser importance than reading) on the way in which the Writing paper was seen by candidates, as there was a clear difference in the scores awarded for the two sections (the Writing paper offered half the marks of the Reading paper at BEC1, one third at BEC2 and two fifths at BEC3).

BEC1 and BEC Preliminary

Table 4.7 shows that for BEC1 there were three different tasks included in the paper. One criticism of the paper focused on the first five items, built around what was essentially a reading and information transfer task. The latter pair of free writing tasks were rated using a relatively simple set of scales. For the first of these tasks, candidates' work was rated on a 5-point scale which was focused on task completion. For the second task, a pair of scores was awarded, one for task completion and the other for language. The latter pair of tasks were both scaffolded using a series of bullet pointed suggestions.

In BEC Preliminary, the first task has been altered and the expected output for the two remaining tasks has been lengthened, each by 10 words. Both of these tasks are scored using a General Impression Mark Scheme (GIMS). In fact, the two tasks use somewhat different versions of the scale, the first containing a set of very basic descriptors, while the second contains a more complex set which focuses both on task completion and language. Both versions are 6-level (0–5)

Table 4.7 BEC1 Writing paper outline

Part	Items	Main Skill Focus	Focus	Format	Marks
7	41–45	Reading of written input	Information transfer	Form completion	5
8	46	Memo writing	Short written output (some scaffolding)	Free writing	5
9	47	Letter writing	Short written output (some scaffolding)	Free writing	10

Total time allowed 70 minutes (40 Reading items + 3 Writing tasks)

scales. The scores for the tasks are weighted, with the second task worth twice the number of marks as the first task. The overall weighting of the Writing paper has been increased, making it worth 25% of the total score for the test (all four papers are now equally weighted at the three BEC levels). This makes the revised paper a clearer reflection of Cambridge ESOL's stated commitment to the inclusion of all four skills in their language tests (Saville 2003:62).

In order to ensure that the Writing paper accurately reflects the amended level of the test, both General Impression Mark Schemes are interpreted at Cambridge/ALTE level 2.

Table 4.8 BEC Preliminary Writing paper outline

Part	Items	Main Skill Focus	Focus	Format	Marks
1	46	Note, message, memo or e-mail writing	Short written output (some scaffolding)	Free writing	10
2	47	Letter writing	Short written output in response to written input (some scaffolding)	Free writing	20

Total time allowed 90 minutes (45 Reading items + 2 Writing tasks)

Figure 4.5 shows the original information transfer task from BEC1. As we can see from this task, the output required of the candidate was simply to retrieve the relevant information from the input (in the form of a very brief memo and receipt) and complete the simple form. The amount of writing was minimal, in fact the task was based on information transfer and all responses could be found in the reading input. For this reason the task was perceived to be more related to reading and as such it was moved from its original position in the writing section (BEC1 Part 7) to the revised reading section (BEC Preliminary Part 7). In addition to the move, the amount of reading input has been increased – one of the variables that has been hypothesised by Norris et al (1998), O'Sullivan & Weir (2000) and Skehan (1998) to impact on task difficulty as it relates to 'code complexity' (number and amount of linguistic input). The revised version of this task can be seen in Figure 4.6.

Figure 4.5 BEC1 Part 6 Writing

WRITING

QUESTIONS 41–47

PART SEVEN

Questions 41–45

- Read the memo and the receipt below.
- Complete the form on the opposite page.
- Write each word, phrase or number **in CAPITAL LETTERS on lines 41–45** on your Answer Sheet.

MEMO

To: Paul Woods, Sales
From: Lynn Thomas, Finance

Re: Your accommodation expenses for the trip to Auckland from 21st to 26th July.

I can't pay you until you send me your expenses claim form.

Thanks.

PAN PACIFIC HOTEL
18 - 24 Eden Avenue, Auckland
Tel: 2388709

RECEIPT

26.7.98

Mr P Woods

5 nights single room with bed & breakfast   NZ$540

cheque / cash / credit card

Accommodation Expenses Claim Form
(please return to Lynn Thomas, Finance)

Name of employee: **(41)** ....

Department: **(42)** ....

Dates of trip: **(43)** ....

Name of hotel: **(44)** ....

Amount claimed: NZ$540

Method of
payment used: **(45)** ....

Source: Cambridge ESOL, BEC Handbook (2000:23)

Figure 4.6 BEC Preliminary Task 7 Reading

PART SEVEN
Questions 41 – 45

- Read the part of the letter and the memo below.
- Complete the form on the opposite page.
- Write a word or phrase (in CAPITAL LETTERS) or a number on lines **41 – 45** on your Answer Sheet.

> With regard to our conversation on the phone yesterday, I can confirm that, due to serious illness, John Brookes has to cancel his flight to Madrid on Saturday 22 June and I therefore request a refund. I enclose the ticket: First Class, flight number UA 453, booking reference 3434/4.

Travelgo Ltd

Memorandum

To:	Julia
From:	Luke
Date:	6 June 2002
Subject:	Refund

Could you please fill in a refund form for this client? Note that the booking reference number is actually 01/3434/A. It was a company booking for a Business Class (not First Class) UATAIR flight from Heathrow. They paid by credit card but it's easier if we send them a cheque for £525.00.

Travelgo Ltd	Refund No: 0055 78A
Booking reference:	**(41)** ....
Ticket details:	
Date of departure:	22/06/02
Flight number:	UA 453 (UATAIR)
Departure from:	Heathrow
Destination:	**(42)** ....
Ticket class:	**(43)** ....
Refund due:	£525.00
Method of Refund:	**(44)** ....
Reason for cancellation: client's	**(45)** ....

Source: Cambridge ESOL BEC Preliminary, Examination Report and Past Examination Papers (2002:32–33)

BEC2 and BEC Vantage

Tables 4.9 and 4.10 show the way in which the Writing paper has been changed at the next level (BEC2 and BEC Vantage).

Table 4.9 BEC 2 Writing paper outline

Items	Main Skill Focus	Focus	Format	Marks
46	Note, message or memo writing	Short written output (30–40 words – very basic scaffolding)	Free writing	5
47	Letter writing	Letter (100–120 words – respond to written inputs)	Free writing	10

Total time allowed 90 minutes (45 Reading items + 2 Writing tasks)

One of the major changes to the structure of the test (described in Chapter 3) is the decision to place more emphasis on writing. It is at BEC Vantage that this decision is first manifested. At this level, we see that there are now separate papers for Reading and Writing – and the weighting system (as with BEC Preliminary) now means that the Writing paper is similar to the other three papers, in that all are worth 25% of the total score for the test.

The first of the two tasks is quite similar in terms of input and expected response, though there is a nod in the direction of contemporary business communication with the inclusion in the specifications of written e-mail communication to the existing list of response formats used in BEC2; the other options are note, message or memo. The other change to this first task is that the response is expected to be slightly longer.

The second writing task is quite different in terms of length of expected response, type of input and output format. The candidate is expected to write a significantly longer text (120–140 words as opposed to 100–120 words at BEC 2), and the input can either be written or presented as tables/graphics/charts. This change in the nature of the input may have an impact on the difficulty of the task, though any impact is lessened by the inclusion of written notes on the graphics in order to make interpreting them less of an issue. The potential problem here is the nature of the information transfer. In the original task, the letter was based on a very basic transfer of information – the fact that the input was read meant that language was provided, for example. The new version asks the candidate to transform information from a chart (which must be interpreted) to a written format. While the written notes may act to negate any significant effect on task difficulty, there is no empirical evidence that the different input types result in significantly different responses. The change from a letter to a report may also be a complicating factor with this task.

Table 4.10 BEC Vantage Writing paper outline

Items	Main Skill Focus	Focus	Format	Marks
1	Note, message, e-mail or memo writing	Short written output (40–50 words – very basic scaffolding)	Free writing	5
2	Correspondence, report or proposal writing	Written output (120–140 words – respond to written inputs)	Free writing	10

Total time allowed 45 minutes (2 Writing tasks)

BEC3 and BEC Higher

The Writing paper at BEC Higher has also been separated from the Reading/ Writing structure of BEC3 (see Tables 4.11 and 4.12). It is at this level that the most clearly defined changes have been made to the paper.

The major changes are:

- output for task 1 has been lengthened to 120–140 words (up from 100 words)
- a choice has been offered in Task 2.

The impact of increasing the required output for the first task is to make the task somewhat more realistic – it being unusual to find a report in the business context that is just 100 words long. While the report might, in an ideal situation, be even longer than the new range, the practical limitations of the test event make writing a longer text impossible unless the test is reduced to a single task. In addition to anecdotal evidence in support of using multiple tasks, Bachman, Lynch and Mason (1995) have presented empirical evidence that having additional tasks has a greater impact on test reliability than having additional raters, so it would be unwise to reduce the number from the present two to a single task.

Table 4.11 BEC3 Writing paper outline

Items	Main Skill Focus	Focus	Format	Marks
51	Report writing	Short written output (100 words – input from simple graphs)	Free writing	10
52	Report writing	Letter (200–250 words – based on limited written input and some scaffolding)	Free writing	20

Total time allowed 100 minutes (50 Reading items + 2 Writing tasks)

The additional time allowed for the Writing paper means that the amount of written output expected of the candidate is now slightly greater than in the original. The other change relates to the fact that by offering a choice of tasks in the second part of the Writing paper, the developers are also offering a choice of output type. Candidates are asked to write on one of the three options, these being a report, a proposal and a piece of business correspondence. The input for all three options is very similar in terms of length and degree of scaffolding (all provide four bullet-pointed guiding points), and all three ask for the same amount of written output. As with any situation where a choice is offered, there is a danger that the different tasks will result in different levels of performance. However, the fact that the input for each choice is so similar suggests that any gains will be attributable to candidate ability – thus the choice can be seen as 'testing for best' – in that a candidate will, it is hoped, opt for the output type which they perceive as offering the best chance for an acceptable performance. As mentioned above, this aspect of the task should be monitored over time to ensure that no unintended bias occurs.

Table 4.12 BEC Higher Writing paper outline

Items	Main Skill Focus	Focus	Format	Marks
1	Report writing – describing, comparing, inferring	Short written output (120–140 words – input from simple graphic)	Free writing	10
2	Report or proposal or correspondence writing	Written output (200–250 words – based on limited written input and some scaffolding)	Free writing (choice from 3)	20

Total time allowed 70 minutes (2 Writing tasks)

Figures 4.7 and 4.8 show the original version of the task and the revised version from BEC Higher respectively. From these two examples we can see that the actual task has not altered, in that the format of the input remains the same in the two test versions. However, in the revised version of the task candidates are offered a choice of writing one of three options, a report (as in the original BEC), a proposal or a letter. The decision to offer candidates a choice is not without problems, and care must be taken to ensure that candidates are not negatively affected by their choice of task. Analysis of trial and test data shows that there has been no negative impact to date – with no significant differences in the scores achieved for the different options across the test population. Of course, this situation must be monitored at each administration.

Changes to the rating procedure

One change that has had an effect on all of the BEC levels except BEC Higher (where the rating procedure has not changed) is the fact that writing performance is now rated using a different scale.

Figure 4.7 BEC3 Part 2 Writing

PART TWO

Question 52

• Your company is planning three staff development courses:

    Time management for all;
    Health and Safety procedures in the workplace;
    Better interpersonal communication skills.

• You have been asked to write a **report**, for the Training Manager, explaining which **one** of these courses you think would be most useful for people who do the same kind of job as you.

• Write the **report**, including the following information:
    • which course you would recommend
    • why it would be the most useful
    • why the others are not so suitable.

• Write **200–250** words on your Answer Sheet.

Source: Cambridge ESOL BEC Handbook (2000:77)

For all tasks and levels, two mark schemes are used:

1. General Mark Scheme: this included six criteria, each with detailed descriptors at five levels or bands:
   These were
   i) content
   ii) vocabulary and structure range
   iii) accuracy
   iv) organisation of information and text
   v) appropriacy of register and format
   vi) effect on target reader.
2. Task Specific Mark Scheme: this gave guidance to the rater on the features of an appropriate response at the different levels.

With the revised BEC papers, the situation differs depending on the test level. While all tasks at all levels are rated using two separate scales (General and Task Specific), at BEC Preliminary level the first of the two tasks is scored using a version of the General Mark Scheme in which task achievement only is addressed.

One of the advantages to using a simplified scale such as this is that the descriptors are easily kept in mind as they are so short. The fact that this scale is used in conjunction with a task specific scale (i.e. the specific 'content points' referred to above are outlined in detail) makes the rating of this task very reliable – as it is relatively easy for raters to make consistent estimates of performance level.

Figure 4.8 BEC Higher Part 2 Writing

PART TWO

Answer **one** of the questions **2**, **3** or **4** below.

Question 2

- A minor accident has recently taken place in your organisation. Your manager has asked you to find out about the accident and write a report summarising the information you have gathered.

- Write your **report**, including the following information:

  - a brief description of the accident

  - what you think caused the accident

  - whether any measures need to be taken to prevent similar accidents happening.

- Write **200 – 250** words on the separate answer paper provided.

Question 3

- Your department has recently taken on a number of new staff. The Human Resources manager of your company has agreed to a request for a series of training sessions that would enable the new employees to work more efficiently. She has asked you to write a proposal for the training.

- Write the **proposal**, outlining the training required, and include the following points:

  - a brief description of the roles of the new staff

  - the type of training they need and why

  - any follow-up training or assessment that might be required.

- Write **200 – 250** words on the separate answer paper provided.

Question 4

- You are helping to arrange an event for all your company's customers, at which your new range of products will be demonstrated.

- Write a **letter** to your customers, including the following information:

  - the nature and purpose of the event

  - details of the event

  - why the event will be worth attending

  - how your customers should respond to your letter.

- Write **200 – 250** words on the separate answer paper provided.

Source: Cambridge ESOL BEC Higher, Examination Report and Past Examination Papers (2002:35)

For the second task at BEC Preliminary and all tasks at BEC Vantage and Higher, a different type of General Impression Mark Scheme is used (see Figure 4.9, which shows the BEC Preliminary version of the new GIMS).

This scheme is far more detailed and includes reference to the criteria used in the original BEC suite, e.g. content, range and accuracy of vocabulary and

Figure 4.9 BEC Preliminary revised General Impression Mark Scheme

Band 5	Full realisation of the task set: • all four content points achieved • confident use of language; errors are minor, due to ambition and non-impeding • good range of structure and vocabulary • effectively organised, with appropriate use of simple linking devices • register and format consistently appropriate. Very positive effect on the reader
Band 4	Good realisation of the task set: • three or four content points achieved • ambitious use of language; some non-impeding errors • more than adequate range of structure and vocabulary • generally well-organised, with attention paid to cohesion • register and format on the whole appropriate. Positive effect on the reader
Band 3	Reasonable achievement of the task set: • three or four content points achieved • a number of errors may be present, but are mostly non-impeding • adequate range of structure and vocabulary • organisation and cohesion is satisfactory, on the whole • register and format reasonable, although not entirely successful. Satisfactory effect on the reader
Band 2	Inadequate attempt at the task set: • two or three content points achieved • numerous errors, which sometimes impede communication • limited range of structure and vocabulary • content is not clearly organised or linked, causing some confusion • inappropriate register and format. Negative effect on the reader
Band 1	Poor attempt at the task set: • one or two content points achieved • serious lack of control; frequent basic errors • little evidence of structure and vocabulary required by task • lack of organisation, causing breakdown in communication • little attempt at appropriate register and forma Very negative effect on the reader
Band 0	Achieves nothing. Either fewer than 25% of the required number of words or totally illegible or totally irrelevant.

grammar, organisation, register, and effect on the reader. The raters award a single impression score based on the descriptors.

The fact that a separate task specific scheme is used for each task and that examiners are familiar with the interpretation levels for the BEC suite, means that the system can result in reliable and consistent rating.

The GMS is interpreted at the following levels:

BEC Preliminary	Cambridge/ALTE Level 2
BEC Vantage	Cambridge/ALTE Level 3
BEC Higher	Cambridge/ALTE Level 4

The great value of this method is that it reinforces the link to the Cambridge/ALTE levels (and therefore to the Common European Framework). While we have seen that the BEC suite examinations have been developed with these external performance criteria in mind, the fact that the rating of an individual's test performance is based directly on the criteria reinforces the link to those criteria and as such offers evidence of test validity.

As can be seen from this section, there have been a number of quite significant changes to the Writing papers, particularly with the choice now offered at BEC Higher for the second writing task. The other changes include an increase in the length of the required output for the initial writing task at all levels, and for Task 2 at BEC Preliminary and BEC Vantage, the separation of the Reading and Writing papers at BEC Vantage and the use of a common General Impression Mark Scheme, but interpreted at different performance levels and tied to the Cambridge/ALTE levels. These changes combine to make the revised Writing papers more reliable and valid – in that they represent a clearer business orientation – in terms of context, output text type and length.

Changes in the Listening papers

From the following description of the old and revised BEC Listening papers, we can see that there have been few changes made. This is because there was a general satisfaction with the Listening papers on the part of the developers and those people who were asked to comment on the test during the review stage.

BEC1 and BEC Preliminary

We can see from Tables 4.13 and 4.14 that there have been few substantive changes to the Listening paper. While the sections remain essentially the same, there has been an attempt made to spread out the items more evenly over the four sub-tests. The revised paper continues to test a variety of sub-skills using a range of test formats, again in keeping with the Cambridge ESOL approach outlined in Chapter 2.

It is at the lowest level that the only substantial change has occurred. In BEC1 Part 2 (see Figure 4.10) the listener is required to identify a series of four numbers from a short listening text and then use these to complete a simple form.

Table 4.13 BEC 1 Listening paper outline

Items	Main Skill Focus	Focus	Format	Marks
1–8	Listening for detail	Information transfer (short conversations/monologues)	MCQ (3 option)	8
9–12	Listening for detail	Information transfer (short conversations/monologues)	Gap filling (numbers)	4
13–22	Listening and writing	Form completion	Gap filling (words and numbers)	10
23–30	Listening for specific information	General comprehension and detailed listening	MCQ (3 option)	8

Total time allowed 40 minutes (30 items)

Table 4.14 BEC Preliminary Listening paper outline

Items	Main Skill Focus	Focus	Format	Marks
1–8	Listening for detail	Information transfer (short conversations/monologues)	MCQ (3 option)	8
9–15	Listening for detail	Information transfer (short conversations/monologues)	Gap filling (words, numbers, letters)	7
16–22	Listening and writing	Form/note completion	Gap filling (1 or 2 words)	7
23–30	Listening for specific information	General comprehension and detailed listening	MCQ (3 option)	8

Total time allowed 40 minutes (30 items)

BEC1 Part 3 (Figure 4.11), then asks the candidates to listen to a conversation for specific 'words or a number'. In a second conversation, the listener completes a form while listening to non-number based details. Between the two parts there are a total of 14 items, though there appears to be an overlap in focus between Parts 2 and 3. This overlap is both confusing (what are the items trying to test?) and at best potentially redundant (if the items are testing the same thing).

Figure 4.10 BEC1 Listening Part 2

PART TWO

Questions 9–12

- Look at the order form below.
- You will hear a customer ordering supplies.
- Listen to the conversation, and write the missing **numbers** in the spaces.
- You will hear the conversation twice.

Ace Computer Supplies

Telephone Order   **Date:** 1.8.98

Company: ALTO Insurance (A.Bell)

Order: (9) .... New Star handbooks

(10) .... E12 telex printer ribbons

Delivery address: (11) .... London Street

Order reference no: (12) BK /..................

Source: Cambridge ESOL BEC Handbook (2000:30)

Figure 4.11 BEC1 Listening Part 3

PART THREE

Questions 13–22

- You will hear two telephone conversations.
- Write **one or two words or a number** in the spaces on each form.
- You will hear each conversation twice.

Conversation One

(Questions 13–17)

- You will hear a customer calling a restaurant.
- Complete the form using the information you hear.

GOLDEN TIGER RESTAURANT
Reservations (company clients)

Caller: Anna Davidson from the

(13) ....

Date: Wednesday **(14)** .... , 1.00 p.m.

Number in party: Six

Special requirements:
Caller requests table near **(15)** ....

and **(16)** .... menu.

Method of payment: monthly **(17)** ....

Conversation Two

(Questions 18 – 22)

- You will hear a staff member arranging a card for a visitor.
- Complete the form using the information you hear.

Visitor's Card Request

Full name of visitor: Martin (18) ....

Date: 10th October

Visiting: (member of staff): Chris (19) ....

(department): **(20)** ....

Site: (21) ....

Reason for visit: (22) ....

Source: Cambridge ESOL 2000: BEC Handbook (2000:31)

The revised paper deals with this problem by expanding Part 2 to include seven items involving listening for specific detail in the form of a 'word, numbers or letters' (see Figure 4.12). As with the original version, there was some support offered to the listener as some of the details in the form were included.

Figure 4.12 BEC Preliminary Listening Part 2

PART TWO
Questions 9 – 15

- Look at the notes below.
- Some information is missing.
- You will hear a man leaving an answerphone message about electrical goods.
- For each question **9 – 15**, fill in the missing information in the numbered space using a **word**, **numbers** or **letters**.
- You will hear the message twice.

Phone Message

COMPANY NAME:	(9) .... Department Store
CONTACT NAME:	(10) Roger ....
PHONE NUMBER:	(11) 01873 ....
URGENT – SEND:	(12) .... fridge/freezer brochures
ALSO INCLUDE:	(13) .... price lists
CHECK AVAILABILITY OF DISHWASHER MODEL NO:	(14) ....
CUSTOMER NEEDS DISHWASHER:	(15) .... mm wide

Source: Cambridge ESOL BEC Preliminary, Examination Report and Past Examination Papers (2002:41)

BEC Preliminary Part 3 (Figure 4.13) then focuses on completing a set of notes with seven items which focus on using 'one or two words'. This task is therefore somewhat different from Part 2, in that the focus is now clearly on words only. The result of these changes is to maintain the same number of items, while making the two parts more clearly distinct.

Figure 4.13 BEC Preliminary Listening Part 3

PART THREE
Questions 16 – 22

- Look at the notes from a staff meeting in a department store.
- Some information is missing.
- You will hear a talk by the store manager.
- For each question **16 – 22**, fill in the missing information in the numbered space using **one** or **two** words.
- You will hear the talk twice.

Staff meeting held on 8 June

Name of new Assistant Manager	(16) Amanda ....
Sportswear Department Promotion opportunities open to	(17) .... staff
Stockroom New	(18) .... will improve stock handling
Design Team Staff training – subject:	(19) ....
Visit From:	(20) ....
Date:	(21) 13th 2002
Subject of talk:	(22) .... policy

Source: Cambridge ESOL BEC Preliminary, Examination Report and Past Examination Papers (2002:42)

BEC2 and BEC Vantage

At the next levels (BEC2/BEC Vantage; BEC3/BEC Higher), we can see that there have been no changes made to the Listening papers (Tables 4.15 to 4.18).

Table 4.15 BEC2 Listening paper outline

Items	Main Skill Focus	Focus	Format	Marks
1–12	Listening for detail	Information transfer (short conversations/monologues)	Form/note completion	12
13–22	Listening to identify topic, context, function etc.	Listening for specific information from 2 short monologues/dialogues	Matching extract to statement (5 items to 8 options)	10
23–30	Listening for specific information	General comprehension and detailed listening	MCQ (3 option)	8

Total time allowed 40 minutes (30 items)

Table 4.16 BEC Vantage Listening paper outline

Items	Main Skill Focus	Focus	Format	Marks
1–12	Listening for detail	Information transfer (short conversations/monologues)	Form/note completion	12
13–22	Listening to identify topic, context, function etc.	Listening for specific information from 2 short monologues/dialogues	Matching extract to statement (5 items to 8 options)	10
23–30	Listening for specific information	General comprehension and detailed listening	MCQ (3 option)	8

Total time allowed 40 minutes (30 items)

BEC3 and BEC Higher

Table 4.17 BEC3 Listening paper outline

Items	Main Skill Focus	Focus	Format	Marks
1–12	Listening for detail	Information transfer (short conversations/monologues)	Note completion	12
13–22	Listening to identify topic, context, function, opinion etc.	Information transfer (short conversations/monologues)	Matching extract to statement (reasons and reactions)	10
23–30	Listening for specific information	General comprehension and detailed listening	MCQ (3 option)	8

Total time allowed 40 minutes (30 items)

Table 4.18 BEC Higher Listening paper outline

Items	Main Skill Focus	Focus	Format	Marks
1–12	Listening for detail	Information transfer (short monologues)	Gap fill, note completion (up to three words or a number)	12
13–22	Listening to identify topic, context, function etc.	Information transfer (short conversations/monologues)	Matching extract to statement (reasons and reactions)	10
23–30	Listening for specific information	General comprehension and detailed listening	MCQ (3 option)	8

Total time allowed 40 minutes (30 items)

The Listening papers reviewed here represent the least altered papers of the BEC suite. The changes that were made were based on feedback from the consultation exercise. The Listening papers of the suite have not been seen, either by the developers or by the stakeholders, as being problematic over the years. They represent a practically effective set of papers that offer a view of listening for specific purposes where the tasks and the language are both set in a business context.

Changes in the Speaking papers

It is in the Speaking papers that the most obvious changes have been made. Criticism of the BEC1 Speaking paper tended to focus on the lack of specificity of the task topics – with half of the test devoted to a personal information exchange task and the other to an information transfer task, which, although it was set in a business context, did not really reflect the type of speaking task typical of the domain (see Table 4.19 and Figure 4.14). In the revised version, the number of tasks has been increased to three (Table 4.20), with the introductory task greatly reduced in scope – the task still operates as a sort of 'low impact' introduction to the test event, in terms of cognitive demand and candidate anxiety.

In terms of the tasks included in the revised version of the test, the second task marks the singular most important change. The introduction of the individual long turn with follow-up questions/comments by another candidate adds an important dimension to the test event, namely that of broadening the potential for the test as a whole to elicit a greater range of language functions. This potential has been demonstrated by O'Sullivan, Weir and Saville (2002) in their report on the development of a set of 'Observation Checklists', used by task writers to predict the linguistic outcomes of Speaking test tasks in terms of informational, interactional and discourse management functions, and again by validation researchers to establish empirically that the predictions could be supported. Essentially, the checklists allow the researcher/validator to generate a profile of a test task in use. This profile, based on the elicitation of language functions, can be used to make working descriptions of the tasks through which meaningful comparisons can then be made. Figure 4.14 represents a mapping of the probable function pattern (or profiles) elicited by the three different tasks used in the revised BEC suite.

The profiles, based on data reported by O'Sullivan, Weir and Saville (2002) and modified to predict the outcome of the tasks in the BEC suite, show how the

Figure 4.14 Profile of language elicited by tasks used in the revised BEC suite Speaking paper

		Task 1	Task 2	Task 3
Informational Functions				
Provide personal information	Present	▓		
	Past	▓		
	Future	▓		
Expressing opinions		▓	▓	▓
Elaborating		▓	▓	▓
Justifying opinions		▓	▓	▓
Comparing		▓	▓	
Speculating		▓	▓	▓
Staging			▓	
Describing a scene		▓		
Expressing preferences		▓	▓	▓
Interactional Functions				
Agreeing		▓	▓	▓
Disagreeing			▓	▓
Modifying				▓
Asking for opinions				
Negotiating of meaning	understanding			▓
	respond to req. clarification	▓		
Managing Interaction				
Initiating				▓
Changing				▓
Reciprocating				▓

Key: Task 1 – one-to-one interview
　　　Task 2 – Individual Long Turn (with follow-up comments etc.)
　　　Task 3 – Two-way interaction (candidate-to-candidate)

three different interaction types tend to generate radically different profiles. They also offer some evidence in favour of including as wide a variety of task structures as possible in this type of test of speaking as it clearly results in a wider range of language functions and offers the candidates an opportunity to display their linguistic range to a greater degree.

The final major changes to the Speaking papers are the introduction of an interlocutor frame and a change in the way in which the scores were awarded (a different rating scale was used) and reported. This change will be discussed after the papers at the different levels are reviewed.

BEC1 and BEC Preliminary

The first part of the BEC1 Speaking paper (Table 4.19) involved a brief (approx. two minute) informal one-to-one interview between the examiner and each of the candidates in turn. This task did not feature input material but was unscripted and based on personal information exchange. As such, it was problematic from the perspective of equivalence (each test was essentially a unique event), lack of specificity (there was no obvious 'business' context) and an associated absence of authenticity. In the revised paper, this first part has been shortened to approximately one minute per candidate and is seen as an opener, designed to settle the candidates.

Table 4.19 BEC1 Speaking paper outline

Structure	Task	Format	Input	Output	Time	Marks
1 interlocutor 1 assessor 2 candidates (possible 3 at end of session)	1	One-to-one interview	Oral questions	Personal information Agreeing, disagreeing, preferences, opinions	4–5 minutes	1 – Higher 2 – Minimum satisfactory
	2	Two-way collaborative task	Written prompt and spoken rubric	Interactional Eliciting and giving information	4 minutes	No Grade – less than satisfactory

Total time allowed 10 minutes (two tasks/parts)

The second task in the BEC1 Speaking paper involved information exchange between the two candidates. Figure 4.15 shows an example of one of the two sets of task cards used by the candidates.

This set of cards shows clearly where the criticism of the BEC1 Speaking paper originated. The main focus of the criticism was the lack of real interaction in performing the task. Basically, the candidates were simply asked to create a series of three questions based on the prompts contained on the 'Your Questions' card. From the example shown we can see that it would be quite easy to complete the task by converting the prompts into simple questions and for one's interlocutor (the other candidate) to respond to these questions with

Figure 4.15 BEC1 Speaking Part 2

International Business Magazine

(2 candidates)

Candidate A

Information

This is the information you need to answer your partner's questions

> **Commercial Life**
>
> for
> * advertising agents
> * account managers
> (from August: special section for designers)
>
> 2 issues per month
> (December – 1 issue only)
>
> Publishers
> Technoprint Ltd. (Switzerland)
> Brown & Burton plc (U.S.A.)

Candidate B

Your Questions

You need to ask your partner for this information about another international business magazine

Title of magazine	....
Suitable for	....
How often published	....
Published by	....

Source: Cambridge ESOL BEC Handbook (2000:36–37)

language taken primarily (or even only) from the text of the card, for example:

Question: [What] [is the] title of [the] magazine?
Response: [It is called] *Commercial Life.*

Another worry about this type of item is the unlikelihood of any extended discourse resulting from the questions asked, certainly if the candidates are expected to stick to the information provided in their prompt cards. This introduces the possibility that the task can only be performed well if the individual candidate is able to create both language and context from the prompt. In other words, successful performance is, to a large extent, dependent on non-language ability such as imagination/creativity or background knowledge.

Table 4.20 BEC Preliminary Speaking paper outline

Structure	Task	Format	Input	Output	Time	Marks
1 examiner 1 observer 2 candidates (possible 3 at end of session)	1	One-to-one interview	Oral questions	Personal information Agreeing, disagreeing, preferences, opinions	2 minutes	1 mark awarded by interlocutor using holistic scale
	2	Individual long turn	Written prompt with bulleted suggestions	Mini presentation	5 minutes (includes 1 minute preparation time)	4 marks awarded by observer using analytic scale (grammar and vocabulary; discourse management; pronunciation; interactive communication)
	3	Two-way collaborative task	Written prompt and spoken rubric	Interactional Eliciting and giving information	5 minutes	

Total time allowed 12 minutes (three tasks/parts)

In the revised version of the paper (outlined in Table 4.20), we can see that the second task is based around an individual long turn (see Figure 4.16). The profile of this task in Figure 4.14 implies that it is quite similar to the first task, though it should be remembered that the profile only tells part of the story – these darkened areas simply show the expected functions in the candidate response; they are not meant to quantify the number of functions. The task involves the candidate in a single long turn, in which they are first given one minute to prepare and then expected to produce at least one minute of continuous output. Finally, there is an opportunity for the candidate who is not speaking to ask a question or make a point related to what has been said and for the speaker to then respond. This will obviously involve the use of a broader variety of linguistic and strategic language use. The final advantage to this type of task is that it is more clearly related to the business context than the information exchange task. Figure 4.16 also indicates that a choice of topic is available to the candidate.

Task 3 in the revised BEC Preliminary (see Figure 4.17) is a two-way (or three-way where there are three candidates tested during one session) inter-action task, in which the candidates are introduced to the task by the interlocutor (see the interlocutor frame in Figure 4.20) and given an additional bullet-pointed prompt card (see Figure 4.17). In this task, the candidates are asked to speak for approximately two minutes, with the interlocutor supporting the presentation where he or she deems it appropriate. Finally, the interlocutor may ask additional questions (again scripted) that are related to the theme of the presentation.

While this task type tends to lead to a broadening of the range of language

Figure 4.16 BEC Preliminary Speaking Part 2

Task Card 11 – Examiner's Copy

A: WHAT IS IMPORTANT WHEN...?

LOOKING FOR A NEW JOB

- CAREER OPPORTUNITIES

- LOCATION OF JOB

- POSSIBILITY OF MAKING BUSINESS TRIPS

B: WHAT IS IMPORTANT WHEN...?

TRAVELLING BY AIR FOR BUSINESS

- FLIGHT DEPARTURE TIMES

- IN-FLIGHT SERVICE

- TRANSPORT TO AND FROM AIRPORTS

Source: Cambridge ESOL BEC Preliminary, Examination Report and Past Examination Papers (2002)

functions elicited (see the discussion above), there is always a danger that the intervention of the interlocutor will reduce the interactive or conversational nature of the event to that of an interview (with the interlocutor engaging in what is essentially a series of individual question-and-answer based interactions with each candidate in turn). This presents the developer with something of a conundrum; if the interlocutor is instructed not to intervene there may be a complete breakdown in the interaction, particularly at this level. On the other hand, this very intervention can alter the nature of the communication! As with almost any other such decision, there is no perfect answer, and the decision here to allow for interventions is based on the only really pragmatic solution – if the interaction breaks down totally there is no language to base a judgement on.

Figure 4.17 BEC Preliminary Speaking Part 3

Rewards for staff

- bonus payment
- party
- day trip
- gift
- shares in the company
- extra day's holiday

Source: Cambridge ESOL, BEC Preliminary, Examination Report and Past Examination Papers (2002)

BEC2 and BEC Vantage

Tables 4.21 and 4.22 show that the format has been changed at this level in the same way.

Table 4.21 BEC 2 Speaking paper outline

Structure	Task	Format	Input	Language	Time	Marks
1 examiner 1 observer 2 candidates (possible 3 at end of session)	1	One-to-one interview	Oral questions	Personal Information exchange Agreeing, disagreeing, preferences, opinions	3–4 minutes	1 – Higher 2 – Minimum satisfactory No Grade – less than satisfactory
	2	Paired task	Written prompt and spoken rubric	Non-personal information transfer Eliciting and giving information	7–8 minutes	

Total time allowed 12 minutes (two tasks/parts)

Table 4.22 BEC Vantage Speaking paper outline

Structure	Task	Format	Input	Output	Time	Marks
1 examiner 1 observer 2 candidates (possible 3 at end of session)	1	One-to-one interview	Oral questions	Personal information Giving opinions, speculating etc.	3 minutes	1 mark awarded by interlocutor using holistic scale
	2	Individual long turn	Written prompt with bulleted suggestions	Mini presentation Giving information and justifying opinions	5 minutes (includes 1 minute preparation time)	4 marks awarded by observer using analytic scale (grammar and vocabulary; discourse management; pronunciation; interactive communication)
	3	Two-way collaborative task + follow-up discussion	Written prompt and spoken rubric Oral prompt for follow-up discussion	Interactional Eliciting and giving information, justifying opinions, making comparisons, agreeing and disagreeing etc.	5 minutes	

Total time allowed 14 minutes (three tasks/parts)

The task shown in Figure 4.18 (Task 2) shows that the candidate is offered a choice from a set of three semi-scaffolded task variations. These are semi-scaffolded in that there are just two bulleted suggestions included in the prompt, with an indication that other points can be added. The prompts are all designed to elicit a single long turn on one of a range of business-related topics. One potential problem with offering a choice, such as has been done here, is that there may be some options that are more difficult for candidates to achieve high scores on. While this can be addressed to a large extent in the design of the task, and in the writing of the different versions of the task through a checklist type framework such as that suggested by O'Sullivan and Weir (2000), it is also necessary to empirically test for bias in the test data.

Figure 4.18 BEC Vantage Speaking Part 2

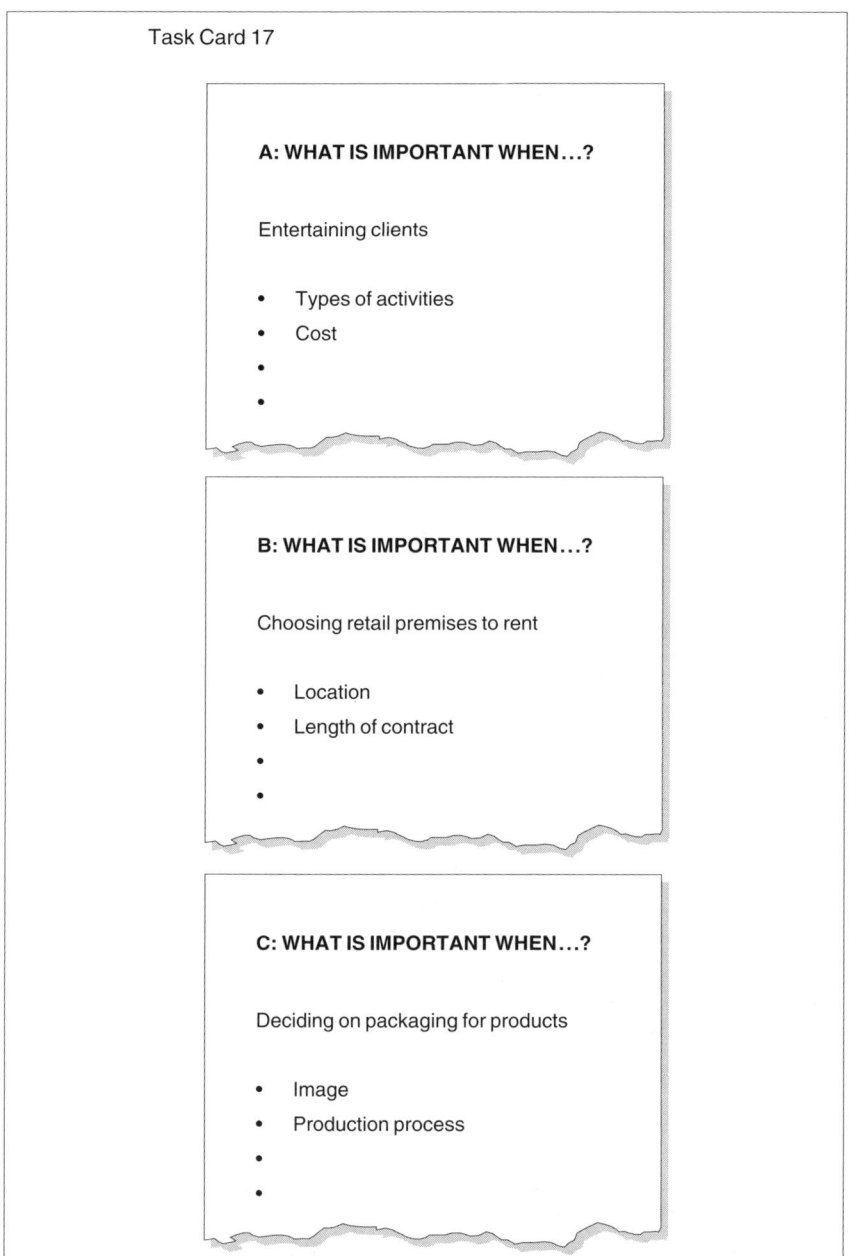

Task Card 17

A: WHAT IS IMPORTANT WHEN...?

Entertaining clients

- Types of activities
- Cost
-
-

B: WHAT IS IMPORTANT WHEN...?

Choosing retail premises to rent

- Location
- Length of contract
-
-

C: WHAT IS IMPORTANT WHEN...?

Deciding on packaging for products

- Image
- Production process
-
-

Source: Cambridge ESOL BEC Vantage, Examination Report and Past Examination Papers (2002:42)

BEC 3 and BEC Higher

Table 4.23 BEC 3 Speaking paper outline

Structure	Task	Format	Input	Language	Time	Marks
1 examiner 1 observer 2 candidates (possible 3 at end of session)	1	One-to-one interview	Oral questions	Personal Information exchange Expressing opinions	3–4 minutes	1 – Higher 2 – Minimum satisfactory No Grade – less than satisfactory
	2	Paired task	Written prompt and spoken rubric	Non-personal information exchange Explaining, persuading, justifying, etc.	4 minutes	
	3	Individual long turn	Written prompt and spoken rubric	Monologue (based on written input) Describing, explaining giving and justifying opinions, etc.	6 minutes	

Total time allowed 14 minutes (three tasks/parts)

Table 4.24 BEC Higher Speaking paper outline

Structure	Task	Format	Input	Output	Time	Marks
1 examiner 1 observer 2 candidates (possible 3 at end of session)	1	One-to-one interview	Oral questions	Personal Information exchange Expressing opinions	3 minutes	1 mark awarded by interlocutor using holistic scale
	2	Individual long turn	Written prompt with bulleted suggestions	Mini presentation Giving information and justifying opinions	6 minutes (includes 1 minute preparation time)	4 marks awarded by observer using analytic scale (grammar and vocabulary; discourse management; pronunciation; interactive communication)
	3	Two-way collaborative task + follow-up discussion	Written prompt and spoken rubric Oral prompt for follow-up discussion	Interactional Eliciting and giving information, justifying opinions, making comparisons, agreeing and disagreeing etc.	7 minutes	

Total time allowed 14 minutes (three tasks/parts)

Figure 4.19 shows the task cards for Part 3 of the BEC Higher. In this task, which is designed to elicit a sample of interaction-based language, candidates are allowed thirty seconds to read the task card and are then expected to speak for approximately three minutes. The topics are clearly business-focused, and can be realistically expected to elicit the sort of profile outlined in Figure 4.14 – with a range of language functions across the three types.

In order to deal with the situation where there are three candidates present, the task has been added to slightly – with an additional element in the expected outcome, see Task 26 in Figure 4.19. There is a potential danger here that the language elicited under the two conditions may be different, as the two conditions involve both different numbers of candidates and different expected outcomes. However, there is no evidence that candidates involved in paired or three-way interactions are biased either towards or against – the format has been successfully used for almost a decade in the Cambridge ESOL Main Suite examinations and has been adopted in other tests around the world. It is certainly an area in which further research is required in order to ensure that there is no unintentional bias present in the Speaking papers of the revised BEC.

Figure 4.19 BEC Higher Speaking Part 3

Task 22   for **two** candidates

Incentive Scheme for Staff

Your company is considering setting up an incentive scheme to improve staff performance. You have been asked to make recommendations for the scheme.

Discuss, and decide together:

- what benefits an incentive scheme for staff would bring to the company

- what types of incentives could be offered

Task 22   for **three** candidates

Incentive Scheme for Staff

Your company is considering setting up an incentive scheme to improve staff performance. You have been asked to make recommendations for the scheme.

Discuss, and decide together:

- what benefits an incentive scheme for staff would bring to the company

- what types of incentives could be offered

- which employees in the company should be targeted

Source: Cambridge ESOL BEC Higher, Examination Report and Past Examination Papers (2002:47–48)

There are obvious advantages to the inclusion of the different task types in the BEC suite. These can be summarised as adding to the test in terms of:

- **authenticity** – since presentations and peer discussion and decision-making are seen as being of particular relevance to the area of business
- **specificity** – the inclusion of these tasks has the effect of making the paper more clearly specific to the language use domain
- **generalisability** – as the task introduces the potential for a wider variety of language function use (see O'Sullivan, Weir and Saville 2002).

Other changes to the Speaking paper

The other major changes to the Speaking papers are the use of an 'interlocutor frame' and the way in which the performances are scored.

The introduction of an interlocutor frame

In the earlier versions of the BEC examinations, the interlocutor frame as we now know it was not used. However, work carried out in the early 1990s, partic-

Figure 4.20 BEC Higher Speaking Part 3 – interlocutor frame

PART 3: Two-way collaborative task and discussion (about 7 minutes)

For 2 candidates

Interlocutor

Now, this part of the test is a discussion activity.

[Hold the card showing the task while giving the instructions below.]

You have about 30 seconds to read this task carefully, and then about 3 minutes to discuss and decide about it together. You're expected to give reasons for your decisions and opinions. You don't need to write anything. Is that clear?

[Place the card in front of the candidates.]

[If necessary, give clarification. Then allow 30 seconds for candidates to absorb the information and to think how to begin. After about 30 seconds, encourage candidates to begin the task, if they have not already done so.]

Are you ready to begin? I'll just listen and then ask you to stop after about 3 minutes. Please speak so that we can hear you.

[Do not join in this stage of the discussion unless it is necessary to prompt the candidates to talk.]

[After the candidates have finished speaking the interlocutor asks questions and finishes the speaking test, as directed on the examiner's copy of the task card.]

Figure 4.20 BEC Higher Speaking Part 3 – interlocutor frame (continued)

Task 22 – Examiner's Copy

> **Incentive Scheme for Staff**
>
> Your company is considering setting up an incentive scheme to improve staff performance. You have been asked to make recommendations for the scheme.
>
> Discuss, and decide together:
>
> - what benefits an incentive scheme would bring to the company
> - what types of incentives could be offered

Interlocutor: *[Select one or more of the following questions as appropriate, to redress any imbalance in Part 3, or to broaden the discussion.]*

- Which incentives do you think are **most effective** for encouraging people to work hard? (Why?)

- What **disadvantages** could there be in incentive schemes? (Why?)

- Is it essential for companies to reward **extra effort**? (Why/Why not?)

- How do you think a company can **inspire loyalty** in employees?

- How do you think the traditional **employer/employee relationship** might change in the future? (Why?)

Thank you. That is the end of the speaking test.

[Retrieve materials.]

Source: Cambridge ESOL BEC Vantage, Examination Report and Past Examination Papers (2002:53–54)

ularly that of Lazaraton (1992, 1996), suggested that the lack of control over the language input was having a measurable impact on the performance of candidates in oral interview type tests.

The introduction of the scripted interlocutor frame allows the test developer to more fully control what is happening in the test event. The frame is a scripted text which guides the examiner through the event, limits the examiner in terms of input (ensuring that all candidates receive the same directions) and timing (guaranteeing that all candidates will have an opportunity to perform all of the tasks provided in the test) – see Figure 4.20 for a copy of the frame that goes with the two candidate version of the task described in Figure 4.19.

We can see from this example that there are times in which clarification may be offered at the discretion of the examiner. Clearly, it would be unwise not to allow for some flexibility as all test events will be in some way different, and candidates of different ability will require more or less help from the examiner. The advantage of allowing the examiner a choice in the follow up questions means that the questions can be chosen to engage with the candidates' output, while still allowing for the control over the event vital to reliability.

Of interest here are the findings of a research study undertaken by O'Sullivan and Lu (2003), who investigated the impact on candidates' linguistic performance of deviations from the interlocutor frame by examiners in the IELTS Speaking test. By making comparisons between transcribed segments of the output of learners taken before and after the deviation, they found that there was no significant impact on a number of measures (discourse features, linguistic accuracy and complexity or fluency). The indication is that as long as the interlocutor maintains the integrity of the test through a systematic, though not dogmatic, use of the interlocutor frame, there will be little perceptible impact on the output of the candidates, thus supporting the decision not to make the interlocutor frame so tight as to eliminate any individual expression on the part of the examiner.

While the Cambridge ESOL move to the paired format has been criticised (Foot 1999) the anecdotal nature of the criticism when coupled with the failure to make a realistic critique of the limitations of the one-to-one interview format limit the value of this criticism. The other major limitation of the criticism was the lack of awareness of the model of language competence which lay behind the move, a problem possibly caused or certainly exacerbated by the lack of published information on the construct at that time. In their response to the criticism, Saville and Hargreaves (1999) provided a well argued rationale for the format, demonstrating the essential weakness in any test design that did not encourage interactive communication – though it should also be pointed out that this strength may also be a weakness, as it is now accepted that the nature of any language of the interaction is co-constructed.

The introduction of a new rating and reporting scale

This original rating procedure has been replaced with a scale which is more typical of the Cambridge ESOL examinations. While the focus is still on the same criteria as were used in the pre-revision tests (grammar and vocabulary, discourse management, pronunciation and interactive communication), the descriptors have been revised and rewritten to reflect the descriptors used in the equivalent Main Suite tests. Using the rating scales in the same way as they are used in the Main Suite, also minimises any negative effect that using a very different type of scale might have on the examiners. Where examiners use a familiar scale, and are making judgements at a level with which they are familiar, there is a far greater likelihood that they will be consistent than if they are asked to use very different scales for each examination they are asked to rate. On the negative side of this is the argument that the rating scales lack any specific business domain orientation. This means that the aspects of language which distinguish the business domain (for example appropriacy of lexis, register, format, and rhetorical structure) are not taken into account, thus questioning the potential of this aspect of the test to tell us about the candidates' ability to perform linguistically in the business domain.

Since the arrangement of the Speaking test now more closely resembles that of the Main Suite examinations in terms of task type and assessment type, more accurate and meaningful comparisons between the Main Suite examinations and external criteria such as the Common European Framework and the three BEC levels can be made (see Figure 4.21 – which represents a schematic diagram of the format of the Main Suite and BEC Speaking tests).

Figure 4.21 Structure of the revised BEC Speaking paper

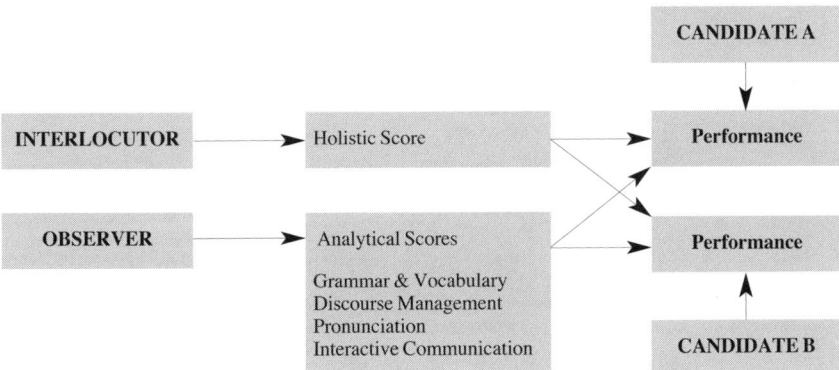

Summary

In this chapter I have tried to outline briefly the changes made to the individual papers in the BEC suite. As you can see from the above, the most significant changes have come as a response to criticisms of the Speaking paper, while the other papers that were considered to be working well were left relatively untouched. This is in line with the 'continuity and change' dimensions referred to in Weir and Milanovic (2003).

Before concluding the chapter, it might be useful to review the BEC examinations in terms of the criteria used to review the other tests in Chapter 1. This will allow the reader to make comparative judgements on the different tests and will, I hope, demonstrate how the value or usefulness of the BEC suite has been increased with this revision.

As the first two of the criteria (a brief introduction to and description of the test) have been dealt with in this chapter, I will focus on the remaining criteria in the brief review contained in Table 4.25. As can be seen from this overview, the changes to BEC have resulted in some areas of significant improvement, and in other areas of similar performance. Even these areas of relatively little or no

Table 4.25 Brief overview of the old and revised BEC suite

	Original BEC	Revised BEC
3. An outline of the construct upon which the test focuses	Not clearly defined, though appears to have been based on a communicative, four skills' definition of the construct.	Now more explicitly designed to reflect the multi-componential approach to competence as typified in Bachman's (1990) model.
4. The test method	A variety of task and item formats are used throughout the different papers.	A variety of task and item formats are used throughout the different papers.
5. Skills' coverage	Listening, Speaking, Reading and Writing	Listening, Speaking, Reading and Writing
6. Measurement qualities	Not available in the public domain.	Reported here in Chapter 2.
7. Degree of specificity/ Authenticity	Relatively specific, though in the case of the Speaking paper, criticised for being too general. In general meets any 'authenticity' criticism, with the exception of the Speaking paper.	Retains former degree of specificity, though revised Speaking paper is much more specific. Tasks across the different papers attempt to engage concepts of both situational and interactional authenticity.
8. Impact of non-language factors	Seem to be unproblematic, though the use of a single interlocutor in the Speaking paper may heighten the impact of any 'interlocutor' effect. Likelihood that background knowledge of the business language domain might impact to some degree on performance in some papers.	Seems to be unproblematic – potential problem in Speaking paper rectified through the introduction of interaction (with peer and examiner) and monologic discourse. The additional specificity in the Speaking paper suggests that background knowledge may impact on performance.
9. Reporting of test performance	Candidates received one grade for Reading, Writing and Listening (A, B or C at levels BEC2 and 3, and A, B, C or D at BEC1). As the Speaking paper was considered a separate entity a separate grade was awarded (1 or 2).	All candidates receive an overall estimate of their ability based on their performance on each of the four papers (each is worth 25% of the total available marks). For BEC Preliminary, results are reported as a Pass with Merit or a Pass or as one of two failing grades – Narrow Fail or Fail. At the other levels there are three passing grades (A, B or C) and two failing grades (D or E). The certificates for all three levels also include a graphical profile (see Figure 3.1). This profile is of particular diagnostic value to the candidate – indicating areas of strength and/or weakness.

change are relevant however, as the lack of change is not due to any inertia, but is based on a thorough review of the entire test system. In fact, this suggests a further criterion for test evaluation, that of systematic self-monitoring. In the case of the BEC suite (as in other Cambridge ESOL examinations) this constant monitoring and revising of tests is a feature which seems to ensure that the tests are continuously being brought up-to-date to reflect changing views of what language ability really consists of, and of how it might best be assessed. It also allows for a test to be constantly monitored for appropriacy as the candidate base changes over time or where the uses of the test evolve.

5 Conclusions and the way forward

Summary

In the first chapter of this book, I reviewed the brief history of the testing of language for business purposes (TLBP). This review demonstrated the relative 'newness' of the area and highlighted the tendency for these tests to be 'industry-driven' with a more pragmatic than theoretical foundation. The only theoretical perspective that has gained recognition is that of Douglas (2000:281), who sees language for specific purpose (LSP) tests as being premised on the fact that language performance varies between specific contexts and that the language of these specific contexts is precise, that it is distinguishable from other language use contexts or domains. Criticism of this definition (Elder 2001) focused on the fact that there were three areas in which LSP tests were problematic. These were:

- specificity
- authenticity
- impact of non-language factors.

Before going on to look at current practice in the area of business language testing, I offered a somewhat different perspective on LSP tests and the above criticism. In this perspective, I suggested that there were four key points that should be taken into account when theorising on LSP testing in general. These were

1. As all tests are in some way 'specific', it is best to think of language tests as being placed somewhere on a continuum of specificity, from the broad general purpose test (such as CPE) to the highly specific test.
2. Very highly specific tests tend to be very poor in terms of generalisability, while the opposite can be said of non-specific (or general proficiency) tests, though this is not a binary choice if we accept that tests can be developed along a specificity continuum.
3. Where a test is situated closer and closer to the more highly specified end of the continuum, the focus on authenticity also changes.
4. The more highly specific a language test is the more it entails a focus on the event rather than on the language of the event. The degree to which non-

language factors impact on a candidate's test performance will reflect the degree of specificity of that test. Therefore, in a highly specific language test it may not be possible to separate the language from the specific event.

Following this, a review of currently available small and large scale tests (in terms of test-taking population) was undertaken. The tests reviewed were looked at from a 9-point perspective based on an overview of the theoretical and practical issues, these were:

1. A brief introduction to the test.
2. A brief description of the test.
3. An outline of the construct upon which the test is based.
4. The test method.
5. Skills' coverage.
6. Measurement qualities.
7. Degree of specificity/authenticity.
8. Impact of non-language factors.
9. Reporting of test performance.

From these reviews it became clear that the practical operationalisation of the TLBP concept appears to be quite uneven in some regards, certainly in terms of the availability of research and/or support material.

Some interesting points can be taken from these reviews

- Large-scale tests tend to have originally been produced at the behest of government agencies (though the trend is that international tests are being produced more and more to meet either perceived or established market needs – in other words the TLBPs are more and more market driven).
- As the markets (and the test-taking population) change there is little sign that the tests have been revised to meet the change, and where change has come, there has been no information on that change made available in the public domain.
- There has not really been a tendency for changes in proficiency language testing practice to be reflected in TLBP practice with regards to context-based, theory-based and scoring validity.
- Few TLBPs include papers related to the four skills of speaking, writing, reading and listening.
- There appears to be a relatively low level of support material available, though the UK-based tests tend to offer practice or past papers at no charge to test takers – these can usually be downloaded from the web (see the References section at the end of this book).
- There is a clear tendency against very highly specific tests, for example a test of language for chartered accountants. Instead, the tests on the market appear to be more general in nature, context-oriented rather than context-focused.

The overview then showed how the review of the Cambridge ESOL Business English Certificate (BEC) suite offered an interesting insight into how such a large scale test system might be revised. The main points highlighted by these chapters are the complexity of the process, for example in demonstrating how different stakeholders' views were taken into account (in different ways), the need for tests to take into account changes in language testing theories and the reinforcement of an all-skills approach.

The implications of this work are twofold, theoretical and practical. The former, is of interest to LSP testing in general, while the latter will focus primarily on the BEC suite of tests though will identify areas of LSP in general that might benefit.

Theoretical implications

Douglas essentially sees *authenticity* as the central issue in his definition of LSP tests:

> . . . a specific purpose language test is one in which test content and methods are derived from an analysis of a specific purpose language use situation, so that test tasks allow for an interaction between the test taker's language ability, on the one hand, and the test tasks on the other (2000:90).

In the first chapter of this book I suggested that it may be better to see this as just one aspect of LSP tests, and instead argue that other central issues were the potential for distinguishing language use in a specific situation and, from the operational perspective, the assessment or evaluation of the performance. Of the points made in Chapter 1, and reiterated above, I would now like to revisit the notion of degree of specificity, because it appears to me to be at the heart of the issue.

In Figures 1.5 and 1.31, I suggested that all tests lie on a 'degree of specificity' continuum. Reflecting now on that suggestion, having reviewed both the literature and current practice in business language testing, I see that it seems to oversimplify the situation. In actual fact, there are a number of elements which combine to help us draw inferences as to the degree of specificity of an LSP test. These elements are related to such concepts as authenticity as well as generalisability and distinguishability.

In order to explain what I mean by this we need to go back to the criticism made by Davies (2001) of the lack of a theoretical basis for LSP testing. In his paper, Davies argues that it is not possible to fully distinguish specific language use domains. The point to be made here is that, by its very nature, language is not easily defined, and the language of a specific use domain is no different. Within any such situation there will be a specific 'core' language, which may refer to a specific use of language or a specific lexicon – see for example the work of Ball (2002) in using a corpus linguistics approach to producing a series of updated wordlists for the BEC suite. As Davies and Elder argue, there is no distinct boundary between this core and what I have labelled here the general language use domain. Instead, there is an area of transition, in which language use is shared with other domains. Figure 5.1 attempts to graphically represent this notion, though it is limited to two dimensions, while the actual situation should be visualised as being multi-dimensional.

Figure 5.1 The notion of core and general language use domains

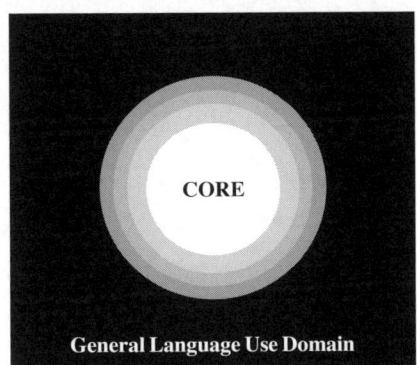

Taking this idea a step further, Figure 5.2, we can now see that the notion of degree of specificity brings with it the related notions of generalisability and situational authenticity. Where a test is seen to be positioned towards the specific end of the continuum, the potential for generalisation from test performance beyond the specific situation is reduced – it is difficult to imagine a test that could be placed at the extreme end of the continuum as this would be focused only on a very limited 'core' language. In the same way, that test would be seen as being more situationally authentic were it manipulated to move it ever closer to the specific end of the continuum. A completely specific language test would therefore be focused only on language unique to a specific use domain and would be tested in use within that domain. Performance on the test could then be related only to that domain. This is clearly neither practical nor desirable.

Figure 5.2 is again limited by my ability to represent the notion of general and core in anything but a two dimensional diagram. In reality, once we move beyond the distinguishable core we are in the domain of general language use – the figure implies that only a part of this domain can be represented in the test sample. What is successfully represented in the figure is the idea that when a test is more 'specific' in its focus, the greater will be the importance of the core and when as the test is more 'general' in focus, a less important role will be played by language from a specific core. The question we must again ask is how do we know that a test is either specific or general in focus?

Figure 5.2 Extension of the 'specificity continuum' concept

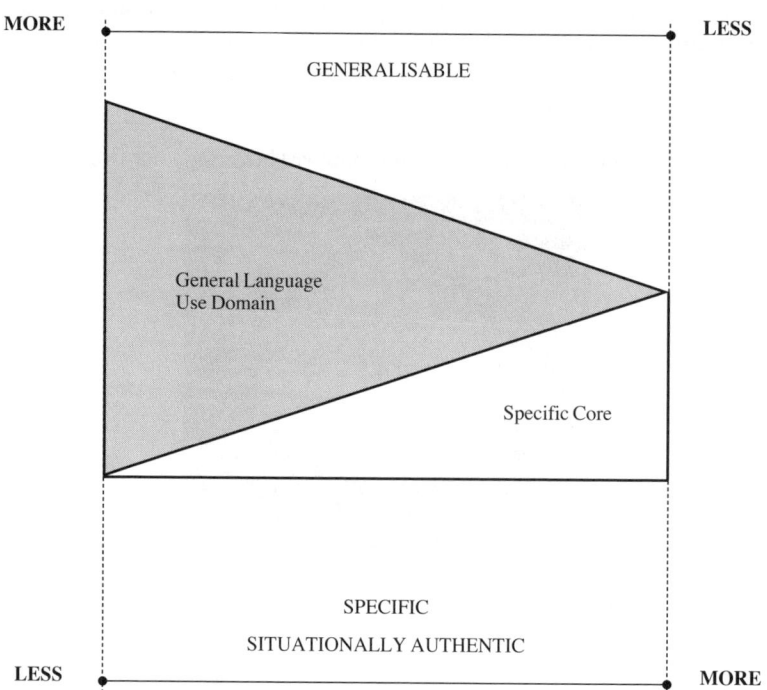

Locating specificity

The notion of specificity, if it is to be of practical use to the test developer, must be tied to an understanding of test validity. One such perception of test validation is suggested by the socio-cognitive spoken language framework discussed by O'Sullivan and Weir (2002) and developed as a series of frameworks for all four skills by Weir (2004). In these frameworks, validity is seen from a socio-cognitive perspective – a perspective which appears similar to that suggested by Chalhoub-Deville (2003) and Chapelle (1998). In the following example, I will refer to the framework developed for validating tests of speaking, though any of the other three frameworks would obviously work equally well.

Figure 5.3 gives an idea of what the entire framework looks like. In this outline, we can see that there are a number of elements, each of which should be attended to by the test developer. Evidence is required at each level, in order to make validity claims for a test. I have added to the framework by highlighting the fact that the test taker can be described in terms of a number of characteristics (physical/physiological; psychological and experiential) and by the internal processing (unique to the individual) which takes place during test performance. The test can be described in terms of its context validity and in terms of the potential for successful test tasks to result in appropriate processing. It is this notion of what Weir (2004) calls theory-based validity that forms the link between the test and the test taker.

Figure 5.3 Format of validation frames

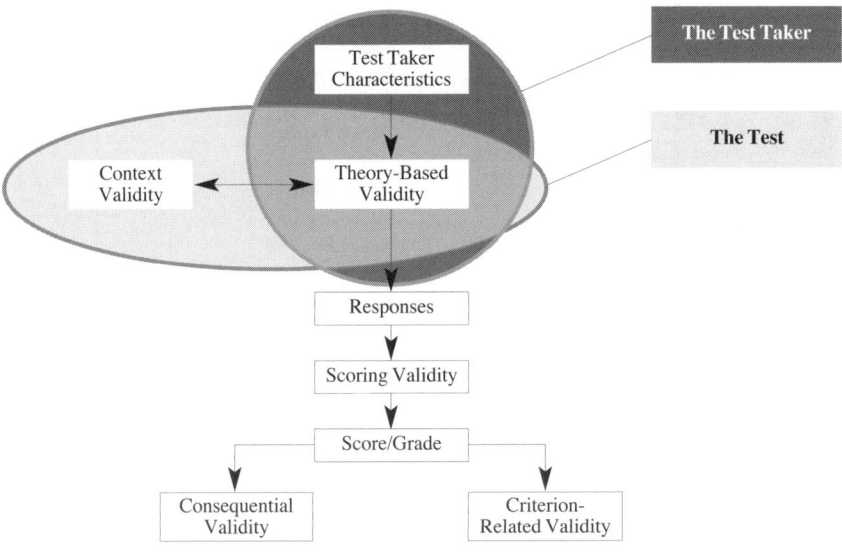

Source: based on Weir (2004)

Since I am hoping to provide a theoretical basis for LSP tests in general and business language tests in particular, I will now demonstrate how I feel the above framework can be shown to be related to the two aspects of authenticity.

Context validity (see Figure 5.4), is concerned with aspects of the demands of the task and text, as well as detailing the test setting. In terms of the view of LSP tests offered here, it should become clear that when we are talking about test specificity, we are actually referring to test context, and this is expressed in the framework as being comprised of task and text demands.

When we consider the difficulty in defining language proficiency and use (for example the 'boundary' issue raised by Davies 2001 and Elder 2001) we can see that context validation is always going to be problematic. The operations and conditions suggested in the framework presented here are based on Weir (1993) and have been used with some success in test development projects for a decade, though they remain tentative in that there is no empirical evidence that these are the only operations and conditions applicable to a test of speaking (see Weir 2004 for a more detailed and updated version of the frameworks).

Figure 5.4 Aspects of context validity for speaking

Context Validity	
Task Demands	**Text Demands**
• Purpose	**Linguistic (Input & Output)**
• Response Format	Mode
• Weighting	Discourse mode
• Known Criteria	Length
• Order of Items	Nature of information
• Time Constraints	Topic familiarity
	Lexical range
Setting:	Structural range
Administration	Functional range
• Physical Conditions	**Interlocutor**
• Uniformity of Administration	Speech rate
• Security	Variety of accent
	Acquaintanceship
	Number
	Gender

Source: Weir (2004)

Test specificity might therefore be expressed as the degree to which the operationalisation of each of these demands can be considered to be uniquely related to a specific language use domain. In practice, this entails making value judgements of the degree of specificity along a continuum for each aspect of both task demands and text demands (see Figure 5.5). This may be seen as being too subjective a task to be of practical use. However, the real value of the exercise is in the breadth of the exercise. Specificity is now seen as a multi-dimensional perspective of a test, and judgements are at least being made on a systematic basis; a criticism of my early reviews of the various tests is that the judgements were essentially intuitive and, as no systematic approach was taken, this intuition may not always have been based on similar criteria (the same criticism can be made of almost all multiple-test reviews).

In order to demonstrate this, I undertook a small experiment in which a group of language specialists was asked to take two test papers (of Reading) and to make judgements on the papers based on a simple Likert scales'-based instrument. The instructions to the specialists asked that they should try to decide where on the scales (one scale for each of the aspects of context validity shown in Figure 5.6) each of the two papers might hypothetically lie, with

Figure 5.5 A multi-componential view of specificity

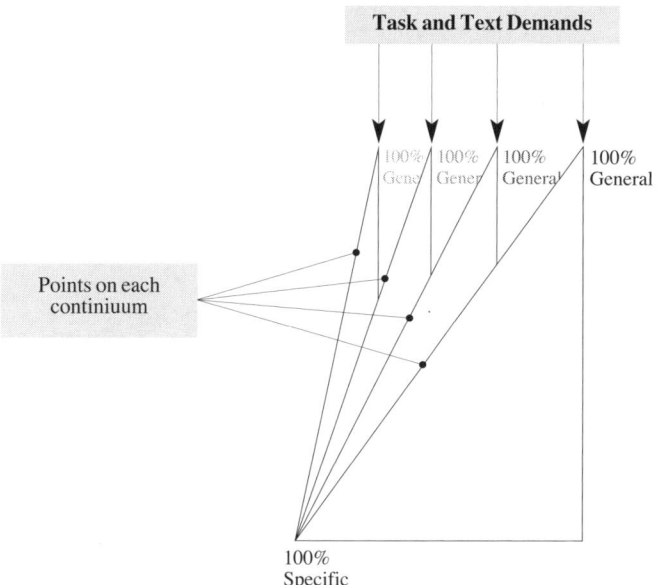

1 meaning 'very specific' and 7 'general' – where an aspect was considered 'neutral' it was decided that a rating of 4 should be awarded. The papers were taken from an LSP test, BEC Vantage, and a general proficiency test, the FCE, as these two tests are designed to allow for inferences to be made at the same CEF level – Level B2. Figure 5.6 shows that there were clear differences seen by the specialists in terms of the task demands. This clearly different profile can be taken as empirical evidence of the distinguishability of LSP and general tests.

Figure 5.6 Differences in task demands between LSP and general proficiency test papers

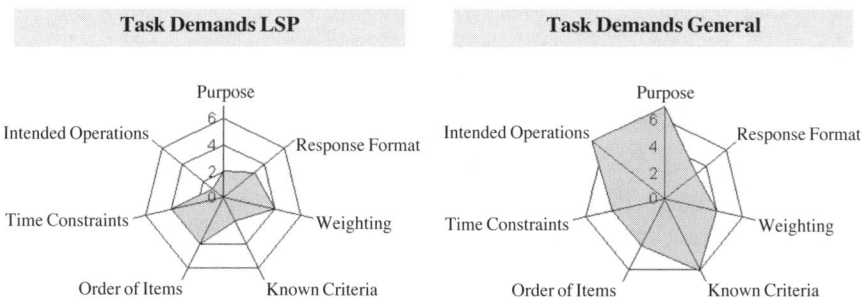

When the participants were asked to repeat the exercise for the same papers but this time with a focus on text demands, the differences are even more obvious (Figure 5.7).

Figure 5.7 Differences in text demands between LSP and general proficiency test papers

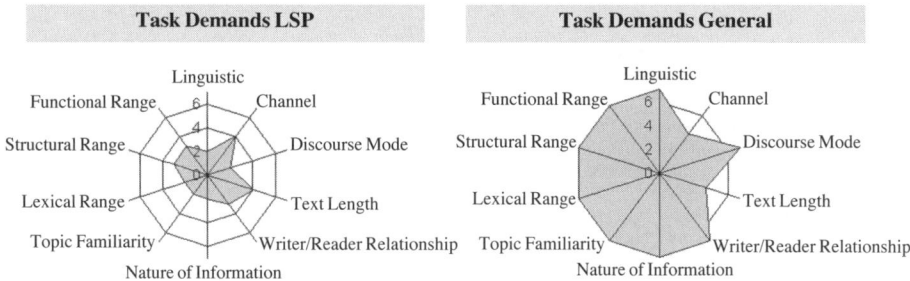

The evidence from this admittedly very small study, suggests that judgements on the degree of specificity of an LSP test can be made in a systematic way. It also suggests that the notion of test specificity is closely linked to that of situational authenticity. Of course it could be argued that even a supposedly 'specific' test such as BEC, or even a 'highly specific' test, such as the one for air traffic controllers described by Teasdale (1994), can never reach a position where the shaded area in the figures is minimised – indicating that the test has achieved a high degree of specificity from all perspectives. The evidence here supports the view that tests can never hope to do more than simulate authenticity, and intuition suggests that this same evidence will be found where other tests are analysed using the methodology suggested here – however highly specific the test developer claims it to be.

The second aspect of validity I will look at is that of theory-based validity (see Weir 2004:Chapter 1), which is concerned with the cognitive processing during test task performance. Test validity, from this perspective, is therefore concerned with the degree to which the processing in the test situation reflects that of the language use domain. While this perspective on test validity is relatively new (though see both Chapelle 1998 and Douglas 2000 for arguments that lend support to this view of validity) there is encouraging evidence from ongoing research in China and Malaysia that evidence can be elicited to support the making of comparative judgements between different test task types.

The symbiotic nature of the relationship between content and theory-based validity can be illustrated by showing how decisions taken with regard to elements of context validity have significant effects on the cognitive processing of test takers who must perform the tasks in the test situation. An example of this can be found in Porter and O'Sullivan (1999) who demonstrated that by

Figure 5.8 Aspects of theory-based validity for speaking

THEORY-BASED VALIDITY		
INTERNAL PROCESSES		**EXECUTIVE RESOURCES**
• Conceptualiser	**MONITORING**	• **Content knowledge**
• Pre verbal message		• Internal
• Linguistic formulator		• External
• Phonetic plan		• **Language knowledge**
• Articulator		• Grammatical
• Overt speech		• Discoursal
• Audition		• Functional
• Speech comprehension		• Sociolinguistic

Source: Weir (2004)

changing the description of the addressee of letters written by Japanese EFL learners, significant changes were observed in terms of both orthography and language use, suggesting that there had been a significant impact on the goal-setting part of the executive processing dimension of written production.

If we show that the cognitive processes involved in an LSP test task performance reflect those of the specific language use domain they are designed to reflect, then we can claim with some confidence that our test task demonstrates interactional authenticity. It is quite possible that such processing may well differ in important respects from general purpose task performance, for example in the recourse to different areas of executive resources. By demonstrating differences in internal processing between LSP and general purpose tasks we are offering an additional argument in favour of the distinguishability of language use domains.

This is obviously pertinent to all areas of language testing, supporting, for example Bachman and Palmer (1996:23) who see authenticity as 'the degree of correspondence of a given language test to the features of the TLU (target language use) task'. The argument here is that we need to go beyond the notion of content validity and situational authenticity to include a working perspective on the interactional aspect of authenticity. This way of looking at validity offers just that perspective.

While it is relatively straightforward to establish the situational authenticity of a test task, it is only by an *a posteriori* empirical exploration of test performance that evidence of the interactional authenticity of any test can be established.

In a way, this brings us back full circle to the definition of LSP tests offered by Douglas, and quoted above. When I quoted Douglas's definition, I suggested that there were limitations to it; however, when these limitations are seen in the light of the twin perspectives of authenticity, we can see that my arguments actually support the definition – though, I hope, adding to it so that the criticisms voiced by Davies, Elder and Douglas himself can be, to some considerable extent, rejected.

Practical implications

Before concluding, I would like to first suggest a series of practical implications for the BEC tests (and other tests of language for specific purposes). There are some implications that are relevant to all papers and others that are specific to each of the four.

Reliability

The issue of reliability is of great importance to all test developers. As we saw in Chapter 2 of this book, there are problems associated with the way in which internal consistency is estimated for tests with truncated populations (existing procedures can result in low estimates as there tends to be restricted variation within the population), and also with the way in which reliability is estimated for tests based on performance such as writing and speaking. Weir (2003b:475) suggests a number of alternatives to the current practice in estimating reliability where a truncated population is involved, as does Luoma (2004:183) who argues that the Standard Error of Measurement (SEM) should be routinely reported 'as a useful quality check'. SEM may serve as a practical device when it comes to dichotomously scored test items, and the internal consistency estimates and SEM reported earlier for the BEC suite are quite satisfactory. However, the fact that SEM is premised on being able to accurately estimate internal consistency means that there is an even greater difficulty with applying the formula to a speaking or writing test. One reason for this is that the most common reported procedure for estimating inter-rater reliability, correlation, is problematic for a number of reasons:

- There is some concern that the intervals represented in rating scales are not equal. This suggests that the researcher/tester should use the Spearman Rank Order Correlation statistic – a less powerful non-parametric estimate of association than Pearson's Rho.
- Correlation statistics can only tell us about the association between the pattern of scoring of raters, not between their level of agreement. So the correlation between the scores awarded by a very harsh rater and a very lenient rater will still be very high if for example the scores they award place the test takers in the same order.
- The correlation between two variables may be due to the impact of other, unobserved variables.

- Even if there are two raters who agree totally, it is possible that they are both either very harsh or lenient – or both inconsistent, but in a similar way.

While I agree that alternatives should be sought, I feel, as does Weir, that those offered to date are simply a short term solution. In the longer term we really need to look more closely at the whole area of reliability. Until recently, it was considered acceptable to discuss test validity in somewhat simplistic terms and it was generally considered acceptable that evidence need only be gathered in relation to a single aspect of validity. Indeed, in the psychology literature it is still common to find a single numerical estimate of test validity. The same view of reliability is common today – with the reporting of a single internal consistency coefficient considered adequate evidence of the reliability of a test.

The format of the validation frames (Figure 5.3), offers, I believe, the basis for a more viable alternative to existing practice. Here, we can see that the notion of reliability has been replaced with the more helpful concept of 'scoring validity'.

Bachman (1990:163–166) argues that test scores are affected by a number of factors: the communicative language ability of the candidate; test method facets (systematic aspects of test delivery for example); personal attributes of the candidate (both individual and group characteristics); and finally random factors (unpredictable and unsystematic factors that impact on test performance). Consideration of the reliability of a test would be greatly improved by conceptualising reliability in terms of these different factors. Weir (2004) suggests that, for tests of reading comprehension, for example, the framework should consist of those elements contained in Figure 5.9.

Figure 5.9 Aspects of scoring validity in tests of reading

SCORING VALIDITY
• Item Analysis
• Internal Consistency
• Reliability
• Stability
• Error of Measurement
• Marker Reliability

Source: Weir (2004)

While this figure is very similar to the suggestions made by Bachman (1990), when we look at the possible aspects of scoring validity for a test of speaking (Figure 5.10) the situation is now quite a lot more complex with the inclusion of a number of new elements in the equation, in particular the rating scale, the rating process and the rater. When we consider the discussion of rating scale development and use in Chapter 1, we can see that this is an area of some interest. In addition, the whole rating process is still relatively unexplored; we continue to know far too little about the effects of rater training (though see Weigle 1994, and Rethinasamy in progress), or of the value of standardisation (see O'Sullivan and Rignall 2001, 2002) or of what happens in the minds of the raters when they are awarding scores (see Lumley 2000).

As for the other areas referred to in Figure 5.10, there is little or no empirical evidence of how they impact on rating performance. O'Sullivan (2002b) argued that the test taker should be described in terms of a series of characteristics (physical, psychological, experiential) and that research should be carried out into the effect on performance of the interaction between these variables and the test event. In the same way that characteristics of the test taker will influence test task performance, it is clear that similar characteristics of the examiner or rater will affect their performance in awarding scores for those performances. There is evidence of how performances can achieve very different scores depending on the examiner (see for example Congdon and McQueen 2000, Engelhard 1994, Fisher 1994, Lamprianou and Pillas 2003, Longford 1994, Lumley, Lynch and McNamara 1994, Lunz and Stahl 1990, Lunz, Wright and Linacre 1990, Myford and Wolfe 2002) but relatively little that I could find on how characteristics of the rater might have some impact on rating performance (though see Lumley 2000, Lumley and McNamara 1995, McNamara and Lumley 1997, O'Sullivan 1999, 2000a, 2002).

Figure 5.10 Aspects of reliability or measurement validity for speaking

SCORING VALIDITY
• Criteria/rating scale
• Rating procedures
▪ Rater Selection
▪ Rater Training
▪ Standardisation/Accreditation
▪ Rating Decisions
▪ Moderation
▪ Consistency
• Raters
• Grading and Awarding

Source: Weir (2004)

Computers

Another area in which there has been a great amount of interest over the past decade in particular is in the delivery of tests using computers. There are a number of issues here that remain somewhat unexplored. In a debate on the use of computers in language testing at the IATEFL conference in Brighton (O'Sullivan 2003) I talked about the fact that computers are used as part of the developmental process, as a delivery mechanism, and as an analysis tool. The potential of computers to positively impact on test development has been referred to elsewhere (for example Chalhoub-Deville 1999, 2001, Brown 1997), while the growing importance of complex statistical analysis tools (such as G-Theory, Multi-faceted Rasch and other IRT-based procedures) would be inconceivable without computers and the programs that make their application a practical consideration.

It is in the area of test delivery that the impact of computers has been most disappointing. While tests such as BULATS, described in Chapter 1, are at the cutting edge of computer-delivery of language tests, even here there is a tendency to limit the test to items that are reminiscent of the old psychometric–structuralist era, that is the test items tend to focus on discrete decontextualised aspects of language use. In fact, there are very few, if any, examples in the literature of really new or innovative item types. One example of how computer delivery of tests of reading comprehension could add to our understanding of the reading construct is the relative ease of designing delivery platforms that allow for an element of timing of tasks, thus allowing the developer to introduce the concept of expeditious reading (see the following section).

In my conclusion to the IATEFL debate I suggested that as language testers we should not be overly dazzled by the technology and look beneath the delivery mechanisms to the underlying tests. I also argued, perhaps a little unkindly, that the tests delivered using computers represented a step backwards in terms of the approach to testing they typically represent. While many tests clearly fall into this category, there are a small number in which efforts have been made to come to terms with the new technology, though the great leap forward first promised by the introduction of computers has not happened.

In the case of testing language for business purposes, for example, we have seen how technology has had a profound impact on the revision of the test – through the impact of the ALTE 'Can Do' statements' projects (in helping to define the levels of the tests) and in the project undertaken to update the business-related wordlists which help define the language use domain which is tested in the BEC suite (Ball 2002).

However, when we consider the notion of theory-based validity it is obvious that there is a great deal of research needed into the degree to which different test delivery mechanisms (e.g. pencil and paper and computer) impact on the cognitive and meta-cognitive processing of test candidates. In other words, does the platform affect the interactional authenticity of the task? This work has only just begun, with O'Sullivan and Weir (2003) investigating this area in terms of delivering a writing test on computer as compared with the more traditional pencil and paper.

Suggestions for future research in specific skills' testing

In the following section I will outline some of the possible areas for research in the testing of the different skills in the area of business language. In this section I will be referring to the BEC suite. However, I believe that the suggestions will be equally applicable to other test systems.

Reading

While there were relatively few changes made to the Reading papers in this revision, this is not to say that there is no additional work needed in the area. Weir (2004) argues for research into the impact of (and need for) expeditious reading (skimming for gist, search reading or scanning for specifics) on candidate performance and though he was looking at the situation from the perspective of general proficiency testing in the revision of the Cambridge ESOL Certificate of Proficiency in English (CPE), the same argument can be made for LSP tests such as BEC. Before this can begin, it is first necessary to look again at the kind of reading undertaken in the domain of business language through continued investigation using needs' analysis techniques such as observation and interviews. The indications from this book are that we should additionally attempt to investigate the cognitive processing associated with these different activities in order to help us gain evidence of the interactional authenticity of future test versions.

Writing

As we saw in Chapter 4, the section related to the changes in the Writing papers indicated that there have been a number of quite significant changes. These changes include the decision to separate the reading and writing skills in BEC Vantage and Higher, and the choice now offered at BEC Higher for the second writing task. There is also an increase in the length of the required output for the initial writing task at all levels and the use of a common General Impression Mark Scheme (GIMS). This GIMS is interpreted at different performance levels and tied to the Cambridge/ALTE levels.

Obviously all of these changes require monitoring and evaluation. For example, in offering a choice of task to the candidates at BEC Higher it is necessary to establish a systematic framework for ensuring that the choices are likely to be equivalent, to routinely trial these different choices, and to establish monitoring systems to ensure that candidates are not negatively affected by their choice – it is possible, for example, that some choices may be inherently more problematic than others. There is also a clear need to ensure that raters see each task as being equal (through training, monitoring of performance and research). There is evidence from speaking test research (McNamara and Lumley 1997) that raters compensate candidates for what they see as poor performance by examiners where they feel that the candidate has been negatively affected; it is also very much worthwhile exploring the impact on scores of raters' perception of the different writing tasks.

The use of the GIMS at the different test levels is also an interesting development. The difficulty with devising and applying rating scales within a test suite which tests at different levels was briefly discussed above. The solution adapted by Cambridge ESOL for the BEC suite marks an effort to standardise the way in which raters come to decisions at the different levels (a vital element of internal consistency – intra-rater reliability) and moves the focus away from the individual rater to the training and standardisation procedures. There are worries about this approach, however. The argument that a specific purpose test will, by its very definition, involve elements of both language ability and domain ability, implies that any rating scale devised for use in this type of test must include some reference to performance in the domain. The 'strong' view of this argument calls for the sort of indigenous scale developed by Abdul-Raof (2002), and while the BEC tests reviewed here would not appear to justify such a scale (as the test is context-oriented rather than context-focused) it may well be that the existing scale does not capture important elements of the performance in context (i.e. of the business language domain). It is a matter for future research to investigate this aspect of scoring validity.

Another effect of using this type of scale (the GIMS) is that the importance of rater training and standardisation becomes even greater than in the past – as it is vital in this system that raters fully understand the process of applying the same scale at different levels and that they are aware of what constitutes acceptable performance at each level. Since there is evidence that systematic feedback during a rating exercise can have a negative effect on rating performance (O'Sullivan and Rignall 2001, 2002) it might be useful to investigate methods of self-retraining (see Kenyon 1997), using the web. For example the kit developed by the Center for Applied Linguistics (CAL) (CAL 2001) offers an opportunity for raters, working in their own time and place, to gain a detailed understanding of a test and its scoring procedures. Raters can also gain certification from CAL on completion of the training programme through an accreditation procedure where their ratings of a set of test performances are compared to those of a set of 'expert raters'. Since this whole area of rater training is relatively unexplored (though see Weigle 1994, 1998) a systematic agenda for research is clearly needed. This agenda should take into account some or all of the following:

- **the rater** – Are there identifiable characteristics which typify the (un)successful rater? (physical, psychological, experiential, individual)
  Are there identifiable behaviours or strategies which typify the (un)successful rater?

- **the scale** – Are there substantive differences in how different scales are applied? (indigenous vs. linguistic for example)

- **the tasks** – Are there particular task types that are susceptible to bias on the part of raters? If so, how is this manifested?
- **rater training** – In what ways do raters benefit from training? What kind of training is most beneficial? (this refers to mode, format and content)
- **rating conditions** – In what ways can manipulation of rating conditions affect rating performance?
- **standardisation** – Does standardisation of raters work? How long should we claim its effects last? Is there a best method – or are different methods suitable for different types of test?

These are just a few of the many possible questions that could be asked of the whole rating process – I have not included any questions related to the inter-action of some or all of these variables, though obviously this is relevant to any research design.

Listening

Though the Listening papers in the BEC suite were basically unaltered in the revision process, there are some issues that might be investigated.

Weir (2003b:477) refers to an internal report from Cambridge ESOL (Field 2000) in which an argument is made for the use of more explicitly authentic texts in the Cambridge Proficiency in English (CPE). Authenticity appears to be seen by Field as being related to both content and delivery. While authenticity of content is dealt with in the BEC suite in terms of the task types and topics that are designed to reflect the business language use domain, the area of delivery has not really been explored in any depth. Aspects of authenticity such as accent, speed of delivery, 'reality' (the degree to which differences between recorded 'real world' texts and purposefully recorded texts affect the listening process) are all in need of exploration. Listening comprehension tests typically involve both aural and read input. Where alternative visual input is included (drawings, charts, still photographs, moving images) listening will be affected. The issue is how and to what extent. While Coniam (2001) suggests that there is evidence that visuals may detract listeners, in general, there has been very little research into the effect on performance of different types of input or of the effects of involving the listener in dealing with a number of different types of input.

Recent advances in neural science have included the development of brain imaging, a procedure that allow us to see what is actually happening in the brain (in terms of neural activity) when people are engaged in high level cognitive tasks. Just et al (2001) used functional magnetic resonance images of brain activity to investigate how trying to perform two non-related tasks affected performance on the two tasks (sentence comprehension, and the mental rotation of three-dimensional objects). Just et al found that when participants attempted to perform the two tasks simultaneously, they did neither task well. In a similar vein, Rubenstein, Meyer and Evans (2001) found that as the difficulty of tasks increased so did the related time costs (where time is lost in switching from one task to another).

The implication here is that the inclusion of additional input to a listening task essentially adds an element to the task which results in test candidates failing to perform that task to the best of their ability (i.e. where a secondary element is not added). Where this additional input is visual (i.e. it is quite different in nature to the original aural input) the difference may well be exaggerated. This would appear to add support to Skehan's (1998) 'code complexity' idea – where manipulation of input will impact on the difficulty of a task – and also the findings of Coniam (2001).

Buck (2001) suggests that other areas of interest to the researcher might include collaborative listening and the identification of the sub-skills of listening. The former presents particular difficulties for the tester, with the problems of identification of the contribution of individual candidates (always problematic with collaborative tasks), though in the area of business language, there may be an argument for including such a task because this type of listening is quite typical of the area. It may well be that such a task could be positioned within the context of the Speaking paper. There appears to be a danger that tests which are made up of a single type of listening task or item may be focusing on too limited an aspect of an individual's listening ability and as such may not allow us to draw broad inferences on candidates' listening ability. Looking back over the BEC suite Listening papers (Chapter 4) we can see that an attempt has been made to identify different focuses for the different elements of the papers. However, the central focus still appears to be on listening for specific details or for information in a text.

Speaking

This was the most changed section of the BEC suite of examinations and still represents a great challenge to language testers, despite some quite major advances during the past decade. As far back as 1972, a major needs analysis undertaken by the LCCIEB identified speaking as an area of particular interest in business English. This is reflected in the general profusion of Speaking papers or separate tests among the examinations reviewed in Chapter 1 – with the exception of the TOEIC tests. However, many of the Speaking papers reviewed suffer from the same non-business orientation as the original BEC Speaking papers.

We saw in Chapter 4 (Figure 4.15) that different types of task tend to result in quite unique profiles of language functions (O'Sullivan, Weir and Saville 2002). This lends support to the inclusion in a test of speaking of tasks that require the candidate to perform under different conditions, in the case of the revised BEC papers these are one-to-one with the examiner, alone in an individual long turn and in interaction with a second (or third) candidate. A score is awarded to each candidate immediately following the test by both the examiner/interlocutor and the examiner/observer. The fact that a single score is awarded by each examiner means that all tasks are treated as one. This may act to reduce the reliability of the scores and at the same time limit the amount of information available to the test developer. The evidence that there are differences between the tasks could be supported by evidence from examiner scores, at present we cannot distinguish between performance on the different tasks in any post examination review. This is certainly an area in which research is required – into the practicality of awarding scores for individual tasks in operational conditions, into the degree to which each task adds to the overall test performance, and into the perception of task importance by the examiners.

It has been argued (McNamara, 1997) that where candidates interact linguistically in order to perform a test task, the resulting language is a reflection of the ability of all concerned in the interaction, that is, the language is co-constructed by the interacting candidates. The difficulty then is in separating the individual from the group or even in identifying unique contributions to the group, since even these apparently unique contributions will have been influenced by the other group members. There is evidence (O'Sullivan 1999, 2000a, 2000b, 2002a) that the affective reaction of an individual candidate to characteristics associated with their interlocutor can have a systematic and significant impact on subsequent performance. However, the number of potential characteristics, and the interactions between these characteristics, means that the whole area is too complex to be dealt with without a programme of extensive research in which the major characteristics are identified and interactions between these characteristics observed. O'Sullivan (2000a) represents a beginning of this process.

In terms of practicality, we seem to be caught between including tasks which require interaction (and both the candidate-to-candidate discussion and the one-to-one interview are such tasks) or limiting speaking tests to individual monologues – though even here I would argue that there is still an audience (perceived in an audio or video recorded format, actual in a 'live' event) so the potential for impact on performance is still a factor. Clearly then, it is necessary to investigate the impact on performance of factors such as interlocutor variables (e.g. sex or age) and candidate perceptions of the interlocutor/audience (e.g. relative language level, age, personality, status etc.). There is also evidence that the effects on candidate performance may be group or culture specific, for example Porter (1991a) reports that Arabic learners and European learners demonstrate very different behaviours depending on particular characteristics associated with their interviewer. A similar phenomenon was noted also by O'Sullivan (2000a, 2000b, 2002a). This implies that the culture of business language may need to be investigated as a separate entity. Ignoring the impact of audience is simply not an option.

Other immediate concerns include monitoring the new interlocutor frames (or scripts) at the different levels and the output language for the different tasks. In terms of the first of these areas, O'Sullivan and Lu (2003) have analysed deviations from the interlocutor frame in the IELTS and shown that there is little impact on the candidate when pre- and post-deviation language is analysed. This type of research is clearly relevant to the BEC Speaking papers as is the work of O'Sullivan, Weir and Saville (2002) in identifying the language functions elicited by speaking test tasks. Brooks (2003) is demonstrating how the checklists can be adapted for use with a specific test, a process that could quite easily be employed in monitoring the BEC Speaking papers.

Apart from these concerns, there are still many other questions to be answered about tests of speaking. O'Sullivan and Weir (2002) have outlined a broad research agenda based on a socio-cultural perspective on language testing based very much on the type of validation framework outlined in Figure 5.3.

Conclusion

I have tried to demonstrate in this book that tests of language for business purposes are different, in their theoretical basis, their content and their intended audience. I do not believe that I have suggested anything that is completely new about the subject, but hope that I have offered a perspective on business language testing (and LSP testing in general) that is supportable from both practical and theoretical perspectives. The book has added support to a definition of LSP tests presented in terms of authenticity (Douglas 2000), though it has suggested that the way we look at authenticity should be with a greater degree of complexity than hitherto conceived.

All tests can be seen as lying on a specificity continuum, between the highly specific and the general purpose. This continuum is multi-componential and includes the twin aspects of authenticity – situational and interactional. A specific purpose test will be distinguishable from other tests (both specific and general purpose) in terms of the domain represented by the demands of its tasks and texts, and in terms of the cognitive processing it elicits.

The book has presented a broad outline of current theory and practice in the testing of language for business purposes. The description of the test development and revision framework which drives the work of Cambridge ESOL and how this led to particular changes in the BEC suite of examinations demonstrates the necessity for a set of clear and unambiguous developmental procedures. Any LSP, or in this case business language, test development or revision project is dependent on having an understanding of the language use domain to be tested, an awareness of the degree to which authenticity decisions impact on the specificity of the test and the ability to deliver instruments of a high quality.

Appendices

APPENDIX 1.1
JOCT Evaluation Criteria

A+   **Superior Japanese communication skills for a wide variety of business situations:**
In addition to Level A abilities, Level A+ speakers can skilfully summarize their ideas, speak convincingly, pick out essential facts, recognize nuances and generally communicate on superior Levels from both technical and cultural perspectives

A   **Thorough Japanese communication skills for normal business situations:**
Level A speakers correctly use the special terms and expressions of business. Speech is fluid and any mistake in pronunciation or grammar does not create problems. Their skills for handling unfamiliar situations are sufficient, although not complete. Overall, however, they have thorough skills for normal communication using business Japanese.

B+   **Require improvement in selected areas to reach Level A:**
Level B+ speakers can use the special vocabulary and expressions of business, but not as well as Level A speakers and sometimes with inadequacies. Speech is fluid, but occasional mistakes with pronunciation, grammar, etc. can cause problems in communication. They sometimes cannot suitably handle unfamiliar situations.

B   **Require improvement in many areas to reach Level A:**
Level B speakers can generally use the special vocabulary and expressions of business, but inadequacies are quite noticeable compared to Level A speakers. Speech is not always fluid and repeated mistakes with pronunciation and grammar cause communication problems. They often cannot suitably handle unfamiliar situations.

C   **Limited communication skills:**
Level C speakers understand the gist of discussions, but limited knowledge of business vocabulary and expressions, as well as Japanese business itself, prevents them from handling matters suitably. Daily conversations are possible, but their communication lacks smoothness. Mistakes in pronunciation and grammar are frequent.

D   **Insufficient Japanese communication skills for business:**
Level D speakers do not have sufficient skills of comprehension and expression, which prevents them from communicating in Japanese to conduct normal business.

APPENDIX 1.2
CEFLS Pilot Test

SAMPLE SCRIPT ONE

THE ROYAL SOCIETY OF ARTS EXAMINATION BOARD

CERTIFICATE IN ENGLISH AS A FOREIGN LANGUAGE
FOR SECRETARIES

PILOT EXAMINATION MAY 1986

Reading and Writing
Test
Two hours

Please write here:

Your name

The name of your
centre

Your number ...10..........

Centre number

You have ten minutes to read the paper before you begin the
examination.

Dictionaries may be used.

15.

Parker Pen Company Ltd has applied for a stand at the National Exhibition Centre in Birmingham. Read the letter below and complete the tasks on pages 2 and 3.

INTERNATIONAL
SUMMER FAIR
22-26 AUGUST 1986

NATIONAL EXHIBITION CENTRE
BIRMINGHAM B40 INT
Telephone: 021-780-4321
Telex: 536647

Mr W Pointer
Marketing Manager
The Parker Pen Company Limited
Newhaven
East Sussex   BN9 OXU

22 May 1986

Dear Mr Pointer

We are pleased to confirm that you have been allocated Stand No 27, Hall 5 (Open Plan Shell Scheme, 10m^2) for the duration of the International Summer Fair, 22-26 August 1986 at the National Exhibition Centre, Birmingham.

Please note that the balance of £630 is due within 28 days.

We recommend that you complete the enclosed questionnaire to secure valuable advance publicity for your products.

Yours sincerely,

P. WALSH
Reservations Administrator

Encs: 4

17.

You are the secretary to Mr W. Pointer, Marketing Manager at the Parker Pen Company, Newhaven, Sussex. He has left you the following letters and instructions in your in-tray. Complete the tasks using the headed paper provided. Set out the letters and memoranda for typing (i.e. with the appropriate formats, including address, date, etc).

16.

TASK 1

Please complete Section II of this questionnaire for me. The information for Section II is attached and needs to be corrected

QU

RETURN THIS FORM TO:-
Condor Public Relations Ltd.
299 Oxford Street,
London W1R 1LA

AL   36

To obtain maximum publicity in the media, it is in your interests to complete this questionnaire, making it as informative as possible and enclosing appropriate sales leaflets if available, and returning it to:

Condor Public Relations Limited
Press & Publicity Officers
International Spring Fair
299 Oxford Street
London W1R 1LA

COMPANY *The Marker Pen Company Limited*

ADDRESS: *The Marker Pen Company Limited*
Newhaven
East Sussex   BN9 0AU

Hall no. *5*   Stand No. *27*

Executive returning this form: *Mr. W. Pointer*

1: Please enclose brief description of items to be exhibited on your stand, and ten black and white photographs. (10" x 8")

18.

TASK 2

Can you correct the typing mistakes and the omission I've indicated so that it can be typed up.

On display will be our complete range of classic, elegant Fountain Pens, Ball Pens, Roller Ball Pens

x   and Pencils, in gold, silver, chrome and stainless steel, made to the highest standards by our quality

x   craftsmen, and attractively gift-boxed.   *attractively*

All our products - from the 25 Range for discerning

x   young people, to the Premier Range which represents *which*
the pinnacle of Parker design and execution - have

x   tradition, style and modern technology *as usual* *in equal*
proportions.

Also exhibited will be our range of smart, functional

x   Desk Sets and accessories.

In addition, we will feature examples of our Marketing

x   Solutions: the Personalised Parker Pen, complete with its discreet clip or emblem to immortalise a company's

x   name or corporate identity, and engraved initials to

x   flatter the client or recipient. Present, troughout the Exhibition will be our Marketing Solutions Adviser to assist in maximising this intimate approach to

x   advertising.

19.

TASK 3

Re National Exhibition Centre Summer Fair,
could you send separate memos to
a) Accounts Dept. and b) Advertising Section :-
Make sure Mrs Safe sends balance due
(£630) to the N.E.C. a.s.a.p., and that
Peter gets the photos ready (10 of them,
10" x 8", black and white.) Best if
he calls me if he has any queries.
I'd also like Accounts to send me up
a copy of the original invoice from
the N.E.C.

MEMORANDUM

THE PARKER PEN COMPANY LIMITED

TO The Accounts Dept.

FROM Mr W Pointer

DATE 17 May 1986

SUBJECT National Exhibition Centre

Please send me a copy
of the original invoice
from N.E.C. and please
ask Mrs Safe to send
the balance due (£630)
to the N.E.C as soon as
possible.

(W Pointer)

21.

20.

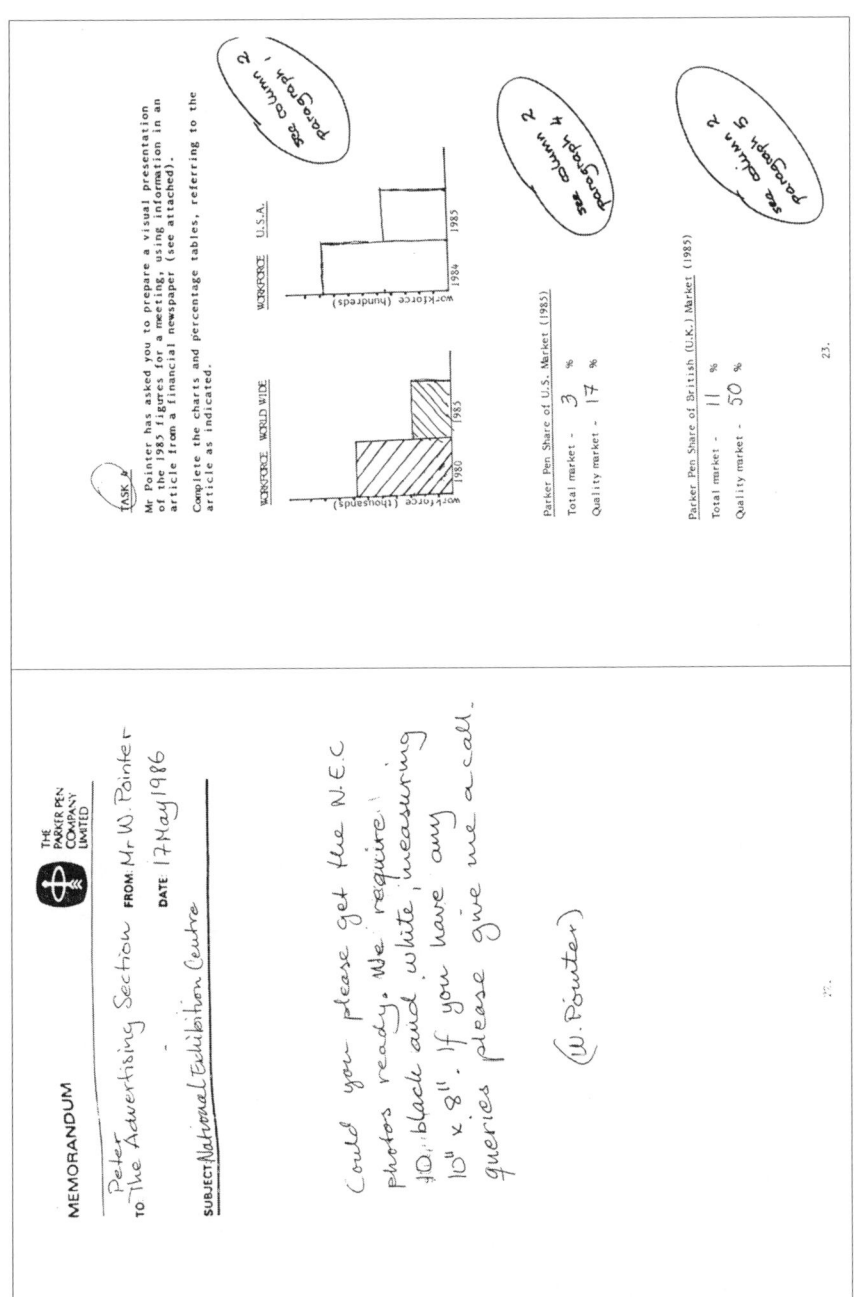

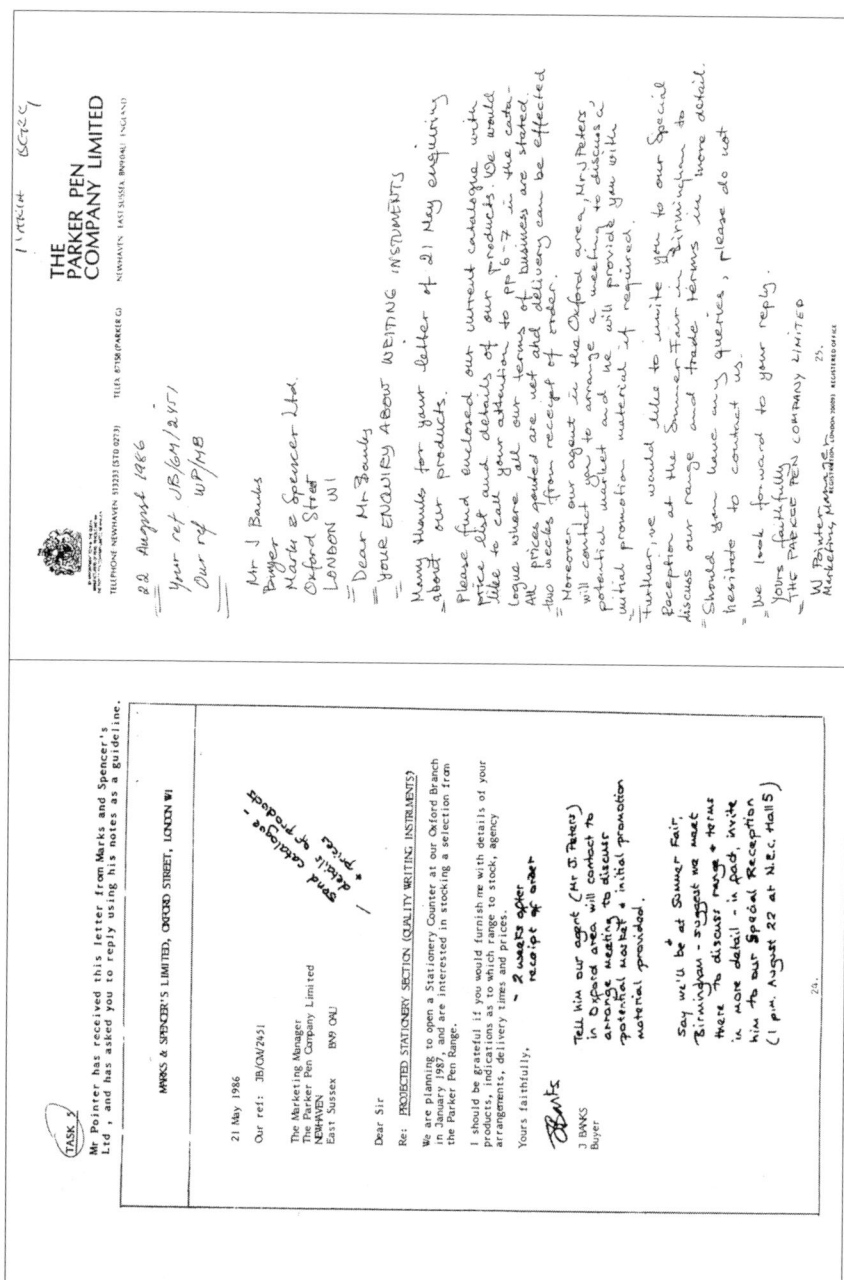

TASK 5

Mr Pointer has received this letter from Marks and Spencer's Ltd, and has asked you to reply using his notes as a guideline.

MARKS & SPENCER'S LIMITED, OXFORD STREET, LONDON W1

21 May 1986

Our ref: JB/CM/2451

The Marketing Manager
The Parker Pen Company Limited
NEWHAVEN
East Sussex BN9 0AU

Dear Sir

Re: PROJECTED STATIONERY SECTION (QUALITY WRITING INSTRUMENTS)

We are planning to open a Stationery Counter at our Oxford Branch in January 1987, and are interested in stocking a selection from the Parker Pen Range.

I should be grateful if you would furnish me with details of your products, indications as to which range to stock, agency arrangements, delivery times and prices.

Yours faithfully,

J BANKS
Buyer

send catalogue of products
detail of prices

- 2 weeks after receipt of order

Tell him our agent (Mr J Peters) in Oxford area will contact to arrange meeting to discuss potential market + initial promotion material provided.

Say we'll be at Summer Fair, Birmingham - suggest we meet there to discuss range + terms in more detail - in pad, invite him to our Special Reception (1 p.m. August 22 at N.E.C. Hall 5)

24.

THE PARKER PEN COMPANY LIMITED

NEWHAVEN EAST SUSSEX BN9 0AU ENGLAND

TELEPHONE NEWHAVEN 513233 (STD 0273)   TELEX 87586 PARKER G

22 August 1986
Your ref JB/CM/2451
Our ref WP/MB

Mr J Banks
Buyer
Marks & Spencer Ltd
Oxford Street
London W1

Dear Mr Banks

YOUR ENQUIRY ABOUT WRITING INSTRUMENTS

Many thanks for your letter of 21 May enquiring about our products.

Please find enclosed our current catalogue with price list and details of our products. We would like to call your attention to pp 6-7 in the catalogue where all our terms of business are stated. All prices quoted are nett and delivery can be effected two weeks from receipt of order.

Moreover our agent in the Oxford area, Mr J Peters will contact you to arrange a meeting to discuss potential market and he will provide you with initial promotion material if required.

Further, we would like to invite you to our Special Reception at the Summer Fair in Birmingham to discuss our range and trade terms in more detail. Should you have any queries, please do not hesitate to contact us.

We look forward to your reply.

Yours faithfully
THE PARKER PEN COMPANY LIMITED
W Pointer
Marketing Manager

25.

M.GF 6

Spoke to John Peters on the phone this morning, and arranged to meet him at 10.30 in the Cavendish Hotel, London next Friday morning, before he meets the Buyer from Marks and Spencer's.

Could you write a letter to confirm this (J. Peters, 18 Walnington Road, Oxford OX2 1PB) and send him a copy of the M. & S. letter.

Also ask him to get together a report on other outlets in Oxford and within a 20 mile radius.

I'll be in at 4.30 to sign it.

26.

THE PARKER PEN COMPANY LIMITED

NEWHAVEN, EAST SUSSEX BN9 0AU, ENGLAND

TELEPHONE NEWHAVEN 515233 (STD 0273)   TELEX 87586(PARKER G)

24 May 1986

Mr J. Peters
18 Walnington Road
OXFORD
OX2 1PB

Dear Mr Peters

CONFIRMATION OF OUR MEETING

With reference to our telephone conversation earlier this morning, I am pleased to confirm the arranged meeting at the Cavendish Hotel in London on Friday 29 May at 10.30.

Enclosed please find a copy of the letter from Marks & Spencer of 21 March.

Please put together a report on other outlets in Oxford and within a 20 mile radius.

I look forward to seeing you

Yours sincerely

W Pointer

REGISTRATION: LONDON 286091 REGISTERED OFFICE: NEWHAVEN, EAST SUSSEX, BN9 0AU

27.

TASK 7

Please telex Metropole Hotel, Birmingham and book me a single room for the duration of the Fair in Birmingham

---

21 Thursday — Sales meeting 12pm The Strand
Euston → Birmingham 17.30-18.50

22 Friday — N.E.C. Summer Fair 9am
(Special reception 1pm Hall 5)

23 Saturday — N.E.C.
(Rep. from Wales 3.30-5ish)

24 Sunday — N.E.C.
(Testifying?)

25 Monday — N.E.C.

26 Tuesday — N.E.C. (End 17.30)
(Accessorial meeting; Good night. Birmingham at 20)

27 Wednesday — Birmingham → Euston (10.33-12.00)

TELEX MESSAGE

35802 BIRMET
87158 PARKER G

PLEASE ARRANGE ACCOMMODATION FOR MR POINTER, ONE SINGLE ROOM WITH BATH FROM 21 AUGUST TO 27 AUGUST PLEASE CONFIRM ASAP. THANKS N BERG, M.A.

28.

APPENDIX 1.3
CEIBT – Test of Reading and Writing – June and November 1992

0208/1   **JUNE**

CERTIFICATE IN ENGLISH
FOR
INTERNATIONAL BUSINESS AND TRADE

TEST OF READING AND WRITING

JUNE 1992

RSA EXAMINATIONS BOARD
UNIVERSITY OF CAMBRIDGE LOCAL EXAMINATIONS SYNDICATE

Time allowed – Two hours

You are also allowed 10 minutes to read the paper.

Please write below:

Your name.. Your number ....

The name of your centre... Centre number ....

Write in ink or ballpoint.
Answer all the questions.
Write the answers to the questions in this answer booklet.

You may use a dictionary.

For Office Use

SB (A)
© R.S.A./U.C.L.E.S. 1992

[**Turn over**

Appendix 1.3

2

BLANK PAGE

3

INFORMATION PAGE

The examination is based on Willoughby Stewart Advertising (WSA), an advertising agency in the south of England. The company has many international clients, including some well-known yacht manufacturers and suppliers.

Don't worry if you know nothing about advertising. We are only testing your English, not your knowledge of this particular business.

You work for WSA in Ringwood, England. WSA plans and administers advertising campaigns and controls the whole process from the original ideas to the final advertisements in the press, in magazines, on street posters and in radio commercials.

WSA has its own photographic studio and graphics department but sends material to outside printers to be printed ready for publication in magazines and trade journals.

Following the instructions and handwritten notes, complete the tasks using the headed paper provided. Write the letters, fax and reports in the appropriate formats, including address, date etc. when necessary. Use your own name to sign the letters, fax etc.

[Turn over

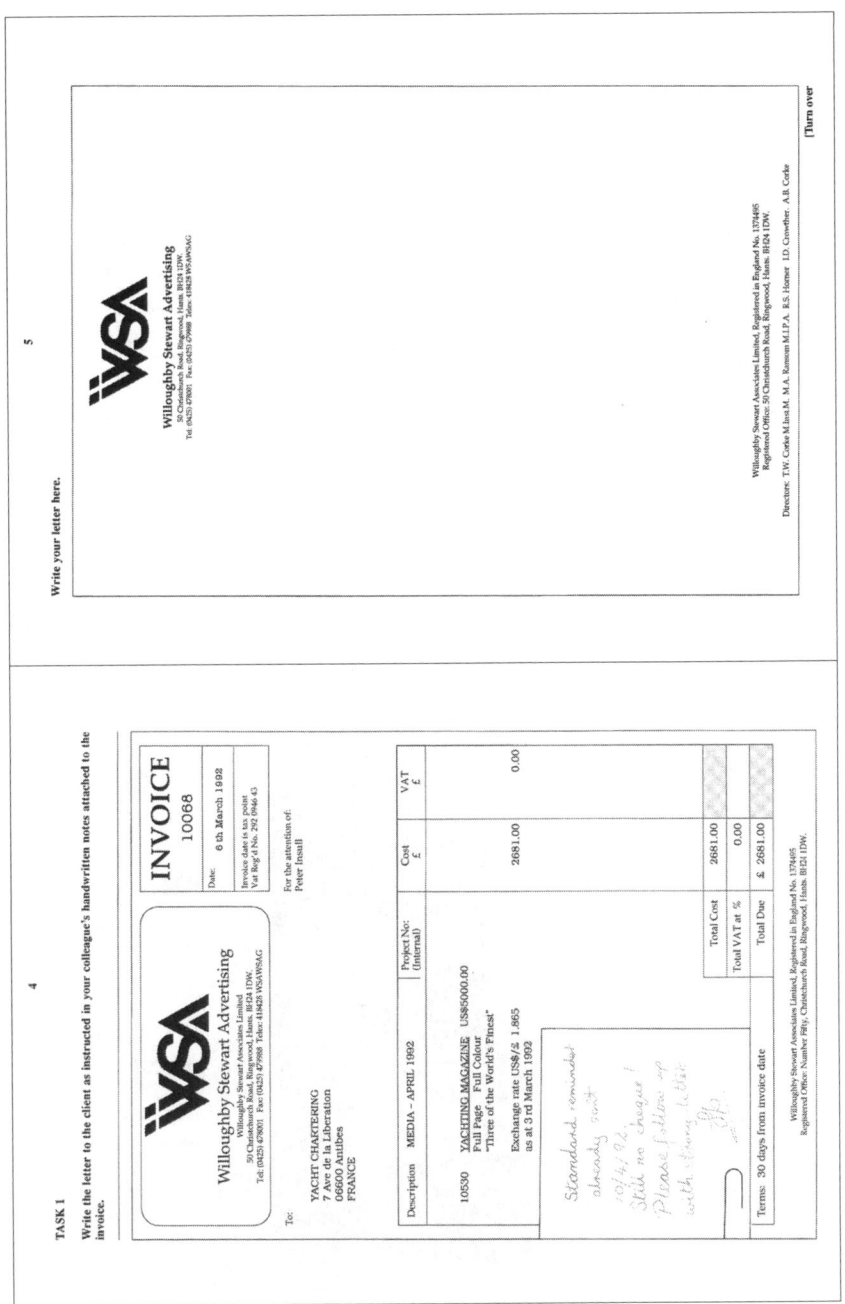

[Turn over

Write your letter here.

Willoughby Stewart Advertising
50 Christchurch Road, Ringwood, Hants. BH24 1DW
Tel (0425) 470001 Fax (0425) 470008 Telex 418428 WSAWSAG

Willoughby Stewart Associates Limited, Registered in England No. 1374495
Registered Office: 50 Christchurch Road, Ringwood, Hants. BH24 1DW.

Directors: T.W. Corke M.Inst.M. M.A. Ransom M.I.P.A. R.S. Horner I.D. Crowther. A.B. Corke

---

TASK 1

Write the letter to the client as instructed in your colleague's handwritten notes attached to the invoice.

Willoughby Stewart Advertising
Willoughby Stewart Associates Limited
50 Christchurch Road, Ringwood, Hants. BH24 1DW
Tel (0425) 470001 Fax (0425) 470008 Telex 418428 WSAWSAG

INVOICE
10068

Date: 6 th March 1992

Invoice date is tax point
Vat Reg'd No. 292 0946 43

To:

YACHT CHARTERING
7 Ave de la Liberation
06600 Antibes
FRANCE

For the attention of:
Peter Insull

Description		Project No: (Internal)	Cost £	VAT £
MEDIA - APRIL 1992				
10530	YACHTING MAGAZINE US$5000.00 Full Page Full Colour "Three of the World's Finest"			
	Exchange rate US$/£ 1.865 as at 3 rd March 1992		2681.00	0.00
		Total Cost	2681.00	
		Total VAT at %	0.00	
		Total Due	£ 2681.00	

Terms: 30 days from invoice date

Standard reminder already sent
10/4/92.
Still no cheque!
Please follow up
with strong letter

Willoughby Stewart Associates Limited, Registered in England No. 1374495
Registered Office: Number Fifty, Christchurch Road, Ringwood, Hants. BH24 1DW.

7

Write your fax here.

Willoughby Stewart Advertising

Willoughby Stewart Associates Limited
50 Christchurch Road, Ringwood, Hants. BH24 1DW.
Tel: (0425) 478001 Fax: (0425) 479988 Telex: 418428 WSAWSAG

FAX MESSAGE

JOB No:

FAX TO:

FAX No:

DATE:

SUBJECT

FAX FROM:

RETURN FAX No: (0425) 479988

SHEETS TO FOLLOW:

IN CASE OF QUERIES ON TRANSMISSION TELEPHONE (0425) 478001

[Turn over]

6

TASK 2

Read the memorandum, correct the 7 errors of spelling in the text of the advertisement proof below and write the fax to be sent with it to the printers (Colthouse Repro Limited, 37 Denmark Road, Bournemouth, Dorset. Fax No. 0202 486302).

M E M O R A N D U M

Job No: 813/6/92

Can you correct the errors on the advertisement proof and write a fax to the printers indicating a change in the deadline (now 15 June, not 22 June) and explaining how we want to alter the layout (see attached advertisement).

Thanks

Trafford

A weekend with the boys.

Sailing means different things to different people. Some sail for the challenge and excitement. Other sail to escape to a word of peace and relaxation. Many do both.

It is for them that we designed the Sigma range – yachts with a dual personality, to satisfy both sides of a sailors nature.

Take the new 35. In Championship Races she's right at home – fast, exciting and highly competitive.

But when you feel like enjoying a gentle cruise with the family, the 35, like the other Sigmas, reveals the other side of her character – docile, comfortable, capable and fully equiped.

Which ever Sigma you choose – the 38 OOD, the new 35 club racer, or the ever popular 33 OOD – you'll won twice the boat ... and have twice the fun.

LONDON BOAT SHOW STAND 64B

33 OOD   35   38 OOD

SIGMA

please underline.

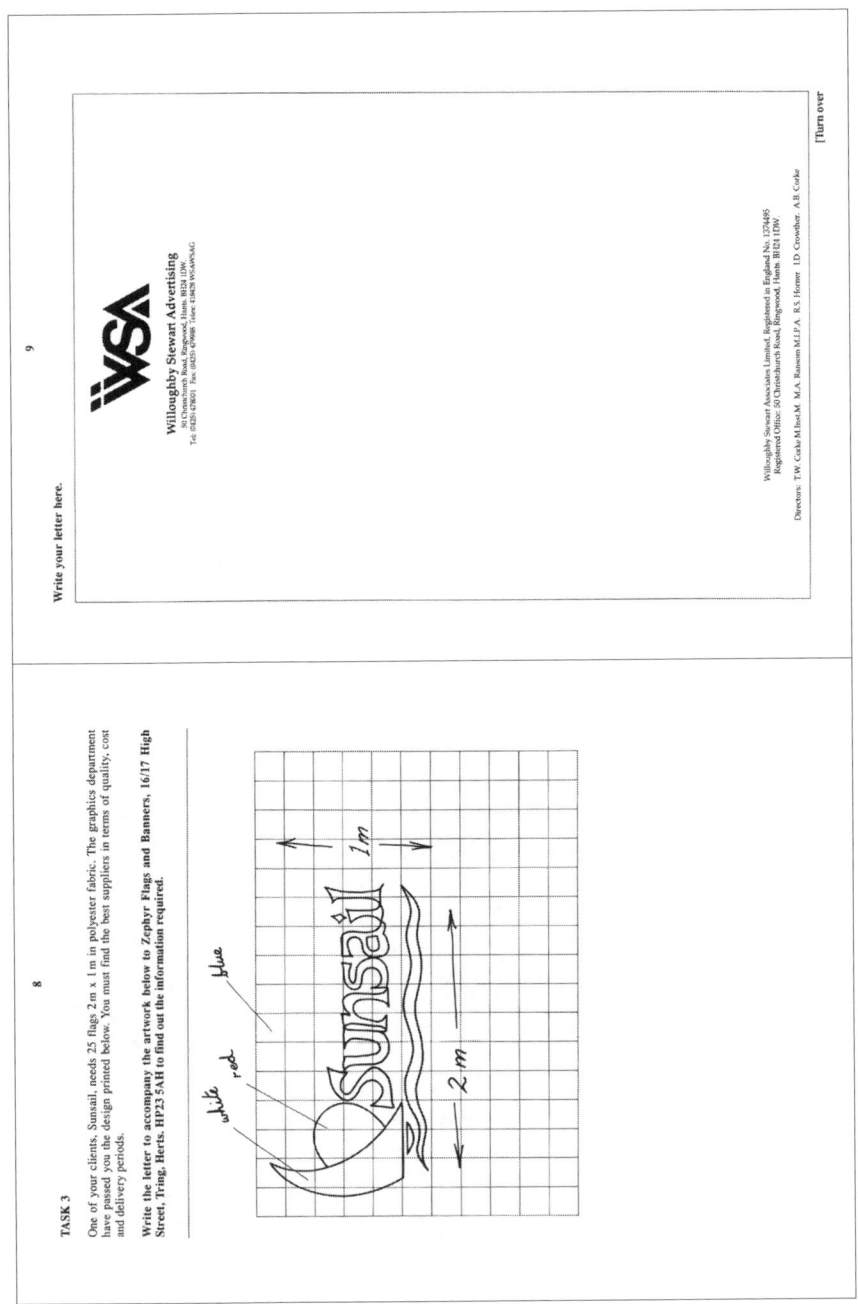

8

TASK 3

One of your clients, Sunsail, needs 25 flags 2 m x 1 m in polyester fabric. The graphics department have passed you the design printed below. You must find the best suppliers in terms of quality, cost and delivery periods.

Write the letter to accompany the artwork below to Zephyr Flags and Banners, 16/17 High Street, Tring, Herts. HP23 5AH to find out the information required.

9

Write your letter here.

Willoughby Stewart Advertising

Willoughby Stewart Associates Limited. Registered in England No. 1376495
Registered Office: 50 Christchurch Road, Ringwood, Hants. BH24 1DW

Directors: T.W. Cocke M.Inst.M. M.A. Ransom M.I.P.A. R.S. Horner I.D. Crowther. A.B. Corke

[Turn over

10

TASK 4

Your company is considering recommending to a client that he should combine his proposed radio commercial with a poster campaign.

Read the article below and write a report for the client summarising the advantages of billboards or posters and the recent improvements in this form of advertising.

You should write no more than 120 words.

Posters make the message stick

A 90-SECOND television advert is at the heart of oil company Texaco's £4m "Children should be seen and not hurt" road safety campaign in which more than four million reflective stickers are being distributed free from the company's service stations.

But television is not the only medium being used by Texaco to carry its message to the public. The TV commercial, first shown last month, is being backed up by a nationwide poster campaign – and to good effect, according to Texaco.

The oil company's co-ordinator of corporate advertising, Maria Miller, attributes part of the campaign's success to billboards. "For us posters were an extremely relevant place to talk about road safety," she says. "We used television to give depth to that message."

Robert Ray, a media planner with D'Arcy Masius Benton & Bowles, the advertising agency handling the Texaco account, agrees. "Television is obviously a very powerful medium. But you can extend the period of visibility and public awareness levels by dovetailing a poster campaign on to a television campaign. It makes a very public statement."

Outdoor advertising is relatively cheap. A two-week nationwide billboard campaign covering 1,200 sites costs about £500,000. By comparison, television companies would demand £20,000 for a 30-second slot on primetime television.

According to the Outdoor Advertising Association, there are about 126,000 poster sites in Britain. The largest are the 48ft by 10ft "supersites", or 96-sheet panels, usually found in city centres. The smallest are the four-sheet panels which adorn thousands of bus-shelters around the country.

Despite the number of sites, the industry took only a small portion of the £8.3 billion spent on advertising last year. Television accounted for £3.2 bn. But for the past 10 years the billboard industry's share of the advertising cake, taking inflation into account, has remained static at about 4 per cent.

Richard Hearne, director of marketing at Arthur Maiden, the country's second largest outdoor advertising contractor, which last year reported a turnover of £23.3 m, admits the industry's expansion has been hampered by its "bucket and paste image".

Before 1985 it was unable to give advertisers any qualitative or quantitative research. Television, for example, has both and newspapers have Jicnars, both systems which give socio-economic breakdowns of relative audiences. In 1985, the industry adopted Outdoor Site Classification and Research (Oscar).

"We've become more market oriented, we're getting out there and selling the medium," says Mr Hearne, who believes the industry should be looking for 1 per cent growth. "That may seem small, but it would bring in an extra £67 m," he says.

The possibility of further restrictions on tobacco advertising, which accounts for about 20 per cent of the market, may make expansion difficult. But the industry believe that in Britain growth can be achieved in a number of areas such as finance and leisure.

In addition there is the chance of limited growth in Eastern Europe. Maiden launched the first poster sites in Moscow earlier this year, other sites have been unveiled in the Czech capital, Prague, and the company is hoping to move into Hungary.

The industry has also spruced up its image. Nigel Mansell, a director of Concord Posterlink, a company which rents sites for clients, such as Rover and Nationwide Anglia, says the number of poster sites has declined but the quality has improved.

Perhaps the most eye-catching are the Ultravision billboards which revolve to show three different ads.

Mr Mansell, whose company had a billings turnover of £42.5 m last year, points out that spring will see the introduction of two-week minimum campaigns as an industry standard.

He forecasts that this should bring lower entry costs and attract new advertisers. The boardings companies are also moving towards shorter billposting times.

Once large-scale poster campaigns could take over a week to get in place, now the large companies can guarantee sites will be ready within 24 to 48 hours.

On the road: Texaco believes its billboard poster campaign has helped get the safety message across

© The Independent 1991

11

Write your report here.

REPORT

Subject _____

[Turn over

BLANK PAGE

TASK 5

The letter below to Mr Smith is from one of WSA's clients. Mr Smith is on holiday until 25 June.

Basing your argument on the information in the bar chart and figures printed on page 14, write the reply trying to persuade the client not to reduce advertising expenditure, and suggest a meeting to discuss ways you can help him.

L.V. Motors Ltd., 1 Royston Rd., Baldock, Herts. SG7 6NT

Tel: (0462) 896095
Fax: (0462) 894018

Mr. T. Smith,
Willoughby Stewart Advertising,
50 Christchurch Road,
Ringwood,
Hants.
BH24 1DW

20 May 1992.

Dear Mr Smith,

Due to the current economic climate affecting our line of business and the subsequent fall in profits over the past few months, we have decided to cut back on our advertising in order to reduce our overall expenditure.

We feel that you have worked hard for us and it is with great regret that we are obliged to suspend for the time being any further advertisements after the present contract terminates at the end of June.

We hope that this situation is only temporary, and look forward to resuming the campaign at a later date.

Yours sincerely,

P Hart

P Hart
Marketing Manager

[Turn over

Appendix 1.3

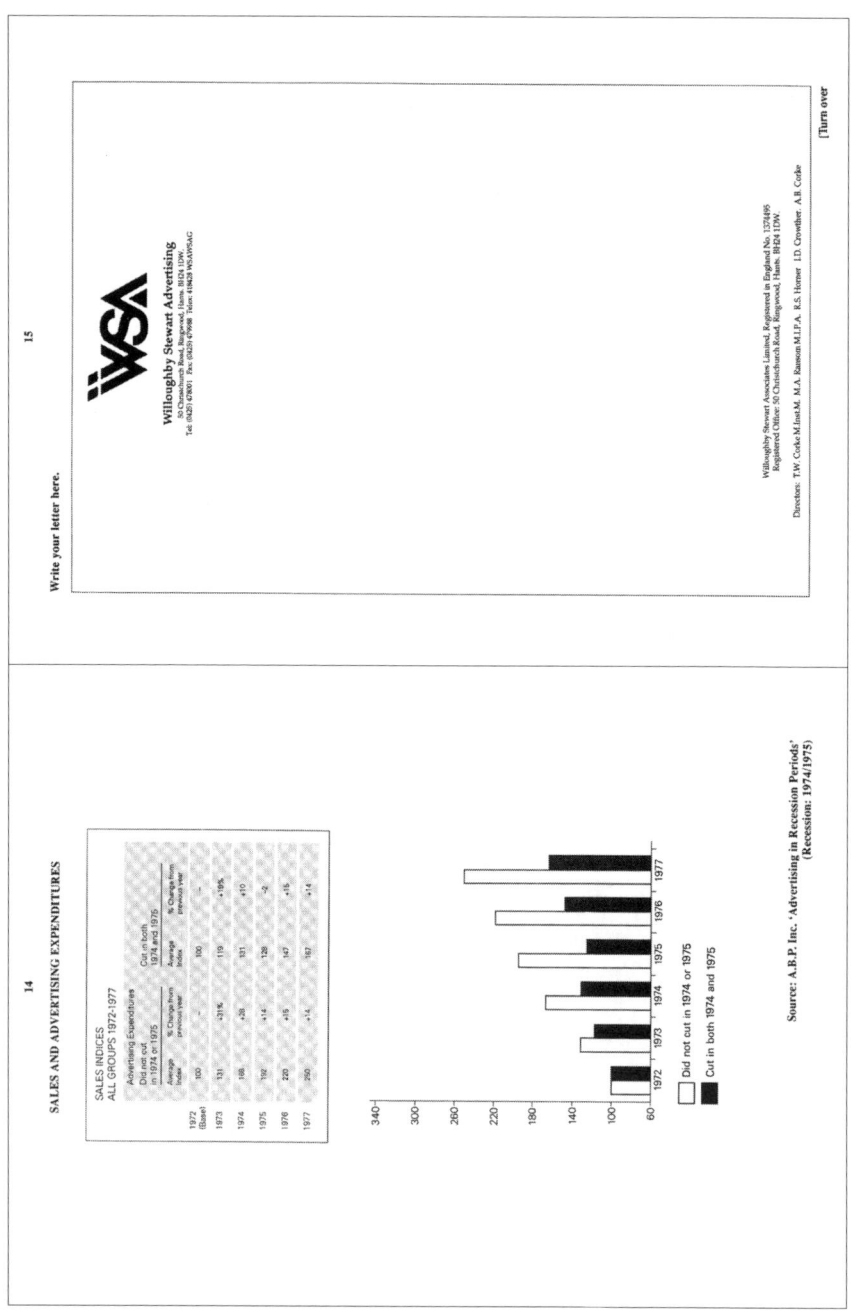

212

16

BLANK PAGE

17

TASK 6

You are attending a Marketing Seminar tomorrow, but still have some work outstanding from today.

Look at the material below and on page 18. Then write a note to your assistant identifying the action you want taken in each case.

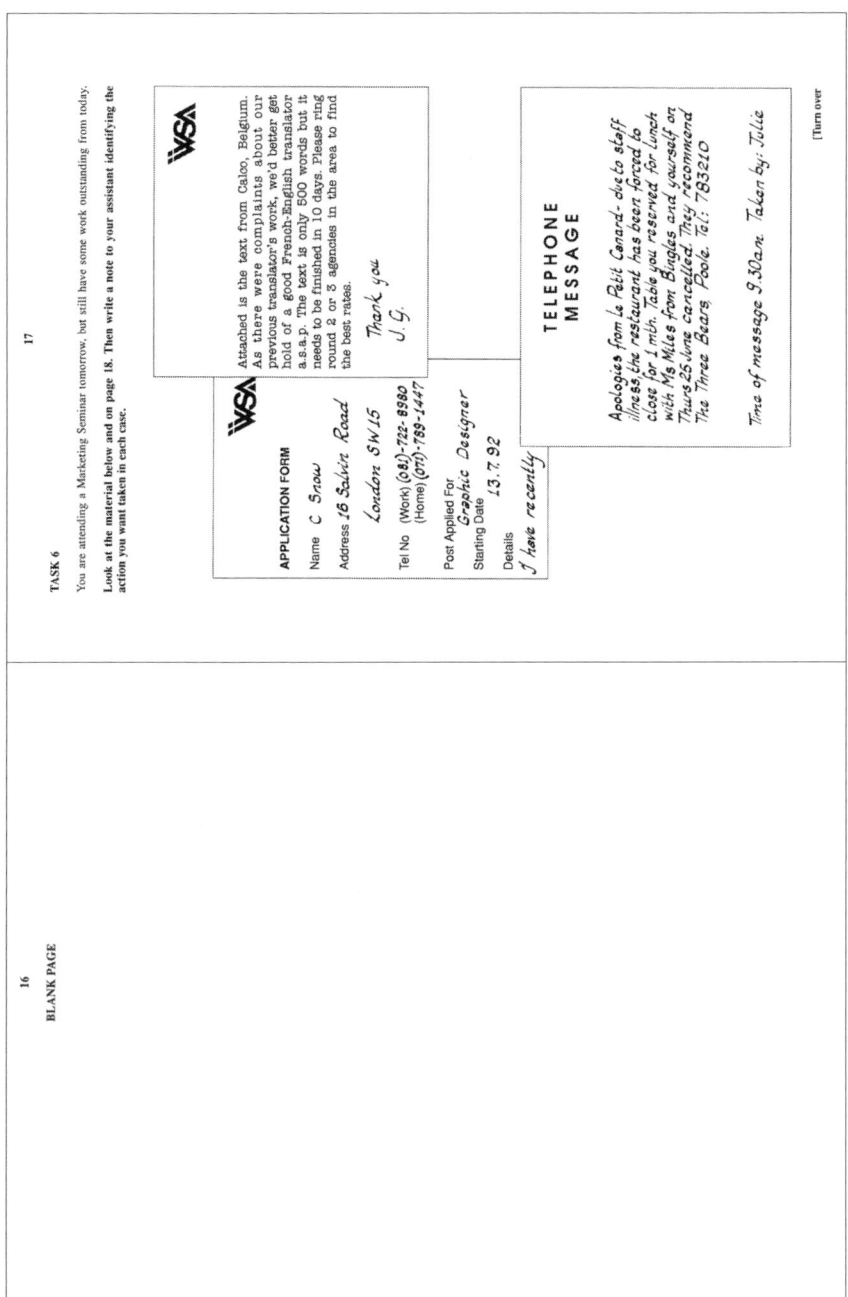

WSA

Attached is the text from Caloo, Belgium. As there were complaints about our previous translator's work, we'd better get hold of a good French-English translator a.s.a.p. The text is only 500 words but it needs to be finished in 10 days. Please ring round 2 or 3 agencies in the area to find the best rates.

Thank you
J. G.

WSA

APPLICATION FORM

Name   C   Snow

Address   16 Salvin Road

  London SW15

Tel No   (Work) (081)-722-8980
  (Home) (071)-789-1447

Post Applied For   Graphic Designer

Starting Date   13.7.92

Details   I have recently

TELEPHONE MESSAGE

Apologies from La Petit Canard - due to staff illness, the restaurant has been forced to close for 1 mth. Table you reserved for lunch with Ms Miles from Biogles and yourself on Thurs 25 June cancelled. They recommend The Three Bears, Poole. Tel: 783210

Time of message 9.30 a.m. Taken by: Julie

[Turn over]

213

18

THE SELWYN PRESS Tel: (0284) 762201 Fax: (0284) 764033
Unit 6, Grantly Estate, Upton, Wiltshire WS7 4SX

12 May 1992

WSA
50 Christchurch Road
Ringwood
Hants

Dear Sirs

We are a national thermographic printing company and have recently opened an office in your area.

We offer a top quality, reliable and confidential trade service at rates you will find difficult to believe possible.

Should you wish to see our brochure and price list, please complete the slip below.

Yours faithfully

D. Mall

D Mall
Production Manager

Please send a copy of your brochure and price list.

Company Name .... Contact Name ....

Company Address ....

MEMORANDUM   WSA

This is to confirm that we should now issue press orders to 'Motor Boat' and 'Yachting' for the inside front cover that will be required to appear in the August issues, at a cost of £6,000 (less agency commission).

Many thanks

C.g.

19

Write your note here.

Action

WSA

Willoughby Stewart Advertising
50 Christchurch Road, Ringwood, Hants. BH24 1DW.
Tel: (0425) 478001 Fax: (0425) 479988 Telex: 418428 WSAWSAG

Willoughby Stewart Associates Limited, Registered in England No. 1374495
Registered Office: 50 Christchurch Road, Ringwood, Hants. BH24 1DW.

Directors: T.W. Corke M.Inst.M. M.A. Ransom M.I.P.A. R.S. Horner I.D. Crowther A.R. Corke

0208/1   **NOV**

CERTIFICATE IN ENGLISH
FOR
INTERNATIONAL BUSINESS AND TRADE

TEST OF READING AND WRITING

NOVEMBER 1992

RSA EXAMINATIONS BOARD
UNIVERSITY OF CAMBRIDGE LOCAL EXAMINATIONS SYNDICATE

Time allowed — Two hours

You are also allowed 10 minutes to read the paper.

Please write below

Your name ....   Your number ....

The name of your centre ....   Centre number ....

Write in pen or biro **not** pencil.
Answer all the questions.
Write the answers to the questions in this answer booklet.

You may use a dictionary.

FOR OFFICE USE
TOTAL =

MML 115410 3/92
                                        [Turn over

3

INFORMATION PAGE

The examination is based on the Aerospace Group of Rolls-Royce plc. The Aerospace Group designs, develops, manufactures and provides technical back-up for engines in civil and military aircraft throughout the world.

Throughout this part of the examination you work in the Technical Sales Department which is part of the Marketing organisation. It provides and presents all the technical information required by Rolls-Royce's customers.

Don't worry if you know nothing about the industry. We are only testing your English, not your knowledge about this particular type of business.

Follow the instructions and handwritten notes and complete the tasks using the headed paper provided. Write the letters, memoranda etc. in the appropriate formats including address, date etc. when necessary. Use your own name to sign the letters when appropriate.

[Turn over

2

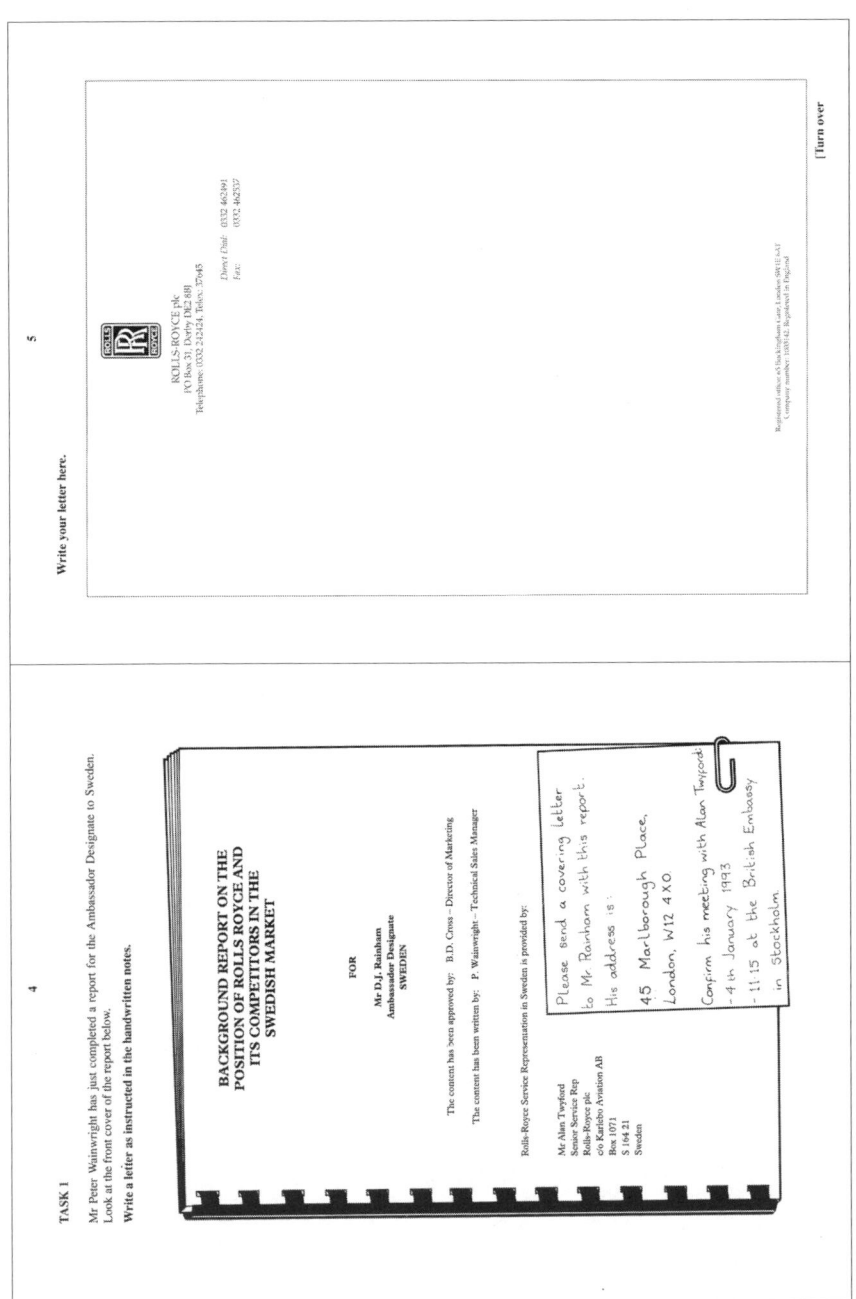

4

TASK 1

Mr Peter Wainwright has just completed a report for the Ambassador Designate to Sweden.
Look at the front cover of the report below.

Write a letter as instructed in the handwritten notes.

BACKGROUND REPORT ON THE POSITION OF ROLLS ROYCE AND ITS COMPETITORS IN THE SWEDISH MARKET

FOR

Mr D.J. Rainham
Ambassador Designate
SWEDEN

The content has been approved by: B.D. Cross – Director of Marketing

The content has been written by: P. Wainwright – Technical Sales Manager

Rolls-Royce Service Representation in Sweden is provided by:

Mr Alan Twyford
Senior Service Rep
Rolls-Royce plc
c/o Karlsbo Aviation AB
Box 11071
S 104 21
Sweden

Please send a covering letter
to Mr Rainham with this report.

His address is:

45 Marlborough Place,
London, W12 4XO

Confirm his meeting with Alan Twyford
- 4th January 1993
- 11.15 at the British Embassy
in Stockholm

5

Write your letter here.

ROLLS-ROYCE plc
PO Box 31, Derby DE2 8BJ
Telephone: 0332 242424, Telex: 37645

Direct Dial: 0332 462391
Fax: 0332 462557

Registered office at Moor Lane, Derby. Registered in England
Company number: 1003142. Registered in England

[Turn over

217

7

TASK 2

Look at the fax below. Using the various office files for information, reply to Aircraft Powerplant by fax.

FAX MESSAGE

Aircraft Powerplant
Charlesville, U.S.A.

Fax: (816) 553-2549

To: Peter Wainwright
Technical Sales Manager
Rolls Royce plc

From: Wain Baker
Date: 20 November 1992

Fax No: 0044 332 462537

No. of Pages: 1

---

1. Re: your fax of 10 November. Can we send a second engineer on the upcoming course?

2. Have mislaid Service Bulletins RR 2450 and RR 2452. Please send one copy of each a.s.a.p.

3. Do you have maintenance cost prediction on SS5E4 yet? Understand this being published middle of this month.

Thanks for prompt servicing of turbine discs, this is an excellent new facility.

Regards

Wain

PLEASE OPEN OUT

FOR TASK 2.

6

218

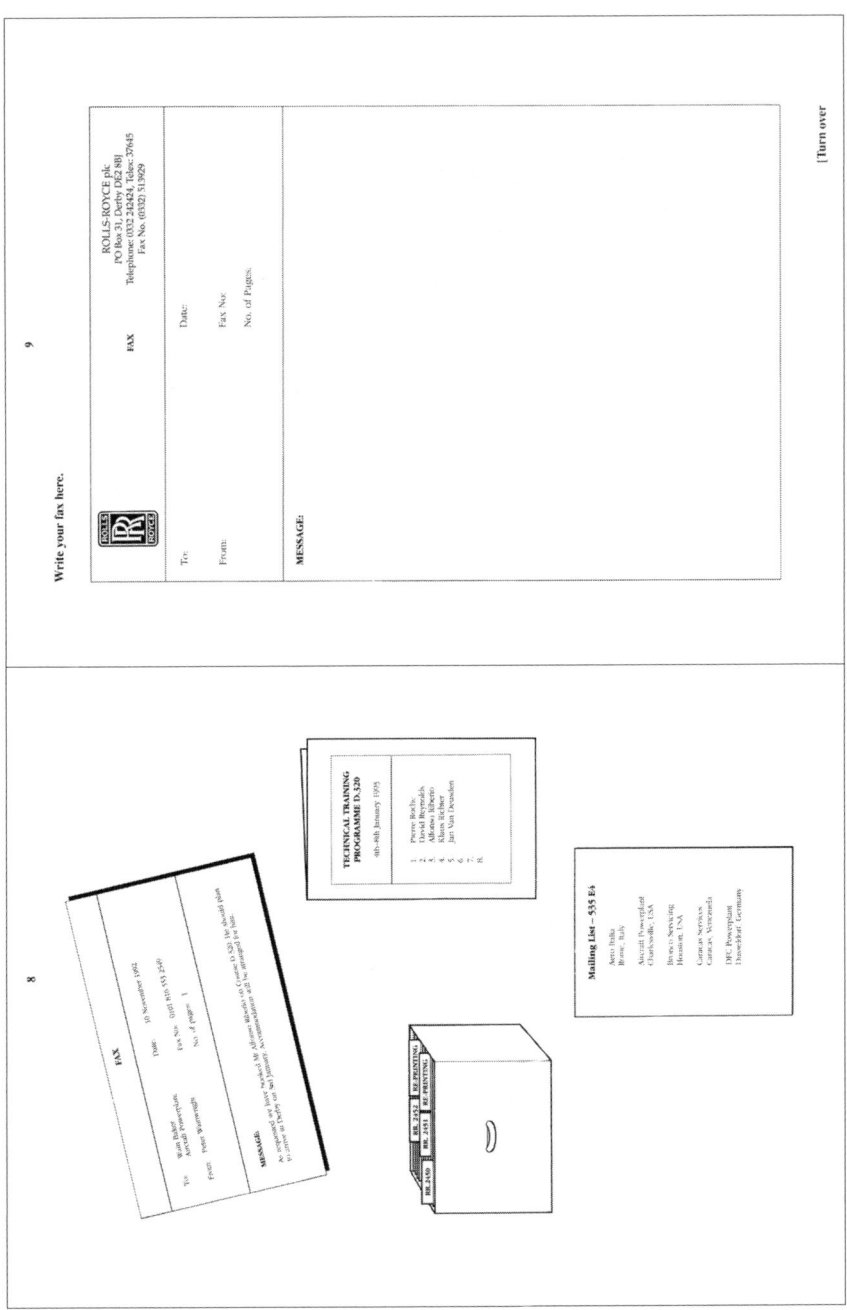

9

Write your fax here.

FAX

ROLLS-ROYCE plc
PO Box 31, Derby DE2 8BJ
Telephone: 0332 242424, Telex: 37645
Fax No. (0332) 51.9929

To:

From:

Date:

Fax No:

No. of Pages:

MESSAGE:

[Turn over

8

FAX

To: Wim Baker
Aerhub Powersytem

From: Peter Wearmouth

Date: 30 November 1992

Fax No: 0.05 835 553 2549

No. of pages: 1

MESSAGE:

**TECHNICAL TRAINING
PROGRAMME D.320**

4th–8th January 1995

1. Pierre Roche
2. David Reynolds
3. Alfonso Alberto
4. Klaus Richter
5. Jan Van Deusden
6.
7.
8.

Mailing List – 535 E4

Aero Italia
Brense, Italy

Aircraft Powersystent
Charlesville, USA

Brenco Servicing
Houston, USA

Caracas Services
Caracas, Venezuela

DFC Powerplant
Dusseldorf, Germany

RR 2450   RR 2451   RE PRINTING   RE PRINTING

TASK 3

Look at the fax and the memo from P. Wainwright below, together with the newspaper article on page 11. Then write a letter in reply.

FAX 010 44 678 9501   DATE 20.11.92

TO: Mr Peter Wainwright
Technical Sales Manager
Rolls Royce Derby

From: Martha Semeidei   –   University of Hamburg
Engineering Department

It was a pleasure to meet you at the conference last week. Your presentation was very interesting. I am bringing a group of students over at the beginning of February and we would very much like to visit the Rolls-Royce Technology Exhibition which you mentioned. Monday, 10th February would be the most convenient for us.

In order to be able to brief the students, could you confirm when and why the Technology Exhibition was set up, the different locations and the aims and format of the exhibition.

INTERNAL MEMO

To: Technical Sales Department

From: Peter Wainwright

Date   20.11.92.

Please reply to Mrs Semeidei on my behalf and confirm that I'll be happy to show her and her group round the Derby Technology Exhibition on 10th Feb. Suggest she arrives around 10 o'clock and ask her if she wants to visit the other centres. Please reply to her questions about the exhibition. If you look at that recent newspaper article, that'll help you to give her a short summary.

TECHNOLOGY REPORT

Expertise on Display

TINY high-tech disc is shown to visitors

The Technology Exhibition builds fine reputations

YEARS ago Rolls-Royce could be criticised, quite fairly, for keeping too quiet about its achievements and its technology.

By John Hutchinson

The Company seemed shy to sell itself on one of its greatest assets, its technical prowess.

The changes of the 1980s have swept away most of that modesty. Reticence about technical achievement has been replaced by the realisation that the skills and inventiveness of Rolls-Royce is employees, properly displayed, make a most influential selling point for Rolls-Royce products.

Nowhere can this new pride in people's achievements be seen to better effect than in Rolls-Royce's Technology Exhibition.

At Derby, Leavesden and Bristol, the three permanent displays that comprise the technology exhibition prove to the outside world that Rolls-Royce is developing and exploiting profitable new techniques to keep the company and its customers ahead of the competition.

"Technology exhibition" may be a dull-sounding title, but the idea soon as you set foot in one of its three guided around the test locations.

Remarkable recent developments in gas turbine technology are shown in a variety of ways: models, graphs, pictures, captions, charts, holograms, and real hardware that you can touch.

"It's an Aladdin's Cave of technology," enthuses Graham Ryder, manager of the Bristol-based exhibition.

"We've had thousands of visitors – customers, potential customers, collaborative partners, government agencies and so on – and most of them have gone away with a new perception of Rolls-Royce.

The idea of a permanent, ever-changing technology exhibition emerged in the 1970s and became reality in the early 1980s.

"Visitors used to be beds, production shops, development areas and so on," explains Graham.

"But, because of the commitment to prod-

uction and development, particular components weren't always available for viewing.

"So top management decided to go for the technology exhibition plan, in which the company's current technological capabilities could be displayed in a clear and professional fashion under a single roof at the main civil, military and small engine factories.

Bristol's display opened in cramped conditions back in 1982 and two years later moved to its current location in Patchway House.

Derby's exhibition was set up in Moor Lane, near the main engineering block, and

Leavesden's display established itself in the laboratory area.

The three individual displays highlight the work of their respective locations while reminding visitors of Rolls-Royce's overall technical abilities. The three displays use a common format, reflecting the depth of thought and planning that has gone into each one.

Rolls-Royce's exhibitions department under Derrick Green has been involved from the start and its ultra-professional approach to the need of getting a clear message across is the key to the technology exhibition's continuing success.

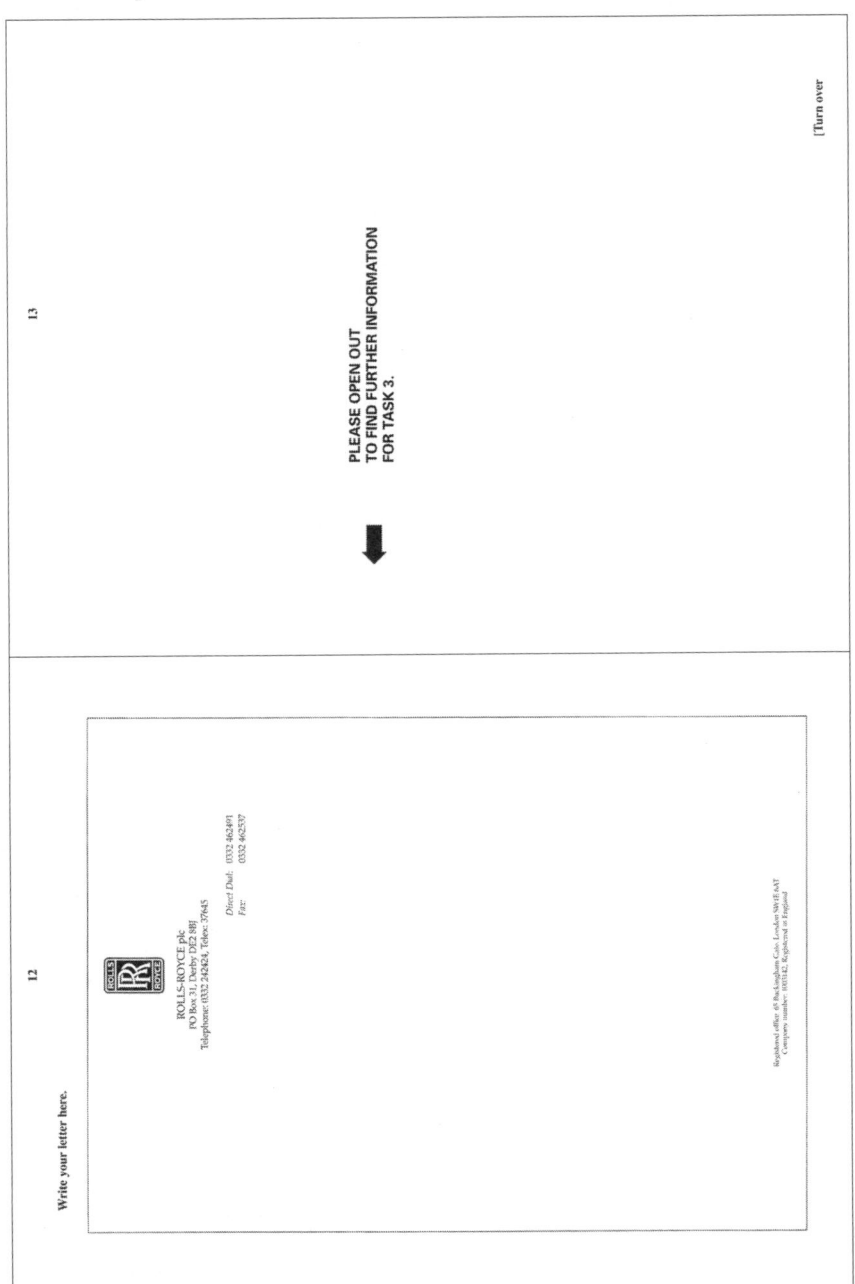

12

Write your letter here.

ROLLS-ROYCE plc
PO Box 31, Derby DE2 8BJ
Telephone: 0332 242424, Telex: 37645

Direct Dial: 0332 462491
Fax: 0332 462537

Registered office: 65 Buckingham Gate, London SW1E 6AT
Company number: 100382, Registered in England

13

**PLEASE OPEN OUT
TO FIND FURTHER INFORMATION
FOR TASK 3.**

[Turn over

14

TASK 4

Look at part of the memo from Peter Wainwright below and follow his instructions.

We've just had confirmation that Iberia has decided to use our Rolls-Royce 535 engines in their new Boeing 737 airliners. Can you write a short article for the 'News in Brief' section of our In-House magazine.

I've jotted down a few notes for you to use.

- Iberia - national carrier - Spain
- operate aircraft - Europe & Africa
- ordered 16 airliners - delivery early 1995
- orders - 535 engine = 1000+
- engine in 3/4 of all Boeing 757 - 13 out of 14 airlines in Europe use it.
- engine - put into service 5+ years ago
  economical / efficient / quiet / reliable

Can you finish off by saying something like - success in Europe important for our worldwide strategy, and finally welcome Iberia to Rolls-Royce family.

Thanks

Peter

15

Write your article here.

NEWS IN BRIEF

[Turn over

TASK 5

Look at the Internal Memorandum below which has been circulated to various departments at Rolls Royce. Reply to the memo as instructed.

INTERNAL MEMORANDUM **COMPANY HEADQUARTERS – DERBY**

From: A Rackham To: PW (FRM) CTH
MNG WDX
HYE TCT
DP

Ref: Tmd/AR2 JMT
Date: 9th November 1992
Tel Ext: 48704

PUBLIC AFFAIRS MARKETING MEETING

The Agenda for the subject meeting scheduled to take place in D.J. Rees' office at 10.15 am on December 10th 1992 is as follows:

1. Engine Projects PR Highlights — *Send apologies*
2. Advertising
3. Airline Briefing
4. Corporate Publicity
5. Paris Air Show — *Will bring all information to next meeting*
6. Outside Requests for Information
7. Any Other Business
8. Date of Next Meeting — *Suggest January 10th*

Sorry for this scribbled note, can you reply to AR for me? I've been called away on business abroad

Frank R. Meadows

Write your reply here.

INTERNAL MEMORANDUM **COMPANY HEADQUARTERS – DERBY**

From:
Ref:
Date:
Tel Ext:

[Turn over

18

TASK 6

Below is part of a brochure (Airline Briefing) which you have been asked to check before sending to the printers.

There are 10 errors or omissions.

Correct the errors and insert the missing words in the right places in the text.

ROLLS ROYCE

AIRLINE BRIEFING

No. 1

The civil aircraft market changing rapidly. Rolls-Royce is in the forefront of these change and in many cases is initiating them.

To keep you up to date with these exicting developments, Rolls-Royce has launched Airline Briefing , which every quarter will keep you in touch with Rolls-Royce its engines.

To do this Rolls-Royce has committed itself developing a range of engines which will be suitably for virtually all airlines. But to be sucessful, a engine must be more than suitable - it offer the lowest cost of ownership by addressing fuel consumption, performance retention, reliability, component lives, ease of maintenance and noise.

BULATS
Business Language Testing Service

English	**Version: EN00**
Standard Test	
Sample Question Paper	

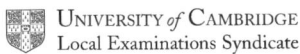

UNIVERSITY *of* CAMBRIDGE
Local Examinations Syndicate

A Member of the Association of Language Testers in Europe (ALTE)

Candidate Information

Candidate name:

Family name: ....

First name: ....

Candidate Number: ....

Examination Centre: ....

Date: ....

Test

About 110 minutes

Listening

About 50 minutes.
As you listen, write your answers in this Question Paper.
When the listening test finishes, you have 5 minutes to copy your answers onto your Answer Sheet.

**Reading &
Language Knowledge**

Spend 60 minutes.
Write your answers on your Answer Sheet.

3

BLANK PAGE

2

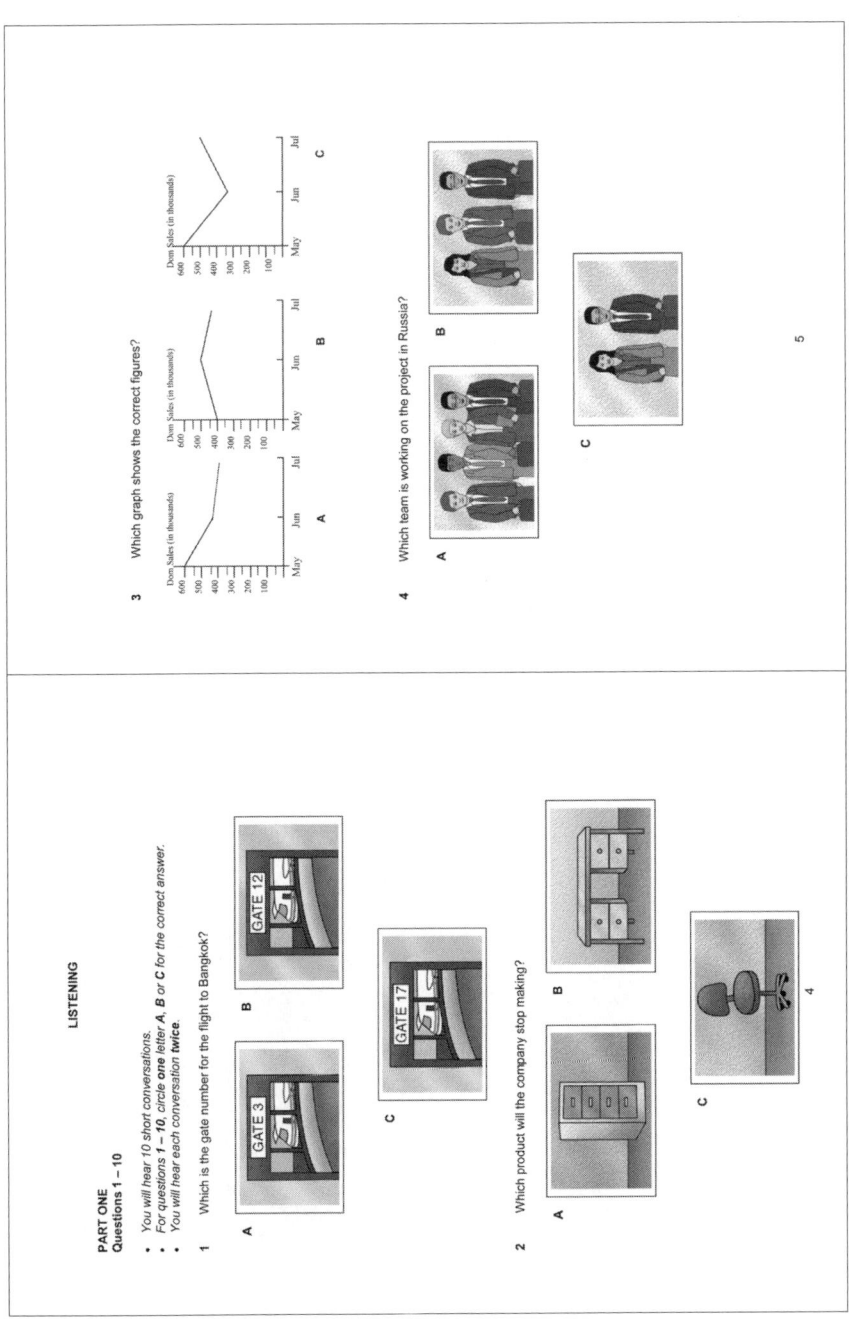

LISTENING

PART ONE
Questions 1 – 10

- *You will hear 10 short conversations.*
- *For questions 1 – 10, circle one letter A, B or C for the correct answer.*
- *You will hear each conversation twice.*

1   Which is the gate number for the flight to Bangkok?

A GATE 3   B GATE 12   C GATE 17

2   Which product will the company stop making?

A   B   C

3   Which graph shows the correct figures?

A   B   C

4   Which team is working on the project in Russia?

A   B   C

Appendix 1.4

5 When will the new product be ready for testing?

A

1	2	3	4	5	6
7	8	9	⑩	11	12	13
14	15	16	17	18	19	20
21	22	23	24	25	26	27
28	29	30	31			

B

1	②	3	4	5	6
7	8	9	10	11	12	13
14	15	16	17	18	19	20
21	22	23	24	25	26	27
28	29	30	31			

C

1	2	3	④	5	6
7	8	9	10	11	12	13
14	15	16	17	18	19	20
21	22	23	24	25	26	27
28	29	30	31			

6 Who is the sales assistant in the shop talking to?

A her boss

B another assistant

C a customer

7 What does Mike do at the training centre?

A He's a student.

B He's a receptionist.

C He's a teacher.

6

8 What does the announcer say about the train to Portsmouth?

A The train will leave at 10.37.

B The departure platform has been changed.

C Passengers will be unable to get food on the train.

9 What does the woman want her colleague to do?

A train new employees

B demonstrate a machine

C give a talk

10 Who is the man on the phone talking to?

A his boss

B a customer

C his assistant

7

PART TWO
Questions 11 – 22

- You will hear three conversations.
- Fill in the numbered spaces on the forms, using the information you hear.
- You will hear each conversation **once** only.

Conversation One
Questions 11 – 14

- Look at the form below.
- You will hear a man calling to place an order.

ORDER FORM

CUSTOMER DETAILS

Name: Ken **(11)** ....

Company: Greenlight Communications
201 Hall Road, Manchester

Tel: 0161 313988   Fax: **(12)** ....

ORDER DETAILS

Item: **(13)** ....   Model: XT519

Quantity/ Amount: **(14)** ....

Conversation Two
Questions 15 – 18

- Look at the form below.
- You will hear a woman making a complaint.

COMPLAINT FORM

Name: Mrs Hector

Address: 31, **(15)** ...., Rossington.

Tel: 01923 951975   Date of Complaint (if different): **(16)** ....

Date: 5 April

Branch: **(17)** ....

Reason for Complaint: Goods damaged due to bad **(18)** ....

Action: Issue credit note.

8

Conversation Three
Questions 19 – 22

- Look at the notes below.
- You will hear a woman calling about an order.

Company: **(19)** ....

In Leon, **(20)** .... Spain.

They want 300 of Model X42 by
(21) .... at the latest.

Despatch by **(22)** .... (they will pay).

9

PART THREE

Section One
Questions 23 – 27

- You will hear five people answer the question 'What do you like about your work?'
- As you listen to each one, decide what the person likes most.
- Choose your answer from the list A – I and write the correct letter in the space provided.
- You will hear the five pieces **once only**.

Example: .... I ....

A	meeting lots of people
B	good salary
C	working on my own
D	variety
E	company has good reputation
F	good office canteen
G	developing useful skills
H	near home
I	foreign travel

23 Person 1 ....

24 Person 2 ....

25 Person 3 ....

26 Person 4 ....

27 Person 5 ....

Section Two
Questions 28 – 32

- You will hear five people talking.
- As you listen, decide what each of them is talking about.
- Choose your answer from the list A – I, and write the correct letter in the space provided.
- You will hear the five pieces **once only**.

Example: .... I ....

A	a plan for a new office
B	a problem at work
C	a business meeting
D	a staff meeting
E	a conference
F	a job interview
G	a new colleague
H	safety precautions
I	a pay rise

28 Person 1 ....

29 Person 2 ....

30 Person 3 ....

31 Person 4 ....

32 Person 5 ....

10

PART FOUR

Section One
Questions 33 – 38

- You will hear a conversation between a university student, Sally, and a company representative, Dan, at a recruitment seminar. Sally is interested in working for Dan's company, Manson's plc.
- For question **33 – 38**, circle **one** letter **A, B** or **C** for the correct answer.
- You will hear the conversation **twice**.

33 Sally finishes her studies

    A in two weeks.
    B in a month.
    C in six weeks.

34 Sally would like to work in

    A marketing.
    B retailing.
    C finance.

35 Manson's have divisions in

    A Europe only.
    B Europe and Hong Kong.
    C Hong Kong only.

36 Manson's want employees who are

    A academically clever.
    B dynamic personalities.
    C keen to learn.

37 In an employee's first year, Manson's offer training in

    A management.
    B sales techniques.
    C market development.

38 Trainees are assessed every

    A 3 months.
    B 6 months.
    C 12 months.

11

Section Two
Questions 39 – 44

- *You will hear a conversation between two employees of a 24-hour supermarket discussing some tenders they have received for a cleaning contract. Helen is a Purchasing officer, and Tony is Head of Maintenance.*
- *For questions 39 – 44, circle one letter A, B or C for the correct answer.*
- *You will hear the conversation twice.*

39 What is the problem with their present contractors?

A They're not honest.
B They're not reliable.
C They're not suitably skilled.

40 Helen thinks that Benton's and Quickco

A offer very different deals.
B don't differ very much.
C have two main differences.

41 When do they want the new cleaners' contract to start?

A in August
B in September
C in December

42 Helen thinks a key factor in deciding who gets the contract is

A the speed of the cleaners.
B the number of the cleaners.
C the cost of the cleaners.

43 Tony is keen for Quickco to get the contract because they

A have a good reputation.
B presented their tender well.
C offered a trial period.

44 How do they feel about their final decision?

A They are confident about it.
B They decide they need some references.
C They want to discuss some issues further.

12

Section Three
Questions 45 – 50

- *You will hear a Personnel Manager interviewing an applicant for a job.*
- *For questions 45 – 50, circle one letter A, B or C for the correct answer.*
- *You will hear the conversation twice.*

45 In his current job, David has to

A see if certain work has been finished.
B assemble parts of a machine.
C help people progress in their careers.

46 Most of the time, David works in

A the Sales Department.
B the main office block.
C the production area.

47 What improvement does David say computers have made?

A Problems are dealt with immediately.
B Production staff have less to do.
C More detailed information is available.

48 In David's opinion, the most common problem is

A human error.
B machine breakdown.
C missing parts.

49 David feels he is suitable for the new job because it requires

A working with similar products.
B problem-solving skills.
C a knowledge of computers.

50 David regards himself as

A a natural leader.
B a good team member.
C a sensitive person.

That is the end of the Listening Section. You now have 5 minutes to copy your answers onto your Answer Sheet.

13

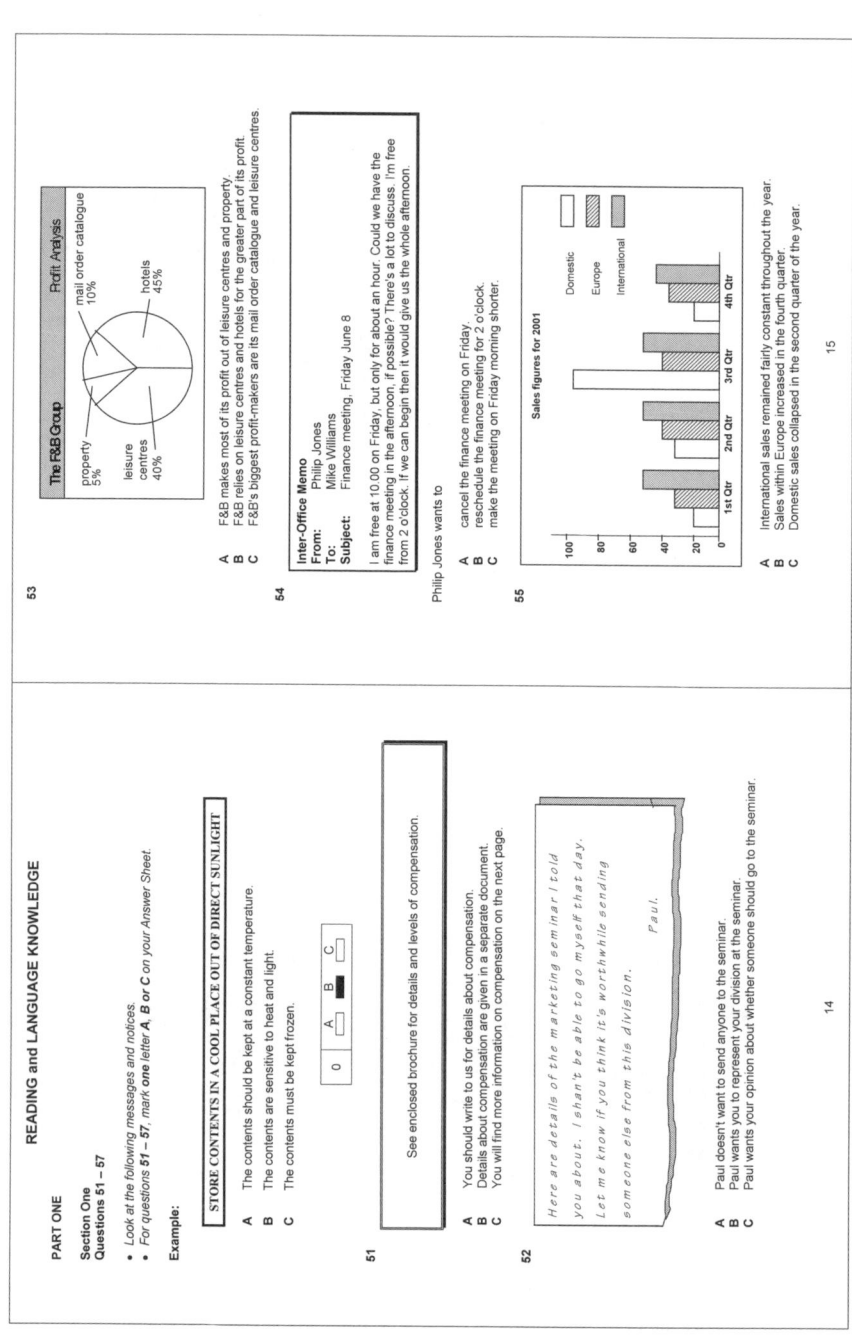

READING and LANGUAGE KNOWLEDGE

PART ONE

Section One
Questions 51 – 57

- Look at the following messages and notices.
- For questions **51 – 57**, mark **one** letter **A**, **B** or **C** on your Answer Sheet.

Example:

STORE CONTENTS IN A COOL PLACE OUT OF DIRECT SUNLIGHT

A The contents should be kept at a constant temperature.

B The contents are sensitive to heat and light.

C The contents must be kept frozen.

	A	B	C
0	☐	■	☐

51

See enclosed brochure for details and levels of compensation.

A You should write to us for details about compensation.

B Details about compensation are given in a separate document.

C You will find more information on compensation on the next page.

52

Here are details of the marketing seminar I told
you about. I shan't be able to go myself that day.
Let me know if you think it's worthwhile sending
someone else from this division.
                                        Paul.

A Paul doesn't want to send anyone to the seminar.

B Paul wants you to represent your division at the seminar.

C Paul wants your opinion about whether someone should go to the seminar.

53

The F&B Group   Profit Analysis

property 5%
mail order catalogue 10%
leisure centres 40%
hotels 45%

A F&B makes most of its profit out of leisure centres and property.

B F&B relies on leisure centres and hotels for the greater part of its profit.

C F&B's biggest profit-makers are its mail order catalogue and leisure centres.

54

Inter-Office Memo
From: Philip Jones
To: Mike Williams
Subject: Finance meeting, Friday June 8

I am free at 10.00 on Friday, but only for about an hour. Could we have the finance meeting in the afternoon, if possible? There's a lot to discuss. I'm free from 2 o'clock. If we can begin then it would give us the whole afternoon.

Philip Jones wants to

A cancel the finance meeting on Friday.

B reschedule the finance meeting for 2 o'clock.

C make the meeting on Friday morning shorter.

55

Sales figures for 2001

(bar chart: 1st Qtr, 2nd Qtr, 3rd Qtr, 4th Qtr; categories Domestic, Europe, International)

A International sales remained fairly constant throughout the year.

B Sales within Europe increased in the fourth quarter.

C Domestic sales collapsed in the second quarter of the year.

56

Storage Units - from £100 each

SAPELE or TEAK melamine wood effect finish.
Also black ash, light oak or white - add 10% to price.
For grey add 17% to price.

A You pay more for teak units than for white ones.
B You pay the same for grey or black ash units.
C You pay less for white units than you do for grey.

57

Symtex Company Results

Sales Target	Sales This Year	Sales Last Year
7,000	7,200	6,700

A This year's sales figures were not as good as last year's.
B Last year's sales figures did not reach the sales target.
C This year's sales failed to reach the sales target.

16

PART ONE

Section Two
Questions 58 – 63

- *Choose the word or phrase which best completes each sentence.*
- *For questions 58 – 63, mark one letter A, B, C or D on your Answer Sheet.*

58 My job frequently involves having to work .... intense pressure.

  A below
  B under
  C beneath
  D underneath

59 This type of decision has to be made at board ....

  A layer
  B rank
  C grade
  D level

60 The Managing Director is now urgently .... to appoint a Head of Operations.

  A seeking
  B pursuing
  C searching
  D hunting

61 The company has decided to .... a share option scheme, starting next year.

  A introduce
  B innovate
  C confer
  D embark

62 Lack of orders has meant that a number of employees have been laid ....

  A down
  B on
  C up
  D off

63 The company has good industrial .... and disputes are rare.

  A workings
  B affairs
  C terms
  D relations

17

PART ONE

Section Three
Questions 64 – 69

- *Read the article below about women who run their own business and answer questions*
  64 – 69 on the opposite page.
- *For questions 64 – 69, mark one letter A, B or C on your Answer Sheet.*

WOMEN RUNNING THEIR OWN BUSINESS

According to recent research, a third of new companies set up in Britain are run by women. Typical examples are Lisa Simons, who started up her own highly successful clothing shops in London with a loan of £15,000 from her bank, and Kate Rogers, who set up *Cellar Cafés* five years ago and sold out to a major restaurant chain this month, at a profit of £3 million.

There are many other examples. *Surprise*, a mail order company selling unusual gifts, had a turnover of $4 million last year. The company was started by Claire Fuller five years ago in a garage, but later moved into premises in the centre of Coventry. Similarly, Nina Taylor started her company, *NC Books*, in an old warehouse in Bristol. A lawyer by training, she had no previous experience of the retail trade but believes that this worked to her advantage. 'Having no knowledge of the book trade,' she says, 'allowed me to bring fresh ideas into the business.'

Young women are also running successful businesses, like Maria Fellows and Christine Craig, both still in their early twenties. Together they set up *Denlows Recruitment Agency* in an office in Liverpool less than two years ago; the firm now has six offices and a staff of 38. Another young woman, American-born Amy Bailey, could not find any good coffee shops in England so she set up *Coffee Choice Company* in 1994. Two years ago a large American group bought the company, although Amy continues to play a leading part in the business.

There are many reasons why women want to run their own businesses. One is that they are increasingly confident that they are capable of doing this. Another is that many no longer want to work for companies which fail to offer satisfying careers. 'Women's businesses are often more successful that those run by men,' says Denise Johnson, of the National Business Bank, 'because women are good at looking ahead and seeing what will be best for a business – they find it very satisfying.'

64 One-third of new British businesses

    A   consist of chain companies
    B   are owned or managed by women.
    C   operate within the food sector.

65 What does the second paragraph tell us about the company called *Surprise*?

    A   The company delivers its products by post.
    B   The company has made a profit every year.
    C   The company operates from a garage.

66 What did Nina Taylor think helped her when she started her business?

    A   having a good knowledge of the law
    B   being the owner of a warehouse
    C   knowing nothing about the book trade

67 What shows that *Denlows Recruitment Agency* has been a success?

    A   It has been in business for more than two years.
    B   It has recruited 25 new employees.
    C   It has opened several new offices.

68 *Coffee Choice Company* was established

    A   to fill a gap in the market.
    B   despite strong competition.
    C   with finance from the US.

69 According to the final paragraph women want to run their own businesses because they

    A   enjoy learning new skills.
    B   like making plans for the future.
    C   prefer working for small companies.

READING and LANGUAGE KNOWLEDGE

Part Two

21

PART ONE

Section Four
Questions 70 – 74

- For questions *70 – 74*, read the text below and think of the word which best fits each space.
- Write only *one* word in each space on your Answer Sheet.

Example:

He is very interested.................computers.

Answer:

| 0 | in | ☐ ☐ |

Maria's Beauty Boutiques

Maria Wilson is the now famous Managing Director of Beauty Boutique International plc, one of ....**(70)**...... world's beauty product chains. The daughter of Spanish immigrants, she ...... **(71)** ..... born and educated in Britain.

She opened her first Beauty Boutique in 1976 and it was ...... **(72)** ..... popular that she opened five more shops in 3 years. ...... **(73)** ..... then business has developed at an amazing rate, and the chain of Beauty Boutiques ...... **(74)** ..... now expanding all over the world.

20

PART TWO

Section One
Questions 75 – 81

- Read these sentences and the job advertisements on the opposite page.
- Which job does each sentence 75 – 81 refer to?
- For each sentence, mark one letter A, B, C or D on your Answer Sheet.

Example:

0   You need to be able to speak two or more foreign languages.

Answer:

0	A	B	C	D
				■

75   You need to have experience of working with newspapers, TV or radio.

76   You have to be able to use a computer efficiently.

77   The job will involve providing senior staff with data.

78   You should have successful sales experience with leading companies.

79   You need to be able to get the best out of people who work for you.

80   Your earnings will depend on how much you sell.

81   You need to show you are suitable for early promotion.

22

A

Financial Analyst   £20-£25,000 + benefits
As a young and enthusiastic finalist/newly qualified accountant, you should demonstrate the potential to progress quickly within the company and to develop an excellent understanding of the commercial needs of the business. With an analytical approach and strong communication skills, you will provide support on purchase price variances, prepare financial reports for the European Head Office and undertake ad hoc projects.

B

Executive Director

The Women's Environment Network (WEN) is looking for a highly motivated, inspiring woman to lead one of Britain's most successful environmental campaigning and information organisations.

Experience required includes management and organisational skills, media, writing and editing experience and a knowledge of the environment and/or women's movement. You will need to run campaigns and motivate a team of about 30 volunteers and paid staff.

C

Wanted:
EXPERIENCED INTERNATIONAL SALESPERSON
representing leading travel company to companies and multinationals in the UK. Applicants are expected to be able to display word-processing skills and familiarity with database software. Basic salary, excellent commission and company car. We have a full-scale London office.

D

Office Equipment
Sales Staff
  ◆ *New Business* ◆
      Sales people
Required by successful office equipment supplier to develop business in Europe. Must have proven ability to sell at senior levels in top companies. The successful applicant will be fluent in at least two foreign languages.

23

236

PART TWO

Section Two
Questions 82 – 86

- Read this letter about buying a computer.
- Choose the best word to fill each space from the words below.
- For each question 82 – 86, mark one word letter A, B, C or D on your Answer Sheet.

1 April

Dear Mr Whitehead

Re: Supply of XR6 Workstations

I have pleasure in confirming our ability to meet your requirements for the Silicon Graphics workstation. In view of your special needs, I suggest that you place your order for the agreed equipment as soon as possible. The ....(82)..... time for hardware for example is 6 weeks from receipt of order to ....(83)..... . Thus, an order placed with us tomorrow will ....(84)..... delivery to your site by the week commencing Monday, 15th May. All orders must be accompanied by a ....(85)..... of 20% of the total amount shown on the attached ....(86)..... .

Yours sincerely

Vincent Law
Sales Manager

	A		B		C		D
82	delivery		arrival		transport		postage
83	institution		initiation		introduction		installation
84	compel		ensure		promise		maintain
85	portion		cost		deposit		discount
86	cheque		quotation		charge		demand

24

PART TWO

Section Three
Questions 87 – 91

- Read the article below about a businessman who made a fortune from his car magazines.
- For each question 87 – 91, write one word in the space on your Answer Sheet.

Example:

He is very interested ....computers.

Answer:

```
0 | in |
```

Millionaire who just loves cars

John Pajackowski is a tall, thin, fit 54 year old who is worth an estimated £145 million thanks to his Car Trader magazines.

Back in ....(87)............ 1960s, John was working in America, selling British sports cars. It was hard work but ....(88)............ he was there, he saw a magazine with pictures of cars for sale. The magazine was regional and anyone ....(89)............ advertise their car in it for a relatively small fee. What impressed John most was that ....(90)............ single advertisement had a picture of the car, unlike normal newspaper adverts, which just provided a written description.

Returning to Britain, John put all of his savings into producing a magazine like the one he ....(91)............ seen in the States. He started in the London region but was soon producing similar magazines for twelve more regions and, by 1990, for three other countries as well.

25

237

PART TWO

Section Four
Questions 92 – 97

- *Choose the word or phrase which best completes each sentence.*
- *For questions 92 – 97, mark one letter A, B, C, or D on your answer sheet.*

92 The successful applicant will have a proven track .... in project management.

   A history
   B record
   C curriculum
   D performance

93 When replying, please .... the above reference number.

   A refer
   B reproduce
   C quote
   D allude

94 Like many companies, we were affected by the .... in the world economy.

   A downside
   B downturn
   C downgrade
   D downfall

95 Once further investment has been .... the plans for growth can be carried out.

   A secured
   B obliged
   C bound
   D forced

96 This approach will enable us to get the maximum benefit from .... of scale.

   A savings
   B compensations
   C resources
   D economies

97 My boss promised to .... on board the suggestions I made at the meeting.

   A take
   B let
   C hold
   D set

PART TWO

Section Five

Questions 98 – 103

- *Read the article below about careers advice and answer questions 98 – 103 on the opposite page.*
- *For questions 98 – 103, mark **one** letter A, B, C or D for the correct answer on your Answer Sheet.*

Keys to unlock path of career fulfilment

It used to be called vocational guidance. Then it became careers advice and counselling. Since the late 1920s there have been various tests to help guide bewildered and guileless school leavers into job categories suited to their interests and abilities. Hence extroverts have been advised, wisely, to go into sales and marketing, where they thrive on the variability, people-contact and air of optimism. Introverts, on the other hand, find the quiet work of accounts, stores and engineering, where they can work alone in a less people-orientated, frenetic atmosphere, more to their taste.

But good careers advisors need to look at other factors when giving advice. For example, career counselling is flawed if it fails to allow for the possibility of people adapting to, and changing, their jobs once they are in them. Most organisations attempt through various explicit (induction, mentoring, training, appraisal) and implicit (reliance on observation) techniques to mould behaviour into an acceptable pattern. This means that attitudes and even aptitudes of employees may be changed over the first year of employment, sometimes, but not always, in the direction desired by the organisation. Thus what was a 'fit' may easily and quickly develop into a *misfit* and vice versa.

Individuals also change their jobs without leaving them. They rearrange furniture, use space and technology differently and personalise different aspects of the job. They can negotiate with colleagues, earn special privileges and use other means to improve their role and output. In this sense, very soon they are doing the job differently from their predecessors, and possibly from the way recommended by the company. However, both adaptation of personal work-style and attempts to change the way of doing the job are more likely to lead to a higher level of 'fit', because the changes are usually all attempts to increase 'fit'.

And jobs themselves change. Organisational restructuring, the development of new technology, changes in the market, and so on, all mean that jobs evolve fairly fast. Because of the speed of technology, all jobs are in a state of flux. Job analysis is therefore becoming less relevant to careers advice. Counsellors analysis has to focus instead on personal potential rather than current knowledge or skill. And the features of such analysis are potential speed and thoroughness in the acquisition of new knowledge and skills.

The areas that are probably most predictive of these are intelligence and personality. Intelligence is probably the best predictor of speed of learning. Often, intelligent people are curious and self-confident and hence happy to tackle new tasks. Intelligent people are better and quicker at analysing both logical and deductive and creative problems. Probably the most important personality dimensions are conscientiousness and neuroticism. Conscientious people soon get a good reputation which serves them in good stead. Coupled with ability, this trait is a sure-fire career winner. On the other hand neuroticism is a deep and abiding handicap. It is not easy to 'cure' and can have a lasting effect on a career. Neurotics are unhappy and tend to be dissatisfied, stressed and complaining in all jobs they have. The consistency of their behaviour leads them to develop a poor reputation in the workplace which of course can be self-fulfilling.

Success in the job in 2020 can be assessed now. We have little idea what the world of work will be like but advisors can do a reasonable job in assessing the potential of the individual within it because they know the predictors of success. And it is these predictors that counsellors need to attend to if they are to give the best advice.

28

---

98 What does the writer say about careers advice in the first paragraph?

  A Those receiving it have sometimes disagreed with it.
  B It has favoured certain types of people over others.
  C Some of the standard advice given has been appropriate.
  D It has acquired a more appropriate title than it used to have.

99 What does the writer say about organisations in the second paragraph?

  A They can turn suitable employees into unsuitable ones.
  B Many of them have a low opinion of careers advisors.
  C They are insensitive to the effect their methods have on employees.
  D Many are unclear about what to expect from employees.

100 The writer says that when individuals make changes to their jobs,

  A they may not be aware that they are doing this.
  B they generally have the best of intentions.
  C they are often afraid of the consequences.
  D they frequently pretend they are not doing this.

101 The writer's main point in the fourth paragraph is that

  A people have become less sure about which career would suit them.
  B people no longer want to stay in the same job for a long time.
  C the speed of change in the world of work has caused confusion.
  D careers advice can no longer focus on the nature of specific jobs.

102 The writer contrasts conscientious people with neurotic people with regard to

  A the kind of advice they can be given.
  B their chances of finding employment.
  C the impression they give to colleagues.
  D their willingness to take advice from others.

103 What is the writer's general view on careers advice in the final paragraph?

  A It has had to allow for the fact that people now have higher aspirations.
  B Whether it is useful or not has become harder to assess.
  C Predicting future developments has become its key ingredient.
  D It has become much less relevant in today's world of work.

29

Appendix 1.4

PART TWO

Section Six
Questions 104 – 110

- *Your secretary has given you this letter to check.*
- *In some lines there is one wrong word.*
- *If there is a wrong word, write the correct word on your answer sheet.*
- *If there is no mistake, put a tick (✓) on your Answer Sheet.*

Example:

One of the items you ordered from our catalogue

0	✓

is <u>temporary</u> out of stock.

00	**temporarily**

Dear Mr Rose ,

It was a pleasure to meet you the other day. I was very grateful

104   that you were able to find some times in your busy schedule to visit us.

105   I thought it should be helpful if I put on paper some of the points we

106   agreed on at our meeting and indicated some with the action points.

107   We agreed which my company will act as your agent in northern

108   Europe. As your agent, we will operate on a commission basis. We will

109   charge you on the rate of 20% for sales up to 2 million Euros. On sales above

110   such figure we will charge commission on a sliding scale up to a maximum

rate of 25%.

Yours sincerely

John Smith

30

BLANK PAGE

31

240

BULATS
Business Language Testing Service

English	**Version: EN40**

Speaking Test

Sample Question Paper

UNIVERSITY *of* CAMBRIDGE
Local Examinations Syndicate

A Member of the Association of Language Testers in Europe (ALTE)

BULATS Speaking Test   Sample Materials

There are **three** parts to the speaking test; in **Part 1**, you will have an **Interview**. This will include questions from the sections below.

- all candidates will be asked questions from **Section 1**;
- people in work will be asked questions from **Section 2**;
- students will be asked questions from **Section 3**;
- all candidates will then be asked questions from **one** of the **Sections 4 - 7**.

This part will last approximately **four** minutes.

PART 1	Interview

Section 1   Introduction
In this part you will be asked questions about your self, where you live and where you study or work.

Section 2   Current work
In this part you will be asked more details about what you do in your job.

Section 3   Current studies
In this part you will be asked more details about your studies.

Section 4   Travel
In this part you will be asked about places you have visited.

Section 5   Language learning
In this part you will be asked about your experiences of studying English.

Section 6   Future career prospects
In this part you will be asked about your future career development.

Section 7   Interests
In this part you will be asked about your hobbies and interests.

In **Part 2** of the test you will be asked to give a short presentation on one of three topics. According to your work experience, the topics may be on general work, technical work, or study.

This part will last approximately **four** minutes.

PART 2	Presentation

INSTRUCTIONS

Please read all THREE topics below carefully.

Choose **ONE** which you feel you will be able to talk about for one minute.
You have one minute to read and prepare your talk.
You may take notes.

Topic A

Describe an important business meeting you attended.
You should say:
    where it was;
    what it was about;
    why it was important.

What were the most interesting moments?

Topic B

Describe someone you particularly enjoy working with.
You should say:
    what this person does;
    what sort of work you do with this person;
    why you like working with this person.

Would you change anything about this person? Give reasons for your answer.

Topic C

Describe the best workplace you have ever had.
You should say:
    where the workplace was;
    what you were doing there;
    why you liked to work there.

Would you change anything about it? Give reasons for your answer.

In **Part 3** of the test you will be asked to take part in a communicative activity with the examiner which is made up of an information exchange and a discussion. According to your work experience, this activity may be on a general work, technical work, or study topic.

This part will last approximately **four** minutes.

PART 3 Communicative Activity

Conference arrangements

You have one minute to read through this task.

Information Exchange

You are making the arrangements for a one-day conference at a local hotel. The Examiner is the Conference Organiser for the hotel and is visiting you to discuss the conference.

Find out this information   i)   the size of the largest conference room
                            ii)   the cost for that room
                            iii)   equipment available

Do you think the hotel is offering you a good service for the price it is charging?

Discussion

Now discuss this topic with the Examiner:

What makes a successful conference?

BULATS

Business Language Testing Service

Deutsch	Version: DE00
Standard Test	
Modelltest	

Mitglied der Vereinigung von Sprachprüfungsanbietern in Europa (ALTE)

**GOETHE INSTITUT
INTER NATIONES**

Kandidateninformation

Name des Kandidaten:
Familienname: ....
Vorname: ....

Kandidatennummer: ....
Prüfungszentrum: ....
Datum: ....

Test

Zeit: ca. 110 Minuten

Hörverstehen

Ca. 50 Minuten
Schreiben Sie während des Hörens Ihre Lösungen in das Aufgabenblatt. Wenn der Test zum Hörverstehen beendet ist, haben Sie 5 Minuten Zeit, um Ihre Lösungen in den Antwortbogen zu schreiben.

Leseverstehen & Sprachkenntnis

60 Minuten
Schreiben Sie Ihre Lösungen in den Antwortbogen.

3

LEERE SEITE

2

Appendix 1.6

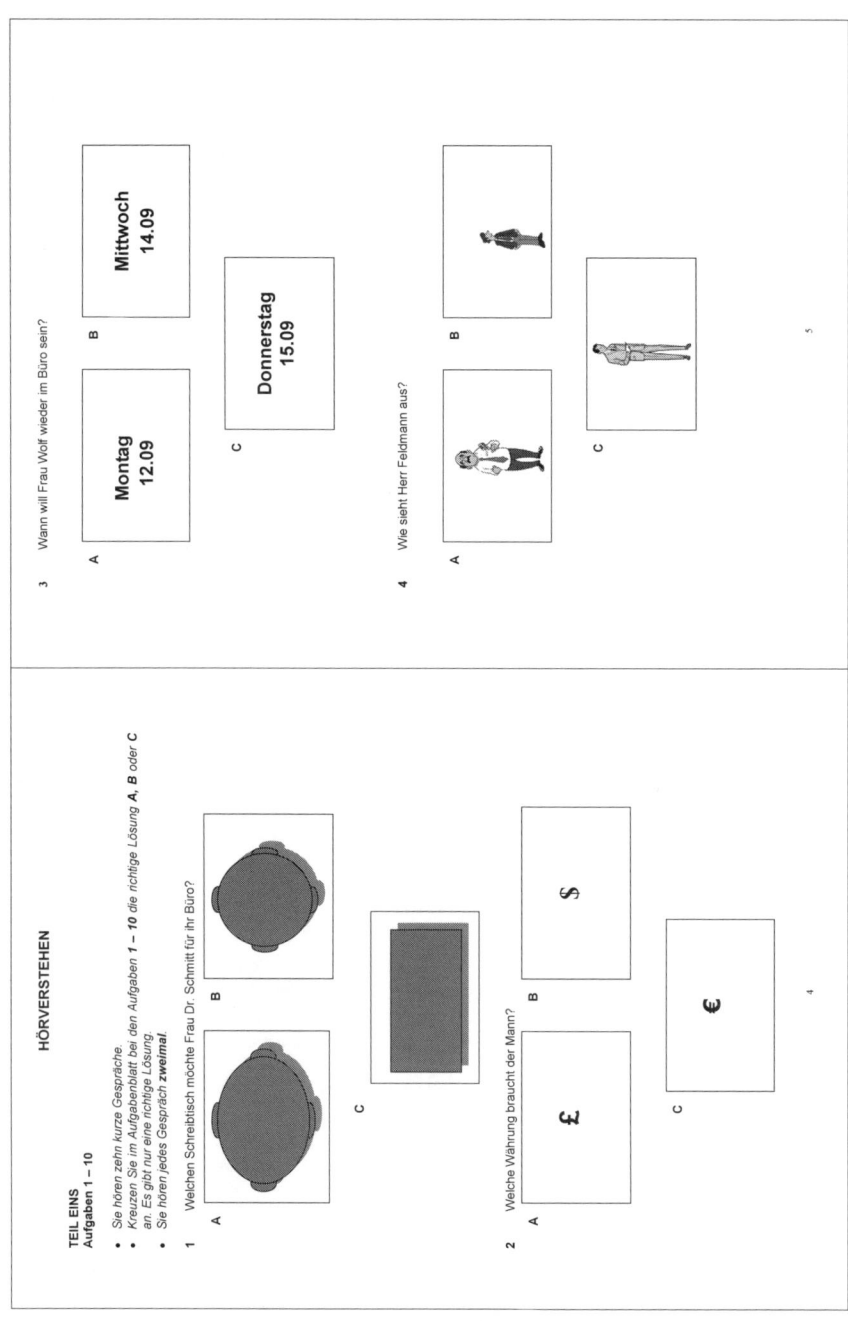

246

5 Was bekommt die Frau des Chefs?

A

B

C

6 Sie hören ein Telefongespräch.
Wann braucht Herr Hoffmann eine Sekretärin?

A Heute Nachmittag

B Morgen Nachmittag

C Sofort

7 Sie hören im Radio eine Nachricht von einer Messe.
Was ist in diesem Jahr anders?

A Das Wetter

B Die Anzahl der Aussteller

C Die Anzahl der Besucher

8 Sie hören ein Gespräch.
Welchen Flug soll das Reisebüro buchen?

A Herr Hilpert will in New York und San Francisco Zwischenstops machen.

B Herr Hilpert will jetzt am 19. April fliegen.

C Herr Hilpert will non stop nach Los Angeles fliegen.

9 Sie hören ein Gespräch.
Wie soll die neue Homepage aussehen?

A Die Homepage soll eine zusätzliche Seite bekommen.

B Die Seite zwei soll neu gestaltet werden.

C Der Inhalt soll gekürzt werden.

10 Sie hören ein Gespräch.
Was sagen die beiden Kolleginnen?

A Sie finden den Chef zu kritisch.

B Sie glauben, dass ein Gespräch Erfolg hat.

C Sie wollen mit dem Chef sprechen.

TEIL ZWEI
Aufgaben 11 – 22

- *Sie hören drei kurze Telefongespräche.*
- *Füllen Sie die nummerierten Lücken in den Formularen mit den Informationen aus, die Sie hören werden. Schreiben Sie Ihre Lösungen in die Formulare, während Sie die Gespräche hören.*
- *Sie hören jedes Gespräch nur einmal.*

Gespräch Eins
Aufgaben 11 – 14

- *Sehen Sie sich das Formular unten an.*
- *Sie hören eine Frau, die einen Auftrag gibt.*

Auftragsformular

Name: *Lia Schröder*

Grund des Anrufs: **(11)** ....

Erreichbar zwischen: **(12)** ....

Adresse: **(13)** .... Tel.: 089/245607

Zahlungswunsch: **(14)** ....

Gespräch Zwei
Aufgaben 15 – 18

- *Sehen Sie sich das Formular unten an.*
- *Sie hören einen Mann, der eine Bestellung macht.*

Bestellung

Name: *Manfred Hausmann*   Kundennummer: **(15)** ....

Artikel: **(16)** .... Nr. L264

Katalog: **(17)** ....

Lieferzeit: **(18)** ....

8

Gespräch Drei
Aufgaben 19 – 22

- *Sehen Sie sich das Formular unten an.*
- *Sie hören eine Frau, die eine Reklamation macht.*

Telefonische Reklamation

Name: *Fa. Hauser & Co.*   Lieferung von: **(19)** ....

Grund der Reklamation: **(20)** ....   Kunden-Nr.: *1028*

Lieferdatum: **(21)** ....

Kundenwunsch: **(22)** ....

9

248

TEIL DREI

Abschnitt Eins
Aufgaben 23 – 27

- *Sie hören fünf kurze Texte. Hören Sie zu und entscheiden Sie, was die Leute über den Gebrauch des „du" oder des „Sie" sagen.*
- *Wählen Sie bei jedem Text Ihre Antwort aus der Liste A – I aus und schreiben Sie den richtigen Buchstaben in die leere Stelle hinter der Nummer.*
- *Sie hören jeden Text nur einmal.*

Beispiel: .... I ....

23 Text 1 ....
24 Text 2 ....
25 Text 3 ....
26 Text 4 ....
27 Text 5 ....

> A   Jede Firma soll eigene Regeln machen.
> B   Das „Sie" für alle schafft klare Verhältnisse.
> C   Das „Du" ist besser für die Zusammenarbeit.
> D   Chefs sollten die Mitarbeiter nicht duzen.
> E   Traditionelle Branchen gebrauchen das „Sie".
> F   Wenn man sich duzt, gibt es keinen Respekt.
> G   Es spielt gar keine Rolle für das Arbeitsklima.
> H   Man kann den Chef nicht duzen.
> I   Man soll nur seine Freunde duzen.

Abschnitt Zwei
Aufgaben 28 – 32

- *Sie hören fünf kurze Texte. Hören Sie zu und entscheiden Sie, was die Leute über einen Auslandsaufenthalt sagen.*
- *Wählen Sie bei jedem Text Ihre Antwort aus der Liste A – I aus und schreiben Sie den richtigen Buchstaben in die leere Stelle hinter der Nummer.*
- *Sie hören jeden Text nur einmal.*

Beispiel: .... I ....

28 Text 1 ....
29 Text 2 ....
30 Text 3 ....
31 Text 4 ....
32 Text 5 ....

> A   Firma muss 1x pro Jahr Flug nach Hause zahlen.
> B   Berufstätigkeit der Ehefrau spielt große Rolle.
> C   Man muss über den Ort genau Bescheid wissen.
> D   Man muss das Klima gut vertragen können.
> E   Man muss im Ausland mehr Geld verdienen.
> F   Gute Schulmöglichkeiten für die Kinder.
> G   Der Aufenthalt soll maximal 3 Jahre dauern.
> H   Man muss die Landessprache gut sprechen.
> I   Der Aufenthalt muss gut für die Karriere sein.

10

TEIL VIER

Abschnitt Eins
Aufgaben 33 – 38

- *Sie hören einen kurzen Vortrag über die Eigenschaften eines guten Verkäufers.*
- *Kreuzen Sie bei den Aufgaben 33 – 38 im Aufgabenblatt die richtige Lösung A, B oder C an. Es gibt nur eine richtige Lösung.*
- *Sie hören das Gespräch zweimal.*

33 Es handelt sich um eine Schulung für
A   Marketing-Manager.
B   Mitarbeiter im Call-Center.
C   Mitarbeiter im Vertrieb.

34 Die Mitarbeiterinnen und Mitarbeiter haben in Krisenzeiten einen sicheren Job, weil
A   das Unternehmen auf starken Absatz angewiesen ist.
B   die Firma viel Geld in ihre Schulungen investiert hat.
C   ihre Gehälter ziemlich niedrig sind

35 Die Mitarbeiterinnen und Mitarbeiter sollen darauf achten,
A   ob der Kunde das Gespräch abbrechen möchte.
B   ob der Kunde noch unsicher ist.
C   wann der Kunde bereit ist, etwas zu kaufen.

36 Der Redner sagt, dass
A   die persönliche Wirkung wichtiger ist als das Produkt.
B   der Verkaufserfolg nur vom Produkt abhängt.
C   der Verkaufserfolg stark vom Auftreten abhängt.

37 Der Redner sagt auch, dass
A   Kenntnisse über den Gesprächspartner sehr nützlich sind.
B   man dem Gesprächspartner nach privaten Dingen fragen sollte
C   man Gespräche über Hobbies vermeiden sollte

38 Der Redner sagt außerdem, dass man
A   bestimmte Fragetechniken gebrauchen sollte.
B   die Fragen dem Gesprächspartner überlassen sollte
C   versuchen sollte, möglichst kurze Fragen zu stellen.

11

Abschnitt Zwei
Aufgaben 39 – 44

- *Sie hören ein Gespräch zwischen zwei Mitarbeitern über ein Problem in ihrer Firma.*
- *Kreuzen Sie bei den Aufgaben 39 – 44 im Aufgabenblatt die richtige Lösung A, B oder C an. Es gibt nur eine richtige Lösung.*
- *Sie hören das Gespräch zweimal.*

39 Frau Scherer und Herr Huber,

   A   beklagen sich über ihre vielen Termine.
   B   sprechen über die Einhaltung von Lieferterminen.
   C   überlegen, wie sie Kunden gewinnen können.

40 Es gab Probleme bei der Verpackung der Waren, weil

   A   die Gläser nicht in die Kartons passten.
   B   dort viele Aushilfen arbeiteten.
   C   eine Maschine nicht funktionierte.

41 Im Auslieferungslager gab es Schwierigkeiten, weil

   A   der Lagermeister erkrankte.
   B   dort Personalmangel herrscht.
   C   falsche Lieferscheine ausgestellt wurden.

42 Herr Huber kritisiert an dem Transportunternehmen, dass

   A   der neue Chef keine Erfahrung hat.
   B   es Gewinne machen will.
   C   es zu viele Aufträge annimmt.

43 Herr Huber schlägt vor,

   A   firmeneigene LKWs anzuschaffen.
   B   mit dem neuen Firmenchef das Problem zu besprechen.
   C   mit einem anderen Transportunternehmen zusammenzuarbeiten.

44 Frau Scherer bittet Herrn Huber,

   A   eine Kalkulation der Transportkosten zu erstellen.
   B   mit mehreren Transportfirmen Kontakt aufzunehmen.
   C   sich für ein neues Transportunternehmen zu entscheiden.

12

Abschnitt Drei
Aufgaben 45 – 50

- *Sie hören ein Gespräch mit Frau Meurer, die in der Personalabteilung einer großen Firma arbeitet. Frau Meurer spricht über die Karrierechancen in technischen Berufen.*
- *Kreuzen Sie bei den Aufgaben 45 – 50 im Aufgabenblatt die richtige Lösung A, B oder C an. Es gibt nur eine richtige Lösung.*
- *Sie hören das Gespräch zweimal.*

45 Es gibt wenig Bewerberinnen für technische Berufe, weil

   A   die Firmen keine Stellen für Frauen ausschreiben.
   B   Frauen die Arbeit in technischen Berufen zu schwer finden.
   C   Frauen glauben, sie seien für technische Berufe ungeeignet.

46 Frau Meurer glaubt, dass

   A   männliche Mitarbeiter die besseren Chancen haben.
   B   technische Berufe immer eine Domäne der Männer bleiben.
   C   technische Berufe besonders zukunftssicher sind.

47 In den technischen Berufen hat die Firma von Frau Meurer

   A   fast keine Bewerbungen von Frauen.
   B   mehr Frauen als Männer eingestellt.
   C   relativ viele Frauen eingestellt.

48 Die Firma von Frau Meurer

   A   bietet Frauen in technischen Berufen höhere Gehälter.
   B   hilft Frauen bei der Finanzierung einer technischen Ausbildung.
   C   lässt Frauen in technischen Berufen schneller aufsteigen.

49 Die Mitarbeiterinnen in der Firma von Frau Meurer

   A   können Beruf und Familie schwer miteinander vereinbaren.
   B   können sich ihre Arbeitszeiten individuell gestalten.
   C   wünschen sich mehr Möglichkeiten der Teilzeitarbeit.

50 Frau Meurer ist der Meinung, dass die

   A   Firmen noch viel mehr für junge Frauen tun könnten.
   B   jungen Frauen ihre Chancen besser wahrnehmen müssten.
   C   Lebenspartner die jungen Frauen nicht genügend unterstützen.

Das ist das Ende des Tests zum Hörverstehen. Übertragen Sie nun Ihre Lösungen auf den Antwortbogen. Sie haben dazu 5 Minuten Zeit.

13

LESEVERSTEHEN und SPRACHKENNTNIS

TEIL EINS

Abschnitt Eins
Aufgaben 51 – 57

• Lesen Sie die folgenden Notizen und Nachrichten.
• Markieren Sie bei den Aufgaben **51 – 57** im Antwortbogen die richtige Lösung **A, B** oder **C**. Es gibt nur eine richtige Lösung.

Beispiel:

| DEN INHALT KÜHL LAGERN UND VOR SONNENLICHT SCHÜTZEN |

A Der Inhalt muss bei gleichbleibender Temperatur lagern.
B Der Inhalt ist empfindlich gegen Hitze und Licht.
C Der Inhalt muss gefroren lagern.

Lösung:

| 0 | A ☐ | B ■ | C ☐ |

51

| *Offizielle Briefe schreiben leicht gemacht* |
| Der Ratgeber mit Beispielen, Anregungen und Mustertexten für Anfragen, Reklamationen, Rechnungen. Bestellen Sie noch heute unsere kostenlose Broschüre. |

Diesen Ratgeber bekommen Sie

A bei Reklamationen.
B gegen Rechnung.
C umsonst.

52

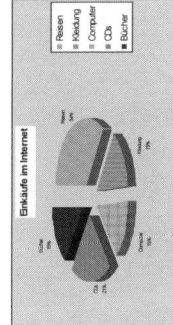

Die Deutschen kaufen im Internet

A mehr Kleider als CDs.
B vor allem Reisen.
C weniger Bücher als Computer.

14

53

| *Liebe Kolleginnen und Kollegen,* |
| *Unsere für letzten Mittwoch geplante Abteilungsbesprechung, die wegen Krankheit ausfallen musste, kann man auch diese Woche nicht stattfinden, da ich am Mittwoch einen wichtigen anderen Termin habe.* |
| *Beste Grüße* |
| *H. Kunstmann* |

Die Abteilungsbesprechung findet diese Woche nicht statt, weil Herr Kunstmann

A einen anderen Termin vorschlägt.
B keine Zeit hat.
C krank ist.

54

| Liebe Mitarbeiter und Mitarbeiterinnen, |
| Die Personalabteilung weist noch einmal darauf hin, dass alle Resturlaube bis Ende April des Folgejahres genommen sein müssen. Nur in Ausnahmefällen, wenn aus betrieblichen Gründen dringend erforderlich, kann ein Urlaubsanspruch auf einen späteren Zeitpunkt, spätestens jedoch bis Ende August des Folgejahres, übertragen werden. |

Die Mitarbeiterinnen und Mitarbeiter

A können einen Teil des Urlaubs im nächsten Frühjahr nehmen.
B können ihren ganzen Urlaub auf das nächste Jahr verschieben.
C müssen ihren Urlaub im laufenden Kalenderjahr nehmen.

55

| *Liebe Kolleginnen,* |
| Frau Martin hat sich wiederholt beschwert über schmutziges Geschirr, das in der Küche herumsteht. Ich denke, sie hat Recht und wir sollten dieses Problem irgendwie regeln. Ich schlage vor, wir setzen uns morgen 11 Uhr kurz zusammen und überlegen gemeinsam, wie wir dieses unliebsame Thema aus der Welt schaffen können. |
| *Wilma Fritz* |

Frau Fritz schlägt vor,

A das Geschirr gemeinsam zu spülen.
B sich über Frau Martin zu beschweren.
C sich zu treffen und das Problem zu diskutieren.

15

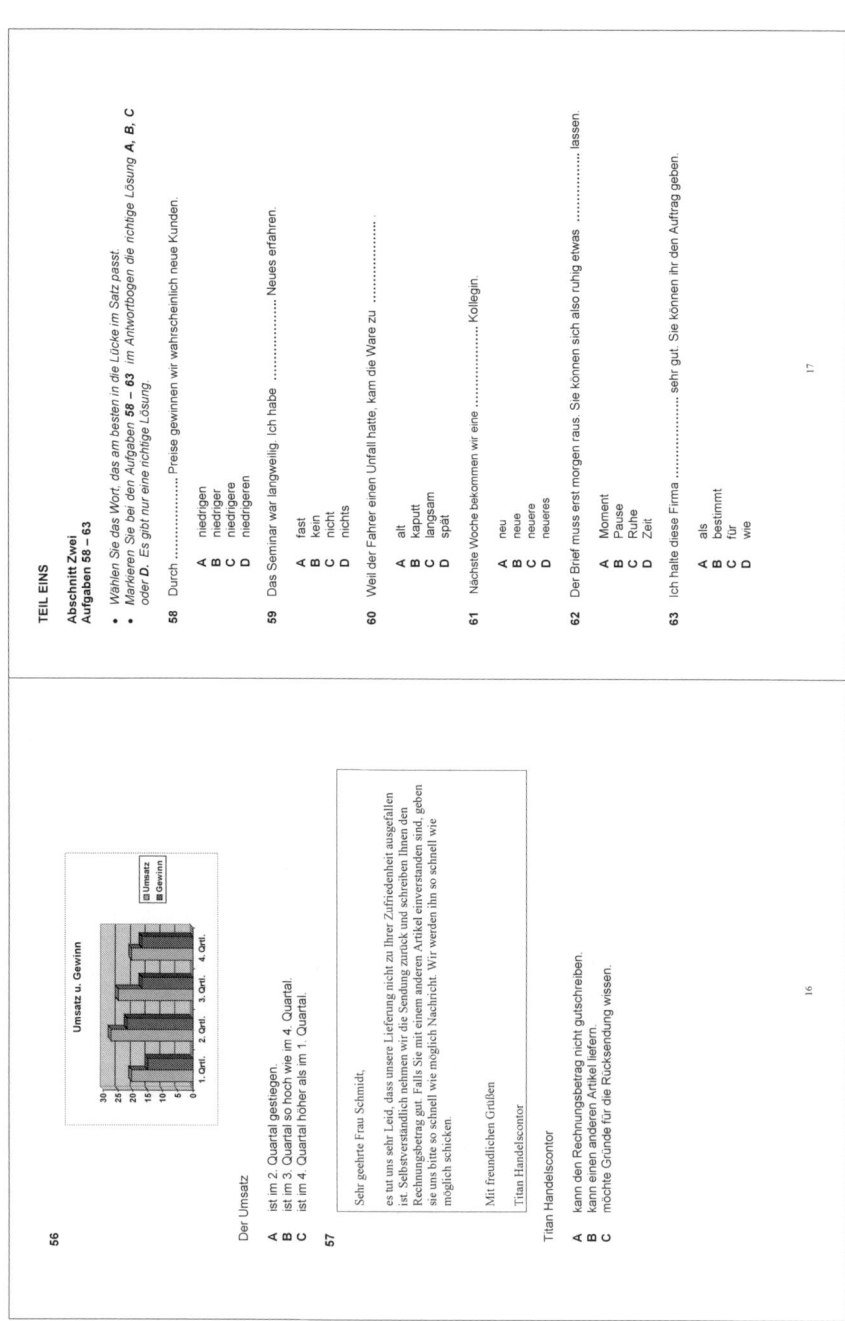

56

Umsatz u. Gewinn

Der Umsatz ....
A ist im 2. Quartal gestiegen.
B ist im 3. Quartal so hoch wie im 4. Quartal.
C ist im 4. Quartal höher als im 1. Quartal.

57

Sehr geehrte Frau Schmidt,

es tut uns sehr Leid, dass unsere Lieferung nicht zu Ihrer Zufriedenheit ausgefallen ist. Selbstverständlich nehmen wir die Sendung zurück und schreiben Ihnen den Rechnungsbetrag gut. Falls Sie mit einem anderen Artikel einverstanden sind, geben sie uns bitte so schnell wie möglich Nachricht. Wir werden ihn so schnell wie möglich schicken.

Mit freundlichen Grüßen

Titan Handelscontor

Titan Handelscontor ....
A kann den Rechnungsbetrag nicht gutschreiben.
B kann einen anderen Artikel liefern.
C möchte Gründe für die Rücksendung wissen.

16

TEIL EINS

Abschnitt Zwei
Aufgaben 58 – 63

• *Wählen Sie das Wort, das am besten in die Lücke im Satz passt.*
• *Markieren Sie bei den Aufgaben 58 – 63 im Antwortbogen die richtige Lösung A, B, C oder D. Es gibt nur eine richtige Lösung.*

58 Durch .... Preise gewinnen wir wahrscheinlich neue Kunden.
A niedrigen
B niedriger
C niedrigere
D niedrigeren

59 Das Seminar war langweilig. Ich habe .... Neues erfahren.
A fast
B kein
C nicht
D nichts

60 Weil der Fahrer einen Unfall hatte, kam die Ware zu ....
A alt
B kaputt
C langsam
D spät

61 Nächste Woche bekommen wir eine .... Kollegin.
A neu
B neue
C neuere
D neueres

62 Der Brief muss erst morgen raus. Sie können sich also ruhig etwas .... lassen.
A Moment
B Pause
C Ruhe
D Zeit

63 Ich halte diese Firma .... sehr gut. Sie können ihr den Auftrag geben.
A als
B bestimmt
C für
D wie

17

TEIL EINS

Abschnitt Drei
Aufgaben 64 – 69

- *Lesen Sie den folgenden Text aufmerksam durch und beantworten Sie die Aufgaben 64 – 69 auf der gegenüberliegenden Seite.*
- *Markieren Sie bei den Aufgaben 64 – 69 im Antwortbogen die richtige Lösung A, B oder C. Es gibt nur eine richtige Lösung.*

Sehr geehrte Damen, sehr geehrte Herren,

Ihre in der Süddeutschen Zeitung erschienene Stellenanzeige hat mich sehr angesprochen. Sie suchen eine zuverlässige Mitarbeiterin, die sich durch Flexibilität auszeichnet, über gute italienische Sprachenkenntnisse und außerdem über Erfahrung in der Planung von Gruppenreisen verfügt.

Weiterhin wünschen Sie Erfahrung im Umgang mit dem PC-Programm START und natürlich eine abgeschlossene Berufsausbildung als Reisekauffrau.

Ich glaube, dass ich alle diese geschilderten Anforderungen erfülle.

Ich bin einsatzfreudig und engagiert, habe meine Italienisch-Kenntnisse an der Dolmetscherschule in Heidelberg erworben und verfüge auch über sehr gute Englisch-Kenntnisse in Wort und Schrift sowie über brauchbare Französisch-Kenntnisse.

Während meiner 3-jährigen Berufstätigkeit war ich vor allem mit der Organisation von Gruppenreisen betraut. Ich habe besonderen Spaß am Umgang mit Menschen, auf deren Wünsche und Bedürfnisse ich mich gut einstellen kann. Für alle von mir organisierten Reisen gab es besonders gute Rückmeldungen.

Aus familiären Gründen plane ich, nach Osnabrück umzuziehen und habe deshalb meinen jetzigen Arbeitsplatz gekündigt.

An Ihrem Unternehmen gefällt mir besonders, dass es ein mittleres Unternehmen mit einer überschaubaren Mitarbeiterzahl ist. Ich glaube, meine Fähigkeiten so besser entfalten zu können als in einem sehr großen Unternehmen.

Gerne würde ich meinen Berufsweg bei Ihnen fortsetzen. Falls Sie meine Bewerbung anspricht, teilen Sie mir bitte einen Termin für ein persönliches Gespräch mit.

Mit freundlichen Grüßen

Ilona Schreiber

18

64 Die ausgeschriebene Stelle verlangt

- A eine abgeschlossene Berufsausbildung.
- B gute Sprachkenntnisse in zwei Fremdsprachen.
- C keine früheren beruflichen Erfahrungen.

65 Die Bewerberin glaubt, dass

- A die Anforderungen hoch sind.
- B sie den Anforderungen genügt.
- C sie die Anforderungen nicht genau kennt.

66 Die Fremdsprachenkenntnisse der Bewerberin sind

- A in Englisch besser als in Französisch.
- B in Französisch besser als in Italienisch.
- C in Französisch nicht ausreichend.

67 Die Bewerberin hat früher

- A Dienstreisen für Firmen organisiert.
- B individuelle Reisen für Firmenmitarbeiter organisiert.
- C Reisen für Gruppen organisiert.

68 Die Bewerberin

- A ist mit ihrem Arbeitsplatz nicht zufrieden
- B möchte aus persönlichen Gründen nach Osnabrück
- C wohnt jetzt in Osnabrück und möchte wegziehen.

69 Die Firma, die die Stelle ausgeschrieben hat, ist

- A die Deutsche Bundesbahn.
- B ein Touristikunternehmen.
- C eine Fluggesellschaft.

19

LESEVERSTEHEN und SPRACHKENNTNIS

Teil Zwei

21

TEIL EINS

Abschnitt Vier
Aufgaben 70 – 74

- Lesen Sie den folgenden Text und überlegen Sie sich für jede der Lücken ein passendes Wort.
- Schreiben Sie für die Lücken **70 – 74** jeweils nur **ein** Wort in den Antwortbogen.

Beispiel:

Er ist sehr .... Computern interessiert.

Lösung:

| 0 | an | ☐ | ☐ |

Ihre Anzeige in der Frankfurter Allgemeinen Zeitung

Aus Ihrer Anzeige entnehme ich, **(70)** .... Ihr Unternehmen talentierte Führungskräfte sucht. Ich habe mein Studium der Betriebswirtschaftslehre vor kurzem abgeschlossen und suche jetzt eine verantwortungsvolle Tätigkeit **(71)** .... frühestmöglichen Zeitpunkt.

Ich glaube, dass ich den beschriebenen Aufgaben aufgrund **(72)** .... Qualifikationen entspreche. Während meines Studiums habe ich ein dreimonatiges Praktikum **(73)** .... einer Firma in den USA verbracht. Deshalb verfüge ich über sehr gute Englischkenntnisse in Wort und Schrift.

Neben Kreativität gehören Belastbarkeit, Verantwortungsbewusstsein und Teamfähigkeit **(74)** .... meinen Eigenschaften.

20

TEIL ZWEI

Abschnitt Eins
Aufgaben 75 – 81

- *Lesen Sie die folgenden Äußerungen und die vier Anzeigen auf der gegenüberliegenden Seite aufmerksam durch.*
- *Welche Anzeige passt zu welcher der Äußerungen 75 – 81?*
- *Markieren Sie im Antwortbogen jeweils einen Buchstaben A, B, C oder D für die richtige Anzeige.*

Beispiel:

0   Sie bekommen im Seminar ein fertiges Konzept.

Lösung:

	A	B	C	D
0	■	□	□	□

75   Dieses Seminar findet in München statt.

76   Sie wollen im Ausland arbeiten und suchen ein Seminar zur Vorbereitung.

77   Sie haben wenig Zeit und suchen deshalb ein virtuelles Seminar.

78   Das Seminar findet an einzelnen Abenden statt.

79   Das Seminar findet zweimal im Jahr statt.

80   Sie suchen ein Seminar, bei dem man nicht alle Termine buchen muss.

81   Sie möchten lernen, wie man sich am besten präsentiert.

22

A

Schreiben Sie Ihren Businessplan online. Das lernen Sie in unserem achtwöchigen Workshop. Wir erlauben Ihnen, welche Inhalte das Papier haben muss und helfen Ihnen, Ihren individuellen Plan einsatzfertig zu erstellen. Nach acht Wochen verfügen Sie über Ihren Plan und haben gleichzeitig das Know-how erworben, um in der Zukunft Ihre Pläne selbstständig erstellen zu können. Das alles via Internet ohne persönliche Zusammenkunft.

B

Können Sie Ihre eigenen Fähigkeiten beim Vorstellungsgespräch richtig vermitteln? Wissen Sie, nach welchen Kriterien Personalentwickler Bewerber auswählen? Beides ist ein wichtiger Schritt zum Wunschjob. Diese Kenntnisse vermittelt Ihnen unser dreitägiges Seminar in München. „Sehen und gesehen werden" für Studenten vor der Job-Suche. Sie können zwischen zwei Terminen jährlich. Für weitere Informationen stehen wir gerne zur Verfügung.

C

Im „Wissensforum" der Frankfurter Allgemeinen Zeitung setzen wir unsere Veranstaltungsreihe fort. An zwölf Abenden referieren Prominente Persönlichkeiten über verschiedene Aspekte der Themen „Erfolg" und „lebenslanges Lernen". Unsere Veranstaltungen können en bloc oder auch einzeln gebucht werden. Reservierungen unter 069/ 25 36 08 bei Frau Schröder.

D

Möchten Sie in einem unserer europäischen Nachbarländer leben und dort auch Ihren Lebensunterhalt verdienen? Dann besuchen Sie unser einwöchiges Seminar „fit für Europa", das Ihnen fundierte Einblicke in unsere Nachbarländer vermittelt. Von Wohnungssuche über Arbeitsrecht bis zur Personalführung, werden in unserem Seminar alle wichtigen Aspekte angesprochen. Wir würden Sie gerne als Teilnehmer begrüßen.

23

255

TEIL ZWEI
Abschnitt Zwei
Aufgaben 82 – 86

- Lesen Sie den folgenden Text aufmerksam durch und wählen Sie für jede Lücke das passende Wort aus der Liste unten aus.
- Markieren Sie für die Lücken **82 – 86** im Antwortbogen die richtige Lösung **A, B, C** oder **D**. Es gibt nur eine richtige Lösung.

Beispiel:

Er möchte, dass Sie ihm den Grund (**0**) ....

0   A ansagen   B sagen   C aussagen   D versagen

Lösung:

0	A	B	C	D

Die erfolgreiche Besprechung

Wenn Sie zu einer Besprechung eingeladen werden, sollten Sie (**82**) .... bestehen, dass sie pünktlich beginnt und sich melden, wenn Sie (**83**) .... , dass die Diskussion zu weit vom Thema abschweift. (**84**) .... derjenige, der eingeladen hat, die Kontrolle über die Besprechung verliert, sollten Sie ihn daran erinnern, dass die Zeit wegläuft und Sie noch viel vor sich haben oder nach der (**85**) .... Besprechung noch wichtige Aufgaben zu erledigen haben. Machen Sie also immer klar, dass Sie (**86**) .... sich an die Tagesordnung zu halten.

82   A dagegen   B damit   C darauf   D darüber
83   A bedauern   B bemerken   C beschließen   D betonen
84   A Nachdem   B Obwohl   C Während   D Wenn
85   A folgenden   B kommenden   C laufenden   D nächsten
86   A vorgehen   B vorgehen   C vorhaben   D vornehmen

24

TEIL ZWEI
Abschnitt Drei
Aufgaben 87 – 91

- Lesen Sie den folgenden Text und überlegen Sie sich für jede der Lücken ein passendes Wort.
- Schreiben Sie für die Lücken **87 – 91** jeweils *nur **ein** Wort* in den Antwortbogen.

Beispiel:

Er ist sehr .... Computern interessiert.

Lösung:

0	an

Ein Seminar zu Zeit- und Selbstmanagement

Der Leitspruch, der sich durch das ganze Seminar zog, war: Sich nicht verzetteln, (**87**) .... klare Prioritäten setzen! Anhand (**88**) .... mehrseitigen Arbeitsblattes fanden die Seminarteilnehmer heraus, in welchen drei Bereichen ihres Zeitmanagements für sie der größte Handlungsbedarf (**89**) ....

Die wichtigste Erkenntnis für alle Teilnehmer des Seminars: Nur (**90**) .... sich darüber im Klaren ist, wohin er in seinem Beruf und in seinem Privatleben langfristig will, der ist auch in der (**91**) .... bei den täglichen Verrichtungen Prioritäten zu setzen.

25

Appendix 1.6

TEIL ZWEI

Abschnitt Vier
Aufgaben 92 – 97

- *Wählen Sie das Wort, das am besten in die Lücke im Satz passt.*
- *Markieren Sie bei den Aufgaben 92 – 97 im Antwortbogen die richtige Lösung A, B, C oder D. Es gibt nur eine richtige Lösung.*

92 Das im letzten Jahr eingeführte Produkt erfreut sich zunehmender ....

   A   Bedeutung
   B   Befriedigung
   C   Begrüßung
   D   Beliebtheit

93 Sie fühlt sich .... ihrer neuen Firma sehr wohl.

   A   auf
   B   in
   C   mit
   D   über

94 Unser Chef weiß mit seinen Mitarbeitern gut ....

   A   umgehen
   B   umgehen soll
   C   umzugehen
   D   wie umgehen

26

---

95 Herr Maier ist noch in einer Besprechung. .... er Sie in einer Stunde zurückrufen?

   A   Kann
   B   Möchte
   C   Muss
   D   Würde

96 Bei deinen Überlegungen solltest du die Wechselkurse nicht außer Acht ....

   A   haben
   B   lassen
   C   nehmen
   D   setzen

97 Ohne seine Hilfe .... wir nie so schnell fertig geworden.

   A   hätten
   B   sind
   C   wären
   D   würden

27

Appendix 1.6

TEIL ZWEI

Abschnitt Fünf
Aufgaben 98 – 103

- Lesen Sie den folgenden Text aufmerksam durch und lösen Sie die Aufgaben auf der gegenüberliegenden Seite.
- Markieren Sie bei den Aufgaben **98 – 103** im Antwortbogen die richtige Lösung **A, B, C** oder **D**. Es gibt nur eine richtige Lösung.

Das verschwendete Kapital

Deutsche Firmen schicken zwar viele Mitarbeiter für teures Geld ins Ausland, deren Wissen nutzen sie aber nicht und verschwenden damit wertvolle Ressourcen. Das ist das Ergebnis einer Studie des Wissenschaftszentrums Berlin, über die in der heutigen Ausgabe von *Wirtschaft Heute* berichtet wird.

Für die Studie wurden zwei große deutsche Firmen untersucht: eine Pharma-Firma mit 20 000 Mitarbeitern und eine Bank mit 30 000 Angestellten. Beide Firmen haben einige hundert Mitarbeiter in allen Teilen der Welt und die Firmenleitungen sind überzeugt, dass internationale Erfahrung wichtig ist und die Mitarbeiter nach ihrer Rückkehr ihr Wissen in die Firma einbringen.

Tatsache ist aber, dass die Firmen nach der Rückkehr der *expatriats* diese kaum nach ihrem Wissen und ihren Erfahrungen fragen. Dabei haben die Mitarbeiter im Ausland viel über ausländische Kultur und Geschäftsgewohnheiten gelernt. Sie kennen z.B. auch die Kreditrisiken, unsichere Kunden oder neue Geschäftsbereiche und verstehen viel besser, wie Ausländer ihre deutschen Geschäftspartner beurteilen. Aber in keiner der beiden Firmen bemühte man sich aktiv darum, das Wissen der Heimkehrer zu nutzen. Kaum einer wurde nach seinen Erfahrungen befragt und nur einem Viertel wurde anschließend eine Stelle angeboten, die einen Bezug zu dem Land hatte, in dem sie gewesen waren. Nur wenige berichteten von Projekten, in denen sie ihr neues Wissen konkret umsetzen konnten.

Es hilft aber nichts. Internationalisierung anzustreben, und dann vorhandene Möglichkeiten nicht zu nutzen. Diese Verschwendung kann sich heute kein Unternehmen mehr leisten. Gründe für diese Versäumnisse der deutschen Firmenleitungen zu finden, ist sehr schwer. Liegt es an zu starrer Organisation, allgemeiner Ignoranz oder sogar an der Angst, dass andere mehr wissen könnten als man selber? Bei den betroffenen Mitarbeitern führte die Haltung der Firmenleitungen meistens zu Frust und Resignation. Von den Firmenleitungen gab es keine Stellungnahme zu den Ergebnissen der Befragung.

28

---

98 In der Studie wurde erforscht, ob die Entsendung von Mitarbeitern ins Ausland

A den Mitarbeitern schadet.
B für die Firma nützlich ist.
C richtig geplant wird.
D zu viel Geld kostet.

99 Bei der Studie handelt es sich um eine

A firmeninterne Studie.
B Umfrage bei Banken und Pharmaunternehmen.
C wissenschaftliche Studie.
D Zeitungsumfrage.

100 Die untersuchten Unternehmen schicken Mitarbeiter ins Ausland, damit sie

A Fremdsprachen lernen.
B im Ausland Filialen aufbauen.
C internationale Erfahrungen sammeln.
D neue Kunden werben.

101 Die Mitarbeiter haben im Ausland Erkenntnisse gewonnen über

A das Deutschlandbild der ausländischen Partner.
B die Kreditwürdigkeit ausländischer Partner.
C die wirtschaftliche Unsicherheit ausländischer Partner.
D potentielle neue Geschäftsbereiche für die Firma.

102 Die zurückgekehrten Mitarbeiter waren frustriert, weil sie

A keine Beförderung auf eine bessere Stelle bekamen.
B mehr Interesse an ihren Erfahrungen erwartet hatten.
C sich an mehr Internationalität gewöhnt hatten.
D sich in ihrer jetzigen Stelle eingeengt fühlten.

103 Die Firmenleitungen

A planen Maßnahmen, um die Situation zu verbessern.
B reagierten nicht auf die Ergebnisse der Studie.
C wissen nicht, wie sie die Situation verbessern sollen.
D wollen keine Mitarbeiter mehr ins Ausland schicken.

29

258

TEIL ZWEI

Abschnitt Sechs
Aufgaben 104 – 110

- *Der nachfolgende Text enthält einige Fehler.*
- *Ist ein Satz ohne Fehler, machen Sie im Antwortbogen ein Häkchen (√) hinter der Nummer.*
- *Ist ein Wort falsch, schreiben Sie die korrekte Form hinter die entsprechende Nummer in den Antwortbogen.*

Beispiel:

Es konnte keine Übereinkurft erzielt werden. | 0 | √ |

<u>Bestätigen</u> Sie bitte den Erhalt der Ware. | 00 | *Bestätigen* |

Lieber Herr Vollmer,

104 Danke für Ihre Anfrage bezüglich der von uns angebotene Drucker. Da

105 Sie die Drucker für Ihr Großraumbüro benötigen und somit auch der

106 Geräuschbelastung eine Rolle spielt, möchte ich Sie die Anschaffung

107 des kompakten DIN A3-Druckers BJ-230 empfehlen. Er gehört zu den

108 leisesten Tintenstrahldruckern der Welt und sind deshalb für ein

Großraumbüro bestens geeignet.

109 Bitte lasse Sie uns Ihre Entscheidung möglichst bald wissen und sagen

110 Sie uns auch, wie vielen Drucker Sie benötigen. Bei einer Bestellung

von mindestens 5 Druckern können wir Ihnen einen Rabatt anbieten.

Mit freundlichen Grüßen

H. Unterberg

LEERE SEITE

30

31

APPENDIX 2.1
ALTE Work Typical Abilities

LEVELS	Listening/Speaking	Reading	Writing
C2 Level 5	CAN advise on/handle complex delicate or contentious issues, such as legal or financial matters, to the extent that he/she has the necessary specialist knowledge.	CAN understand reports and articles likely to be encountered during his/her work, including complex ideas expressed in complex language.	CAN make full and accurate notes and continue to participate in a meeting or seminar.
C1 Level 4	CAN contribute effectively to meetings and seminars within own area of work and argue for or against a case.	CAN understand correspondence expressed in non-standard language.	CAN handle a wide range of routine and non-routine situations in which professional services are requested from colleague or external contacts.
B2 Level 3	CAN take and pass on most messages that are likely to require attention during a normal working day.	CAN understand most correspondence, reports and factual product literature he/she is likely to come across.	CAN deal with all routine requests for goods or services.
B1 Level 2	CAN offer advice to clients within own job area on simple matters.	CAN understand the general meaning of non-routine letters and theoretical articles within own work area.	CAN make reasonably accurate notes at a meeting or seminar where the subject matter is familiar and predictable.
A2 Level 1	CAN state simple requirements within own job area, such as 'I want to order 25 of...'.	CAN understand most short reports or manuals of a predictable nature within his/her own area of expertise, provided enough time is given.	CAN write a short, comprehensive note of request to a colleague or a known contact in another company.
A1 ALTE breakthrough level	CAN take and pass on simple messages of a routine kind, such as 'Friday meeting 10 am'.	CAN understand short reports or product descriptions on familiar matters, if these are expressed in simple language and the contents are predictable.	CAN write a simple routine request to a colleague, such as 'Can I have 20X please?'.

APPENDIX 3.1
BEC 1 Sample Paper

Candidate Name _____

Centre Number

Candidate Number

UNIVERSITY OF CAMBRIDGE LOCAL EXAMINATIONS SYNDICATE
Examinations in English as a Foreign Language

BUSINESS ENGLISH CERTIFICATE 1　　　　**0230/1**
Test of Reading and Writing

SAMPLE PAPER　　　　　　　　　　1 hour 10 minutes

Additional materials:
　Answer sheets

TIME　　1 hour 10 minutes

INSTRUCTIONS TO CANDIDATES

Do not open this paper until you are told to do so.

Write your name, Centre number and candidate number in the spaces at the top of this page. Write these details in pencil on your Answer Sheets **if these are not already printed.**

Write all your answers in **pencil** on your Answer Sheets – **no extra time is allowed for this.**

Read carefully the instructions for each part, and the instructions for completing your Answer Sheets.

Try to answer all the questions.

At the end of the examination hand in both this question paper and your Answer Sheets.

INFORMATION FOR CANDIDATES

There are forty-seven questions on this question paper:
　　Reading Questions 1 – 40
　　Writing Questions 41 – 47

This question paper consists of 15 printed pages and 1 blank page.

SB (SLC/TC) 011603/1
© UCLES 1999

[Turn over

2

READING

QUESTIONS 1–40

PART ONE

Questions 1–5

- Look at questions 1–5.
- In each question, which sentence is correct?
- For each question, mark **one letter (A, B or C)** on your Answer Sheet.

Example: 0

Don't forget –
flight BA692 6.45 pm

The plane arrives at

A quarter to seven in the morning.
B quarter past six in the evening.
C quarter to seven in the evening.

The correct answer is C, so mark your Answer Sheet like this

	A	B	C
0			▭

1

For further information on our full range of products, please complete and return the form below.

You can find out more about these products by

A requesting a form.
B buying any product.
C sending your details.

3

2

OFFICE HOURS
MON - THURS   8.30 - 5.00
FRI   8.30 - 4.00
SAT   CLOSED
SUN   CLOSED

A The office closes early on Fridays.
B The office closes at the same time every day.
C The office is open at the weekend.

3

CONFERENCE VISITORS' INFORMATION DESK
Please note:
Lunch is available only if booked when you registered

Lunch is available for

A all visitors to the conference.
B people who have already requested it.
C anyone who wants to book now.

4

Filing Cabinet Specifications

Height: 102 cm
Width: 47 cm
Colours: Brown or Grey

This product is available in different

A sizes.
B colours.
C sizes and colours.

5

FREE CALCULATOR WITH ALL ORDERS OVER $50

You can get a free calculator

A if you spend more than fifty dollars.
B if you order more than fifty items.
C if you make more than fifty orders.

[Turn over

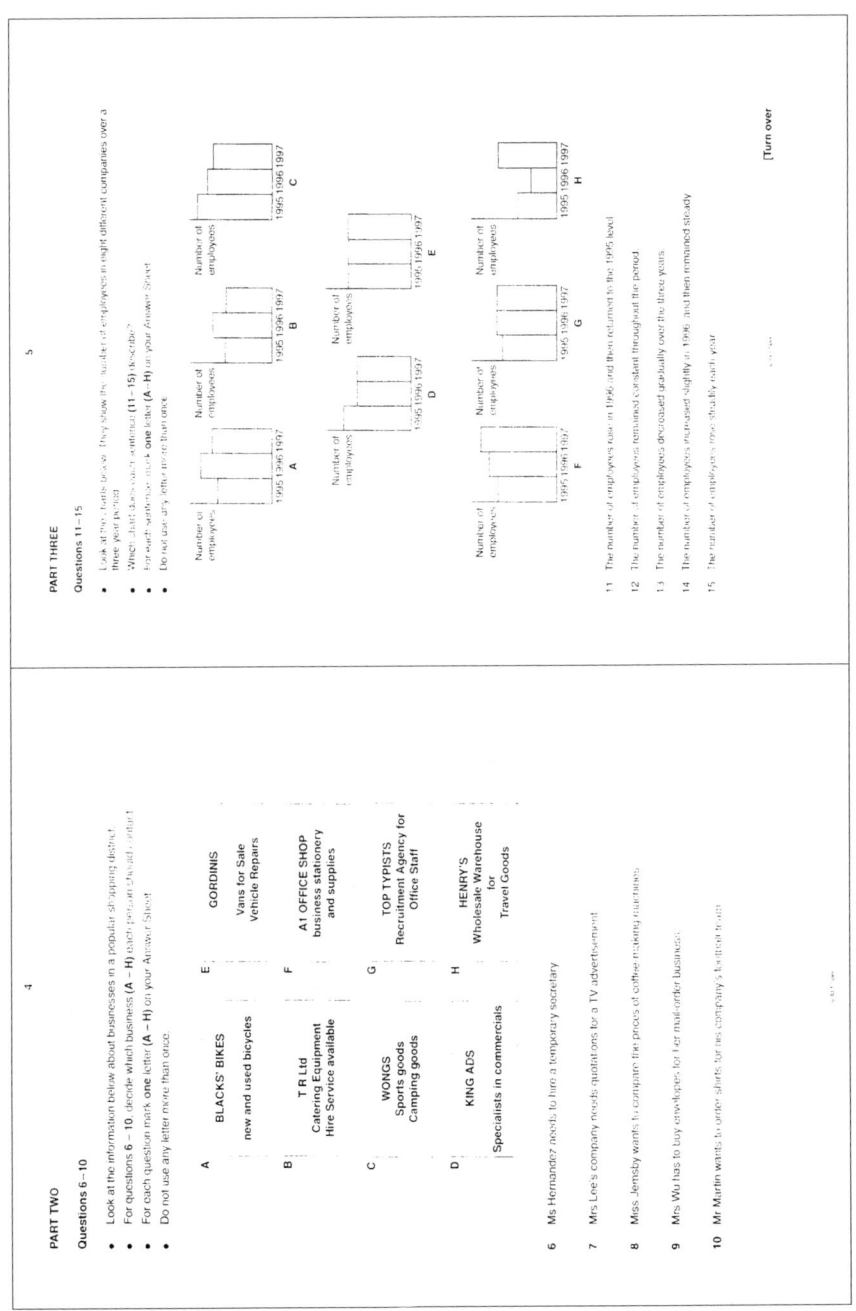

PART TWO

Questions 6–10

- Look at the information below about businesses in a popular shopping district.
- For questions 6 – 10, decide which business (A – H) each person should contact.
- For each question mark one letter (A – H) on your Answer Sheet.
- Do not use any letter more than once.

A
BLACKS' BIKES
new and used bicycles

B
T R Ltd
Catering Equipment
Hire Service available

C
WONGS
Sports goods
Camping goods

D
KING ADS
Specialists in commercials

E
GORDINIS
Vans for Sale
Vehicle Repairs

F
A1 OFFICE SHOP
business stationery
and supplies

G
TOP TYPISTS
Recruitment Agency for
Office Staff

H
HENRY'S
Wholesale Warehouse
for
Travel Goods

6   Ms Hernandez needs to hire a temporary secretary

7   Mrs Lee's company needs quotations for a TV advertisement

8   Miss Jemisty wants to compare the prices of coffee making machines

9   Mrs Wu has to buy envelopes for her mail-order business

10 Mr Martin wants to order shirts for his company's football team

PART THREE

Questions 11–15

- Look at the bar charts below. They show the number of employees in eight different companies over a three year period.
- Which chart does each sentence (11 –15) describe?
- For each sentence mark one letter (A – H) on your Answer Sheet.
- Do not use any letter more than once.

11 The number of employees rose in 1996 and then returned to the 1995 level.

12 The number of employees remained constant throughout the period.

13 The number of employees decreased gradually over the three years.

14 The number of employees increased slightly in 1996, and then remained steady.

15 The number of employees rose steadily each year.

[Turn over

Appendic 3.1

PART FOUR

Questions 16–22

- Read the report below about a company's sales.
- Are sentences **16–22** on the opposite page 'Right' or 'Wrong'?
- If there is not enough information to answer 'Right' or 'Wrong', choose 'Doesn't say'.
- For each sentence **16–22**, mark **one** letter (**A**, **B** or **C**) on your Answer Sheet.

Company Sales Highest Yet

Business at Shanghai International is breaking all records. Shanghai International is a joint venture between a British firm, whose headquarters are just outside London, and a Chinese firm based in Shanghai. The company produces paint and has benefitted enormously from the development of shipbuilding in China. Last year was the best yet for the company, with total sales up by 50% in quantity and 60% in value on the previous year. Shanghai International now sells eight times more paint than when it started in 1990, and is growing faster than any other paint production operation in South-East Asia. Sales have doubled since it moved to a new factory two years ago, and the possibility of further expansion is already being discussed, with plans to build a plant in Dalian, in the north of China.

Shanghai International now provides China's biggest shipbuilding companies with more than 50% of their paint requirements. To deal with the sharp rise in production, the company has recently built two new warehouses at the present factory site.

7

16 The companies which own Shanghai International are from different countries.

   A Right   **B** Wrong   **C** Doesn't say

17 Shanghai International supplies paint to a number of different industries.

   A Right   **B** Wrong   **C** Doesn't say

18 Last year, Shanghai International sold 60% more paint than in the year before.

   A Right   **B** Wrong   **C** Doesn't say

19 Shanghai International moved to a new site because the old factory was too small.

   A Right   **B** Wrong   **C** Doesn't say

20 Shanghai International is considering setting up a new operation in northern China.

   A Right   **B** Wrong   **C** Doesn't say

21 Shanghai International supplies China's biggest shipbuilders with all the paint they need.

   A Right   **B** Wrong   **C** Doesn't say

22 The company has added two new warehouses as a result of the increase in production.

   A Right   **B** Wrong   **C** Doesn't say

[Turn over

PART FIVE

Questions 23–30

- Read the information sheet below about conference centres.
- Answer questions 23–30 on the opposite page.

EASTBY COMMERCIAL DEVELOPMENT OFFICE
Conference Centre Information

Conference organisers often have difficulty finding a suitable place to hold a conference. We would like to suggest four conference centres in our area where you are certain to find good service and value.

THE CORNWELL CONFERENCE CENTRE
The Cornwell is twenty kilometres from Eastby and is most easily reached by car or coach. It has two conference rooms, each holding up to three hundred people, and three seminar rooms, each designed for a maximum of forty. There is also a first-class restaurant. There are excellent telephone, fax and e-mail facilities. The price per head also covers bed and breakfast in a nearby hotel.

THE EASTBY BUSINESS CENTRE
Companies needing a good social programme as well as meeting rooms are well looked after at the EBC. The management can arrange concerts and discos on request. The EBC is located opposite the main entrance to the City Museum on Bateman Street. As parking space is not available at the Centre, the management recommends that guests leave their cars in the Eastby Railway Station car park, which is free.

THE GREENHILL CENTRE
The Greenhill, only five kilometres from Eastby, is a good choice for small conferences and meetings. It is popular with many companies based in the area and its highly-trained reception staff speak a number of foreign languages. There are three comfortable meeting rooms, seating ninety people in total, all well equipped with audio-visual aids. The Centre offers a special price if all three rooms are hired together. Guests can stay overnight in the nearby Greenhill Hotel, which has outdoor tennis courts.

THE METRO REGENT
The Metro Regent is a large, modern hotel in beautiful gardens, with a conference hall suitable for up to two hundred people. It is only ten minutes by train from Eastby city centre, which has many tourist attractions. Cars and minibuses can be rented from the hotel. There is a busy programme of conferences at the Metro Regent, especially in the summer, so early booking is advisable. The hotel is closed for the whole of November and for the New Year.

- For questions 23–26, choose the correct answer.
- For each question, mark **one** letter (**A, B** or **C**) on your Answer Sheet.

23 The cost per person at the Cornwell includes

A   telephone calls.

B   all meals.

C   hotel accommodation.

24 The Eastby Business Centre advises conference guests to park

A   outside the main entrance.

B   at Eastby Railway Station.

C   opposite the City Museum.

25 The Greenhill Centre is frequently used by

A   local companies.

B   foreign companies.

C   television companies.

26 The most popular time for holding conferences at the Metro Regent is

A   New Year.

B   Summer.

C   November.

- For questions 27–30, use the information in the text to match each conference centre with the service it offers (A–G).
- For each question, mark the correct letter (A–G) on your **Answer Sheet**.
- Do not use any letter more than once.

27   The Cornwell Conference Centre

28   The Eastby Business Centre

29   The Greenhill Centre

30   The Metro Regent

A   discounts

B   secretarial support

C   excellent food

D   games room

E   organised entertainment

F   sightseeing trips

G   vehicle hire

[*Turn over*

10

PART SIX

Questions 31–40

- Read the text below about company pay policy.
- Choose the correct word to fill each gap, from **A**, **B** or **C** on the opposite page.
- For each question, mark **one letter** (**A**, **B** or **C**) on your Answer Sheet.

Company Pay Policy

Company pay policy should have two main goals. Firstly, the policy should provide **(31)** ...... acceptable level of reward. This will make it possible **(32)** ...... the company to hire and keep employees. Secondly, if should encourage individual employees to seek promotion within the company by **(33)** ...... rewards for additional responsibility and improved skills. The aim is to make employees see themselves **(34)** ...... part of a team.

Pay policy should therefore be decided at the **(35)** ...... level in the organisation. The Personnel Manager is normally the one **(36)** ...... takes the final decision. However, that does not mean that **(37)** ...... members of the management team do **(38)** ...... have responsibility as well. The issue is **(39)** ...... important that one manager cannot deal with it alone. Everyone in a company is responsible for making sure **(40)** ...... pay policy is successful.

11

	A	B	C
31	this	the	an
32	for	to	by
33	offer	offered	offering
34	in	as	like
35	highest	higher	highly
36	which	whose	who
37	another	other	others
38	neither	never	not
39	too	so	such
40	any	much	many

[Turn over

12

WRITING

QUESTIONS 41–47

PART SEVEN

Questions 41–45

- Read the memo and the receipt below.
- Complete the form on the opposite page.
- Write each word, phrase or number in **CAPITAL LETTERS** on lines **41–45** on your Answer Sheet.

MEMO

To: Paul Woods, Sales
From: Lynn Thomas, Finance

Re: Your accommodation expenses for the trip to Auckland from 21st to 26th July.

I can't pay you until you send me your expenses claim form.

Thanks.

PAN PACIFIC HOTEL
18 - 24 Eden Avenue, Auckland
Tel: 2388709

RECEIPT   26.7.98

Mr P Woods

5 nights single room with bed & breakfast   NZ$540

cheque / cash / credit card

02/001 Spec

13

Accommodation Expenses Claim Form
(please return to Lynn Thomas, Finance)

Name of employee: (41) ....

Department: (42) ....

Dates of trip: (43) ....

Name of hotel: (44) ....

Amount claimed: NZ$540

Method of
payment used: (45) ....

02/001 Spec

[Turn over

267

Appendic 3.1

14

PART EIGHT

Question 46

- You need some office furniture for a new employee in your department.
- Write a memo to Eric Ford in the Purchasing Department.

- telling him what furniture you need
- explaining why you need it
- asking him to tell you when the furniture will arrive.

- Write **about 20 – 30 words**.
- **Write on your Answer Sheet. Do not write in capital letters.**

Memo

To: Eric Ford, Purchasing

15

PART NINE

Question 47

- Read the letter below.

We would be grateful if you could give us information about two of your cleaning products, Super Floor Cleaner and General Cleaner.

We would like to know the discount you can offer if we buy 30 litres of each product.

We would also like to know when you could deliver these quantities; this would ideally be before 18th October.

Yours sincerely

Helen Wong

Helen Wong
Supervisor
Office Cleaning Services

- Write a letter to Ms Wong

- thanking her for her enquiry
- telling her about your discounts
- confirming that you can deliver by the required date
- asking her to phone if she would like further details.

- Write **50 – 70 words**.
- **Write on your Answer Sheet. Do not write in capital letters. Do not include any addresses.**

Candidate Name _____

Centre Number

Candidate Number

UNIVERSITY OF CAMBRIDGE LOCAL EXAMINATIONS SYNDICATE

Examinations in English as a Foreign Language

BUSINESS ENGLISH CERTIFICATE 1　　**0230/2**

Test of Listening

SAMPLE PAPER　　　　Approx. 40 minutes
(including 10 minutes' transfer time)

Additional materials:
　Answer sheet

TIME　　Approx. 40 minutes (including 10 minutes' transfer time)

INSTRUCTIONS TO CANDIDATES

Do not open this paper until you are told to do so.

Write your name, Centre number and candidate number in the spaces at the top of this page. Write these details in pencil on your Answer Sheet **if these are not already printed.**

Listen to the instructions for each part carefully.

Try to answer all the questions.

Write your answers on this question paper.

At the end of the test you will have 10 minutes to copy your answers onto your Answer Sheet.

Read the instructions for completing your Answer Sheet carefully.

Write all your answers in **pencil**.

At the end of the examination hand in both this question paper and your Answer Sheet.

INFORMATION FOR CANDIDATES

Instructions are given on the tape.

You will hear everything twice.

There are thirty questions on this question paper.

This question paper consists of 9 printed pages and 3 blank pages.

S9 (CW/KG) Ol9069/1
© UCLES 1999

[Turn over

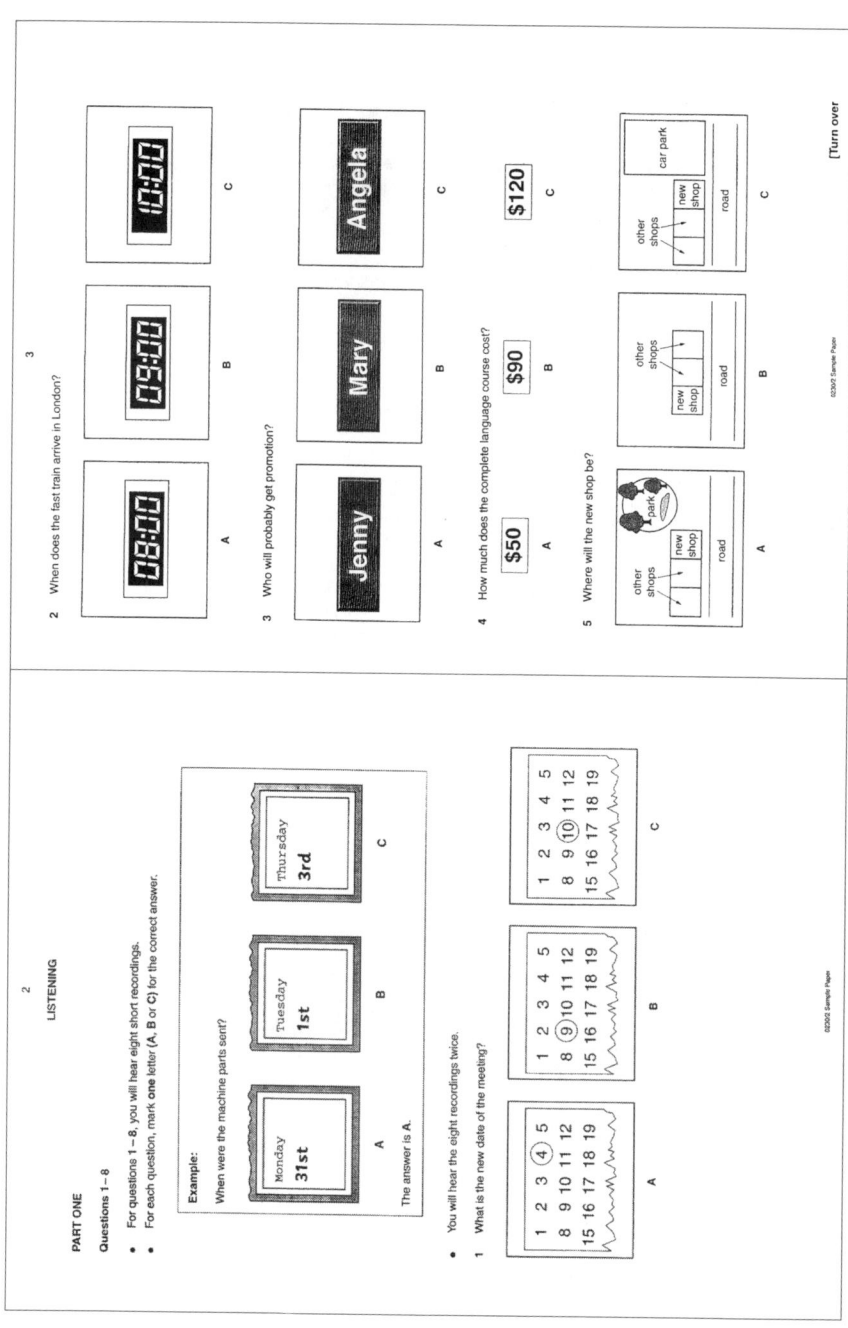

2

3 When does the fast train arrive in London?

08:00   09:00   10:00
A   B   C

3 Who will probably get promotion?

Jenny   Mary   Angela
A   B   C

4 How much does the complete language course cost?

$50 $90 $120
A   B   C

5 Where will the new shop be?

A   B   C

©2005 Sample Paper

[Turn over

2

LISTENING

PART ONE

Questions 1 – 8

- For questions 1 – 8, you will hear eight short recordings.
- For each question, mark **one** letter (**A**, **B** or **C**) for the correct answer.

Example:

When were the machine parts sent?

Monday   Tuesday   Thursday
31st   1st   3rd
A   B   C

The answer is A.

- You will hear the eight recordings twice.

1 What is the new date of the meeting?

1 2 3 ④ 5
8 9 10 11 12
15 16 17 18 19
A

1 2 3 4 5
8 ⑨ 10 11 12
15 16 17 18 19
B

1 2 3 4 5
8 9 ⑩ 11 12
15 16 17 18 19
C

©2005 Sample Paper

270

4

6 Where is the fair this year?

in Nice	in London	in Barcelona
A	B	C

7 Which floor is Mr Lee's office on?

3rd Floor	4th Floor	5th Floor
A	B	C

8 What does the woman need to do before the conference?

A   make the travel arrangements

B   type up the sales figures

C   discuss her lecture

5

PART TWO

Questions 9–12

- Look at the order form below.
- You will hear a customer ordering supplies.
- Listen to the conversation, and write the missing **numbers** in the spaces.
- You will hear the conversation twice.

Ace Computer Supplies

Telephone Order   **Date:** 1.8.98

Company: ALTO Insurance (A.Bell)

Order: (9) .... New Star handbooks

(10) .... E12 telex printer ribbons

Delivery address: (11) .... London Street

Order reference no: (12) BK /..................

[Turn over

6

PART THREE

Questions 13 – 22

- You will hear two telephone conversations.
- Write **one or two words or a number** in the spaces on each form.
- You will hear each conversation twice.

Conversation One

(Questions 13–17)

- You will hear a customer calling a restaurant.
- Complete the form using the information you hear.

GOLDEN TIGER RESTAURANT
Reservations (company clients)

Caller: *Anna Davidson from the* ....

.... (13)

Date: *Wednesday* **(14)** ...., *1.00 p.m.*

Number in party: *Six*

Special requirements:
Caller requests table near **(15)** ....
and **(16)** .... *menu.*

Method of payment: *monthly,* **(17)** ....

Conversation Two

(Questions 18 – 22)

- You will hear a staff member arranging a card for a visitor.
- Complete the form using the information you hear.

Visitor's Card Request

Full name of visitor: Martin (18) ....

Date: *10th October*

Visiting: (member of staff): Chris (19) ....

.... **(department):** .... **(20)**

Site: (21) ....

Reason for visit: (22) ....

7

272

8

PART FOUR

Questions 23–30

- Listen to a meeting between a safety officer and a production manager about how safety and security can be improved at their factory.
- For each question 23–30, mark one letter (A, B or C) for the correct answer.
- You will hear the conversation twice.

23 What is the first subject discussed?

A the increase in injuries
B the reporting of dangerous behaviour
C the causes of accidents

24 Where are the notices going to be put?

A in the staff canteen
B in the production department
C in all the corridors

25 Which people do not have to wear any special clothes at the factory?

A company visitors
B sales staff
C administration staff

26 Which of the factory staff wear orange coats?

A quality control
B technicians
C security

27 Who gives out visitors' cards?

A personnel officers
B department managers
C security officers

9

28 Which gate is often left open?

A the North gate
B the West gate
C the South gate

29 Security at the open gate is improved by using

A extra staff.
B special locks.
C cameras.

30 When is the next meeting?

A April
B May
C June

You now have 10 minutes to transfer your answers to your Answer Sheet.

273

BEC 1   SAMPLE SPEAKING TEST

International Business Magazines

(2 candidates)

Candidate A

Information

This is the information you need to answer your partner's questions.

> ### *Commercial Life*
>
> for
> - advertising agents
> - account managers
>
> (from August: special section for designers)
>
> 2 issues per month
> (December - 1 issue only)
>
> Publishers:
> Technoprint Ltd (Switzerland)
> Brown & Burton plc (U.S.A)

BEC 1   SAMPLE SPEAKING TEST

International Business Magazines

(2 candidates)

Candidate A

Your Questions

You need to ask your partner for this information about an international business magazine.

Title of magazine   ....

Topics covered   ....

Available from   ....

Price of magazine   ....

BEC 1   SAMPLE SPEAKING TEST

International Business Magazines

(2 candidates)

Candidate B

Information

This is the information you need to answer your partner's questions.

International Finance

Regular articles include:
- top 100 investments worldwide
  - business trends
  - banking news

On sale in Europe & Asia (all major bookshops)

$3.50 per issue
($4 including post)

Appendic 3.1

International Business Magazines

(2 candidates)

Candidate B

Your Questions

You need to ask your partner for this information about another international business magazine.

Title of magazine	....
Suitable for	....
How often published	....
Published by	....

APPENDIX 3.2
BEC 2 Sample Paper

	Centre Number	Candidate Number

Candidate Name _____

UNIVERSITY OF CAMBRIDGE LOCAL EXAMINATIONS SYNDICATE
Examinations in English as a Foreign Language

BUSINESS ENGLISH CERTIFICATE 2   **0231/1,2**

Test of Reading and Writing

SAMPLE PAPER   1 hour 30 minutes

Additional materials:
  Answer sheets

TIME   1 hour 30 minutes

INSTRUCTIONS TO CANDIDATES

Do not open this paper until you are told to do so.

Write your name, Centre number and candidate number in the spaces at the top of this page. Write these details in pencil on your Answer Sheets **if these are not already printed**.

Write all your answers in **pencil** on your Answer Sheets – **no extra time is allowed for this**.

Read carefully the instructions for each part, and the instructions for completing your Answer Sheets.

Try to answer all the questions.

At the end of the examination hand in both this question paper and your Answer Sheets.

INFORMATION FOR CANDIDATES

There are forty-seven questions on this question paper:
  Reading Questions 1 – 45
  Writing Questions 46 and 47

This question paper consists of 13 printed pages and 3 blank pages.

SB (SLC) QK95120/1
© UCLES 1999

[Turn over

2

READING

QUESTIONS 1 – 45

PART ONE

Questions 1 – 7

- Look at the sentences below and the book reviews on the opposite page.
- Which book does each sentence 1 – 7 refer to?
- For each sentence, mark **one letter (A, B, C or D) on your Answer Sheet.**
- You will need to use some of these letters more than once.

Example:

0   It is the work of a successful writer.

	A	B	C	D
0				

1   It describes activities which have become increasingly popular.

2   It gives important information as briefly as possible.

3   It deals with an area that has received little attention previously.

4   It describes methods that can help with team-building.

5   It is suitable for people with varying degrees of commercial experience.

6   It was previously published with a different title.

7   It is written for people from different types of professional background.

3

A

The Trainer's Pocketbook

Formerly known as *The Instructor's Pocketbook*, the eighth edition of this short guide covers 'all the essentials of training', from creating the right learning environment to the use of audio-visual equipment. This 78-page book concentrates on presenting the key facts in summary form.

B

The Handbook of Health and Safety

This is a comprehensive guide intended for managers, union safety representatives and anyone teaching for Occupational Health & Safety examinations. Apart from the usual subjects of legal obligations and risk prevention, it focuses on a relatively neglected issue, that of health concerns about computer use – particularly those associated with keyboard work.

C

Writing Effective Advertisements

This guide has been put together by best-selling author John Newton and looks at the reasons why some advertisements are more successful than others. Ideal both for someone starting up in business and for the established business person, it contains useful information on advertisement layout and content.

D

Using Management Games

This second edition, which reflects the growing trend to use management games as training tools, acts as a guide to exercises designed to increase group effectiveness. The writer explains the ways in which exercises, for example puzzles and communication games, can be used to improve group co-operation.

[Turn over]

4

PART TWO

Questions 8 – 12

- Read the article below about how companies can make their employees want to stay.
- Choose the best sentence from the list on the opposite page to fill each of the gaps.
- For each gap **8 – 12**, mark **one** letter **(A – I) on your Answer Sheet**.
- Do not use any letter more than once.

Keeping Good Employees

The difficulty of holding on to good, experienced staff has always been a major issue with the majority of companies. High staff turnover can result in many problems. **(example)** ..... I .....

Most companies hope to recruit the right type of person in the first place. However, too much emphasis on qualifications and not enough on personality often leads to a company attracting the right standard, but not the right kind, of person. **(8)** .... They can also be used to identify existing staff who are suitable but who, initially, may not have been considered.

It is important for companies to understand why employees move on to another employer. **(9)** .... They can be the key to identifying any problem areas that might exist within an organisation. It is essential, therefore, that employers who are about to disappear are interviewed before they depart, in order to discover why they are leaving.

Analysis of these interviews has shown that a lack of appreciation is one of the main factors causing employees to look elsewhere for work. Managers should provide regular feedback to their staff. **(10)** .... If this is not done, employees will think their efforts are not appreciated.

Communications within the organisation are another consideration. **(11)** .... This can be avoided through regular departmental and inter-departmental meetings, which are extremely valuable as a means of passing on information throughout the company, and keeping employees up to date with recent developments. They also serve to provide the opportunity for employees to express their opinions.

Paying staff according to how they perform is another way of recognising employees' efforts. If the company benefits from an employee's extra effort, it is only reasonable that the employee should also receive some financial benefit. It is, however, important to avoid offering some members of staff the opportunity to improve their pay while excluding others. **(12)** .... In cases where such difficulties might exist, a planned career progression for an individual staff member means that the person knows exactly what to expect from the job and what is required from them.

5

example
A B C D E F G H I

A For example, when good work has been done it must be praised.

B This can easily happen, since it is not always possible to introduce productivity measurements into every employee's work.

C In particular, employers are recognising that these requirements will change as time goes by.

D Selection tests can be used to indicate a candidate's suitability for the job they are applying for.

E The methods of training do not necessarily have to mean increased costs.

F The reasons for staff resigning and the benefits offered by their new employers must be recorded.

G Options to consider are part-time working and job share schemes, which benefit both employer and employee.

H If these are poor, employees will feel left out.

I One of the most serious of these is the cost of continually having to find and train replacements.

[Turn over

279

6

PART THREE

Questions 13 – 20

• Read the text below about exports from Chile and answer questions **13 – 20** on the opposite page.

CHILE INVESTS IN FRUIT AND VEGETABLES

Chile has become one of Europe's favourite sourcing countries for fruit and vegetables. In fact it has taken less than ten years for Chile to establish itself as Latin America's largest exporter of fruit and vegetables, with Europe the largest consumer. Fresh produce exports are one of the country's main growth sectors, with over 36 million tons of fruit and seven million tons of vegetables exported world-wide each year.

1. Much of the country's agriculture is carried out in the fertile Maipo Valley, which is also famous as a wine-growing area. The Mediterranean climate and fertile soil provide ideal growing conditions, helped by a comparative absence of insects and disease. Being located in the southern hemisphere is another advantage and, at certain times of the year, fruit such as grapes and certain vegetables can be obtained only from Chile.

2. The Chileans recognise that investment is the key to continued success, and have invested heavily in food-processing and packaging technology in order to build up sales of value-added foods, such as frozen and tinned fruit and vegetables, in addition to the original juices and jams. Raspberries are their largest frozen fruit export, with some 19,000 tons exported each year, and asparagus, with 3,500 tons, their largest frozen vegetable export. There has been a dramatic rise in the export sales of frozen fruit and vegetables, which have increased by as much as 4000% in some cases.

3. A very important player in this success story has been the Frutos del Maipo Corporation. Frutos del Maipo was formed in 1978, originally to provide fruit for jam producers in Chile. Using both fresh and frozen fruit, it now supplies the national industry all year round, as well as the principal markets of Europe, the USA and Japan. Its sales last year reached 8,000 tons and were valued at US$12m, representing 30% of the Chilean market.

4. The UK is Chile's fourth largest European importer of frozen produce, importing over three million tons, valued at US$6m. The distance between Santiago and the UK means that most of this fruit and vegetable cargo is transported by air. British Airways has benefited from the dramatic increase in exports to the UK, adding a third direct weekly flight to Santiago. BA's World Cargo Division has seen a 45% growth in the movement of fresh goods from Chile to the UK in the last year. According to Rodrigo Casal of British Airways World Cargo, this trade between Chile and the UK will continue to grow at a rapid rate.

02311-2 Sample W99

7

Questions 13 – 16

• For questions **13 – 16**, choose the best title for each numbered paragraph from the list below.
• For each numbered paragraph **1 – 4**, mark **one** letter (**A – G**) on your Answer Sheet.
• Do not use any letter more than once.

13 Paragraph 1 ....

14 Paragraph 2 ....

15 Paragraph 3 ....

16 Paragraph 4 ....

A	Developing the export range
B	The importance of the US and Japan
C	Protection from disease
D	A Chilean company's success
E	Competition from technology
F	Natural advantages
G	Increased freight business

Questions 17 – 20

• Using the information in the text, complete each sentence **17 – 20** with a phrase **A – G** from the list below.
• For each question **17 – 20**, mark **one** letter (**A – G**) on your Answer Sheet.
• Do not use any letter more than once.

17 The biggest importers of Chilean fruit and vegetables are ....

18 Chile has realised the importance of using ....

19 A particularly large increase occurred in exports of ....

20 Frutos del Maipo started by supplying ....

A	frozen fruit and vegetables
B	other Latin American countries
C	the jam industry
D	up-to-date processing methods
E	modern air-freight terminals
F	European countries
G	juices and jams

02311-2 Sample W99

[Turn over

PART FOUR

Questions 21 – 35

- Read the letter below.
- Choose the correct word **A**, **B**, **C** or **D** on the opposite page to fill each gap.
- For each question **21 – 35**, mark **one letter** (**A**, **B**, **C** or **D**) **on your Answer Sheet**

8

RICHMAN RING:
International Movers

Our ref: F/2J   21st March 1998

Dear Mr Ratanara,

Re: Removal of business equipment from Singapore to Hong Kong

Thank you for your telephone enquiry I am **(example)** .... to provide you with the quotation that you requested. **(21)** .... addition to this, I am including further details of our service. The price is **(22)** .... on the items that you mentioned in your phone call and will, of course, vary if you decide to add extra items or **(23)** .... some.

In order to keep the cost as low as **(24)** .... , we will move your equipment when it is most convenient for us. We will try to **(25)** .... your move with those of other clients which ask us to transport goods at around the same time. I am sure you will **(26)** .... that if we were to make a special trip just for your equipment the cost would be much **(27)** .... This means that **(28)** .... you requested a move on 23 June, this precise date may not be possible. However, we regularly transport goods **(29)** .... Singapore and Hong Kong, and we would **(30)** .... to be able to move your equipment within two or three days of your requested date.

The **(31)** .... does not include packing. You informed us that you prefer to **(32)** .... out your own packing since **(33)** .... of your equipment is quite fragile.

I hope that these initial details meet with your **(34)** .... , and ask that you do not hesitate to **(35)** .... is if you require any further advice.

Yours sincerely,

Dave Ring

Dave Ring
Transport Manager

9

Example

	A sending	B communicating	C writing	D working

example A B C D

	A	B	C	D
21	A in	B With	C On	D By
22	A built	B created	C based	D made
23	A decrease	B prevent	C omit	D leave
24	A realistic	B possible	C probable	D desired
25	A associate	B gather	C mix	D combine
26	A understand	B satisfy	C wish	D hope
27	A appreciated	B higher	C heavier	D superior
28	A still	B even	C despite	D although
29	A among	B beside	C between	D along
30	A forecast	B think	C choose	D expect
31	A guess	B value	C estimate	D judgement
32	A send	B carry	C bring	D take
33	A part	B section	C piece	D bit
34	A kindness	B approval	C permission	D allowance
35	A dial	B connect	C reach	D contact

[Turn over

Appendix 3.2

10

PART FIVE

Section A

Questions 36 – 40

- Read the memo below about a health and safety matter.
- In most of the lines **36 – 40** there is **one extra word** which does not fit. One or two lines, however, are correct.
- If a line is correct, write **CORRECT** on your Answer Sheet.
- If there is an extra word in the line, write the **extra word** in **CAPITAL LETTERS on your Answer Sheet.**

Examples:

0   Before signing up the delivery note, could you please check   `0` `U` `P`

00   that the consignment is complete and undamaged.   `00` `C` `O` `R` `R` `E` `C` `T`

We recently had a health and safety incident at one of our sites

36   which was not properly recorded. The accident did not involve with

37   any member of the permanent staff, but which happened to an

38   electrical contractor working at the new site. Will you please ensure in

39   future that Central Administration are informed immediately of any

40   accident occurring on company property and that all of details are

recorded in the Accident Book kept in Central Administration.

11

Section B

Questions 41 – 45

- Read the letter below.
- In each line **41 – 45** there is **one wrong word.**
- For each line **41 – 45**, write the **correct word in CAPITAL LETTERS** on your Answer Sheet.

Examples:

0   I hope that you are happiness with the plans.   `0` `H` `A` `P` `P` `Y`

00   Can you answer my letter to once?   `00` `A` `T`

I am writing further to our telephone conversation yesterday. We confirm

41   order number 4539 about 200 tables and 800 chairs in white, from your

42   Skandia range of office furniture. As explaining yesterday, our clients have

43   very definite requirements with regarding to the dates. Would you therefore

44   please confirm what you can in fact arrange shipment of the goods and

45   guarantee deliver within the time-scale we provisionally agreed, i.e. by

1 August. We look forward to receiving your confirmation.

[Turn over

12

WRITING

QUESTIONS 46 and 47

PART ONE

Question 46

- You are the Research and Development Director of an engineering company, which is a subsidiary of a larger corporation. The Chairman of the corporation is visiting your company next week.

- Write a memo of **30 – 40 words** to all your staff:
  - informing them of the visit
  - telling them why the visitor is coming
  - telling them when he will arrive and asking them to be at the welcome reception for him.

- **Write on your Answer Sheet. Do not write in capital letters.**

13

PART TWO

Question 47

- You are responsible for planning the magazine advertising of your company's new product, which is a polish for cars. You have just received the letter below from the magazine that you are going to advertise with. You have also received a memo from your Marketing Manager about the advertising campaign.

- Write a letter of **100 – 120 words** to Mr Ellwood at the magazine, telling him about the changes to the advertisement booking, and asking him for any other information that you require.

- Do not include postal addresses.

- **Write on your Answer Sheet. Do not write in capital letters.**

Dear Ms Boddington,

Thank you for your advertisement booking, the details of which I confirm below.

Name of Company: Autocare Products
Name of Product: Supergloss

Details of advert: ½-page black & white
Advert will appear in: June, July and August issues of the magazine
Cost of advert: $350 per issue (4 issues = $1050)
Discount: 5% for early booking
Total Cost: $997.50

We trust that this is satisfactory.

Yours sincerely,

Jack Ellwood
Jack Ellwood
Advertising Sales Manager

MEMO

To Cathy Boddington

From John Humphrey

Re: New product advertising

The Managing Director has approved an increase of budget on this campaign, so we can go for colour advertisements.

Could you contact the magazine and get them to change this? Please check the price and the possibility of a bigger discount.

Also tell them to get the product name right - **Supagloss**.

Thanks

John

Candidate Name _____

Centre Number

Candidate Number

UNIVERSITY OF CAMBRIDGE LOCAL EXAMINATIONS SYNDICATE
Examinations in English as a Foreign Language

BUSINESS ENGLISH CERTIFICATE 2   **0231/3**

Test of Listening

SAMPLE PAPER

Approx. 40 minutes
(including 10 minutes' transfer time)

Additional materials:
Answer sheet

TIME   Approx. 40 minutes (including 10 minutes' transfer time)

INSTRUCTIONS TO CANDIDATES

Do not open this paper until you are told to do so.

Write your name, Centre number and candidate number in the spaces at the top of this page. Write these details in pencil on your Answer Sheet **if these are not already printed**.

Listen to the instructions to each part carefully.

Try to answer all the questions.

Write your answers on this question paper.

At the end of the test you will have 10 minutes to copy your answers onto your Answer Sheet.

Read the instructions for completing your Answer Sheet carefully.

Write all your answers in **pencil**.

At the end of the examination hand in both this question paper and your Answer Sheet.

INFORMATION FOR CANDIDATES

Instructions are given on the tape.

You will hear everything twice.

There are thirty questions on this question paper.

_____
This question paper consists of 7 printed pages and 1 blank page.

SB (CW/JB) QK95121/1
© UCLES 1999

[Turn over

2

PART ONE

Questions 1 – 12

- You will hear three telephone conversations or messages.
- Write **one or two words** or a **number** in the numbered spaces on the notes or forms below.
- You will hear each recording twice.

Conversation One
(Questions 1 – 4)

- Look at the notes below.
- You will hear a secretary giving information to her boss about his schedule.

9.30 **(1)** ....

11.00 **(2)** ....

14.00 **(3)** ....

(4) ....

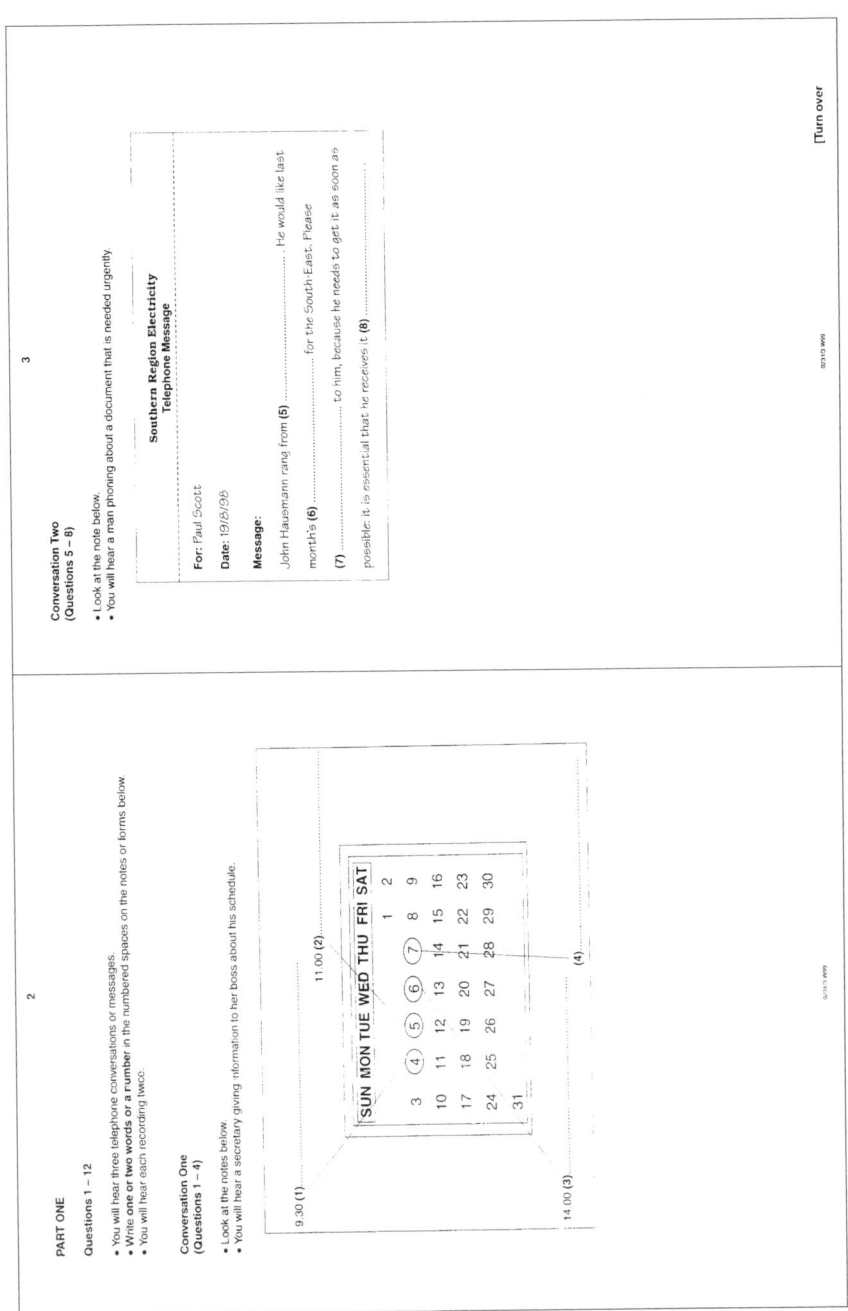

SUN	MON	TUE	WED	THU	FRI	SAT
					1	2
3	4	5	6	7	8	9
10	11	12	13	14	15	16
17	18	19	20	21	22	23
24	25	26	27	28	29	30
31						

3

Conversation Two
(Questions 5 – 8)

- Look at the note below.
- You will hear a man phoning about a document that is needed urgently.

Southern Region Electricity
Telephone Message

For: Paul Scott

Date: 19/8/98

Message:

John Hausmann rang from **(5)** .... He would like last month's **(6)** .... for the South-East. Please **(7)** .... to him, because he needs to get it as soon as possible: it is essential that he receives it **(8)** ....

[Turn over

4

Conversation Three
(Questions 9 – 12)

• Look at the form below.
• You will hear a staff development officer booking a new member of staff on an in-house training course.

ABP IN-HOUSE TRAINING: COURSE BOOKINGS

Course: (9) ....

Level: (10) ....

Name: Ms Amy Choi

Position/job: (11)

Name of Line Manager: Mr Lim

Position/job of Line Manager: (12)

02717-W99

PART TWO

Questions 13 – 22

Section One
(Questions 13 – 17)

• You will hear five short recordings. Each speaker is making an informal progress report on their work.
• For each recording, decide what the job of the speaker is.
• Write **one letter (A – H)** next to the number of the recording.
• Do not use any letter more than once.
• You will hear the five recordings twice.

13 ....

14 ....

15 ....

16 ....

17 ....

A	financial analyst
B	public relations officer
C	market researcher
D	product designer
E	sales manager
F	computer programmer
G	machine operator
H	personnel officer

Section Two
(Questions 18 – 22)

• You will hear another five recordings.
• For each recording, decide what the main reason is for the phone call.
• Write **one letter (A – H)** next to the number of the recording.
• Do not use any letter more than once.
• You will hear the five recordings twice.

18 ....

19 ....

20 ....

21 ....

22 ....

A	to get information
B	to express agreement
C	to ask advice
D	to give a warning
E	to make an apology
F	to pay a compliment
G	to offer help
H	to express interest

02717-W99

[Turn over

6

PART THREE

Questions 23 – 30

- You will hear someone talking about Marketing.
- For each question **23 – 30**, mark one letter (**A**, **B** or **C**) for the correct answer according to what the speaker says.
- You will hear the recording twice.

23 The '4 Cs' theory has replaced the '4 Ps' theory because it concentrates on

   A   companies.
   B   customers.
   C   computers.

24 Communicating with customers is more important than just

   A   promoting your product.
   B   knowing your product.
   C   preparing your product.

25 Your costings should reflect the

   A   quantity you expect to sell over a specific period.
   B   customers' willingness to pay for the whole package.
   C   effort required to manufacture the product.

26 Consumers may switch to your product if it is

   A   cheaper than anyone else's.
   B   easier for them to buy.
   C   advertised on television.

27 Convenience shopping suits people who

   A   don't like driving.
   B   like small shops.
   C   don't have much spare time.

28 The chairman of Sony was successful because he

   A   enjoyed marketing his products.
   B   invented the loudspeaker.
   C   predicted what people might want.

7

29 The speaker says that every business must have

   A   permanent staff
   B   annual meetings.
   C   a marketing plan.

30 The attitude of many unsuccessful companies to marketing is that it is

   A   time-consuming.
   B   worthless.
   C   expensive.

You now have 10 minutes to transfer your answers to your Answer Sheet.

287

Appendix 3.2

BEC 2   SAMPLE SPEAKING TEST

Set 1   Business Travel

(2 candidates)

Candidate A

Information

This is the information you need to answer your partner's questions.

Action Airways

Over 30 destinations worldwide (daily flights)

Special Business Class fares
eg New York - Singapore $975 return
(incl. taxi to/from city centre)

Business Class services:
- choice of meals
- personal TV & video
- phone, fax, e-mail

Discussion

Discuss with your partner what to consider when choosing an airline to fly with. Consider **cost, facilities provided**, and any other points you think are important.

BEC 2   SAMPLE SPEAKING TEST

Business Travel
(2 candidates)

Candidate A

In this activity you will exchange information with your partner about business travel by air.

Your Questions

Find out from your partner this information about Eagle Airways.

Destinations offered ....

Special services for companies ....

Discounts available ....

BEC 2   SAMPLE SPEAKING TEST

Business Travel
(2 candidates)

Candidate B

In this activity you will exchange information with your partner about business travel by air.

Information

This is the information you need to answer your partner's questions.

Eagle Airways

Flights from New York to Paris, Amsterdam, Berlin & Rome
(no flights Sundays)

For company bookings only:
- check-in by telephone
- free transfer to and from hotel at destination

15% discount for groups (min.6)

Discussion

Discuss with your partner what to consider when choosing an airline to fly with. Consider **cost, facilities provided**, and any other points you think are important.

BEC 2 SAMPLE SPEAKING TEST

Business Travel

(2 candidates)

Candidate B

Your Questions

Find out from your partner this information about Action Airways.

Destinations offered ....

Ticket prices ....

Services for passengers ....

	Centre Number	Candidate Number

Candidate Name _____

UNIVERSITY OF CAMBRIDGE LOCAL EXAMINATIONS SYNDICATE
Examinations in English as a Foreign Language

BUSINESS ENGLISH CERTIFICATE 3   **0232/1,2**

Test of Reading and Writing

SAMPLE PAPER   1 hour 40 minutes

Additional materials:
 Answer sheets

TIME   1 hour 40 minutes

INSTRUCTIONS TO CANDIDATES

Do not open this paper until you are told to do so.

Write your name, Centre number and candidate number in the spaces at the top of this page. Write these details in pencil on your Answer Sheets **if these are not already printed.**

Write all your answers in **pencil** on your Answer Sheets – **no extra time is allowed for this.**

Read carefully the instructions for each part and the instructions for completing your Answer Sheets.

Try to answer all the questions.

At the end of the examination hand in both this question paper and your Answer Sheets.

INFORMATION FOR CANDIDATES

There are fifty-two questions in this question paper:
    Reading Questions 1–50
    Writing Questions 51 and 52

This question paper consists of 13 printed pages and 3 blank pages.

CC (KS) 011164A/1
© UCLES 1999

[Turn over

3

Writing a business proposal is not an easy task, so here are some tips designed to help you write a winning proposal.

A

Get as much helpful information about the client as possible – annual reports, company periodicals, publicity. Sometimes there is a point of contact, i.e. someone who is involved in drafting the request for proposals, and who can answer technical questions about the form and content of your proposal. Call the person – they may reveal some information that can give you a competitive edge or at least a more customised approach to solving the prospective client's problem. Sometimes they even have a checklist of items they look for in each proposal and will be prepared to tell you about it if you ask.

B

Prospective clients want to make sure you understand what they need before you start proposing a way to meet that need. If a reader needs to save money, you must slant all your ideas toward the goal of achieving cost effectiveness. If, for example, your department has a lot of experience in a specific area, then this fact should not just be mentioned repeatedly but woven into a sentence highlighting how this experience is of potential advantage to the client.

C

Proposals are evaluated by a wide range of readers, from top management to technical evaluators to budget analysers. These readers will focus on different sections of a proposal, perhaps missing out whole segments. All readers, however, should be able to evaluate the first section of a proposal, which is a summary of the document. The length can vary greatly – it may sometimes be only one paragraph but in a very formal report it may run to several pages.

D

The worst thing you can do is offer value judgements which the client can refute. You want to seem serious, fair, objective and factual. Only after you build a foundation of fact can you offer a few judgements. Otherwise, you are likely to invite the reader to take issue with you. The facts are your findings and should be labelled as such; opinions are conclusions and should be labelled that way. If you use adjectives like 'powerful', 'wide ranging', 'significant', etc., make sure you support them with helpful details for them to study.

E

In proposal writing there is a tendency to rely on standard formats, i.e. static, standard sentences, paragraphs or pages that seem to fit all situations, and do not change from proposal to proposal. No company sees itself as being like any other and so the last thing you want is for a prospective client to believe you are just recycling old solutions. You must try to recode the ideas to fit the needs of the particular client and try not to copy old ideas because you cannot be bothered to generate new ones.

[Turn over

2

READING

PART ONE

Questions 1–8

- Look at the sentences below and at the five pieces of advice on writing a proposal on the opposite page.
- Which piece of advice does each sentence refer to?
- For each sentence 1–8 mark **one** letter **A, B, C, D** or **E** on your Answer Sheet.
- You will need to use some of these letters more than once.

Example

You may be able to speak to someone about the proposal.

0	A	B	C	D	E

1   You should back up all claims you make

2   Don't repeat the content of previous proposals.

3   Emphasise the ways in which your particular expertise could help the client.

4   Companies may already have prepared some ideas about what they expect in the proposal.

5   Remember that proposals are studied by more than one person

6   Be aware that all clients regard themselves as unique.

7   You should separate verifiable information from your personal point of view.

8   Start with a statement that will be accessible to everyone who studies it

4

PART TWO

Questions 9–14

- Read this text from a business magazine.
- Choose the best sentence from the opposite page to fill in each of the gaps.
- For each gap **9–14**, mark **one** letter **A–H** on your Answer Sheet.
- Do not use any letter more than once.
- There is an example at the beginning (0).

CORK

Saudi Arabia has oil. South Africa has diamonds. Portugal has cork. **0** **H** Roughly 170,000 tonnes, or 55% of world production, is stacked in Portugal's dusty warehouses, boiled in its vats, ground into crumbs and punched into corks. That is twice as much as in Spain, the country's nearest rival. This is partly because the climate in Portugal is so suitable for growing cork trees, but that is not the only reason. Portugal even boasts a cork-manufacturing equivalent to Saudi Arabia's Aramco and South Africa's De Beers: a family run firm, Amorim, controls a third of the country's cork market.

For most of its 120 years Amorim was indistinguishable from hundreds of other Portuguese cork makers. **9** While the less successful competition have small factories and manufacture only stoppers for bottles, Amorim has built large factories and has developed a wider range of cork-based products. **10** It makes 70% of the world's cork flooring, and almost 95% of the cork-based seals Portugal produces to be used in car engine production.

This does not mean that Amorim has everything its own way. **11** And there is some evidence that the demand for corks is in decline. Makers of spirits such as whisky and gin gave up cork in the 1960s; many cheaper wines now have plastic corks. A Norwegian company, Cortex, has patented a cork made from man-made materials which it claims is superior to the real thing. **12** But the world uses 25 billion traditional corks a year, and it is hard to imagine a good quality bottle of wine without one.

If Amorim is vulnerable, it is because the technology needed to make wine corks is so easy to master. Its 15% or so of the world market does not give the firm enough power to control prices. However, its influence is growing. **13** For the past few years, it has been buying up cork distributes in almost 30 countries. **14**

Just as it is difficult to imagine the world without Aramco's oil or in Saudi Arabia or De Beer's diamonds in South Africa, so Amorim's cork looks as sure as anything else in this world to remain an integral part of the world's manufacturing.

A   In these newer markets the figures show the firm is dominant.

B   However, the firm has managed to grow to its current size, with annual sales of 53 billion escudos ($340 million), because it has used economies of scale.

C   It hopes to be making 200 million of its synthetic corks a year by the end of the decade.

D   That had been the reason for the company's control

E   Moreover, it is beginning to distribute for smaller Portuguese producers.

F   That may be explained by the company's latest strategy.

G   Only one per cent of covered floors are made of cork, for example.

H   A third of the world's output is grown there.

[Turn over

293

6

PART THREE

Questions 15–20

- Read the following article about general managers, and the questions on the opposite page.
- Each question has four suggested answers or ways of finishing the sentence, **A**, **B**, **C** and **D**
- Mark **one** letter **A**, **B**, **C** or **D** on your Answer Sheet for the answer you choose.

General Managers (GMs) are a part of public management and play a key role in organisations. Depending on the size of the organisation a GM can be, for example, a senior manager responsible for a division or a subsidiary company or a less senior manager in charge of a department or section. They are a link between top management, who make policy decisions, and junior managers, who carry out these policies. Top management work, though GMs and they can make the difference between good and bad policy, and a motivated or demotivated workforce. The relationships GMs have with their bosses, subordinates and each other are very important for the success or failure of an organisation. GMs within the same organisation need to have good working relationships with each other in order to apply policies in the same way throughout the organisation. At the same time, GMs are also required to make broad policies into plans that suit their particular division or departments.

In a company conflicts between the activities of various departments will inevitably arise, and it is the job of the GM to act as a link between the departments. Research has shown that the personality of a GM is very important in helping to resolve these departmental problems. The research has also shown that GMs far as the personalities of GMs are concerned. GMs are ambitious people who have balanced temperaments and are good with people. In addition, good GMs combine these personality traits with a detailed knowledge of their business. This work hard to fit into and is accepted by the culture of their particular organisation. It has also been demonstrated that good performance GMs have three sets of skills.

First, they need agenda-setting skills, so that they can identify and communicate others of the most important objectives of a project. Second, GMs need to develop networking skills. Good GMs deliberately attempt to develop contacts within and outside the organisation. Such a network of contacts means that the GM is aware of issues and can act on them quickly. To develop agenda-setting and networking skills it is essential for a GM to be skilled in dealing with people. This is particularly important as they spend such a large amount of time working with employees at all levels of a company.

In terms of work, tasks and attitude, the research has shown that the work of a GM is done in short bursts, with managers working on many different subjects which can sometimes has a different aim. GMs discuss a wide range of subjects in an unconnected way and tend to ask questions rather than talk. They acquire large amount of information which they pass on to top management. A reason there with decisions. In order to collect this information they must learn to react to situation and change circumstances consequently, both the approach and role of a GM has to adapt to the situation in which they are operating. There are flexible skills necessary.

7

15 According to the writer, the key role of a General Manager is to

A help to formulate company policy
B communicate between groups of people
C interpret plans made by senior management
D accept changes in responsibility.

16 GMs must have good relationships with each other in order to

A carry out policies uniformly
B manage each other's departments
C motivate junior management
D find out the differences between departments

17 What does the writer say about problems between departments?

A They can be caused by resentment of GMs.
B GMs may feel unable to intervene.
C Ambition rather than knowledge will help a GM to solve them.
D GMs can help solve them by effective liaison

18 We are told that agenda-setting skills

A are more important than networking skills.
B help a manager develop networking skills.
C depend on having skills in dealing with people
D are the basis to interpersonal skills

19 What does research show about the way managers work?

A They work in short bursts of contact.
B Their work is completed very quickly
C Managers do many things at the same time.
D Managers appreciate orders.

20 The main reason why GMs collect a lot of information is

A in order to be clear to give instructions
B because they cannot avoid constantly changing
C to enable them to carry out difficult projects.
D to help them to encourage people to agree.

[Turn over

8

PART FOUR

Questions 21–30

- Read the article below about computer culture in the USA.
- Choose the best word from the opposite page to fill each gap.
- For each question **21–30** mark **one** letter **A, B, C** or **D** on your Answer Sheet.
- There is an example at the beginning **(0)**.

Computers today in the USA

It is remarkable how quickly computers have ......(0)...... so important in the USA. In the early 1980s, most commentators ......(21)...... it for granted that the American economy was slowing down and that Germany and Japan were the economies which would dominate global business at the end of the century. This is an example of the ......(22)...... of forecasters. They were proved wrong by a generation of brilliant people working in the United States who made computers smaller, faster and ......(23)...... of performing tasks that no-one twenty years ago would have thought possible. The industrial heroes of our time do not mine ore or produce steel – they make and programme computers.

If you do not use a computer, it is difficult to understand how useful they are. Twenty years ago, business people were just beginning to ......(24)...... the impact computers would have on their operations. When they were told that the revolution would ......(25)...... major changes over the next 20 years, the imaginative ones expanded their imaginations; the people who did not ......(26)...... believe in it thought they would have enough time to ......(27)...... the problem later. Now that the revolution has occurred, it seems to have come ......(28)...... very quickly.

Many, especially the newly computer literate, are finding it hard to ......(29)...... up. But though it is difficult they must, or they will be left ......(30)......, just as those who used a pen were overtaken by those who used a typewriter. Not all change may be progress, but all progress involves change.

9

Example

0	A	B	C	D
		▮		

0	A become	B turned	C gained	D developed
21	A said	B took	C thought	D gave
22	A scarcity	B inadequacy	C shortage	D unsuitability
23	A achievable	B accessible	C feasible	D capable
24	A grasp	B grip	C grab	D grapple
25	A lead	B cause	C result	D raise
26	A rather	B almost	C quite	D nearly
27	A cope	B repair	C deal	D resolve
28	A about	B back	C to	D forward
29	A make	B keep	C stay	D go
30	A over	B away	C behind	D off

[Turn over

10

PART FIVE

Questions 31–40

- Read the article below about making cuts in budgets.
- For each question **31–40** write **one** word in **CAPITAL LETTERS** on your Answer Sheet.

Example 0 [B] [E] [ ] [ ] [ ] [ ] [ ]

Marketing and Advertising Budgets

The marketing and advertising budget is often the first to ......(0)...... cut when a company's business targets are not being met. These are the findings of a survey of 100 Finance Directors from large companies. ......(31)...... directors questioned placed marketing and advertising at the top of the list for cuts when a company is ......(32)...... pressure, ahead of human resources, training, research and development and information technology. Given this finding, it is not surprising that marketing is also given a very low priority for investment.

The survey indicates that marketing expenditure has not increased ......(33)...... line with company turnover: 79 per cent of those questioned said turnover had ......(34)...... up, while only 30 per cent had increased marketing budgets. It also seems that 18 per cent did not know whether marketing expenditure in their companies had grown ......(35)...... not. For those Marketing Directors ......(36)...... are used to getting larger budgets, the days of automatic rises appear to be over. Finance Directors ......(37)...... also commonly involved in discussions about marketing and advertising each month. Even though the case for increasing budgets has ......(38)...... be argued more rigorously these days, in 19 per cent of companies ......(39)...... is no named director with responsibility for reporting on marketing at board level. Just 22 per cent of companies claimed to have representation ......(40)...... the board from the marketing director.

11

PART SIX

Questions 41–50

- In **most** lines of the following text, there is **one** unnecessary word. It is either grammatically incorrect or does not fit in with the sense of the text.
- For each numbered line **41–50**, find the unnecessary word and then write the word in **CAPITAL LETTERS** on your Answer Sheet. Some lines are correct. If a line is correct, write **CORRECT** on your Answer Sheet. The exercise begins with two examples **(0)** and **(00)**.

Examples 0 [D] [O] [N] [F] [ ] [ ] [ ]
         00 [C] [O] [R] [R] [E] [C] [T]

Education or experience?

0   Recently there has been much debate done about what should qualify a person
00 for promotion in the business world. In the past, a new employee would
41 start by delivering the office mail. He would then work his way up the ladder,
42 gaining higher and more responsible positions, eventually leading to the management.
43 But with the rapid growth of getting business courses and qualifications there is
44 now another way. Many of people who aim for top management can miss out on the
45 'mail delivery' stages by studying for a period and gaining on one of the numerous
46 business qualifications now available. There is some criticism of this accelerated
47 promotion. It is felt that it results in knowledge without experience, and such
48 knowledge type is inevitably incomplete. On the other hand the growth in business
49 courses has led to much more highly skilled business practices. The answer seems
50 to be that both experience and qualifications have their value, but as it should

    not be forgotten that experience is a qualification in itself.

[Turn over

12

WRITING

PART ONE

Question 51

- The bar charts below show the number of visits made to Waitco supermarket by different categories of customers.

- Using the information from the bar charts, write a short **report** summarizing the changes in the customer profile between 1996 and 1998.

- Write about **100** words on your Answer Sheet.

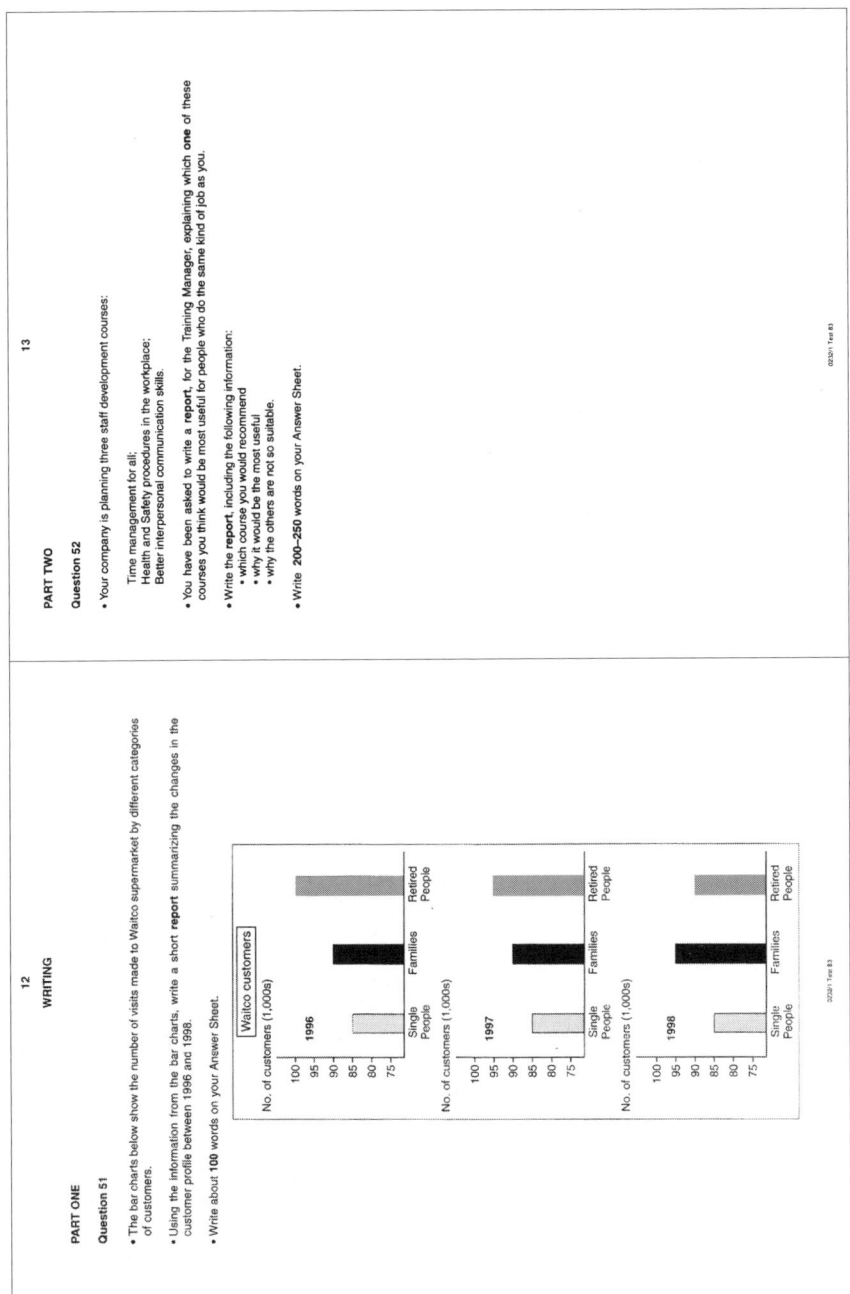

13

PART TWO

Question 52

- Your company is planning three staff development courses:

  Time management for all;
  Health and Safety procedures in the workplace;
  Better interpersonal communication skills.

- You have been asked to write a **report**, for the Training Manager, explaining which **one** of these courses you think would be most useful for people who do the same kind of job as you.

- Write the **report**, including the following information:
  - which course you would recommend
  - why it would be the most useful
  - why the others are not so suitable.

- Write **200–250 words** on your Answer Sheet.

Candidate Name

Centre Number

Candidate Number

UNIVERSITY OF CAMBRIDGE LOCAL EXAMINATIONS SYNDICATE
Examinations in English as a Foreign Language

BUSINESS ENGLISH CERTIFICATE 3   **0232/3**

Test of Listening

SAMPLE PAPER

Approx. 40 minutes
(including 10 minutes' transfer time)

Additional materials:
Answer sheet

TIME   Approx. 40 minutes (including 10 minutes' transfer time)

INSTRUCTIONS TO CANDIDATES

Do not open this paper until you are told to do so.

Write your name, Centre number and candidate number in the spaces at the top of this page. Write these details in pencil on your Answer Sheet **if these are not already printed.**

Listen to the instructions for each part carefully.

Try to answer all the questions.

Write all your answers on this question paper.

At the end of the test you will have 10 minutes to copy your answers onto your Answer Sheet.

Read the instructions for completing your Answer Sheets carefully.

Write all your answers in **pencil.**

At the end of the examination hand in both this question paper and your Answer Sheet.

INFORMATION FOR CANDIDATES

Instructions are given on the tape.

You will hear everything twice.

There are thirty questions in this question paper.

This question paper consists of 5 printed pages and 3 blank pages.

CC (KS) 011164B/1
© UCLES 1999

[Turn over

2

PART ONE

Questions 1–12

- You will hear a speaker addressing a group of investors attending a dinner to celebrate a confectionery company's one hundredth birthday.
- As you listen, for questions **1–12**, complete the notes using up to **three** words or a number.
- You will hear the recording twice.

Rewards for shareholders

1 They will be able to try the company's new .... product.

2 They will also receive a .... per share.

The present situation

3 Sales have decreased in the last ....

4 Shares are expected to increase in value by .... in the near future.

5 The company's main rivals are enormous .... companies.

Company history

6 The company was originally a ....

7 It recently became an ....

The future

8 The company has set a high .... for the future.

9 It does not intend to offer .... on its products.

10 The company will spend more money on ....

11 The company anticipates trade with countries in ....

12 The company expects bigger sales to the .... industry

---

3

PART TWO

Questions 13–22

- You will hear five different people talking about a meeting they have just attended.
- For each extract there are two tasks. For Task One, choose the reason for each meeting from the list **A–H**. For Task Two, choose the way that each person reacted to the meeting from the list **A–H**.
- You will hear the recording twice.

TASK ONE – REASON

- For questions **13–17**, match the extracts with the reasons, listed **A–H**.
- For each extract, choose the reason for the meeting.
- Write **one** letter **A–H** next to the number of the extract.

13 ....

14 ....

15 ....

16 ....

17 ....

A	to discuss sales targets
B	to present a new idea
C	to demonstrate a new product
D	to elect a new chairman
E	to analyse a problem
F	to discuss expansion
G	to decide on redundancies
H	to vote to issue shares

TASK TWO – REACTION

- For questions **18–22**, match the extracts with the reactions, listed **A–H**.
- For each extract, choose the way the speaker reacted.
- Write **one** letter **A–H** next to the number of the extract.

18 ....

19 ....

20 ....

21 ....

22 ....

A	thought it was very interesting
B	felt nervous about speaking
C	was not happy with the decisions made
D	found it confusing
E	disagreed strongly with someone
F	thought it was very boring
G	lost his/her temper with someone
H	agreed with the final decision

[Turn over

4

PART THREE

Questions 23–30

- You will hear a radio presenter interviewing a business woman called Linda Taylor.
- For each question 23–30 mark **one** letter, **A, B** or **C**, for the correct answer.
- You will hear the recording twice.

23 What do we learn about Linda Taylor?

   A She has set up an airline.
   B She has recently bought out an airline.
   C She is in charge of an airline.

24 What new development has taken place at BellAir?

   A They have installed new machinery.
   B They have opened a new workshop.
   C They have bought modern planes.

25 What problems did they have to resolve?

   A New engineers had to be employed.
   B The legal process was difficult.
   C Some staff had to be re-trained.

26 She has formed an alliance with Sunlines in order to increase BellAir's

   A involvement in tourism.
   B profit margins.
   C number of flights.

27 BellAir ticket prices have been reduced on

   A domestic flights.
   B all flights.
   C international flights.

28 What change has been made in the marketing arrangements?

   A An outside consultancy has been contracted.
   B A new director has been appointed.
   C The present department has been expanded.

29 Linda went into aviation to

   A fulfil a dream.
   B earn a high salary.
   C follow family tradition.

30 What does Linda think is the key to success?

   A believing in yourself
   B having good qualifications
   C making people trust you

That is the end of the Listening Test. You now have ten minutes to transfer your answers to your Answer Sheet.

Part 2 Sample Task

For two candidates:

TRAINING REVIEW

Your company intends to review its annual training budget. You have been asked to contribute ideas to this review:

Discuss, and decide together:

- what aspects of training should be given priority in a company

- how to evaluate training effectively

For three candidates:

INTERNATIONAL TRADE SHOW

Your company has won an international competition to be represented at a trade show abroad. You have been given the job of organising the company's stand.

Discuss, and decide together:

- which aspects of the company you should focus on

- which features of the country should be emphasized

- which kinds of people and equipment will be needed on the stand

Part 3 Sample Task

A	**Time Management:** how to organise your work time effectively
B	**Marketing:** the importance of establishing a clear brand name for a product
C	**Staff Management:** how to motivate employees to be responsible for their own productivity

APPENDIX 4.1
BEC Preliminary Sample Paper

	Centre Number	Candidate Number
Candidate Name _____		

UNIVERSITY OF CAMBRIDGE LOCAL EXAMINATIONS SYNDICATE
Examinations in English as a Foreign Language

BUSINESS ENGLISH CERTIFICATE   **0351/1,2**
Preliminary
Test of Reading and Writing   **Test 023**

Wednesday   **5 JUNE 2002**   Morning   1 hour 30 minutes

Additional materials:
  Answer Sheets

TIME   1 hour 30 minutes

INSTRUCTIONS TO CANDIDATES

Do not open this paper until you are told to do so.

Write your name, Centre number and candidate number in the spaces at the top of this page. Write these details in pencil on your Answer Sheets **if these are not already printed.**

Write all your answers in **pencil** on your Answer Sheets – **no extra time is allowed for this**.

Read carefully the instructions for each part, and the instructions for completing your Answer Sheets.

Try to answer all the questions.

At the end of the examination hand in both this question paper and your Answer Sheets.

INFORMATION FOR CANDIDATES

There are forty-seven questions on this question paper:
  Reading Questions 1 – 45
  Writing Questions 46 – 47

This question paper consists of 17 printed pages.

SP (AT/SLC) S25800/4

READING
QUESTIONS 1 – 45

PART ONE
Questions 1 – 5

- Look at questions 1 – 5.
- In each question, which sentence is correct?
- For each question, mark one letter (A, B or C) on your Answer Sheet.

Example: 0

Don't forget –
flight BA692   6.45 pm

The plane arrives at

A quarter to seven in the morning.
B quarter past six in the evening.
C quarter to seven in the evening.

The correct answer is C, so mark your Answer Sheet like this:

0   A   B   C

1

FOR MORE INFORMATION ABOUT ANY OF THE JOB VACANCIES ON THIS LIST, PHONE 0845 1234, QUOTING THE REFERENCE NUMBER

Phone 0845 1234 for

A a list of current job vacancies.
B a reference number for one of these vacancies.
C details about jobs on the list.

2

We guarantee delivery to your door within 24 hours, if the goods are in stock.

A All customers are guaranteed next-day delivery.
B Goods are delivered next day, depending on availability.
C Any goods out of stock are delivered with your next order.

3

Print | To | cc | Subject: Expenses
Accounts
Sales Department

Send in all receipts for expenses by the last day of this month.

Accounts will

A need to have details of expenses before next month.
B settle all expenses at the end of this month.
C return your receipts by the end of the month.

4

SCHRODERS

Special Offer on photocopier rentals.
First 3000 copies free. After that each copy just 3p.

A Any photocopies from Shroders will cost: 3p each.
B Each copy costs 3p less after the first 3000 copies.
C For the first 3000 copies, Shroders make no charge.

5

Staff are reminded that all arrangements for leave must be approved in advance by line managers.

Staff must

A inform their manager if they are absent.
B get permission to take time off.
C remind their manager of when they are on leave.

PART TWO
Questions 6 – 10

- Look at the business advertisements below.
- For questions 6 – 10 on the opposite page, choose which company (**A – H**) each person needs to consult.
- For each question, mark one letter (**A – H**) on your Answer Sheet.
- Do not use any letter more than once.

A — Selling abroad? Call **EXPORT EXPERTS!**

B — **WEBMASTERS** Business Website designers

C — *PRONTO SECRETARIAL SERVICES* **Office tasks quickly completed.**

D — - - - - **RAPIDPRINT** - - - - **For all your printing**

E — HEADLINE RECRUITMENT AGENCY **We find the staff you need.**

F — IT TRAINERS *Leaders in the training field*

G — THORN'S TRAVEL AGENCY Experts in foreign business travel

H — CLARK'S **Technical Publishers**

6 A publishing company wants to select a computer course for new staff.

7 A marketing director requires five hundred leaflets to promote a new product.

8 The sales manager of a software company has to arrange several trips abroad for her staff.

9 The manager of a small printing company requires advice on entering foreign markets.

10 A human resources manager has to appoint an executive secretary urgently for the Managing Director.

PART THREE
Questions 11 – 15

- Look at the chart below. It shows the amounts by which a company's expenditure on materials, labour and overheads were above budget.

- Which month does each sentence (11 – 15) on the opposite page describe?

- For each sentence, mark one letter (A – H) on your Answer Sheet.

- Do not use any letter more than once.

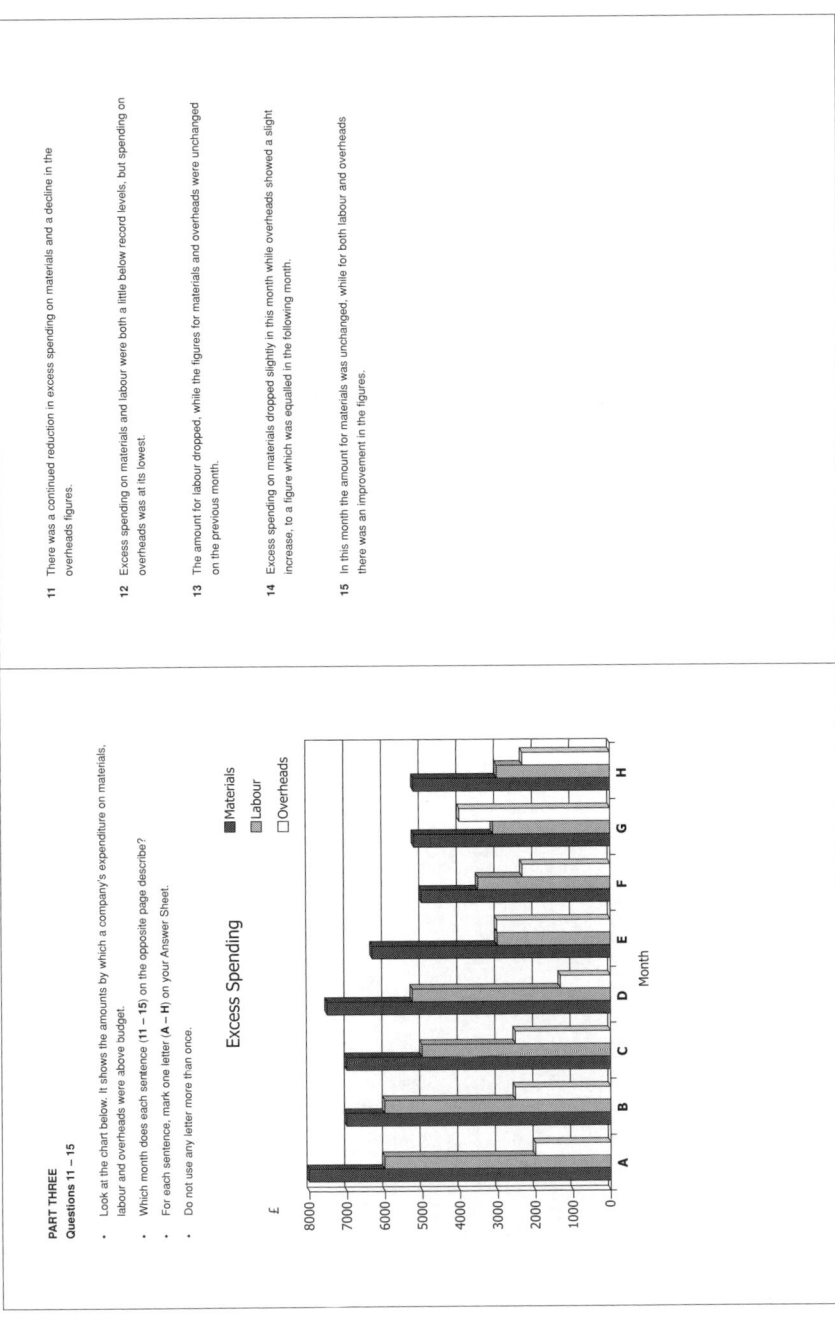

Excess Spending

£

■ Materials
▨ Labour
☐ Overheads

Month

11 There was a continued reduction in excess spending on materials and a decline in the overheads figures.

12 Excess spending on materials and labour were both a little below record levels, but spending on overheads was at its lowest.

13 The amount for labour dropped, while the figures for materials and overheads were unchanged on the previous month.

14 Excess spending on materials dropped slightly in this month while overheads showed a slight increase, to a figure which was equalled in the following month.

15 In this month the amount for materials was unchanged, while for both labour and overheads there was an improvement in the figures.

PART FOUR
Questions 16 – 22

- Read the newspaper article below about an organisation which protects its members' original designs.

- Are sentences **16 – 22** on the opposite page 'Right' or 'Wrong'? If there is not enough information to answer 'Right' or 'Wrong', choose 'Doesn't say'.

- For each sentence **16 – 22**, mark one letter (**A**, **B** or **C**) on your Answer Sheet.

PAC Wins Again

Last year, Scotland-based Glenmore Jewellery became the fortieth member of the organisation PAC (Protection Against Copying) to take successful legal action to protect its products. Glenmore, which sells hand-made jewellery designed and produced by local artists, was angry to discover a competitor, Nevis, selling copies of these designs. Nevis has now agreed to stop selling the products, as well as to pay Glenmore's legal costs.

Another Scottish company, Highland Design, also asked for PAC's help last year; as a result, Grampian Gifts has agreed to stop selling glass designs similar to products made by Highland Design. Grampian will also pay Highland Design 50% of the profit it has made on these ranges over the last four years.

"Recently there's been a sharp rise in the number of reports received from members," says James Ellis, PAC's Chief Executive. "This demonstrates that designers clearly feel we can help them. If they discover copies of their designs at exhibitions, for example, they are advised to contact us immediately."

PAC, with over 700 members world-wide, has an almost 100% success rate in legal action taken to defend the interests of the individuals and companies it represents.

16 Glenmore makes all the jewellery that it sells.

    A Right   **B** Wrong   **C** Doesn't say

17 Glenmore is the best-known brand of traditional Scottish jewellery design.

    A Right   **B** Wrong   **C** Doesn't say

18 Nevis has a large stock of unsold copies of Glenmore jewellery.

    A Right   **B** Wrong   **C** Doesn't say

19 Grampian Gifts has to pay all its profits for the last four years to Highland Design.

    A Right   **B** Wrong   **C** Doesn't say

20 The number of members who contact PAC has increased.

    A Right   **B** Wrong   **C** Doesn't say

21 Designers should report any copies of their work which they see at exhibitions.

    A Right   **B** Wrong   **C** Doesn't say

22 PAC has won the majority of cases of legal action it has taken for its members.

    A Right   **B** Wrong   **C** Doesn't say

PART FIVE

Questions 23 – 28

- Read the article below about a businessman's plans for developing a shopping centre.
- For each question 23 – 28, on the opposite page, choose the correct answer.
- Mark one letter (**A**, **B** or **C**) on your Answer Sheet.

Shaking Up the Business

Since becoming Chief Executive of the Star City shopping centre and exhibition halls, Peter Maurice feels he has done a lot. Now, though, he wants to change the whole feeling of the business. 'Visitors should feel we are looking after them,' he says. 'Very often the public go into a shop and find so much there that they can't decide what to buy, so they don't buy anything. Keep it simple, that's the key to retailing.'

At Star City, staff are encouraged to tell managers, including Maurice himself, what they think of them. 'The things they say about me are what I expect, because I'm fairly self-aware – I know what I'm like and that I can make people a little angry. But I'm very much in favour of change, and everyone knows that a lot needs to be done.'

He learnt his management techniques the hard way. 'At 23 I went into business and lost money; I had to learn fast. Then, at 32, I won an export contract to Hong Kong. I admire the strength of character and the ambition of the people there, and brought back two very significant words: "No problem". Then I took a course at Harvard Business School. It was very hard work, but worth it.'

As well as running Star City, Peter Maurice controls Big Events, which organises exhibitions. At the moment, Big Events is working on plans for a boat show to rival the Capital Boat Show, which in 2004 is moving from its traditional site at Star City to a new venue.

Maurice has created an unusual company structure. 'The financial director and commercial director are responsible to me directly, but in my first week here, the head of Marketing resigned. Then the same happened with Human Resources. I said to both teams: "Do you want to self-manage?" That's when they decided to do – it can work if you have people who work well together and can report to you as a team,' he explains.

For the immediate future, Maurice will continue with the essential work of updating the centre. After that, he plans to look at ways of expanding Star City beyond the present conferences and exhibitions, to include major shows and concerts. 'I want a lively centre full of exciting events, where my well-trained staff are ambassadors for the company.'

23 In Peter Maurice's opinion, what prevents many customers from making purchases?

A The shop hasn't got what they want.
B Nobody is available to serve them.
C There is too much to choose from.

24 Maurice's staff say that he

A sometimes annoys them.
B is trying to do too much too quickly.
C needs to be more self-aware.

25 What does Maurice say he learnt from his experience in Hong Kong?

A how to run a successful import-export business
B the importance of being confident and having a positive attitude
C that he needed to go back to business school

26 What is Maurice's exhibitions company, Big Events, planning to do in 2004?

A take control of the Capital Boat Show
B move the Capital Boat Show to a larger venue
C hold an event to compete with the Capital Boat Show

27 Which of these departments has a director who reports to Peter Maurice?

A Finance
B Marketing
C Human Resources

28 Maurice's long-term ambition for the centre is to

A retrain all the staff at the centre.
B modernise the centre.
C bring entertainment to the centre.

PART SIX
Questions 29 – 40

• Read the advertisement below about an exhibition.

• Choose the correct word to fill each gap, from **A**, **B** or **C** on the opposite page.

• For each question **29 – 40**, mark one letter (**A**, **B** or **C**) on your Answer Sheet.

Business Show of the Year
14–18 September 2002
London

Business 2002 is a key event aimed at people intending to set up **(29)** _____ business. This year's exhibition **(30)** _____ provide visitors with valuable information on products and services essential for **(31)** _____ a small business. **(32)** _____ is also free advice on **(33)** _____ to obtain finance, getting the best out of Information Technology and dealing with the **(34)** _____ problems of health and safety in the workplace. Entrance to the exhibition is free and **Business 2002** hopes to **(35)** _____ at least 5,000 visitors a day. Companies **(36)** _____ took part last year said it was well worth the cost.

If you would like further information **(37)** _____ having a stand at the **Business 2002** exhibition, contact **(38)** _____ on 020 5493 7721 for an exhibitors' pack.

We **(39)** _____ arranged special reduced travel and hotel rates for standholders. So don't **(40)** _____ the opportunity, book a stand now.

29	A	on	B	in	C	at
30	A	will	B	shall	C	would
31	A	run	B	runs	C	running
32	A	This	B	There	C	It
33	A	which	B	that	C	how
34	A	many	B	some	C	any
35	A	attract	B	attracting	C	attracts
36	A	whose	B	who	C	what
37	A	to	B	with	C	about
38	A	ours	B	our	C	us
39	A	are	B	have	C	were
40	A	pass	B	fail	C	miss

PART SEVEN

Questions 41 – 45

- Read the part of the letter and the memo below.
- Complete the form on the opposite page.
- Write a word or phrase (in CAPITAL LETTERS) or a number on lines **41 – 45** on your Answer Sheet.

With regard to our conversation on the phone yesterday, I can confirm that, due to serious illness, John Brookes has to cancel his flight to Madrid on Saturday 22 June and I therefore request a refund. I enclose the ticket: First Class, flight number UA 453, booking reference 3434/4.

Travelgo Ltd

Memorandum

To:	Julia
From:	Luke
Date:	6 June 2002
Subject:	Refund

Could you please fill in a refund form for this client? Note that the booking reference number is actually 01/3434/A. It was a company booking for a Business Class (not First Class) UATAIR flight from Heathrow. They paid by credit card but it's easier if we send them a cheque for £525.00.

Travelgo Ltd   **Refund No: 0055 78A**

Booking reference: **(41)** ....

Ticket details:

Date of departure: 22/06/02

Flight number: UA 453 (UATAIR)

Departure from: Heathrow

Destination: **(42)** ....

Ticket class: **(43)** ....

Refund due: £525.00

Method of Refund: **(44)** ....

Reason for cancellation: client's   **(45)** ....

Appendix 4.1

WRITING

QUESTIONS 46 – 47

PART ONE

Question 46

- You have noticed that staff using company cars are forgetting to fill them with petrol on their return.

- You also want to remind staff of procedures for parking company cars and depositing keys.

- Write a **memo** to all staff:

  - explaining what to do about petrol after using a company car

  - saying where to leave the car

  - telling staff what to do with the keys.

- **Write 30 – 40 words.**

- **Write on your Answer Sheet.**

Memorandum

To:	**All staff**
From:	**Office Manager**
Date:	**6 June 2002**
Subject:	**Company Cars**

_____

_____

_____

_____

_____

_____

PART TWO

Question 47

- Read this part of a fax from Mr David Craven, one of your company's customers.

> We ordered eight LP4 electric motors from you last month. It is now 3 June and we still have received nothing, even though you informed us that we would have the motors by 30 May. We need to know when we will receive these motors as our own work will be held up if they do not arrive within the next few days.

- Write a **letter** to Mr Craven:

  - apologising for what has happened

  - explaining the delay

  - saying when you will send the motors

  - offering a reduction on the bill.

- **Write 60 – 80 words.**

- **Write on your Answer Sheet. Do not include any postal addresses.**

Candidate Name_____

Centre Number

Candidate Number

UNIVERSITY OF CAMBRIDGE LOCAL EXAMINATIONS SYNDICATE
Examinations in English as a Foreign Language

BUSINESS ENGLISH CERTIFICATE
Preliminary

0351/3

Test of Listening

Test 023

Wednesday   **5 JUNE 2002**   Morning   Approx. 40 minutes
(including 10 minutes'
transfer time)

Additional materials:
    Answer Sheet

TIME   **Approx. 40 minutes (including 10 minutes' transfer time)**

INSTRUCTIONS TO CANDIDATES

Do not open this paper until you are told to do so.

Write your name, Centre number and candidate number in the spaces at the top of this page. Write these details in pencil on your Answer Sheet **if these are not already printed.**

Listen to the instructions for each part carefully.

Try to answer all the questions.

Write your answers on this question paper.

At the end of the test you will have 10 minutes to copy your answers onto your Answer Sheet.

Read the instructions for completing your Answer Sheet carefully.

Write all your answers in **pencil**.

At the end of the examination hand in both this question paper and your Answer Sheet.

INFORMATION FOR CANDIDATES

Instructions are given on the tape.
You will hear everything twice.
There are thirty questions on this paper.

_____
This question paper consists of 8 printed pages.

SP (SC/KN) S25767/2

Appendix 4.1

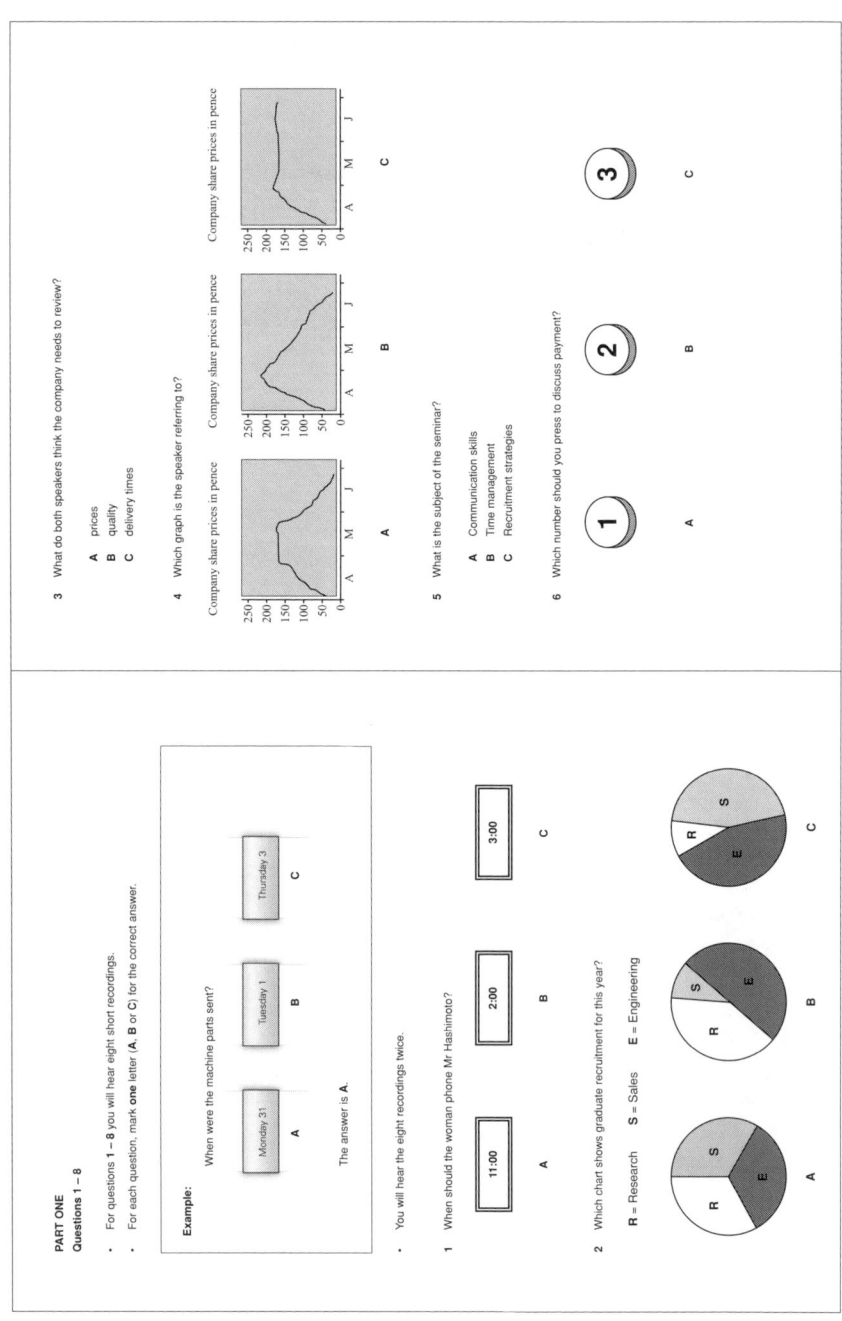

PART ONE
Questions 1 – 8

• For questions 1 – 8 you will hear eight short recordings.
• For each question, mark **one** letter (**A**, **B** or **C**) for the correct answer.

Example:

When were the machine parts sent?

Monday 31   Tuesday 1   Thursday 3

A   B   C

The answer is **A**.

• You will hear the eight recordings twice.

1   When should the woman phone Mr Hashimoto?

11:00   2:00   3:00

A   B   C

2   Which chart shows graduate recruitment for this year?

R = Research   S = Sales   E = Engineering

A   B   C

3   What do both speakers think the company needs to review?

A   prices
B   quality
C   delivery times

4   Which graph is the speaker referring to?

Company share prices in pence   Company share prices in pence   Company share prices in pence

A   B   C

5   What is the subject of the seminar?

A   Communication skills
B   Time management
C   Recruitment strategies

6   Which number should you press to discuss payment?

1   2   3

A   B   C

312

7 What does the woman want information about?

A. AIRLINE TICKETS

B. CAR HIRE

C. HOTEL

8 What does the man order?

A

B

C

PART TWO

Questions 9 – 15

- Look at the notes below.
- Some information is missing.
- You will hear a man leaving an answerphone message about electrical goods.
- For each question 9 – 15, fill in the missing information in the numbered space using a **word, numbers** or **letters**.
- You will hear the message twice.

Phone Message

COMPANY NAME:	(9) _____ Department Store
CONTACT NAME:	(10) Roger _____
PHONE NUMBER:	(11) 01873 _____
URGENT – SEND:	(12) _____ fridge/freezer brochures
ALSO INCLUDE:	(13) _____ price lists
CHECK AVAILABILITY OF DISHWASHER MODEL NO:	(14) _____
CUSTOMER NEEDS DISHWASHER:	(15) _____ mm wide

Appendix 4.1

PART THREE
Questions 16 – 22

- Look at the notes from a staff meeting in a department store.
- Some information is missing.
- You will hear a talk by the store manager.
- For each question **16 – 22**, fill in the missing information in the numbered space using **one** or **two** words.
- You will hear the talk twice.

Staff meeting held on 8 June

Name of new Assistant Manager   (16) Amanda ....

Sportswear Department
Promotion opportunities: re   (17) .... staff

Stockroom
Now   (18) .... will improve stock handling

Design Team
Staff meeting – before: (19) ....

Visit
From: (20) ....
Date: (21) 15th 2002
Subject of talk: (22) .... policy

PART FOUR
Questions 23 – 30

- You will hear an interview with Michael Wright, a managing director, talking about his company, ALC.
- For each question **23 – 30**, mark **one** letter (**A**, **B** or **C**) for the correct answer.
- You will hear the interview twice.

23 Michael's company first started in business
   A producing parts for lorries.
   B doing lorry repairs.
   C building special lorries for clients.

24 Michael joined ALC because he wanted to
   A continue as an engineer.
   B run the production department.
   C be a director.

25 At the time Michael became a director, ALC was
   A doing good business.
   B buying new equipment.
   C negotiating a contract.

26 Michael suggested that the company should
   A change its production methods.
   B aim to take over its biggest rivals.
   C increase its production rate.

27 One of the reasons ALC started producing ambulances was because
   A a customer had asked it to.
   B the company already had a good design.
   C the market for ambulances was fairly stable.

314

TEST OF SPEAKING

Tasks are included from Parts 2 and 3 of the Test of Speaking, together with the script followed by the Interlocutor for these Parts.

Material is not included for Part 1, in which the Interlocutor asks the candidates questions directly rather than asking them to perform tasks.

---

28 When it started producing ambulances, ALC's main problem was

  A competing with another company.
  B having to cut its prices.
  C losing a contract.

29 Michael feels ALC is unusual because the directors

  A are responsible for marketing the products.
  B have little contact with managers.
  C work on the production line.

30 Now ALC is now aiming to

  A improve its cash flow.
  B recruit more staff.
  C do more training.

You now have 10 minutes to transfer your answers to your Answer Sheet.

Task Card 11

A: WHAT IS IMPORTANT WHEN...?

Looking for a new job

- Career opportunities
- Location of job
- Possibility of making business trips

B: WHAT IS IMPORTANT WHEN...?

Travelling by air for business

- Flight departure times
- In-flight service
- Transport to and from airports

BEC Preliminary June 2002

In using the keys and marking notes in practice testing, it should be remembered that scores in individual papers or questions are subject to weighting during the actual examination processing.

Task Sheet 23

Rewards for staff

- bonus payment
- party
- day trip
- gift
- shares in the company
- extra day's holiday

Task Card 14

A: WHAT IS IMPORTANT WHEN...?

Joining a computer skills course

- Course materials
- Trainer
- Number of participants in group

B: WHAT IS IMPORTANT WHEN...?

Choosing a delivery company

- Speed of service
- Cost
- Personal recommendation

Appendix 4.1

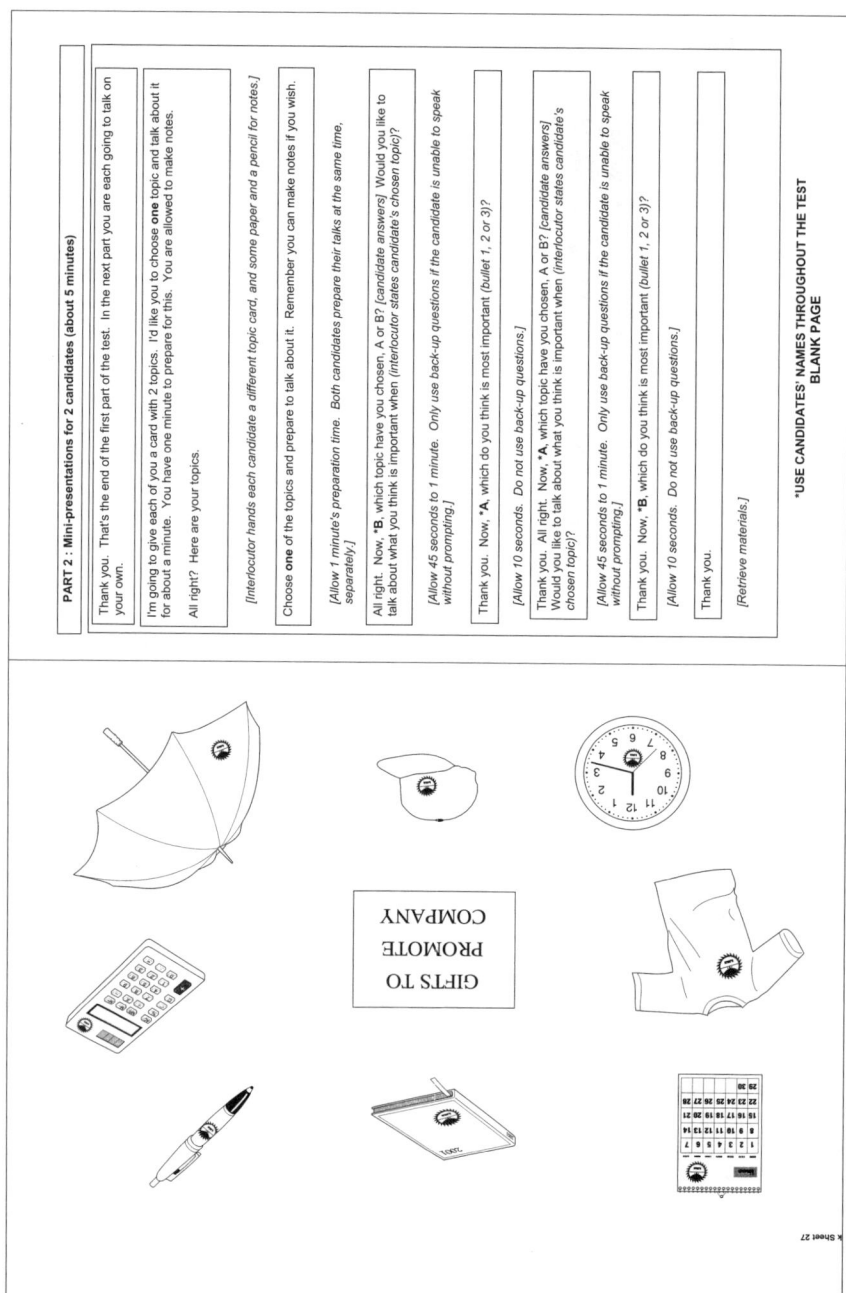

PART 2 : Mini-presentations for 2 candidates (about 5 minutes)

Thank you. That's the end of the first part of the test. In the next part you are each going to talk on your own.

I'm going to give each of you a card with 2 topics. I'd like you to choose **one** topic and talk about it for about a minute. You have one minute to prepare for this. You are allowed to make notes.

All right? Here are your topics.

[Interlocutor hands each candidate a different topic card, and some paper and a pencil for notes.]

Choose **one** of the topics and prepare to talk about it. Remember you can make notes if you wish.

[Allow 1 minute's preparation time. Both candidates prepare their talks at the same time, separately.]

All right. Now, *B, which topic have you chosen, A or B? [candidate answers] Would you like to talk about what you think is important when (interlocutor states candidate's chosen topic)?*

[Allow 45 seconds to 1 minute. Only use back-up questions if the candidate is unable to speak without prompting.]

Thank you. Now, *A, which do you think is most important (bullet 1, 2 or 3)?*

[Allow 10 seconds. Do not use back-up questions.]

Thank you. All right. Now, *A, which topic have you chosen, A or B? [candidate answers] Would you like to talk about what you think is important when (interlocutor states candidate's chosen topic)?*

[Allow 45 seconds to 1 minute. Only use back-up questions if the candidate is unable to speak without prompting.]

Thank you. Now, *B, which do you think is most important (bullet 1, 2 or 3)?*

[Allow 10 seconds. Do not use back-up questions.]

Thank you.

[Retrieve materials.]

*USE CANDIDATES' NAMES THROUGHOUT THE TEST
BLANK PAGE

GIFTS TO
PROMOTE
COMPANY

k Sheet 27

Task Card 11 – Examiner's Copy

A: **WHAT IS IMPORTANT WHEN...?**

LOOKING FOR A NEW JOB

CAREER OPPORTUNITIES

LOCATION OF JOB

POSSIBILITY OF MAKING BUSINESS TRIPS

Are **career opportunities** the most important thing about a new job? (Why/Why not?)
Is the **location** of the job important? (Why/Why not?)
How important is the opportunity to make **business trips**? (Why/Why not?)

Select from the following additional prompts (if the above have already been covered):

Is **salary** the most important thing about a job? (Why/Why not?)
Are **training opportunities** important? (Why/Why not?)
Is a **friendly working environment** important in a new job? (Why/Why not?)

B: **WHAT IS IMPORTANT WHEN...?**

TRAVELLING BY AIR FOR BUSINESS

FLIGHT DEPARTURE TIMES

IN-FLIGHT SERVICE

TRANSPORT TO AND FROM AIRPORTS

Are **flight departure times** important? (Why/Why not?)
How important is the **service on a flight**? (Why/Why not?)
Is it essential to have good **transport to and from the airports**? (Why/Why not?)

Select from the following additional prompts (if the above have already been covered):

How important is the **food** on a plane? (Why/Why not?)
How important is the **amount of luggage** passengers can take on a business flight? (Why/Why not?)
Which **airport facilities** are useful for business travellers? (Why?)

PART 2 : Mini-presentations for 3 candidates (about 6 minutes)

Thank you. That's the end of the first part of the test. In the next part you are each going to talk on your own.

I'm going to give each of you a card with 2 topics. I'd like you to choose **one** topic and talk about it for about a minute. You have one minute to prepare for this. You are allowed to make notes.

All right? Here are your topics.

[Interlocutor hands each candidate a different topic card, and some paper and a pencil for notes.]

Choose **one** of the topics and prepare to talk about it. Remember you can make notes if you wish.

[Allow 1 minute's preparation time. All candidates prepare their talks at the same time, separately.]

All right. Now, ***B**, which topic have you chosen, A or B? *[candidate answers.]* Would you like to talk about what you think is important when *(interlocutor states candidate's chosen topic)*?

[Allow 45 seconds to 1 minute. Only use back-up questions if the candidate is unable to speak without prompting.]

Thank you. Now, ***C**, which do you think is most important *(bullet 1, 2 or 3)?*

[Allow 10 seconds. Do not use back-up questions.]

All right. Now, ***A**, which topic have you chosen, A or B? *[candidate answers.]* Would you like to talk about what you think is important when *(interlocutor states candidate's chosen topic)?*

[Allow 45 seconds to 1 minute. Only use back-up questions if the candidate is unable to speak without prompting.]

Thank you. Now, ***B**, which do you think is most important *(bullet 1, 2 or 3)?*

[Allow 10 seconds. Do not use back-up questions.]

All right. Now, ***C**, which topic have you chosen, A or B? *[candidate answers.]* Would you like to talk about what you think is important when *(interlocutor states candidate's chosen topic)?*

[Allow 45 seconds to 1 minute. Only use back-up questions if the candidate is unable to speak without prompting.]

Thank you. Now, ***A**, which do you think is most important *(bullet 1, 2 or 3)?*

[Allow 10 seconds. Do not use back-up questions.]

Thank you.

[Retrieve materials.]

Task Card 13 – Examiner's Copy

A: WHAT IS IMPORTANT WHEN…?

ARRANGING A BUSINESS TRIP ABROAD

TYPE OF TRANSPORT

ACCOMMODATION

CONTACT PERSON

Is the **type of transport** important? (Why/Why not?)
How important is the **accommodation** available? (Why/Why not?)
Is it important to have a **contact person** abroad? (Why/Why not?)

Select from the following additional prompts (if all the above are covered):

How important is the **cost** of the trip? (Why/Why not?)
Is it important to have **colleagues with you** on a business trip? (Why/Why not?)
Is it essential to **speak the language**?(Why/Why not?)

B: WHAT IS IMPORTANT WHEN…?

CHOOSING OFFICES TO RENT

LOCATION

FACILITIES

COST

Is **location** the most important thing to consider? (Why/Why not?)
What kinds of **facilities** in the offices are essential? (Why?)
How important is **cost**? (Why/Why not?)

Select from the following additional prompts (if the above have already been covered):

Why is it important to consider the **size** of the premises?
How important is the **condition** of the building? (Why/Why not?)
Are parking spaces **for staff essential?** (Why/Why not?)

Task Card 14 – Examiner's Copy

A: WHAT IS IMPORTANT WHEN…?

JOINING A COMPUTER SKILLS COURSE

COURSE MATERIALS

TRAINER

NUMBER OF PARTICIPANTS IN GROUP

Are **course materials** the most important thing to consider? (Why/Why not?)
Is it important who the **trainer** is? (Why/Why not?)
How important is the **number of participants** in the group? (Why/Why not?)

Select from the following additional prompts (if the above have already been covered):

Are opportunities to **get qualifications** essential? (Why/Why not?)
How important is **cost**? (Why/Why not?)
Why is it important to consider the **time and length** of each lesson?

B: WHAT IS IMPORTANT WHEN…?

CHOOSING A DELIVERY COMPANY

SPEED OF SERVICE

COST

PERSONAL RECOMMENDATION

Is **speed of service** the most important thing to consider? (Why/Why not?)
How important is **cost**? (Why/Why not?)
Is it important to ask other people for their **recommendations**? (Why/Why not?)

Select from the following additional prompts (if the above have already been covered):

Is it essential for the delivery company to include **insurance**? (Why/Why not?)
How important is the **size** of the delivery company? (Why/Why not?)
How important are **discounts** from the company? (Why/Why not?)

PART 3: Collaborative task and discussion (about 5 minutes for 2 candidates)
(about 7 minutes for 3 candidates)

Task 23

Now, in this part of the test you are going to talk about something together.

I'm going to describe a situation.

Your company has performed very well this year, and the managers want to thank all the staff. Talk together for about *2 minutes about ways of rewarding staff and decide which one is the best.

Here are some ideas to help you.

[Place the task sheet in front of the candidates so that they can both (all) see it.]

Think about the ideas for a few seconds.

I'll just describe the situation again.

Your company has performed very well this year, and the managers want to thank all the staff. Talk together for about *2 minutes about ways of rewarding staff and decide which one is the best.

Now talk together. Please speak so that we can hear you.

*[Allow candidates about *2 minutes to complete the task without intervention. Prompt only if absolutely necessary.]*

***3 minutes [for 3 candidates]*

[Retrieve materials.]

Interlocutor: *[Select one or more of the following questions as appropriate, to redress any imbalance between candidates in Part 3, or to extend the discussion.]*

- Is there any other reward you would like? (Why?)
- Is it important for all staff to receive the same type of reward? (Why/Why not?)
- What kind of place would be suitable for a company trip? (Why?)
- How important is it to reward staff for good work? (Why?/Why not?)
- Should companies have a regular programme of social events for staff? (Why/Why not?)

Thank you. That is the end of the speaking test.

PART 3: Collaborative task and discussion (about 5 minutes for 2 candidates)
(about 7 minutes for 3 candidates)

Task 27

Now, in this part of the test you are going to talk about something together.

I'm going to describe a situation.

A large retail company is choosing some gifts to help promote the company. Talk together for about *2 minutes about the possible gifts and decide which three gifts would be most suitable.

Here are some ideas to help you.

[Place the task sheet in front of the candidates so that they can both (all) see it.]

Think about the ideas for a few seconds.

I'll just describe the situation again.

A large retail company is choosing some gifts to help promote the company. Talk together for about *2 minutes about the possible gifts and decide which three gifts would be most suitable.

Now talk together. Please speak so that we can hear you.

*[Allow candidates about *2 minutes to complete the task without intervention. Prompt only if absolutely necessary.]*

***3 minutes [for 3 candidates]*

[Retrieve materials.]

Interlocutor: *[Select one or more of the following questions as appropriate, to redress any imbalance between candidates in Part 3, or to extend the discussion.]*

- What kind of gift would you find the most useful? (Why?)
- Do you think promotional gifts should be expensive? (Why/Why not?)
- Why is it important for companies to give gifts to their clients?
- Who should companies give promotional gifts to? (Why?)
- What other ways are there to promote a company?

Thank you. That is the end of the speaking test.

Answer Keys

Reading

Part 1

1 C
2 B
3 A
4 C
5 F

Part 2

6 F
7 D
8 G
9 A
10 E

Part 3

11 F
12 D
13 C
14 B
15 H

Part 4

16 B
17 C
18 C
19 B
20 A
21 A
22 A

Part 5

23 C
24 A
25 B
26 C
27 A
28 C

Part 6

29 B
30 A
31 C
32 B
33 C
34 A
35 A
36 B
37 C
38 C
39 B
40 C

Part 7

41 01/3434/A
42 Madrid
43 Business (Class)
44 (a)/(by) cheque
45 illness/ sickness/ sick/ unwell/ not well

Listening

Part 1

1 B
2 C
3 A
4 A
5 A
6 B
7 C
8 A

Part 2

9 Naughton
10 Woodes
11 453339
12 250
13 8
14 JO165
15 590 (mm)

Part 3

16 Hill
17 junior sales
18 (new) software (programme(s))
19 window/shop display
20 (the/our) Chairman/(Company) Chairman
21 (13th of) July
22 export(s)/exporting (policy)

Part 4

23 B
24 C
25 C
26 A
27 C
28 A
29 A
30 B

Writing Sample Scripts

Part 1

Script A

Dear colleagues,

After using the company cars, please fill them up with petrol and leave the cars in front of our building on our company car parking places. Then give the car key to our team secretary.

Many thanks.

> **Script A**
> All content points achieved within the specified word limit with no ambiguity and minimal effort from the reader. Some simple linking devices are used. The style is friendly but not informal.
>
> Band 5

Script B

I'll remind you that you must fill the company car with petrol on their return. After that you follow the procedures for parking as you know and deposit the keys in the blu basket.

> **Script B**
> The first and third content points are achieved but the reader would not know 'where to leave the car' as specified in the question. Otherwise the quality of the language and style is adequate for this level and no misunderstandings are created. It would be accepted that people working within the company would know what the 'blue basket' was and where it was located.
>
> Band 3

Script C

Please fill the company cars have been drived in case the next one couldn't drive it again.

And also following the instructions of the parking order. Please leave the deposit of the key is well.

Thank you

> **Script C**
> Although the candidate has tried to address the content points, none of them has been achieved, either because of insufficient language control (point 1) or because the instructions are too vague (points 2 and 3). Band 1 is awarded rather than Band 0 as the candidate has written 38 words and the response is not totally irrelevant.

Part 2

Script D

Dear Mr Craven,

Thank you for your fax on the 3 June.

I apologise about the delay of our product. I regret to inform you that the motors are out of stock right now. We will obtain in 2 days. In addition, we will send the motors to you this friday on the 7 June. I would like to give you 5% discount.

If you require more information, pleas don't be so hesitate to contact us. Thank you for your co-operation.

Your sincerely

J Scharrenberg

> **Script D**
> All content points have been achieved. Despite some inaccuracies, the message is well organised and is always clear. Some good functional language is used and the tone of the letter is apologetic and respectful to the customer.
> **Band 5**

Script E

Dear Mr Craven,

We have, just received your fax dated 3 June and we apologise for what has happened.

We must close our office for one week because we have been stolen.

You will receive these motors by 15 June and we have reduced at 10% on the bill.

If you need more information don't hesitade to contact our driver on 777.39.77.

Yours sincerely,

Hanna Visconti

> **Script E**
> There is a good range of tenses, an appropriate style and some very good functional language. The information is well organised but the candidate could have made more effort to link the sentences and paragraphs together. The second content point requires considerable interpretation on the part of the reader.
> **Band 4**

Script F

Dear Mr Craven:

My apologis for the delay, I'm realy sorry but the delay was because the motors arrived later in my company, I'm going to send the motor tomorro at 9.00 am, I like to give to you a discount in the total price the discount is 20% off in the total.

Sorry for all the unconvenience.

Your faithfuly

Ignacio Dazzi
Manager

> **Script F**
> The letter is well laid out with an appropriate salutation and close. All 4 content points have been achieved but there are a number of errors in spelling, punctuation and sentence structure. The text is quite short. There is a barely adequate range of structure and vocabulary displayed for this level.
> **Band 3**

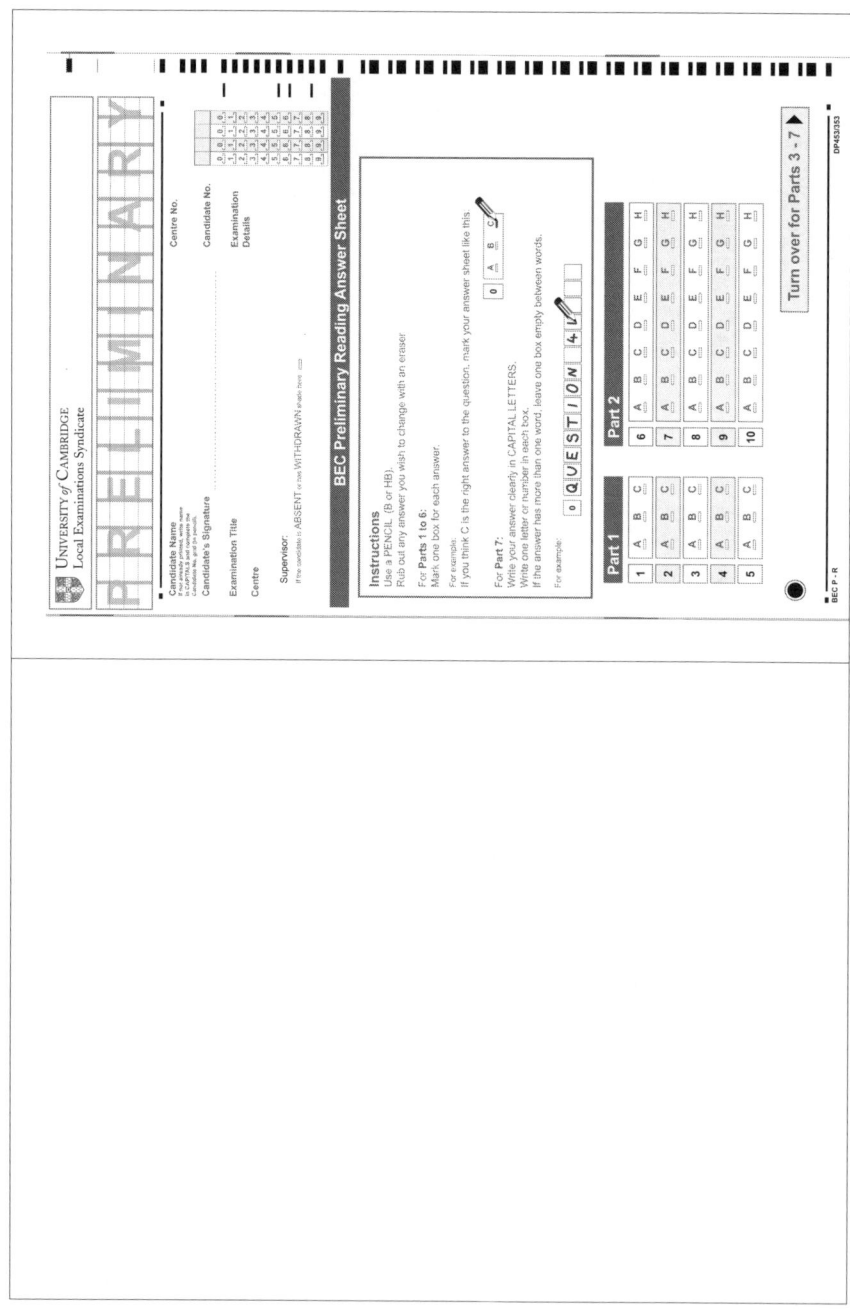

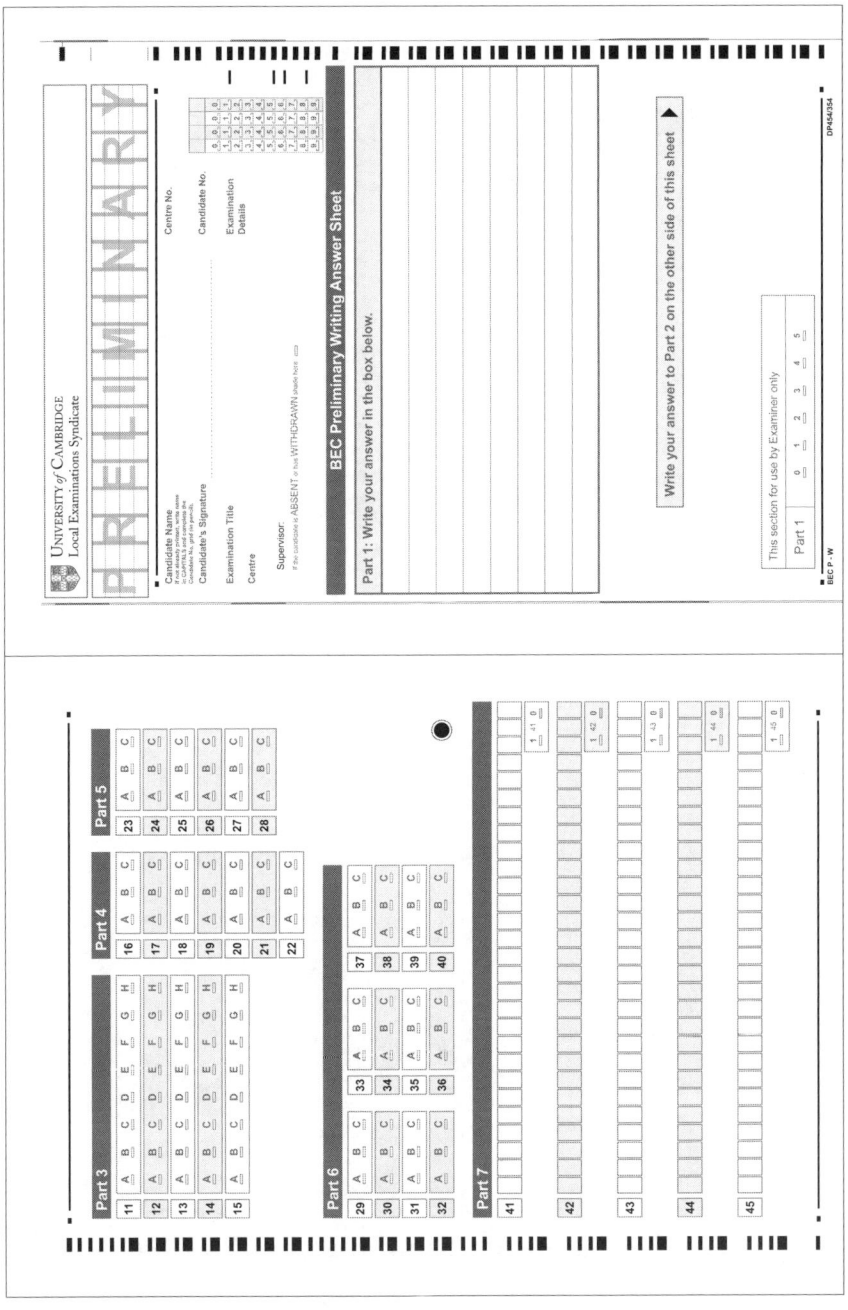

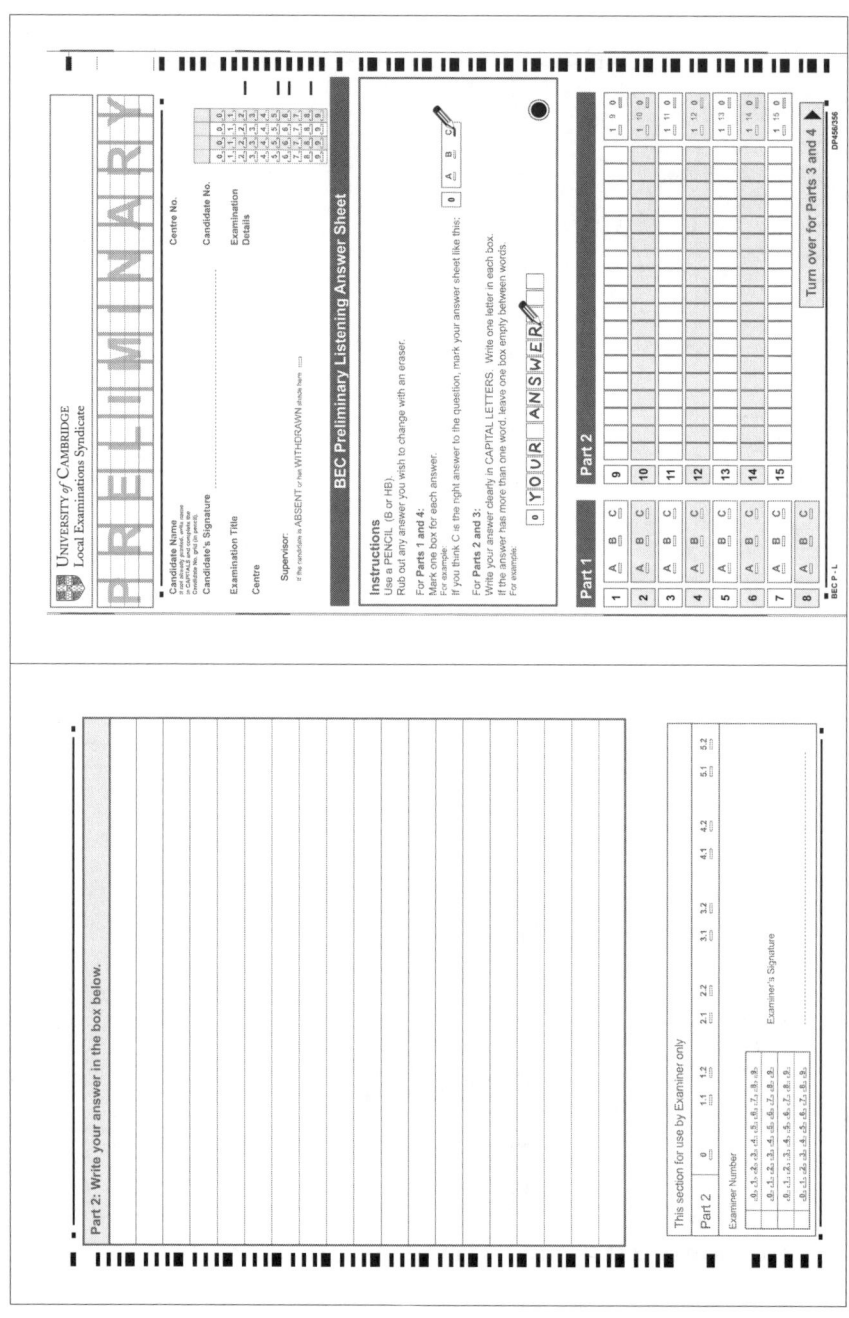

Feedback Form

BEC Preliminary Examination Report June 2002

We are interested in hearing your views on how useful this report has been.

We would be most grateful if you could briefly answer the following questions and return a photocopy of this page to the following address:

BEC Reports Co-ordinator
Cambridge ESOL
1 Hills Road
Cambridge
CB1 2EU
UK

Fax: 44 1223 460278

1. Please describe your situation: (e.g. EFL teacher, Director of Studies, Examinations Officer, Local Secretary, etc)

2. Have you prepared candidates for BEC Preliminary?

3. Do you plan to prepare candidates for BEC Preliminary in the future?

4. How have you used this report? (e.g. to provide feedback to other teachers, for examination practice, etc.)

5. Which parts of this report did you find most useful?

6. Which parts were not so useful?

7. What extra information would you like to see included in this report?

8. Your name: (Optional)

Centre/School:

Thank you.

APPENDIX 4.2
BEC Vantage Sample Paper

UNIVERSITY OF CAMBRIDGE LOCAL EXAMINATIONS SYNDICATE
Examinations in English as a Foreign Language

BUSINESS ENGLISH CERTIFICATE   **0352/1**
Vantage

Test of Reading   **Test 023**

Thursday   **6 JUNE 2002**   Morning   1 hour

Additional materials:
Answer Sheet

TIME   1 hour

INSTRUCTIONS TO CANDIDATES

Do not open this paper until you are told to do so.

Write your name, Centre number and candidate number in the spaces at the top of this page. Write these details in pencil on your Answer Sheet **if these are not already printed**.

Write all your answers in **pencil** on your Answer Sheet – **no extra time is allowed for this**.

Read carefully the instructions for each part and the instructions for completing your Answer Sheet.

Try to answer all the questions.

At the end of the examination hand in both this question paper and your Answer Sheet.

INFORMATION FOR CANDIDATES

There are forty-five questions on this question paper.

This question paper consists of 10 printed pages.

SP (SLC) S26502/3

Changes in Performance Feedback

A

In the past, feedback about your performance used to mean a quiet chat with the boss. But now 360-degree feedback – the system where employees are also given feedback from peers and from the people they manage – is taking root in corporate culture. The system is characterised by greater participation and has grown out of the desire of companies to create more open working environments where people work better together and ideas and opinions are exchanged between teams and across levels of seniority.

B

PCs linked to the company IT network are set to become the feedback machines. Many firms introducing 360-degree feedback are using Personal Development Planner software. Feedback on an individual, which is based on a questionnaire relating to attributes needed for that person's role in the company, is collected using this electronic system. All the information gathered is analysed and the end result is a suggested development plan. The advantage is that individuals make requests for the feedback themselves and receive the results directly.

C

Sarah Rains, from the pharmaceutical company Optec, said, 'Now feedback is available on our network, we encourage managers to choose how they use it. It is a flexible tool and we tell them that waiting for the annual event of a formal appraisal needn't apply.' At the engineering company NT, 250 technical managers have been through the feedback process. Jack Palmer, a senior manager there, said, 'We needed to develop the interpersonal skills of these technically-minded people. In particular, we wanted to build on their team-working and coaching skills.'

D

So, how is the new feedback culture likely to affect you? It could form the basis of your personal development programme, providing pointers to your strengths and also to those areas you need to develop more. Or feedback could be used for 'succession planning', where companies use the information to speculate on who has the right skills to move into more senior positions. As yet, few organisations have stretched the role of feedback so far as to link it to salaries. But one thing is clear: the future will bring even wider participation by all members

---

PART ONE
Questions 1 – 7

- Look at the statements below and the information on the opposite page about feedback on staff performance.
- Which section (**A, B, C** or **D**) does each statement **1 – 7** refer to?
- For each statement **1 – 7**, mark one letter (**A, B, C** or **D**) on your Answer Sheet.
- You will need to use some of these letters more than once.

Example:

   0   the reluctance of companies to base pay on staff feedback

	A	B	C	D
0	⬜	⬜	⬜	▬

1   staff being reminded that it is not essential to restrict feedback to once a year

2   the way in which feedback could identify people suitable for promotion

3   the aim of improving staff communication throughout an organisation

4   the feedback obtained on an employee being linked to requirements for a particular job

5   aspects of a group of employees' work that were identified as requiring improvement

6   feedback indicating both positive and negative aspects of an individual's work

7   the participation of less senior personnel in a member of staff's feedback

PART TWO
Questions 8 – 12

- Read the article below about working in international teams.
- Choose the best sentence from the opposite page to fill each of the gaps.
- For each gap **8 – 12**, mark one letter (**A – G**) on your Answer Sheet.
- Do not use any letter more than once.
- There is an example at the beginning, (**0**).

International Teams

An international team can be defined as a group of people who come from different nationalities and work together towards a common goal. (**0**) .....G..... . The fact that they are spread out presents a range of opportunities and challenges that teams working in the same place do not experience.

One trend in particular which is creating the need for more international teams is that we are in the middle of a dramatic information revolution. (**8**) .... Thus, these teams can now spend as much time working apart as together. They can access and share information as never before. Business will increasingly be done in an 'information space', with information becoming a product in its own right. (**9**) .... Doing this through the internet and e-mail is inexpensive and relatively easy, in both technologically developed and developing countries.

A question commonly asked by managers is whether these teams actually work. Can they deliver improved performance? After a decade of work experience and research with international teams, I believe the answer is positive. (**10**) .... What's more, many of those companies which have actually introduced

international teams have focused only on the performance of the teams, without taking into account the context in which they are introduced. Context plays a key role in the likelihood of their success.

Creating the right context for international teams needs more than a quick fix, though. It requires a long-term commitment. (**11**) .... On the contrary, companies need to focus on the way they operate, and possibly initiate a complete review of their practices before introducing an international team.

Given these challenges, what should organisations do to make sure that their international teams are successful? Much has been written about effective team processes in general, and the first thing to say is that most of these guidelines apply equally to international teams. Experience has shown that international teams are simply more complex versions of national teams. (**12**) .... While these elements may have a variety of interpretations in different cultures, they are as important to international teams as they are to national teams.

Example:

A If an organisation is just beginning to work globally and has only recently created international teams, it often underestimates the level of support needed by teams.

B It is now well-established that any team will have a greater chance of success if it has clear goals, a strong sense of commitment, appropriate leadership and good interpersonal relationships.

C The recognition of this has created many more knowledge workers, that is, people who create, exchange and broadcast information as knowledge.

D Organisations must understand that operating globally affects every aspect of business, and they cannot simply set up international teams and assume that everything else can remain unchanged.

E The first major impact of this is that satellite technology is increasingly allowing team members to participate in discussions wherever they are, at any time they choose.

F Unfortunately, however, few organisations until now have been prepared to make the necessary investment to gain the potential benefits that international teams offer.

G Unlike most national teams, international teams often work apart and across cultures and time zones, for extended periods of time.

PART THREE

Questions 13 – 18

- Read the article below about leadership in business and the questions on the opposite page.

- For each question **13 – 18**, mark one letter (**A, B, C** or **D**) on your Answer Sheet for the answer you choose.

The Effective Leader

From workplace surveys I have found that most people want to be – and feel they could be – more effective leaders. Certainly they want their leaders to be more effective. But what do we mean by effective leadership in business? It would appear a simple question. Unfortunately, effectiveness is more easily recognisable when it is absent. Leaders who attempt to use business jargon and try out the latest ideas are too often seen as figures of fun. Whilst people frequently agree on what ineffective leadership is, clearly knowing what not to do is hardly helpful in practice.

Huge amounts of research have been done on this very wide subject. When you look at leadership in different ways, you see different things. While descriptions of leadership are all different, they are all true – and this is where disagreement arises. However, leadership is specific to a given context. The effectiveness of your actions is assessed in relation to the context and to the conditions under which you took them.

For a magazine article I wrote recently, I interviewed a publishing executive, author of several well-known publications, about what effective leadership is. It was significant that, at first, he did not mention his own company. He talked at length about what was happening in the industry – the mergers, takeovers and global nature of the business. Before he was able to describe his own objectives for the new publishing organisation he was setting up, he had to see a clear fit between these proposals and the larger situation outside. Obvious? Of course. But I have lost count of the number of leaders I have coached who believed that their ideas were valid whatever the situation.

At this point I should also mention another example, that of a finance director whose plan of action was not well received. The company had joined had grown steadily for twenty years, serving

clients who were in the main distrustful of any product that was too revolutionary. The finance director saw potential challenges from competitors and wanted his organisation to move with the times. Unfortunately, most staff below him were unwilling to change. I concluded that although there were certainly some personal skills he could improve upon, what he most needed to do was to communicate effectively with his subordinates, so that they all felt at ease with his different approach.

Some effective leaders believe they can control uncertainty because they know what the organisation should be doing and how to do it. Within the organisation itself, expertise is usually greatly valued, and executives are expected, as they rise within the system, to know more than those beneath them and, therefore, to manage the operation. A good example of this would be the firm of accountants I visited. Their business was built on selling reliable expertise to the client, who naturally wants uncertainty to be something only other companies have to face. Within this firm, giving the right answer was greatly valued, and mistakes were clearly to be avoided.

I am particularly interested in what aims leaders have and what their role should be in helping the organisation to achieve its strategic aims. Some leaders are highly ineffective when the aim doesn't fit with the need, such as the manufacturing manager who was encouraged by her bosses to make revolutionary changes. She did, and was very successful. However, when she moved to a different part of the business, she carried on her programme of change. Unfortunately, this part of the business had already suffered badly from two mismanaged attempts at change. My point is that what her people needed at that moment was a steady hand, not further changes – she should have recognised that. The outcome was that within six months staff were calling for her resignation.

---

13 In the first paragraph, the writer says that poor leaders

- **A** do not want to listen to criticism.
- **B** do not deserve to be taken seriously.
- **C** are easier to identify than good ones.
- **D** are more widespread than people think.

14 Why does the writer believe there is disagreement about what effective leadership is?

- **A** Definitions of successful leadership vary according to the situation.
- **B** There are few examples of outstanding leaders available to study.
- **C** Leaders are unable to give clear descriptions of their qualities.
- **D** The results of research on the subject have concluded little.

15 The publishing executive's priorities for leadership focused on

- **A** significant and long-term aims.
- **B** internal organisational aspects.
- **C** professional skills and abilities.
- **D** overall business contexts.

16 According to the writer, the finance director was unsuccessful because

- **A** staff were uncomfortable with his style.
- **B** existing clients were suspicious of change.
- **C** competitors had a more dynamic approach.
- **D** colleagues gave little support to his ideas.

17 Staff at the accountancy firm who were promoted were required to

- **A** correct mistakes.
- **B** have a high level of knowledge.
- **C** maintain discipline within the organisation.
- **D** advise clients on responding to uncertainty.

18 The example of the manufacturing manager is given to emphasise that

- **A** managers need support from their employers.
- **B** leaders should not be afraid of being unpopular.
- **C** effective leaders must be sensitive to staff needs.
- **D** managers do not always understand the attitudes of staff.

PART FOUR

Questions 19 – 33

- Read the extract below from the annual report of a company with manufacturing interests around the world.

- Choose the best word to fill each gap from **A, B, C** or **D** on the opposite page.

- For each question **19 – 33**, mark one letter (**A, B, C** or **D**) on your Answer Sheet.

- There is an example at the beginning, (**0**).

Example:

	A	B	C	D
	extension	expansion	accumulation	inflation

0 [A] [B ▦] [C] [D]

Manufacturing Strategy

During the last year, we announced the significant (**0**) ......**B**...... of our plastic sheeting plant in Malaysia, which, together with the acquisition of the Javanese factory, will approximately double the Group's manufacturing (**19**) .... The cost of this development is within (**20**) ...... and will be approximately $5.6m, of which $2.7m was incurred during the previous year. It is on schedule to (**21**) ...... increasing volumes from October 2002.

Following the (**22**) ...... of plastic tubing manufacture from Germany to Thailand, we have effectively doubled the capacity of this facility at an (**23**) ...... cost of $12m. The project is set to cost less than the original (**24**) ...... and is on target for increased production by June 2003.

In February, we announced our (**25**) ...... to sell our factory in Ireland. This decision is in line with the Group's strategy of (**26**) ...... on our core categories of branded products.

In June, we announced investment in a new state-of-the-art UK manufacturing facility for specialist plastic components. This facility will be (**27**) ...... by mid-2003 and will increase the Group's capacity to manufacture products efficiently in-house. At the same time it will (**28**) ...... about 200 new jobs in an area of high unemployment. The factory is to cost approximately $24m, towards which government (**29**) ...... of up to $4m are already available. Sadly, as part of this move, we announced the (**30**) ...... of our Blackburn facility, which is due to take place in the early part of 2003.

As part of our commitment to effective external communications with all our stakeholders, in October we (**31**) ...... the corporate website, which is now providing up-to-date information on the Group, and we look forward to receiving (**32**) ...... from users of the site. Existing product websites are now in the (**33**) ...... of being redesigned as part of the global rebranding strategy.

	A	B	C	D
19	output	yield	total	mass
20	budget	income	account	fund
21	forward	transfer	advance	deliver
22	replacement	rearranging	relocation	redistribution
23	aimed	imagined	accepted	expected
24	guess	judgement	estimate	conviction
25	focus	object	intention	purpose
26	concentrating	planning	attending	directing
27	running	implementing	executing	organising
28	appoint	result	employ	create
29	scholarships	grants	allocations	gifts
30	finish	closure	ending	conclusion
31	dispatched	prompted	launched	effected
32	attitude	approach	outlook	feedback
33	practice	progress	process	procedure

PART FIVE
Questions 34 – 45

- Read the article below about market research.
- In most of the lines **34 – 45** there is one extra word. It is either grammatically incorrect or does not fit in with the meaning of the text. Some lines, however, are correct.
- If a line is correct, write **CORRECT** on your Answer Sheet.
- If there is an extra word in the line, write **the extra word** in CAPITAL LETTERS on your Answer Sheet.
- The exercise begins with two examples, **(0)** and **(00)**.

Examples:

| 0 | I | N | C | O | R | R | E | C | T |

Market Research

0	Market research involves in collecting and sorting facts and opinions from specific groups
00	of people. The purpose of research can vary from discovering the popularity of a political
34	party to assessing whether is a product needs changing or replacing. Most work in
35	consumer research involves interviewers employed by market research agencies, but
36	certain industrial and social research is carried out by any specialist agencies. Interviews
37	may be with individuals or groups and can last anything as from a few minutes to an hour or
38	more. In some interviews, people may be asked to examine or try out products before
39	giving up their opinion. Successful interviewers tend to like meeting people and should not
40	only be shy of addressing strangers. Interviewers are usually expected to work
41	unsupervised, organising their own workload. Self-discipline is absolutely essential, and
42	as are motivation and energy. There are no specific age limits for such a work, though
43	many agencies prefer to employ older applicants with experience of meeting people.
44	Market research agencies which frequently organise training, where trainees learn how to
45	recognise socio-economic groups and practise approaching to the public. For information
	on market research training and qualifications, contact the Market Research Association.

333

Candidate Name _____

	Centre Number	Candidate Number

UNIVERSITY OF CAMBRIDGE LOCAL EXAMINATIONS SYNDICATE

Examinations in English as a Foreign Language

BUSINESS ENGLISH CERTIFICATE   **0352/2**

Vantage

Test of Writing   **Test 023**

Thursday   **6 JUNE 2002**   Morning   45 minutes

Additional materials:
  Answer Paper

TIME   45 minutes

INSTRUCTIONS TO CANDIDATES

Do not open this paper until you are told to do so.

Write your name, Centre number and candidate number in the spaces at the top of this page and on each sheet of answer paper used.

Read the instructions carefully.

Answer both questions.

Write your answers on the separate answer paper provided.

Write clearly in pen, not pencil. You may make alterations but make sure that your work is **easy to read**.

If you use more than one sheet of paper, fasten the sheets together.

At the end of the examination hand in both this question paper and your answer paper.

INFORMATION FOR CANDIDATES

Part 2 carries twice as many marks as Part 1.

This question paper consists of 3 printed pages.

SP (SLC/KS) S26977/2

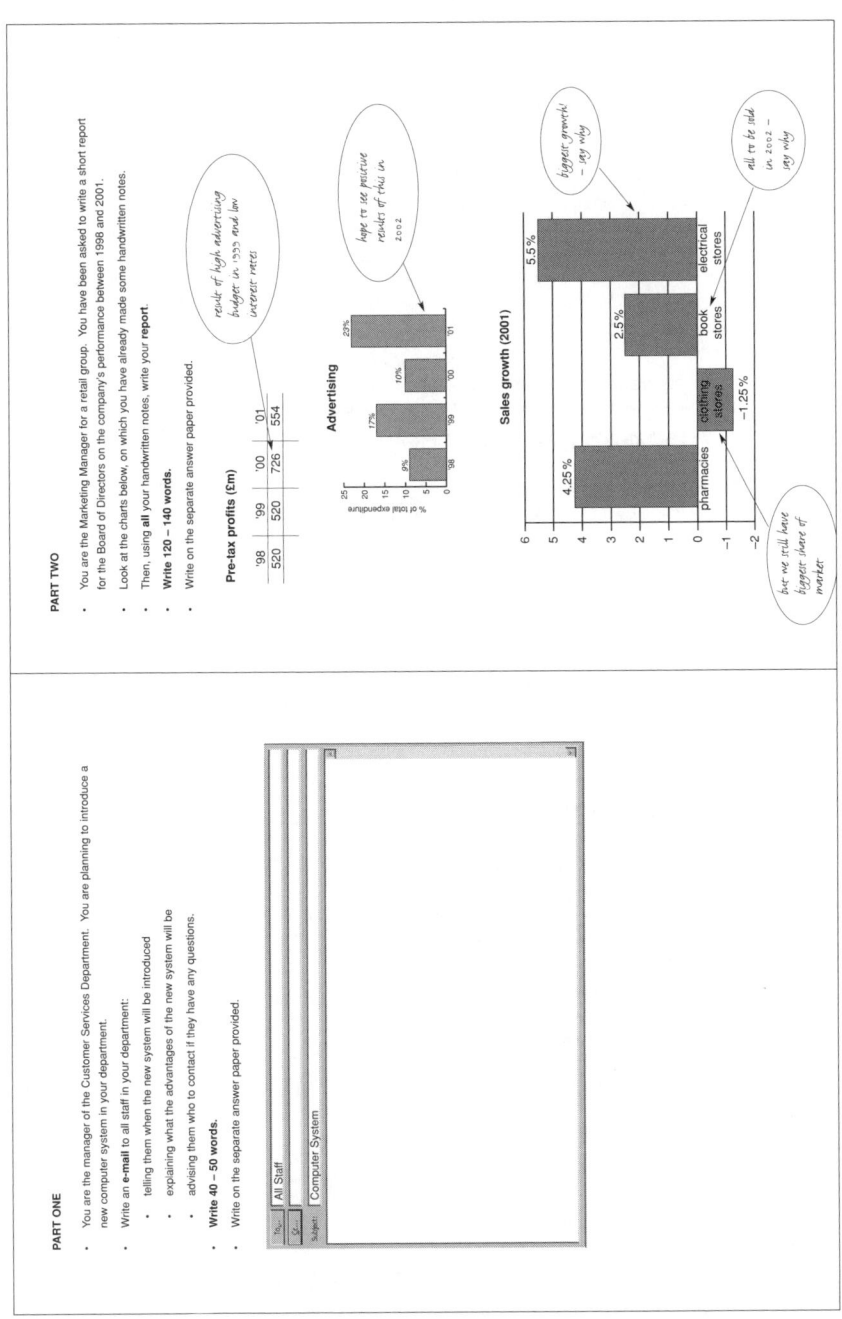

PART ONE

- You are the manager of the Customer Services Department. You are planning to introduce a new computer system in your department.

- Write an **e-mail** to all staff in your department:
  - telling them when the new system will be introduced
  - explaining what the advantages of the new system will be
  - advising them who to contact if they have any questions.

- Write **40 – 50 words.**

- Write on the separate answer paper provided.

To: All Staff
Subject: Computer System

PART TWO

- You are the Marketing Manager for a retail group. You have been asked to write a short report for the Board of Directors on the company's performance between 1998 and 2001.

- Look at the charts below, on which you have already made some handwritten notes.

- Then, using **all** your handwritten notes, write your **report.**

- Write **120 – 140 words.**

- Write on the separate answer paper provided.

Pre-tax profits (£m)

	'98	'99	'00	'01
	520	520	726	554

result of high advertising budget in 1999 and low interest rates

Advertising

% of total expenditure: '98 9%, '99 17%, '00 10%, '01 23%

hope to see positive results of this in 2002

Sales growth (2001)

pharmacies 4.25%, clothing stores –1.25%, book stores 2.5%, electrical stores 5.5%

bigger growth – say why

will it be sold in 2002 – say why

but we still have bigger share of market

Appendix 4.2

	Centre Number	Candidate Number

Candidate Name _____

UNIVERSITY OF CAMBRIDGE LOCAL EXAMINATIONS SYNDICATE

Examinations in English as a Foreign Language

BUSINESS ENGLISH CERTIFICATE   **0352/3**

Vantage

Test of Listening   **Test 023**

Thursday   **6 JUNE 2002**   Morning   Approx. 40 minutes
(including 10 minutes'
transfer time)

Additional materials:
  Answer Sheet

TIME   Approx. 40 minutes (including 10 minutes' transfer time)

INSTRUCTIONS TO CANDIDATES

Do not open this paper until you are told to do so.

Write your name, Centre number and candidate number in the spaces at the top of this page. Write these details in pencil on your Answer Sheet **if these are not already printed**.

Listen to the instructions for each part carefully.

Try to answer all the questions.

Write your answers on this question paper.

At the end of the test you will have 10 minutes to copy your answers onto your Answer Sheet.

Read the instructions for completing your Answer Sheet carefully.

Write all your answers in **pencil**.

At the end of the examination hand in both this question paper and your Answer Sheet.

INFORMATION FOR CANDIDATES

Instructions are given on the tape.
You will hear everything twice.
There are thirty questions on this paper.

This question paper consists of 7 printed pages.

SP (CW) S22995/2

336

PART ONE
Questions 1 – 12

- You will hear three telephone conversations or messages.
- Write **one or two words** or **a number** in the numbered spaces on the notes or forms below.
- You will hear each recording twice.

Conversation One
(Questions 1 – 4)

- Look at the note below.
- You will hear a man calling his office.

Telephone message

Martin Hayes phoned from the (1) ....

There is a problem: the (2) .... haven't
arrived. (They were sent by our last week.)

Another thing he needs more (3) ....

He's attending a (4) .... this morning, so
call him back around lunchtime.

Conversation Two
(Questions 5 – 8)

- Look at the note below.
- You will hear a woman calling about a job application.

MESSAGE

For: Jill

Sara (5) .... called this morning about the
post of (6) ....

They'd like you to attend a (7) .... on the
28th, they'll confirm this by letter.

In the meantime, can you send her details of your
(8) ....

Appendix 4.2

Conversation Three
(Questions 9 – 12)

* Look at the note below.
* You will hear a man phoning about some arrangements for a meeting.

WHILE YOU WERE OUT

Message for: *Laura O'Neil*   **From:** *Chris Darcy*

Message

Chris (HR) phoned about meeting of **(9)** ....

next week. There's going to be announcement about

(10) .... *and wants you to make*   *of the new company,*

presentation on. **(11)** ....   *in your*

Could you also cover **(12)** ....

presentation?

PART TWO
Questions 13 – 22
Section One
(Questions 13 – 17)

* You will hear five short recordings.
* For each recording, decide which aspect of working conditions the speaker is talking about.
* Write one letter (**A – H**) next to the number of the recording.
* Do not use any letter more than once.
* You will hear the five recordings twice.

13 ....

14 ....

15 ....

16 ....

17 ....

A	career prospects
B	health and safety
C	working hours
D	holiday allowance
E	training courses
F	disciplinary procedures
G	job security
H	pay increases

Section Two
(Questions 18 – 22)

* You will hear another five recordings.
* For each recording, decide what each speaker is trying to do.
* Write one letter (**A – H**) next to the number of the recording.
* Do not use any letter more than once.
* You will hear the five recordings twice.

18 ....

19 ....

20 ....

21 ....

22 ....

A	nominate a supplier
B	present sales figures
C	support a proposal
D	refuse an increment
E	agree to expenditure
F	claim damages
G	negotiate a contract
H	request a postponement

PART THREE
Questions 23 – 30

- You will hear a radio interview with a leading industrialist and business consultant, Philip Spencer.
- For each question 23 – 30, mark one letter (**A, B** or **C**) for the correct answer.
- You will hear the recording twice.

23 When visiting companies, Philip Spencer's objective is to

   A improve staff productivity.
   B identify problem areas.
   C retrain weak management.

24 Problems at Manson's had continued after Spencer's first visit because of

   A poor distribution systems.
   B inadequate market research.
   C outdated production methods.

25 Difficulties at Criterion Glass stemmed from lack of attention to

   A competitors' designs.
   B quality of merchandise.
   C consumer demand.

26 Philip Spencer blames his early business difficulties on

   A inexperience with new companies.
   B lack of knowledge of the financial sector.
   C bad advice from established organisations.

27 He defends his unusual personal style by saying that

   A it is important in business to make a strong impression.
   B his business ideas are more important than his appearance.
   C most business people are too serious and traditional.

28 He thinks he was appointed chairman of LBI because the company

   A knew of his successes with failing companies.
   B felt he had a positive image with the public.
   C liked his fearless approach to problem-solving.

29 According to Philip Spencer, successful managers are distinguished by their

   A concern for detail.
   B desire to make money.
   C strong leadership.

30 His final advice to people starting in business is to

   A make every effort to prevent mistakes.
   B find the best sources of information.
   C maintain a positive attitude at all times.

You now have 10 minutes to transfer your answers to your Answer Sheet.

TEST OF SPEAKING

Tasks are included from Parts 2 and 3 of the Test of Speaking, together with the script followed by the Interlocutor for these Parts.

Material is not included for Part 1, in which the Interlocutor asks the candidates questions directly rather than asking them to perform tasks.

Task Card 17

A: WHAT IS IMPORTANT WHEN...?

Entertaining clients

- Types of activities
- Cost
-
-

B: WHAT IS IMPORTANT WHEN...?

Choosing retail premises to rent

- Location
- Length of contract
-
-

C: WHAT IS IMPORTANT WHEN...?

Deciding on packaging for products

- Image
- Production process
-
-

Task Card 18

A: WHAT IS IMPORTANT WHEN...?

Selecting staff for promotion

- Attitude to work
- Current performance
-
-

B: WHAT IS IMPORTANT WHEN...?

Considering a career change

- Further study or training
- Opportunities for future promotion
-
-

C: WHAT IS IMPORTANT WHEN...?

Planning an advertising campaign

- Market research
- Selecting appropriate media
-
-

Task Card 20

A: WHAT IS IMPORTANT WHEN...?

Dealing with complaints from clients

- Offering an apology
- Suggesting a solution to the problem
- •
- •

B: WHAT IS IMPORTANT WHEN...?

Setting prices for new products

- Production costs
- Competitors' prices
- •
- •

C: WHAT IS IMPORTANT WHEN...?

Aiming to reduce staff turnover

- Financial incentives
- Career structure
- •
- •

Task 29

Work Experience Programme

The manufacturing company you work for has decided to offer a two-week work experience programme for a small group of students from a local business college.

You have been asked to help with the preparations for this programme.

Discuss the situation together, and decide:

- what kinds of work experience the company might offer
- how the participants should be selected

Task 33

For **three** candidates

Work Experience Programme

The manufacturing company you work for has decided to offer a two-week work experience programme for a small group of students from a local business college.

You have been asked to help with the preparations for this programme.

Discuss the situation together, and decide:

- what kinds of work experience the company might offer
- how the participants should be selected
- what feedback and evaluation should take place after the programme has finished

---

PART 2 : Mini-presentations for 2 candidates (about 6 minutes)

Thank you. That's the end of the first part of the test. In the next part you are each going to give a short presentation.

I'm going to give each of you a choice of 3 topics. I'd like you to choose **one** of the topics and give a short presentation on it for about a minute. You will have about a minute to prepare for this and you can make notes if you wish while you prepare. After you have finished your talk, your partner will ask you a question.

All right? Here are your topics.

[Interlocutor hands each candidate a different topic card, and some paper and a pencil for notes.]

Choose **one** of the topics to talk about. You can make notes.

[Allow 1 minute's preparation time. Both candidates prepare their talks at the same time, separately.]

All right. Now, *B, which topic have you chosen, A, B or C? [candidate answers] Would you like to talk about what you think is important when (interlocutor states candidate's chosen topic).

[Allow 45 seconds to 1 minute. Only use back-up questions if the candidate is unable to speak without prompting.]

Thank you. Now, *A, please ask *B your question about his/her talk.

[Allow 10 seconds. Do not use back-up questions.]

Thank you. All right. Now, *A, which topic have you chosen, A, B or C? [candidate answers] Would you like to talk about what you think is important when (interlocutor states candidate's chosen topic).

[Allow 45 seconds to 1 minute. Only use back-up questions if the candidate is unable to speak without prompting.]

Thank you. Now, *B, please ask *A your question about his/her talk.

[Allow 10 seconds. Do not use back-up questions.]

Thank you.

[Retrieve materials.]

*USE CANDIDATES' NAMES THROUGHOUT THE TEST

PART 2 : Mini-presentations for 3 candidates (about 8 minutes)

Thank you. That's the end of the first part of the test. In the next part you are each going to give a short presentation.

I'm going to give each of you a choice of 3 topics. I'd like you to choose **one** of the topics and give a short presentation on it for about a minute. You will have about a minute to prepare for this and you can make notes if you wish while you prepare. After you have finished your talk, one of your partners will ask you a question.

All right? Here are your topics.

[Interlocutor hands each candidate a different topic card, and some paper and a pencil for notes.]

Choose **one** of the topics to talk about. You can make notes.

[Allow 1 minute's preparation time. All candidates prepare their talks at the same time, separately.]

All right. Now, ***B**, which topic have you chosen, A, B or C? *[candidate answers]* Would you like to talk about what you think is important when (*interlocutor states candidate's chosen topic*)?

[Allow 45 seconds to 1 minute. Only use back-up questions if the candidate is unable to speak without prompting.]

Thank you. Now, ***C**, please ask ***B** a question about his/her talk.

[Allow 10 seconds. Do not use back-up questions.]

Thank you. All right. Now, ***A**, which topic have you chosen, A, B or C? *[candidate answers]* Would you like to talk about what you think is important when (*interlocutor states candidate's chosen topic*)?

[Allow 45 seconds to 1 minute. Only use back-up questions if the candidate is unable to speak without prompting.]

Thank you. Now, ***B**, please ask ***A** a question about his/her talk.

[Allow 10 seconds. Do not use back-up questions.]

All right. Now, ***C**, which topic have you chosen, A, B or C? *[candidate answers]* Would you like to talk about what you think is important when (*interlocutor states candidate's chosen topic*)?

[Allow 45 seconds to 1 minute. Only use back-up questions if the candidate is unable to speak without prompting.]

Thank you. Now, ***A**, please ask ***C** a question about his/her talk.

[Allow 10 seconds. Do not use back-up questions.]

Thank you.

[Retrieve materials]

*USE CANDIDATES' NAMES THROUGHOUT THE TEST

Task Card 17 – Examiner's Copy

A: **WHAT IS IMPORTANT WHEN…?**

ENTERTAINING CLIENTS

TYPES OF ACTIVITIES

COST

What **types of activities** are important to consider? (Why?)
Is it essential to consider **cost**? (Why/Why not?)

Select from the following additional prompts (if the above have already been covered):

How important is the **venue**? (Why/Why not?)
Is it important which **company personnel** are involved in entertaining clients? (Why/Why not?)

B: **WHAT IS IMPORTANT WHEN…?**

CHOOSING RETAIL PREMISES TO RENT

LOCATION

LENGTH OF CONTRACT

Is **location** the most important thing to consider? (Why/Why not?)
Why is the **length of the contract** important?

Select from the following additional prompts (if the above have already been covered):

How important is **cost**? (Why/Why not?)
How important is it to consider the **condition** of the premises?(Why/Why not?)

C: **WHAT IS IMPORTANT WHEN…?**

DECIDING ON PACKAGING FOR PRODUCTS

IMAGE

PRODUCTION PROCESS

Why is **image** important ?
How important is it to consider the **production process**? (Why?)

Select from the following additional prompts (if the above have already been covered):

How important is the **cost** of the packaging? (Why/Why not?)
Is it essential to carry out **market research** before deciding on the packaging? (Why/Why not?)

Task Card 18 – Examiner's Copy

A: **WHAT IS IMPORTANT WHEN…?**

          SELECTING STAFF FOR PROMOTION

          ATTITUDE TO WORK

          CURRENT PERFORMANCE

Is the employee's **attitude to work** the most important thing to consider? (Why/Why not?)
Is it essential to consider an employee's **current performance**? (Why/Why not?)

Select from the following additional prompts (if the above have already been covered):

How important is it to consider the employee's **ambition**?   (Why/Why not?)
How important is it for the candidate to have **appropriate skills** for the new post?   (Why?)

B: **WHAT IS IMPORTANT WHEN…?**

          CONSIDERING A CAREER CHANGE

          FURTHER STUDY OR TRAINING

          OPPORTUNITIES FOR FUTURE PROMOTION

Why is it important to consider **further study or training**?
Is it important to consider **opportunities for further promotion**? (Why/Why not?)

Select from the following additional prompts (if the above have already been covered):

Is it essential to consider **financial rewards**?   (Why/Why not?)
How important are **flexible working arrangements** when considering a career change?
(Why/Why not?)

C: **WHAT IS IMPORTANT WHEN…?**

          PLANNING AN ADVERTISING CAMPAIGN

          MARKET RESEARCH

          SELECTING APPROPRIATE MEDIA

How important is it to carry out **market research**?   (Why/Why not?)
Is **selecting the appropriate media** the most important thing? (Why/Why not?)

Select from the following additional prompts (if the above have already been covered):

How important is it to **budget effectively**? (Why?)

Task Card 20 – Examiner's Copy

A: **WHAT IS IMPORTANT WHEN…?**

          DEALING WITH COMPLAINTS FROM CLIENTS

          OFFERING AN APOLOGY

          SUGGESTING A SOLUTION TO THE PROBLEM

Is **offering an apology** the most important thing? (Why/Why not?)
Is it essential to **suggest a solution** to the problem? (Why/Why not?)

Select from the following additional prompts (if the above have already been covered):

How important is it to offer **compensation**? (Why/Why not?)
Why is it important to investigate the **cause** of the problem?

B: **WHAT IS IMPORTANT WHEN…?**

          SETTING PRICES FOR NEW PRODUCTS

          PRODUCTION COSTS

          COMPETITORS' PRICES

Are **production costs** the most important thing to consider? (Why/Why not?)
Why is it essential to consider **competitors' prices**?

Select from the following additional prompts (if the above have already been covered):

How important is it to consider **average spending** levels of the target markets?   (Why?)
Why is it important to consider **product image**?

C: **WHAT IS IMPORTANT WHEN…?**

          AIMING TO REDUCE STAFF TURNOVER

          FINANCIAL INCENTIVES

          CAREER STRUCTURE

Are **financial incentives** the most important thing to consider?   (Why/Why not?)
How important is it to have a **career structure** for employees? (Why?)

Select from the following additional prompts (if the above have already been covered):

How important is organising **social events** for staff?   (Why/Why not?)
Is it important to **involve staff** in decision making in the company? (Why/Why not?)

PART 3 : Collaborative task and discussion for 2 candidates (about 5 minutes)

Now, in this part of the test you are going to discuss something together.

[Point to the card showing the task while giving the instructions below.]

You have about 30 seconds to read this task carefully, and then about 3 minutes to discuss and decide about it together. You should give reasons for your decisions and opinions. You don't need to write anything. Is that clear?

[Place the card in front of the candidates so that they can both see it.]

[If necessary, give clarification. Then allow 30 seconds for candidates to absorb the information and to think how to begin.]

I'm just going to listen and then ask you to stop after about 3 minutes. Please speak so that we can hear you.

[After the candidates have finished speaking, the interlocutor asks questions and finishes the speaking test as directed on the examiner's copy of the task card.]

PART 3 : Collaborative task and discussion for 3 candidates (about 7 minutes)

Now, in this part of the test you are going to discuss something together.

[Point to the card showing the task while giving the instructions below.]

You have about 30 seconds to read this task carefully, and then about 4 minutes to discuss and decide about it together. You should give reasons for your decisions and opinions. You don't need to write anything. Is that clear?

[Place the card in front of the candidates so that they can all see it.]

[If necessary, give clarification. Then allow 30 seconds for candidates to absorb the information and to think how to begin.]

I'm just going to listen and then ask you to stop after about 4 minutes. Please speak so that we can hear you.

[After the candidates have finished speaking, the interlocutor asks questions and finishes the speaking test as directed on the examiner's copy of the task card.]

Task 33 – Examiner's Copy

For three candidates

Work Experience Programme

The manufacturing company you work for has decided to offer a two-week work experience programme for a small group of students from a local business college.

You have been asked to help with the preparations for this programme.

Discuss the situation together, and decide:

what kinds of work experience the company could offer
how the participants should be selected
what feedback and evaluation should take place after the programme has finished

Interlocutor: *[Select one or more of the following questions as appropriate, to redress any imbalance or to broaden the discussion.]*

What **other preparations** would the company need to make before receiving work experience students? (Why?)

What are the **advantages** to a company of offering a work experience programme to business students?

What do you think is the **most useful** kind of work experience for business students? (Why?)

What **help** would you give a student on their first day of work experience? (Why?)

Which areas of business would **you** like to have more experience of? (Why?)

In what ways can businesses develop **close links with the community**?

Thank you. That is the end of the speaking test.

[Retrieve materials.]

PART 3 : Collaborative task and discussion for 3 candidates (about 7 minutes)

Now, in this part of the test you are going to discuss something together.

[Point to the card showing the task while giving the instructions below.]

You have about 30 seconds to read this task carefully, and then about 4 minutes to discuss and decide about it together. You should give reasons for your decisions and opinions. You don't need to write anything. Is that clear?

[Place the card in front of the candidates so that they can all see it.]

[If necessary, give clarification. Then allow 30 seconds for candidates to absorb the information and to think how to begin.]

I'm just going to listen and then ask you to stop after about 4 minutes. Please speak so that we can hear you.

[After the candidates have finished speaking, the interlocutor asks questions and finishes the speaking test as directed on the examiner's copy of the task card.]

Answer Keys

Reading

Part 1

1	C
2	D
3	A
4	B
5	C
6	D
7	A

Part 2

8	E
9	C
10	F
11	D
12	B

Part 3

13	C
14	A
15	D
16	A
17	B
18	C

Part 4

19	A
20	A
21	D
22	C
23	C
24	C
25	C
26	A
27	A
28	D
29	B
30	B
31	D
32	D
33	C

Part 5

34	is
35	CORRECT
36	any
37	as
38	CORRECT
39	up
40	only
41	and
42	a
43	CORRECT
44	which
45	to

Listening

Part 1

1 (retail) exhibition
2 stands
3 price (-) lists

4 (press) conference
5 Middlemiss /Middle Miss
6 Sales Exec(utive)
7 (company) presentation
8 referees

9 (the) shareholders
10 (planned) merger
11 (combined) sales
12 expected savings

Part 2

13	E
14	B
15	H
16	F
17	C
18	D
19	H
20	C
21	A
22	F

Part 3

23	B
24	C
25	C
26	B
27	B
28	C
29	A
30	C

Writing Sample Scripts

Part 1

Script A

To: All Staff

c.c.

Subject: Computer System

I would like to inform you about new computer system which is scheduled to provide in the beginning of next month.

This new system is installed a flexible programme which is able to obtain information about various customers' needs.

If you have any questions, please contact to Mr. Smith, IT Systems Manager.

> **Script A**
> All content points are achieved though point 2 (explanation of the advantages of the new system) is slightly unclear. There is an adequate range of language though some awkwardness.
>
> **Band 3**

Script B

Dear Staff

To all staff in Customer Services Department we will introducing new computer system in our department on 2 July 2002.

The new system ,exelli will help us to calculate all the figars by giving the very lettle information and by this new system we consuming our time.

Please don't hasitate if you have quaction or information and advice call Mary Black on 020 7885 9207/

All the best

> **Script B**
> This answer attempts to address all the content points but is seriously affected by a lack of control over grammar and vocabulary exhibiting frequent basic errors. These errors obscure the meaning and have a very negative effect on the target reader. This answer is over the prescribed length for this part of the test but was not penalised directly for this.
>
> **Band 1**

Script C

I am writing to inform you that a new computer system will be introduced as from June 13th. It will enable all staff to access on-line courses available on our intranet.

For any questions, please contact Mrs Brown, EDP Department.

Best regards.

Script C
A concise and very effective answer which covers all content points clearly and effectively. It has a very positive effect on the target reader.

Band 5

Part 2

Script D

As marketing manager I have to inform about our company's performance since 1988 to 2001, and because of this I have to deal with the pre-tax profits, advertising and sales growth.

*1.   Pre-tax profits (£m)

In 1998, our profits were £520m, in 1999 £520m, in 2000 £726m and in 2001 £559m. We can appreciate that the year with the biggest profit was in 2000: this is the result of a high advertising budget in 1999 and low interest rates. The rest of the years have been low, so I think we have to do the same as in 1999n next year.

*2.   Advertising

In 1998 was a 9% of total expenditure, in 1999 17%, 2000 10% and in 2001 a 23%. This last one has been the highest per cent of total expenditure and I hope to see there positive results in 2002 and the following years.

* 3   We have to deal with different issues, as wages, their growth was about 4.25%: our clothing stores was in 1.25%, but this is not a big problem because we still have biggest share of market. A 2.5% in book stores, but all have to be sold in 2002 because we are going to end with this group.

The biggest growth was the electrical stores with a 5.5%: this is because our retail group is being specialised in this kind of stores and we have to carry on with this growth..

Thank you very much for your attention and I am sure that the following years' will be better than these are.

Script D

All content points are addressed and there is good organisation though cohesion and linking is sometimes poor. The register and format is reasonable and there is evidence of adequate range. There are some errors and awkwardness of phrasing, e.g. 'going to send with this group', 'is being specialised in this kind of stores'. Overall the target reader would be informed.

Band 3

Script E

Report on: "FCB" performance between 1998 and 2001

INTRODUCTION

This report aims to show the situation of our company about pre-tax profits, advertising and sales growth between 1998 and 2001.

FINDINGS

In 1998 and 1999 pre-tax profits remained stable at £m520, then they sharply rose in 2000 thanks to high advertising and low interest rates in 1999. Unfortunately profits fell at £m554 last year.

Advertising situation has fluctuated during the four years and I hope the company will have positive results in 2002.

Sales of clothing stores had a little decrease last year, but F.CB still has the biggest share of market. Pharmacies performance was good and electrical stores registered a big growth in sales due to an efficient advertisement.

I have decided to sell all the book stores in 2002 to sell all the book stores in 2002 to concentrate the company efforts on the clothing ones.

CONCLUSION

It is concluded that the situation of our company is not bad, and FCB will be able to achieve positive results in 2002.

RECOMMENDATION

It is recommended that this year FCB should increase pre-tax profit and clothing stores sales and try to reduce advertising costs.

Script E

The answer is effectively organised with good use of cohesive devices and headings and only minor errors. Unfortunately point 2, regarding the expected positive impact of the extra spending on advertising in 2001, is not adequately addressed, and so the target reader would not be fully informed. This keeps this answer in band 2.

Band 2

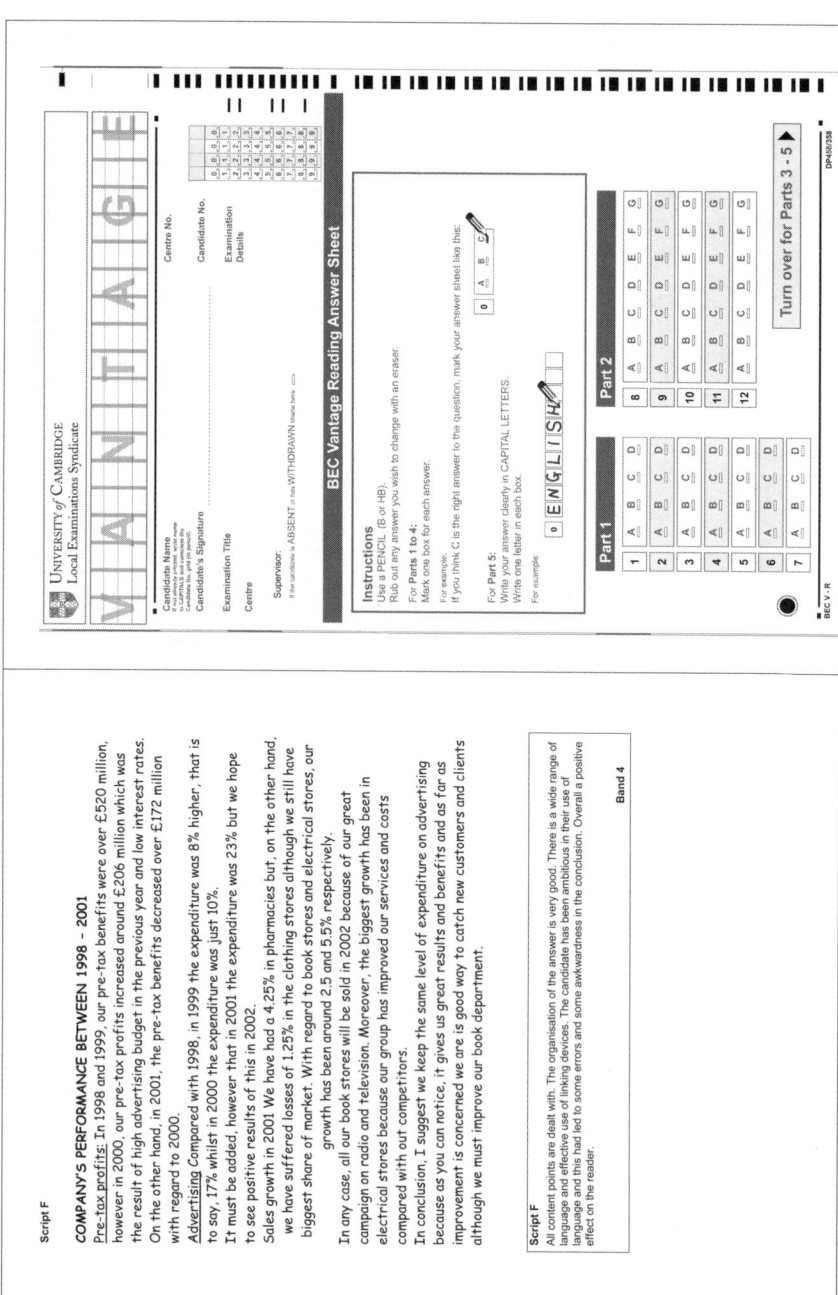

Script F

COMPANY'S PERFORMANCE BETWEEN 1998 - 2001

<u>Pre-tax profits:</u> In 1998 and 1999, our pre-tax benefits were over £520 million, however in 2000, our pre-tax profits increased around £206 million which was the result of high advertising budget in the previous year and low interest rates. On the other hand, in 2001, the pre-tax benefits decreased over £172 million with regard to 2000.

<u>Advertising</u> Compared with 1998, in 1999 the expenditure was 8% higher, that is to say, 17% whilst in 2000 the expenditure was just 10%.

It must be added, however that in 2001 the expenditure was 23% but we hope to see positive results of this in 2002.

Sales growth in 2001 We have had a 4.25% in pharmacies but, on the other hand, we have suffered losses of 1.25% in the clothing stores although we still have biggest share of market. With regard to book stores and electrical stores, our growth has been around 2.5 and 5.5% respectively.

In any case, all our book stores will be sold in 2002 because of our great campaign on radio and television. Moreover, the biggest growth has been in electrical stores because our group has improved our services and costs compared with out competitors.

In conclusion, I suggest we keep the same level of expenditure on advertising because as you can notice, it gives us great results and benefits and as far as improvement is concerned we are is good way to catch new customers and clients although we must improve our book department.

Script F

All content points are dealt with. The organisation of the answer is very good. There is a wide range of language and effective use of linking devices. The candidate has been ambitious in their use of language and this had led to some errors and some awkwardness in the conclusion. Overall a positive effect on the reader.

Band 4

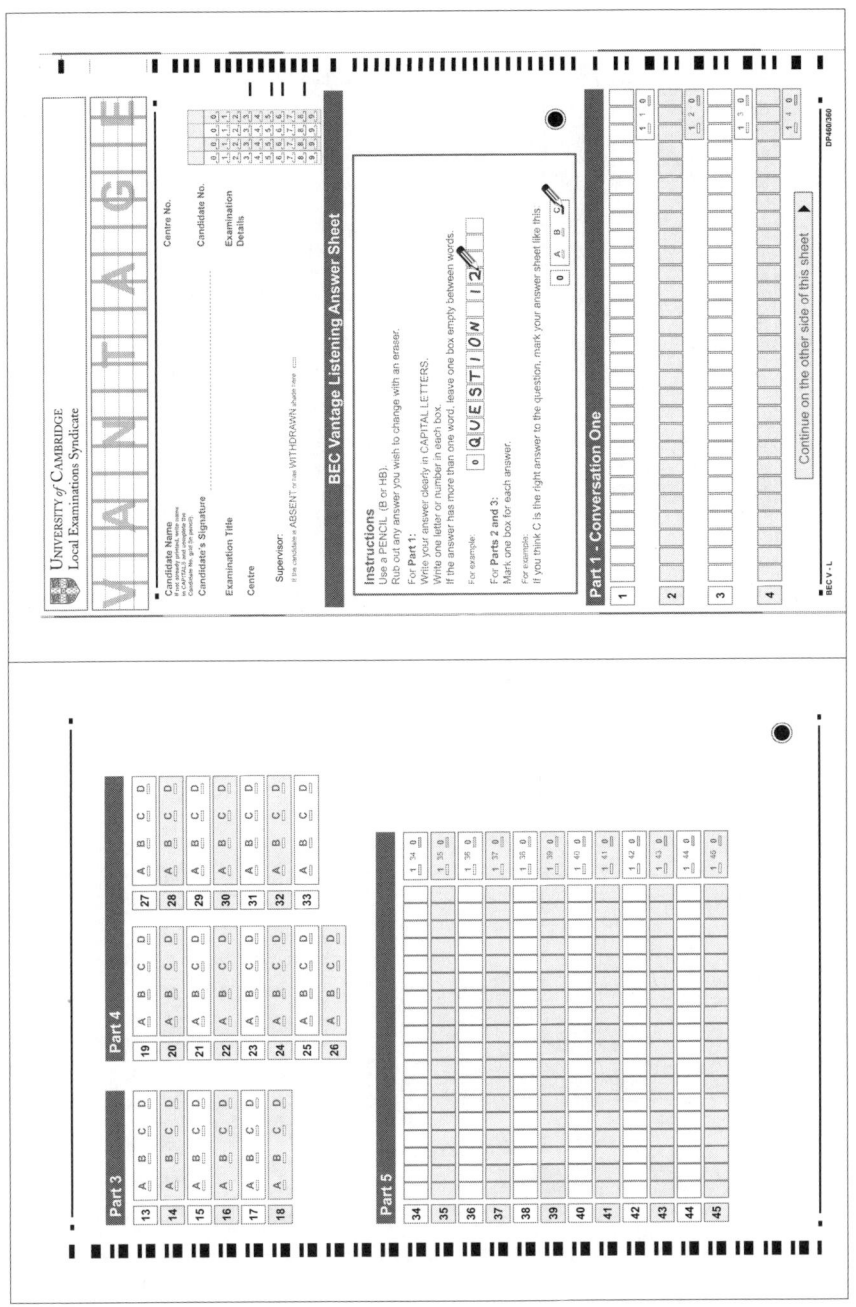

Appendix 4.2

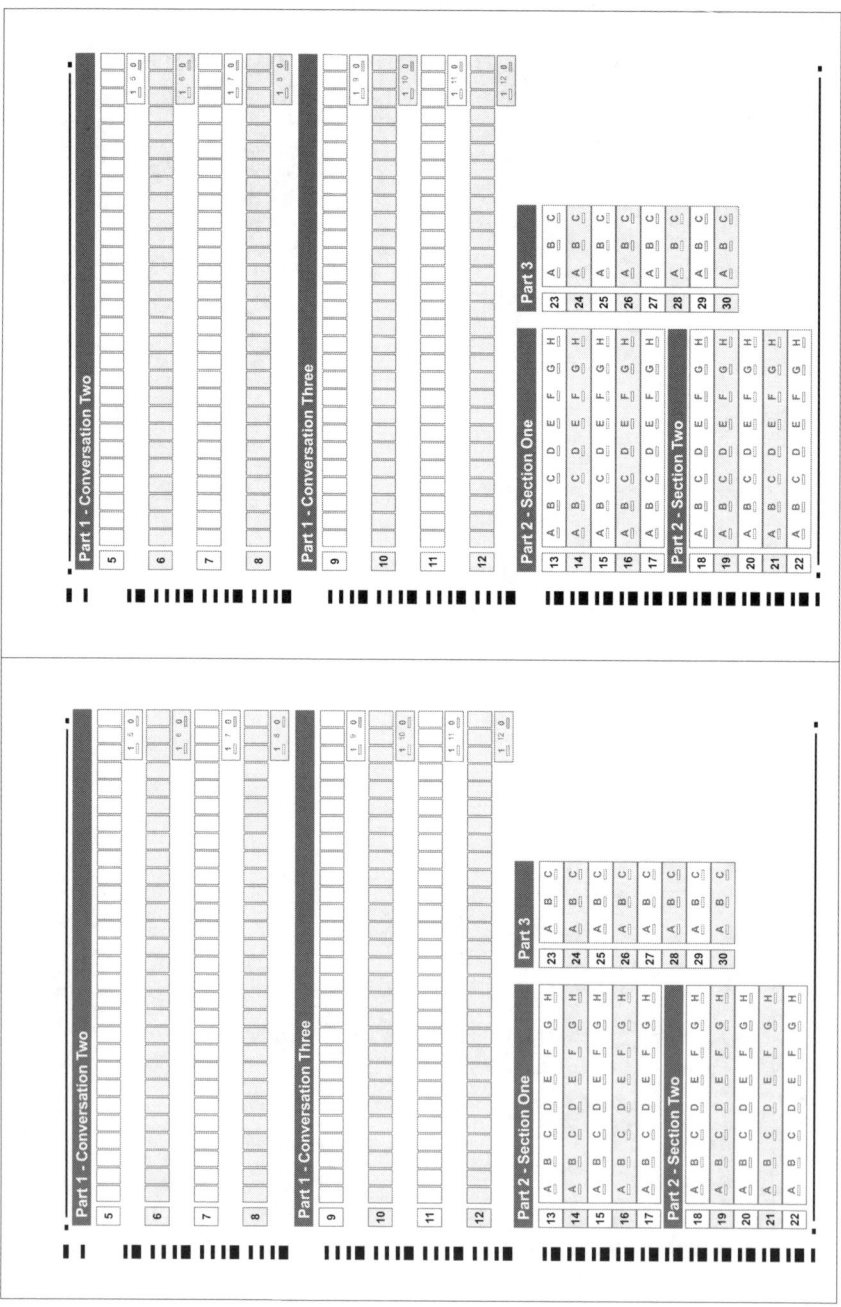

352

APPENDIX 4.3
BEC Higher Sample Paper

		Centre Number	Candidate Number
Candidate Name			

UNIVERSITY OF CAMBRIDGE LOCAL EXAMINATIONS SYNDICATE

Examinations in English as a Foreign Language

BUSINESS ENGLISH CERTIFICATE

0353/1

Higher

Test of Reading

Test 023

Wednesday **5 JUNE 2002** Morning 1 hour

Additional materials:
Answer Sheet

Time 1 hour

INSTRUCTIONS TO CANDIDATES

Do not open this paper until you are told to do so.

Write your name, Centre number and candidate number in the spaces at the top of this page. Write these details in pencil on your Answer Sheet **if these are not already printed.**

Write all your answers in **pencil** on your Answer Sheet – **no extra time is allowed for this.**

Read carefully the instructions for each part and the instructions for completing your Answer Sheet.

Try to answer all the questions.

At the end of the examination hand in both this question paper and your Answer Sheet.

INFORMATION FOR CANDIDATES

There are fifty-two questions on this question paper.

This question paper consists of 11 printed pages.

SP (NF) S31428
© UCLES 2002

Appendix 4.3

PART ONE
Questions 1 – 8

- Look at the statements below and at the extracts from five job advertisements on the opposite page.

- Which advertisement (**A, B, C, D** or **E**) does each statement **1 – 8** refer to?

- For each statement **1 – 8**, mark one letter (**A, B, C, D** or **E**) on your Answer Sheet.

- You will need to use some of these letters more than once.

- There is an example at the beginning, (**0**).

Example:

    0   This company is offering a job only on a temporary basis.

            0 A   B   C   D   E

1   This company is known for dealing with problems quickly.

2   This company plans to take over other companies.

3   This company has as its clients some of the country's leading companies.

4   This company is not turning out as many goods as it could sell.

5   The person appointed to this post will deliver assistance to other companies.

6   This company wants to change the main focus of its attention.

7   This company's goods are expensive.

8   The person appointed to this job will have to show an ability to deal with ever-changing market conditions.

A

HEAD OF PRODUCTION

Success for this £40 million food production plant has come as a result of clear national market focus, coupled with quality products commanding premium prices. Demand continues to outstrip the ability to produce and new product lines have been enthusiastically received by the market place. To ensure that the business meets its demanding customer requirements in a well-controlled and professional fashion, a Head of Production is now needed to install good manufacturing practices and to ensure that the production staff are moulded more positively into a cohesive and responsive unit.

B

OPERATIONS MANAGER

We are a major stationery company. After years of impressive success in ground-breaking new products and customer relationship development, our present objective is to drive manufacturing processes higher up the agenda and we are now committed to manufacturing innovation. We wish, therefore, to appoint a Senior Operations Manager to impart the very latest in manufacturing development. Drive, enthusiasm and a passion for excellence are required, as is the ability to win a similar response from colleagues at all levels.

C

Project Manager

We are seeking to appoint a Project Manager to work on a two-year contract with the fish processing industry. Applicants must have a degree in food science or business discipline with a minimum of three years' experience, preferably in the seafood industry, and must be able to demonstrate an understanding of the current issues facing the fish processing industry. Duties will include leading a small team of researchers, assessing the needs of client companies and providing them with support, primarily through the organisation of technical workshops.

D

Managing Director

We are an international packaging and printing group and have ambitious plans for future expansion both through organic growth and by acquisition. We are now seeking a successor to our present Managing Director who is due to retire in three months' time. The successful candidate will have to display technical competence in the industry and will have a demonstrable track record of managing a high technology business. The new MD will be expected to build on our enviable blue-chip customer base through secure and profitable business development activities.

E

HEAD OF CUSTOMER SERVICE

We are looking for someone with team management, database and process development skills to head our customer service department. The person appointed will be responsible for managing operational delivery and performance. He or she will have to demonstrate experience in the management of fluctuating supply and demand situations. The company, a leader in the provision of services to businesses in the telecommunications sector, has a strong reputation for quality and speed of solution delivery. We are poised to implement an explosive growth plan and are targeted to treble in size by 2004.

PART TWO
Questions 9 – 14

- Read this text from an article about job interviews.
- Choose the best sentence from the opposite page to fill each of the gaps.
- For each gap 9 – 14, mark one letter (**A – H**) on your Answer Sheet.
- Do not use any letter more than once.
- There is an example at the beginning, (**0**).

Interviewing on screen

The problems of global recruitment are disappearing rapidly. The reason for this lies in the technology, that could redefine the traditional job interview, **0** **H** These give them access to the global recruitment market, enabling them to interview and assess their choice of candidates on screen, for example via video-conference link, CD-Rom display or electronic file transfer.

The development of the use of technology as a method of recruitment has brought considerable benefits to recruitment practices. For example, it means great savings in terms of both time and the travel budget. **9** One problem with face-to-face interviews is that body language is bound to play an important part in them. **10** This necessarily leads to an inherent unfairness in such interviews. Putting distance between candidate and interviewer with the use of a video camera can help to overcome this problem as body language will be less obvious. **11** It could prove an unfair advantage, or possibly disadvantage, if used only with those unable to attend a face-to-face interview.

A great deal has been made in recent years of NLP (neuro-linguistic programming), which includes the science of body language, and its value in job interviews. **12** Others, however, reject the new technology simply because they are afraid of it. The benefits of technology, though, are too great to ignore, when one considers that the best person for a particular job may decide not to attend for interview if he or she has to travel a considerable distance.

Appointing senior executives is increasingly seen as a global business. Companies which intend to select candidates for jobs from a wider pool will have little choice but to bear the cost of overseas travel to conventional interviews, or to embrace the new technology. **13** Inevitably, companies will be seeking more cost-effective ways of recruiting quality candidates, and for this, virtual interviewing may offer a solution.

The greatest value of face-to-face interviews is at the stage of final selection. **14** Nevertheless, there are many positive aspects of using technology as a recruitment tool. Times are changing, and unless the die-hards who ignore new technology change with them, they may find themselves left behind.

Example:

A At the same time, the economic climate suggests that there is a very real prospect of leaner budgets in future.

B We are instinctively inclined to feel more positive to people who are similar to us.

C However, some experts feel that the main advantage of on-screen interviewing is that it addresses flaws in the conventional interview.

D For this reason there will always be a place for it.

E For some posts, applicants may be able to choose between a face-to-face interview and an on-screen interview.

F Some people in industry consider this to be a far more reliable approach to selection than a high-tech interview.

G But for it to be completely fair, the on-screen method would have to be used with all candidates.

H Employers now have at their disposal a range of communication tools.

Appendix 4.3

PART THREE
Questions 15 – 20

- Read the following article about different-sized management consultancies and the questions on the opposite page.
- For each question **15 – 20**, mark one letter (**A, B, C** or **D**) on your Answer Sheet for the answer you choose.

A few years ago, when Carol Nichols arrived as head of human resources with NVCT, the fast-expanding telecoms and software services company, she knew that from day one working with management consultancy firms would be an integral part of her role. 'I had already decided on the kind of consultancies I wanted to employ', she says. 'When I started, I was pretty much a one-woman department. So it was important for me to form partnerships to help me support the growth of the department and the company. What I wanted was smaller consultancies with whom I could establish personal relationships – firms which would grow with us, and be flexible enough to respond to our changing needs.'

Paul Eden, Managing Director of NVCT, confirms the desirability of smaller consultancies. Larger firms have a tendency to use one person to sell, and another to deliver, with the result that clients may not really know who or what they are buying. With a smaller firm, you are buying the consultant as much as the product – the person rather than the brand.

Penny White, financial services group Interco's Head of Strategic Management, highlights other advantages of the smaller consultancy. 'A smaller consultancy recognises that it cannot do everything, and is much more willing to work with other preferred consultants for the good of the client,' she says. 'And on fees, smaller consultancies can be less rigid and more cost-effective, simply because their overheads are lower. That is not to say that they need to undercut to win business, but part of a small consultancy's strategy must be to thoroughly investigate how to add value to everything it does. Larger consultancies are gaining expertise in business psychology and applying it to running change programmes, but they still tend to bring in their own team to implement projects, which means that when they move on, the know-how goes with them, leaving the client with a knowledge vacuum, not the integrated training that small firms, in particular, really need.'

But the larger consultancies do have their advocates. Bill Dawkins, editor of Consultancy Today: 'One area where the industry giants have an edge is where major global companies require a standardised service across a number of different countries. Such clients are frequently spending substantial sums of money in consulting engagements, and, not surprisingly, they are seeking the reassurance of a recognised and respected brand which they know they can trust to deliver.'

When it comes to choosing which kind of consultancy to use, there is no right or wrong in any absolute sense. By their very nature, smaller entrants are able to move more swiftly than the larger firms. But the question is whether they have the necessary substance and track record behind them to see larger-scale programmes through. Choose a smaller consultancy for pilot implementations where you want 'look and see' solutions in a short space of time. Then turn to a larger firm for full implementation and transformation programmes. Increasingly, the choice between big and small is not mutually exclusive, but complementary. The two often find themselves working together on the same project - creating a combination neither of them can achieve on its own.

15 Carol Nichols preferred to use smaller consultancies because

A she had previous experience of them.
B they could develop alongside her company.
C she would be able to have control over them.
D they would improve her department's reputation.

16 Paul Eden says one advantage of smaller consultancies is that

A clients benefit from continuous individual contact.
B they have a clearer understanding of clients' brands.
C clients feel they get a better return on their investment.
D they are able to sell their ideas to clients more effectively.

17 Penny White points out that smaller consultancies can

A be flexible about co-operating with other firms.
B spend time researching a wide range of issues.
C provide useful introductions to other firms.
D advise firms on ways to reduce overheads.

18 Penny White says that larger consultancies do not

A train their consultants to work with smaller companies.
B appreciate the function of psychology in business.
C deliver the results that projects are set up to achieve.
D transfer their expertise fully to their clients.

19 According to Bill Dawkins, larger consultants

A are able to pass on economies of scale to clients.
B have a deeper understanding of industrial issues.
C represent a more secure investment for some clients.
D differentiate their advice according to country.

20 The writer concludes by recommending using smaller consultancies

A in situations requiring quick results.
B for monitoring projects' progress.
C in conjunction with each other.
D for the finer details of projects.

PART FOUR
Questions 21 – 30

- Read the article below about pricing policies.
- Choose the correct word to fill each gap from **A, B, C** or **D** on the opposite page.
- For each question **21 – 30**, mark one letter (**A, B, C** or **D**) on your Answer Sheet.
- There is an example at the beginning, **(0)**.

Pricing policies

Whenever a product or service is made ......**(0)**...... for sale, one of the most important ......**(21)**...... to be made is the one related to the price to be charged. To have no coherent policy ......**(22)**...... price – merely to 'think of a number' – is to ......**(23)**...... trouble.

The basic point as far as pricing is ......**(24)**...... is to answer the question, ...**(25)**...... what level should we pitch our prices?' A relatively high price (in comparison to the competition) ......**(26)**...... that the product has something special about it not found in the other products. In other words, the customer is expected to pay a ......**(27)**...... for the extra-special qualities to be found in the product. This also applies to services like any form of maintenance or repair work. Unfortunately, it is a well-established economic law that the higher the price, the lower the ......**(28)**...... sold. Nonetheless, both ends of the market can be equally profitable.

The question of discounts is important too. Some organisations offer discounts out of ......**(29)**...... , while others never give any kind of discount. A 'quantity discount' can attract customers: the more they buy, the lower the unit price. 'Prompt-payment discounts' are another ......**(30)**...... to the customer (usually retailers), whereby if payment is made quickly (say, within ten days), the amount payable is less than it would normally be.

Example:

	A	B	C	D
0	available	convenient	appointed	obtainable

0 A ■ B ☐ C ☐ D ☐

	A	B	C	D
21	decisions	considerations	conclusions	resolutions
22	relating	observing	regarding	accounting
23	appeal	welcome	request	invite
24	implicated	concerned	included	referred
25	At	To	By	With
26	expresses	marks	exhibits	indicates
27	premium	bonus	commission	reward
28	mass	volume	bulk	capacity
29	practice	course	procedure	habit
30	inducement	motive	influence	provocation

PART FIVE
Questions 31 – 40

- Read the article below about the importance of the office environment.
- For each question **31 – 40**, write one word in CAPITAL LETTERS on your Answer Sheet.
- There is an example at the beginning, **(0)**.

Example:

| 0 | A | N | |

Beautiful is best

Is your office ......**(0)**...... attractive and comfortable place? Is it specifically designed to ensure that whatever stresses you encounter in the course of your work, your surroundings make life just that little bit ......**(31)**...... bearable? ......**(32)**...... you greeted every morning by cut flowers, the smell of freshly brewed coffee and a colour scheme that ......**(33)**...... easy on the eye? Or do you have to settle for a desk covered with the pen marks of numerous former employees and a stationery cupboard that can be opened only with a pickaxe?

If the second scenario sounds more familiar, you are by ......**(34)**...... means alone. A recent survey found that 38% of employees feel the interior design of the office they work in prevents them from performing ......**(35)**...... the best of their abilities.

Many employers refuse to entertain the thought of improving and updating their offices ......**(36)**...... of the costs involved. In the long run, however, it might be unwise to be too tight-fisted ......**(37)**...... it comes to employees' comfort. The working environment ......**(38)**...... a direct effect on productivity, and 78% of bosses ......**(39)**...... responded to the survey agreed that a pleasant office is a major influence in attracting and retaining good-quality workers. Employee under-performance can not only spell financial loss ......**(40)**...... also fuels personal frustration when the employee feels unfulfilled. And it's highly likely that the dissatisfied secretary will look to greener pastures – or cleaner offices.

PART SIX
Questions 41 – 52

- Read the text below about the hotel industry.
- In most of the lines **41 – 52** there is one extra word. It is either grammatically incorrect or does not fit in with the sense of the text. Some lines, however, are correct.
- If a line is correct, write **CORRECT** on your Answer Sheet.
- If there is an extra word in the line, write **the extra word** in CAPITAL LETTERS on your answer sheet.
- The exercise begins with two examples, **(0)** and **(00)**.

Examples:

0	N	I	L	L			
00	C	O	R	R	E	C	T

POOR SUPPORT FOR HOTEL STUDENTS

0	Is there anyone in the hotel industry who will, instead of just complaining that they
00	can't find reliable qualified staff, not to mention retain them, is actually prepared
41	to help students with continued professional development? At present time I'm an
42	associate member of a professional body in the hotel management. In order to
43	upgrade to full membership, I decided how to undertake the Professional Certificate.
44	As part of the course, I had requirement to complete an assignment on front-office
45	operations. This seemed straightforward, but I couldn't yet find one establishment
46	that was prepared to allow me to visit and gather the information I required. Some of
47	the 12 hotels I contacted, only two actually had the decency to explain that 'normally
48	it would be OK', but at the moment they couldn't spare the time or staff. Just as for
49	the rest, it was simply 'No'. Would someone please tell to me, and all the other
50	dedicated hospitality professionals out there who are trying to further on their career
51	prospects via continued professional development, exactly how we attain the
52	qualifications that the industry requires us, when the industry seems unwilling to help?

Candidate Name _____

	Centre Number	Candidate Number

UNIVERSITY OF CAMBRIDGE LOCAL EXAMINATIONS SYNDICATE
Examinations in English as a Foreign Language

BUSINESS ENGLISH CERTIFICATE   **0353/2**
Higher

Test of Writing   **Test 023**

Wednesday   **5 JUNE 2002**   Morning   1 hour 10 minutes

Additional materials:
   Answer Paper

TIME   1 hour 10 minutes

INSTRUCTIONS TO CANDIDATES

Do not open this paper until you are told to do so.

Write your name, Centre number and candidate number in the spaces at the top of this page and on each sheet of answer paper used.

Read the instructions carefully.

This paper requires you to complete **two** tasks.

Answer the Part 1 task and **one** task from Part 2.

Write your answers on the separate answer paper provided.

Write clearly in pen, not pencil. You may make alterations but make sure that your work is **easy to read**.

If you use more than one sheet of paper, fasten the sheets together.

At the end of the examination hand in both this question paper and your answer paper.

INFORMATION FOR CANDIDATES

Part 2 carries twice as many marks as Part 1.

This question paper consists of 3 printed pages.

SP (SM/JB) S30782
© UCLES 2002

PART ONE

Question 1

- The graph below compares the export sales of a company called LTG with its domestic sales from 1997 to 2001.

- Using the information from the graph, write a short **report** comparing the two sets of sales figures during this period.

- Write about **120 – 140** words on the separate answer paper provided.

LTG SALES

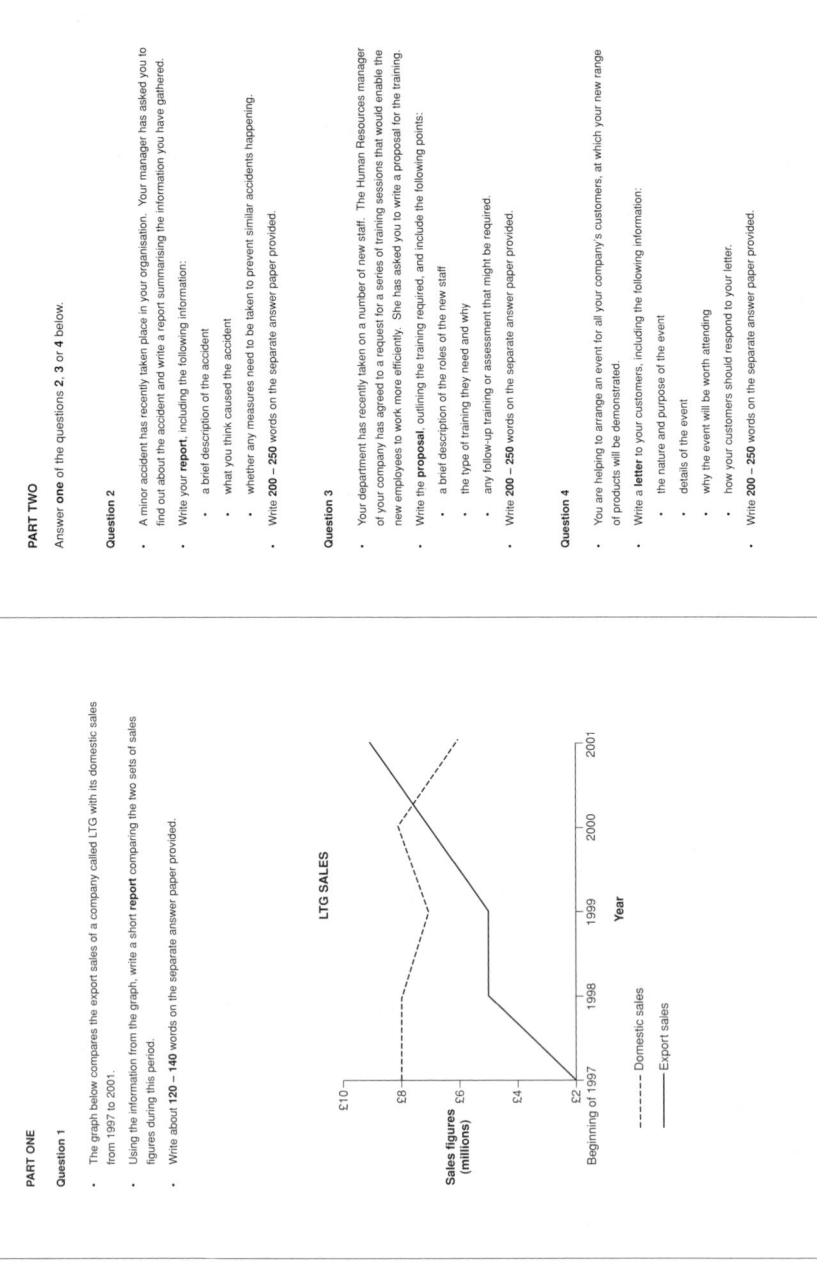

PART TWO

Answer **one** of the questions **2**, **3** or **4** below.

Question 2

- A minor accident has recently taken place in your organisation. Your manager has asked you to find out about the accident and write a report summarising the information you have gathered.

- Write your **report**, including the following information:
  - a brief description of the accident
  - what you think caused the accident
  - whether any measures need to be taken to prevent similar accidents happening.

- Write **200 – 250** words on the separate answer paper provided.

Question 3

- Your department has recently taken on a number of new staff. The Human Resources manager of your company has agreed to a request for a series of training sessions that would enable the new employees to work more efficiently. She has asked you to write a proposal for the training.

- Write the **proposal**, outlining the training required, and include the following points:
  - a brief description of the roles of the new staff
  - the type of training they need and why
  - any follow-up training or assessment that might be required.

- Write **200 – 250** words on the separate answer paper provided.

Question 4

- You are helping to arrange an event for all your company's customers, at which your new range of products will be demonstrated.

- Write a **letter** to your customers, including the following information:
  - the nature and purpose of the event
  - details of the event
  - why the event will be worth attending
  - how your customers should respond to your letter.

- Write **200 – 250** words on the separate answer paper provided.

	Centre Number	Candidate Number

Candidate Name _____

UNIVERSITY OF CAMBRIDGE LOCAL EXAMINATIONS SYNDICATE
Examinations in English as a Foreign Language

BUSINESS ENGLISH CERTIFICATE　　　　　**0353/3**
Higher
Test of Listening　　　　　　　　　　　　　　　　**Test 023**

Wednesday　　**5 JUNE 2002**　　　Morning　　　Approx. 40 minutes
　　　　　　　　　　　　　　　　　　　　(including 10 minutes' transfer time)

Additional materials:
　Answer Sheet

TIME　Approx. 40 minutes (including 10 minutes' transfer time)

INSTRUCTIONS TO CANDIDATES

Do not open this paper until you are told to do so.

Write your name, Centre number and candidate number in the spaces at the top of this page. Write these details in pencil on your Answer Sheet **if these are not already printed**.

Listen to the instructions for each part carefully.

Try to answer all the questions.

Write your answers on this question paper.

At the end of the test you will have 10 minutes to copy your answers onto your Answer Sheet.

Read the instructions for completing your Answer Sheet carefully.

Write all your answers in **pencil**.

At the end of the examination hand in both this question paper and your Answer Sheet.

INFORMATION FOR CANDIDATES

Instructions are given on the tape.

You will hear everything twice.

There are thirty questions on this paper.

This question paper consists of 5 printed pages.

SP (SM) S30783
© UCLES 2002

Appendix 4.3

PART ONE
Questions 1 – 12

- You will hear the Chairman of Masons, an international retailer, reporting to a meeting of shareholders.
- As you listen, for questions **1 – 12**, complete the notes using up to **three** words or a number.
- You will hear the recording twice.

MASONS

Annual report to shareholders

Review

1 Annual profits rose by ....

2 £89.4m profit in the ....

3 560,000 square metres of new ....

4 Retail turnover up by ....

Developments

5 New .... issued at end of the year.

6 York store has developed new ....

7 Intense competition necessitated many ....

8 .... make up a quarter of food products.

9 Competitors have slower ....

10 Each Masons store has a different ....

The future

11 Profits will be affected over the next eighteen months by ....

12 Our present plan for .... will guarantee long-term profits.

PART TWO
Questions 13 – 22

- You will hear five different people talking about running their own business.
- For each extract there are two tasks. For Task One, decide the reason they decided to set up their own business from the list **A – H**. For Task Two, decide what problem they encountered while running their business from the list **A – H**.
- You will hear the recording twice.

TASK ONE – THE REASON

- For questions **13 – 17**, match the extracts with the reasons, listed **A – H**.
- For each extract, decide why the speaker set up his or her own business.
- Write **one** letter (**A – H**) next to the number of the extract.

13	A I wanted more free time.
14	B I had been made redundant.
15	C I felt that I lacked job security.
16	D I found a particular product appealing.
17	E I wanted more rewards for my work.
	F I found that the necessary capital was available to me.
	G I wanted to develop a part-time hobby.
	H I wanted to work from home.

TASK TWO – THE PROBLEM

- For questions **18 – 22**, match the extracts with the problems, listed **A – H**.
- For each extract, decide what problem each speaker encountered while running their business.
- Write **one** letter (**A – H**) next to the number of the extract.

18	A I nearly ran out of funding.
19	B I had problems with suppliers.
20	C I had difficulty recruiting staff.
21	D I underestimated the set-up costs.
22	E I had to work too many hours.
	F I suddenly had to change location.
	G I had production problems.
	H I needed more market research.

362

PART THREE

Questions 23 – 30

- You will hear a radio interview with a company trainer.
- For each question **23 – 30**, mark one letter (**A, B** or **C**) for the correct answer.
- You will hear the recording twice.

23 According to Melanie Chambers, many training programmes fail to

  A encourage workers to study alone.
  B deal with what workers lack.
  C offer workers the skills they ask for.

24 The interviewer suggests that Human Resource managers have

  A problems hiring the right kind of staff.
  B insufficient interest in certain aspects of their work.
  C difficulty taking an in-depth view of performance.

25 Melanie cites the example of *Glymo Electrics* to show that managers may

  A have selfish reasons for not training staff.
  B be held responsible for poor training programmes.
  C be justified in ignoring inadequacies in staff performance.

26 Melanie says that the most important thing about basic skills training is that

  A it must focus on individual skills and not integrate them.
  B it should be specifically tailored to employees' jobs.
  C it should be taught in the work environment.

27 Melanie and the interviewer agree that the results of a training programme

  A can take managers by surprise.
  B often exceed employees' expectations.
  C may not be immediately obvious.

28 According to Melanie, how do some managers react when their staff show initiative as a result of training?

  A They fail to notice it.
  B They appreciate the change.
  C They feel threatened by it.

29 How does Melanie believe that managers should contribute to the training process?

  A by teaching some sessions of the training programmes themselves
  B by examining the content of employee training programmes
  C by reporting on the overall success of training programmes

30 In introducing staff training, Melanie says that it is important that employees

  A are consulted about the content of courses.
  B are not made to feel they must participate.
  C do not misunderstand its purpose.

That is the end of the Listening Test. You now have ten minutes to transfer your answers to your Answer Sheet.

363

TEST OF SPEAKING

Tasks are included from Parts 2 and 3 of the Test of Speaking, together with the script followed by the Interlocutor for these Parts.

Material is not included for Part 1, in which the Interlocutor asks the candidates questions directly rather than asking them to perform tasks.

Task Card 3

A: **Personnel Management:** the importance to a company of having well motivated staff

B: **Strategic Planning:** how to decide whether to purchase or rent company premises

C: **Sales:** how to ensure that price levels for new products are set appropriately

Task Card 1

A: **Customer Relations:** the importance of making customers feel valued

B: **Company Growth:** the importance to a company of controlling expansion

C: **Marketing:** how to ensure that agents maintain a high level of effectiveness when representing a company

Task 22

Incentive Scheme for Staff

Your company is considering setting up an incentive scheme to improve staff performance. You have been asked to make recommendations for the scheme.

Discuss, and decide together:

- what benefits an incentive scheme for staff would bring to the company
- what types of incentives could be offered

Task Card 4

A: **Communication Skills:** the importance of foreign language training for selected employees

B: **Advertising:** how to select a suitable agency to handle a company's advertising

C: **Finance:** how to decide whether to float a company on the stock-market

Task 26

For **three** candidates

Incentive Scheme for Staff

Your company is considering setting up an incentive scheme to improve staff performance. You have been asked to make recommendations for the scheme.

Discuss, and decide together:

• what benefits an incentive scheme for staff would bring to the company
• what types of incentives could be offered
• which employees in the company should be targeted

PART 2: Mini-presentations (about 6 minutes)

For 2 candidates

Interlocutor

Now, in this part of the test, I'm going to give each of you a choice of three different topics. I'd like you to select one of your topics and talk about it for about **ONE** minute. You'll have around a minute to prepare this. You're allowed to make notes, if you want to.

All right? Here are your topics. You can make notes on the spare paper while you are preparing to talk. Please don't write anything on your topic card.

[Hand each candidate a different topic card, e.g. Sets 1 and 5, and some spare paper and a pencil for notes. Allow 1 minute's preparation time. Both candidates prepare their talks at the same time, separately.]

All right. Now, *B, would you begin by telling us which topic you've chosen?

When you've finished talking, *A will ask you a question about your talk. *A, you're allowed to take notes while *B is talking.

*B, would you like to begin?

[Candidate B speaks for 1 minute. Only interrupt if he/she is unable to speak without prompting.]

Thank you. *A, is there anything you'd like to ask *B?

*[If candidate B's talk does not generate a question from candidate A, the Interlocutor may feel it appropriate to ask a question instead, **if time allows**.]*

* USE CANDIDATES' NAMES THROUGHOUT THE TEST

Part 2: Mini-presentations (about 8 minutes)

For 3 candidates

Interlocutor	Now, in this part of the test, I'm going to give each of you a choice of three different topics. I'd like you to select one of your topics and talk about it for about **ONE** minute. You'll have around a minute to prepare this. You're allowed to make notes, if you want to. All right? Here are your topics. You can make notes on the spare paper while you are preparing to talk. Please don't write anything on your topic card. *[Hand each candidate a different topic card each, e.g. Sets 1, 5 and 8, and some spare paper and a pencil for notes. Allow 1 minute's preparation time. All candidates prepare their talks at the same time, separately.]* All right. Now, *B, would you begin by telling us which topic you've chosen? When you've finished talking, *A and *C will each ask you a question about your talk. *A and *C, you're allowed to take notes while *B is talking. *B, would you like to begin? *[Candidate B speaks for 1 minute. Only interrupt if he/she is unable to speak without prompting.]* Thank you. *A and C, is there anything you'd like to ask *B? *[If candidate B's talk does not generate a question from candidate A or C, the Interlocutor may feel it appropriate to ask a question instead, if time allows.]*

* USE CANDIDATES' NAMES THROUGHOUT THE TEST

Thank you, *B. Now, *A, it's your turn. When you've finished talking, *B will ask you a question about your talk. *B, you're allowed to take notes while *A is talking.

All right? *A, do you need a few seconds to think about your topic again?

[Allow candidate A ten seconds if necessary.]

Can you tell us which topic you've chosen to talk about, *A?

Would you like to begin? *[Use only if candidate does not start the talk immediately.]*

[Candidate A speaks for 1 minute. Only interrupt if he/she is unable to speak without prompting.]

Thank you. *B, is there anything you'd like to ask *A?

[If candidate A's talk does not generate a question from candidate B, the Interlocutor may feel it appropriate to ask a question instead, if time allows.]

Thank you.

[Retrieve materials.]

* USE CANDIDATES' NAMES THROUGHOUT THE TEST

PART 3: Two-way collaborative task and discussion (about 7 minutes)

For 2 candidates

Interlocutor

Now, this part of the test is a discussion activity.

[Hold the card showing the task while giving the instructions below.]

You have about 30 seconds to read this task carefully, and then about 3 minutes to discuss and decide about it together. You're expected to give reasons for your decisions and opinions. You don't need to write anything. Is that clear?

[Place the card in front of the candidates.]

[If necessary, give clarification. Then allow 30 seconds for candidates to absorb the information and to think how to begin. After about 30 seconds, encourage candidates to begin the task, if they have not already done so.]

Are you ready to begin? I'll just listen and then ask you to stop after about 3 minutes. Please speak so that we can hear you.

[Do not join in this stage of the discussion unless it is necessary to prompt the candidates to talk.]

[After the candidates have finished speaking the interlocutor asks questions and finishes the speaking test, as directed on the examiner's copy of the task card.]

Thank you, *B. Now, *C, it's your turn. When you've finished talking, *A and *B will each ask you a question about your talk. *A and *B, you're allowed to take notes while *C is talking.

All right, *C, do you need a few seconds to think about your topic again?

[Allow candidate C ten seconds if necessary.]

Can you tell us which topic you've chosen to talk about, *C?

Would you like to begin? *[Use only if candidate does not start the talk immediately.]*

*[Candidate *C speaks for 1 minute. Only interrupt if he/she is unable to speak without prompting.]*

Thank you. *B and *A, is there anything you'd like to ask *C?

[If candidate C's talk does not generate a question from candidate A or B, the Interlocutor may feel it appropriate to ask a question instead, if time allows.]

Thank you, *C. Now, *A, it's your turn. When you've finished talking, *B and *C will each ask you a question about your talk. *B and *C, you're allowed to take notes while *A is talking.

[Allow candidate A ten seconds if necessary.]

Can you tell us which topic you've chosen to talk about, *A?

Would you like to begin? *[Use only if candidate does not start the talk immediately.]*

[Candidate A speaks for 1 minute. Only interrupt if he/she is unable to speak without prompting.]

Thank you. *C and *B, is there anything you'd like to ask *A?

[If candidate A's talk does not generate a question from candidate B or C, the interlocutor may feel it appropriate to ask a question instead, if time allows.]

Thank you all.

[Retrieve materials.]

* USE CANDIDATES' NAMES THROUGHOUT THE TEST

Task 22 – Examiner's Copy

Incentive Scheme for Staff

Your company is considering setting up an incentive scheme to improve staff performance. You have been asked to make recommendations for the scheme.

Discuss, and decide together:

- what benefits an incentive scheme would bring to the company
- what types of incentives could be offered

Interlocutor: *[Select one or more of the following questions as appropriate, to redress any imbalance in Part 3, or to broaden the discussion.]*

- Which incentives do you think are **most effective** for encouraging people to work hard? (Why?)
- What **disadvantages** could there be in incentive schemes? (Why?)
- Is it essential for companies to reward **extra effort**? (Why/Why not?)
- How do you think a company can **inspire loyalty** in employees?
- How do you think the traditional **employer/employee relationship** might change in the future? (Why?)

Thank you. That is the end of the speaking test.

[Retrieve materials.]

| PART 3: Three-way collaborative task and discussion (about 9 minutes) |

For 3 candidates

| Interlocutor | Now, this part of the test is a discussion activity. |

[Hold the card showing the task while giving the instructions below.]

You have about 30 seconds to read this task carefully, and then about 5 minutes to discuss and decide about it together. You're expected to give reasons for your decisions and opinions. You don't need to write anything. Is that clear?

[Place the card in front of the candidates.]

[If necessary, give clarification. Then allow 30 seconds for candidates to absorb the information and to think how to begin. After about 30 seconds, encourage candidates to begin the task, if they have not already done so.]

Are you ready to begin? I'll just listen and then ask you to stop after about 5 minutes. Please speak so that we can hear you.

[Do not join in this stage of the discussion unless it is necessary to prompt the candidates to talk.]

[After the candidates have finished speaking the interlocutor asks questions and finishes the speaking test, as directed on the examiner's copy of the task card.]

Answer Keys

Reading

Part 1		Part 4		Part 6	
1	E	21	A	41	time
2	D	22	C	42	the
3	D	23	D	43	how
4	A	24	B	44	requirement
5	C	25	A	45	yet
6	B	26	D	46	some
7	A	27	B	47	CORRECT
8	E	28	A	48	just
		29	D	49	to
Part 2		30	A	50	on
9	C			51	CORRECT
10	B	**Part 5**		52	us
11	G	31	more		
12	F	32	are		
13	A	33	is		
14	D	34	no		
		35	to		
Part 3		36	because		
15	B	37	when		
16	A	38	has		
17	A	39	who/that		
18	D	40	it		
19	C				
20	A				

Listening

Part 1		Part 2		Part 3	
1	11%	13	D	23	B
2	Financial Services Division	14	A	24	C
3	selling space	15	F	25	A
4	5.5%	16	C	26	B
5	mail order catalogue	17	H	27	A
6	display format	18	H	28	C
7	price reductions	19	G	29	B
8	new (product) lines	20	C	30	C
9	innovation rate/rate of innovation	21	A		
10	layout	22	E		
11	(new/major) investments				
12	expansion				

Task 26 – Examiner's Copy

For three candidates

Incentive Scheme for Staff

Your company is considering setting up an incentive scheme to improve staff performance. You have been asked to make recommendations for the scheme.

Discuss, and decide together:

- what benefits an incentive scheme would bring to the company
- what types of incentives could be offered
- which employees in the company should be targeted

Interlocutor: *[Select one or more of the following questions as appropriate, to redress any imbalance in Part 3, or to broaden the discussion.]*

- Which incentives do you think are **most effective** for encouraging people to work hard? (Why?)
- What **disadvantages** could there be in incentive schemes? (Why/Why not?)
- Is it essential for companies to reward **extra effort**? (Why/Why not?)
- How do you think a company can **inspire loyalty** in employees?
- How do you think the traditional **employer/employee relationship** might change in the future? (Why/Why not?)

Thank you. That is the end of the speaking test.

[Retrieve materials.]

Writing Sample Scripts

Part 1

Script A

LTG SALES

1. *Terms of References*

   As an student in Park Lane College, I have been asked to write a report comparing the two sets of sales (domestic and export sales) from 1997 to 2001.

2. *Proceedings*

   I have used a graph comparing the export sales of LTG with its domestic sales from 1997 to 2001.

3. *Findings*

   Domestic Sales: From 1997 till 1998 sales kept steadily in £8, decreasing in 1999 to £7, then increase steadily to £8 in 2000 and then again decrease to £6 in 2001.
   Export Sales: In 1998 increase sharply from £2 to £5, steadily till 1999 and then increase dramatically to £9 in 2001.

4. *Conclusion*

   Domestic Sales has kept steadily in £8, altering its sales £1 up and down, although from 2000-2001 decreased to £6.
   Export Sales has increased sharply through all that years (1997-2001).

> **Script A**
>
> This task fails to reach an adequate standard on both task achievement and language. It lacks range and the appropriate language for a description of a graph. **Band 2**

Script B

Generally speaking, between 1997 and 2001, the amount of LTG sales have levelled off, passing from £10 millions to nearly £15 millions. But domestic and Export sales have evolved differently.

As the company have developped its Export sales, the amount of this sale have increased dramatically, except in 1998 when it remained constant, from £2 millions to nearly £9 millions.

On the other hand, we can notice that domestic sales have been neglected, as its amount first remained constant in 1997, then fluctuated slightly between 1998 and 2000, to finally fall steadily to £6 millions.

Perhaps, the strategy of LTG is to improve currently its exportations without quite giving away its domestic market.

> **Script B**
>
> All major content points are included and the answer is well organised with clear paragraphing, an introduction and a conclusion. The language, however, is adequate rather than good for this level. **Band 3**

Script C

This report compares the domestic and export sales made by LTG from 1997 to 2001 by using a graph as a reference.

The first thing that immediately catches the eye when looking at the graph is that while exports have done very well growing dramatically between 1997 and 2001, domestic sales are decreasing.

In 1997 domestic sales stood at £8,000,000. Between 1998 and 1999 they dropped to £7,500,000. This loss was followed by a timid growth in 2000, with sales rising to £8,000,000 again. However, this tendency soon stopped and in 2001 sales fell to £6,000,000.

Exports on the contrary, have been constantly growing. They rapidly rose from £5,000,000 in 1998-1999 to nearly £10,000,000 in 2001.

Therefore I would recommend LTG to concentrate exclusively on foreign customers.

> **Script C**
>
> There is one minor content omission - no starting figure for exports. Apart from that the answer is well-organised with clear paragraphing, introduction and conclusion. There are few errors and a reasonably good range of language. **Band 4**

Part 2

Script D   Question 2

Introduction

The aim of this report is to describe the accident that has recently taken place in our organisaton and to see if any measures can be taken to prevent similar accidents happening.

Findings

The key findings are outlined below.

It was found that recent dates related to appointments with clients, final contracts that had to be signed and several invoices that had to be sent, had been missed. This was due to the fact that our computer agenda stopped working for several days last week.

This was probably as a result of either a technical problem of the computer system itself or just an electricity black out. Therefore, the department has already called some technicians to have everything checked.

Conclusion

It is clear that our organisation can not miss important dates just because it keeps all the information in a computer system.

It is obvious that some measures need to be taken to avoid that similar accidents will happen again in the future.

Recommendation

It is therefore suggested that our employee register all the information and the dates not only in the computer agenda but in a papery one too.

In this way, if something happens to the computer system, our organisation will be able anyway to gather the information it needs and not to loose the dates!

Script D

This answer does not adequately deal with the task set, describing an incident rather than an accident.

Band 2

Script E   Question 3

A Proposal for Training New Employees

This proposal outlines relevant training for our recently hired new project managers. Their duties consist of taking the overall responsibility of the projects, meeting the timetables, organising the project work and motivating the participants.

Training at the very beginning is needed to make sure that the new employees can focus their efforts efficiently. The proposed training would include lessons in management and project work. Language lessons would improve our new project managers' ability to communicate with foreign project participants. Lessons in management and project work are needed to understand the dynamics of business life and co-operation.

Our customers follow very carefully how we perform things we have promised. As a last item in the proposed training would be lessons in teamwork. It is important to emphasize the meaning of good teamwork for the new employees. A good co-operation with colleagues and sharing of work and information brings usually the best results, too.

After the basic training proposed in this paper, it would be good if we could follow, how the new employees are able to use in their work the new knowledge gained in the training. For this purpose we could arrange a feedback meeting about two months after the basic training.

Summary – Training needed
- *management & project work*
- *languages*
- *teamworking skills.*

Script E

There is a reasonable achievement of the task, assuming that HR knows which department has 'recently hired new project managers'. Language and vocabulary are adequate.

Band 3

Appendix 4.3

Script F

Question 4

Mr. Black
St. John's Hospital
'Address'

4 June 02

Dear Mr. Black,

Oslo Pharmaceutical Trade Fair

I am writing to invite you to a trade fair taking place in Oslo in July this year.

The Oslo Pharmaceutical Trade Fair is arranged every fifth year and is one of the greatest trade fairs run in Scandinavia. The most important pharmaceutical companies in Northern Europe will attend this fair, and Amersham Health will have a stand there. The different companies attending will present their products.

The fair will be arranged from 5-7 July 2002, starting at 10 am. The event will take place at 'Sjølyst conference centre' just outside Oslo.

Amersham Health AS will present and demonstrate the new pharmaceutical products of the company. We will focus on our ultrasound contrast media. In addition, lecturers related to research products will be held. We will aim to give detailed information about our products. It should be of particular interest for radiologists and medical doctors to see how our ultrasound contrast media, Optison®, can facilitate investigations of heart perfusion. This alone should make the fair worth visiting.

We would appreciate if you or any of your colleagues would like to attend this event. We would be grateful if you could respond by fax or e-mail by 25 June 02. Please see the letter heading for details.

I look very much forward to hearing from you.

Yours sincerely
Marianne W. Wulff
Amersham Health AS.

Script F

This answer shows a good realisation of the task set with all major content points included. There are few errors, but the range of language could be improved upon, particularly the over-reliance on 'will'.

Band 4

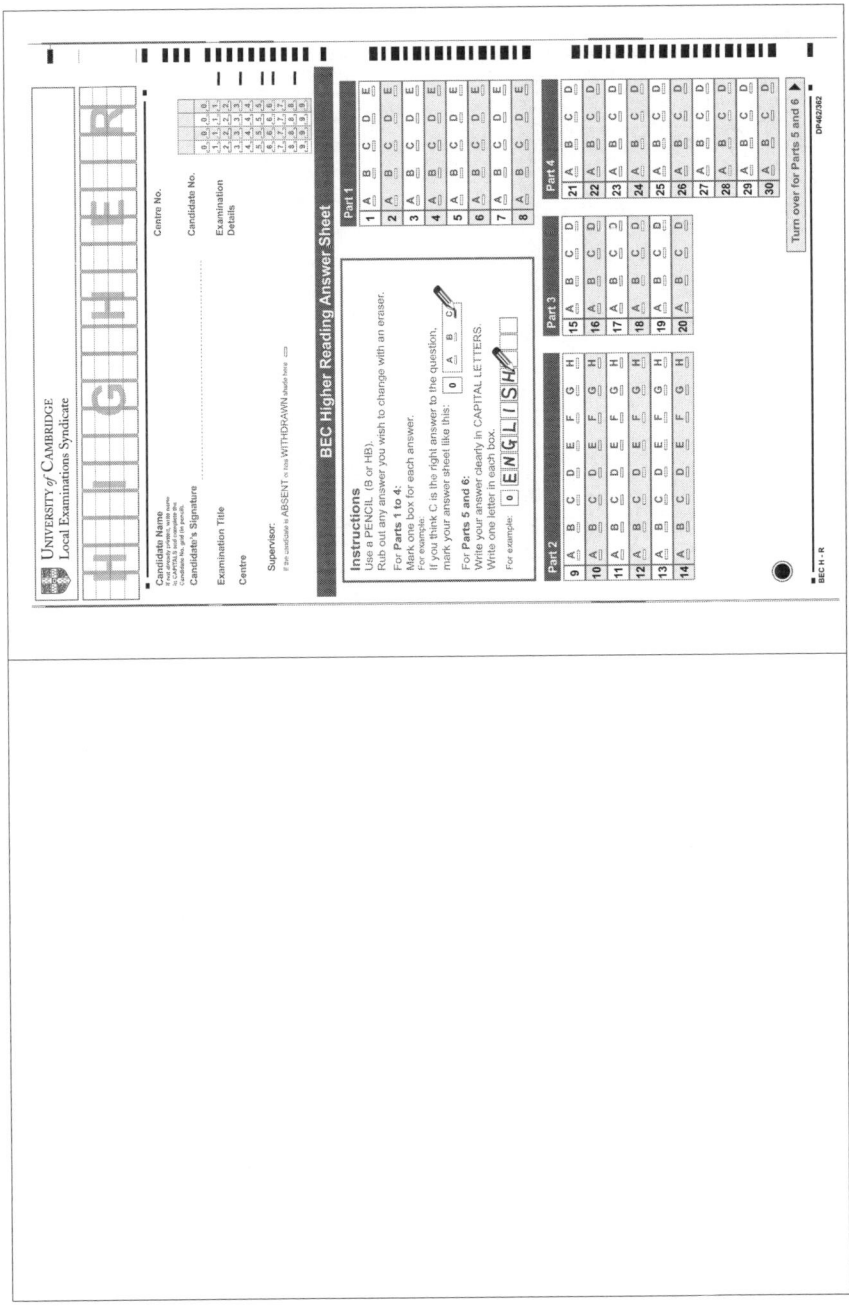

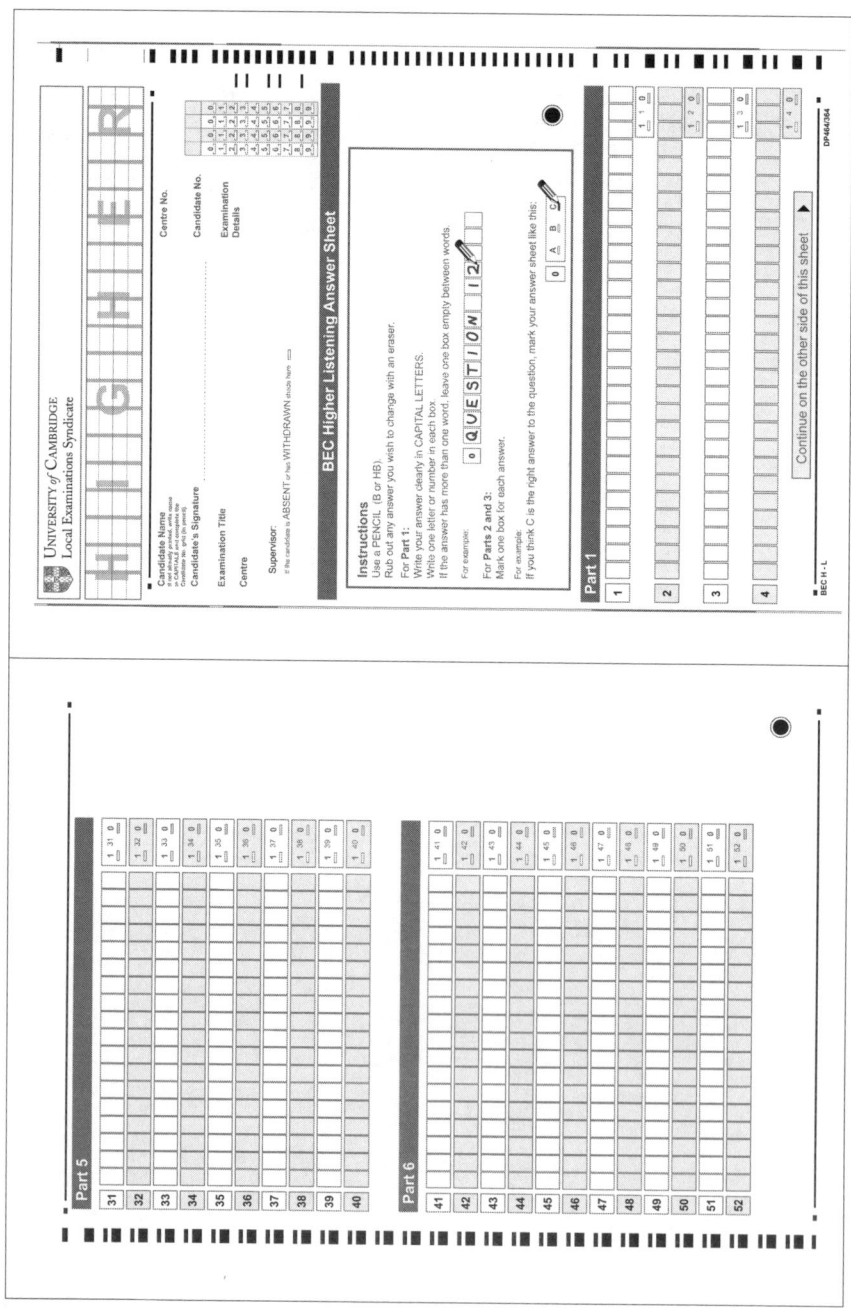

Feedback Form

BEC Vantage Examination Report June 2002

We are interested in hearing your views on how useful this report has been.

We would be most grateful if you could briefly answer the following questions and return a photocopy of this page to the following address:

BEC Reports Co-ordinator
Cambridge ESOL
1 Hills Road
Cambridge
CB1 2EU
UK

Fax: 44 1223 460278

1. Please describe your situation: (e.g. EFL teacher, Director of Studies, Examinations Officer, Local Secretary, etc)

2. Have you prepared candidates for BEC Vantage?

3. Do you plan to prepare candidates for BEC Vantage in the future?

4. How have you used this report? (e.g. to provide feedback to other teachers, for examination practice, etc.)

5. Which parts of this report did you find most useful?

6. Which parts were not so useful?

7. What extra information would you like to see included in this report?

8. Your name: (Optional) _____

Centre/School: _____

Thank you.

Part 1 - Conversation Two

Part 1 - Conversation Three

Part 2 - Section One

Part 2 - Section Two

Part 3

Additional information on tests of language for business purposes

Tests of European language for business purposes: ALTE members

CEF Levels	Italian	English	French	German	Spanish
C2			DSEC (Diplôme Supérieur d'Etudes Commerciales)		DEN (Diploma de Espanol de los Negocios)
C1	CIC (Certificato di Italiano Commerciale) advanced	BEC (Business English Certificate) Advanced		PWD (Prüfung Wirtschaftsdeutsch International)	
B2		BEC (Business English Certificate) Intermediate		ZDf B (Zertifikat Deutsch für den Beruf)	CEN (Certificado de Espanol de los Negocios)
B1	CIC (Certificato di Italiano Commerciale) Intermediate	BEC (Business English Certificate) Preliminary			
A2					
A1					

* BULATS is currently available in English, French, German and Spanish

Contact information for business language test developers

Organisation	Address	Website
Pitman qualifications	City and Guilds Pitman Qualifications 1 Giltspur Street London EC1A 9DD United Kingdom Fax: +44 (0) 20 7294 3502	www.pitmanqualifications.com
LCCIEB	LCCIEB Corporate Headquarters 112 Station Road Sidcup Kent DA15 7BJ United Kingdom Phone: +44 (0) 20 8309 3000 Fax: +44 (0) 20 8302 4169	www.lccieb.com/Lcci/Home/Index.asp
TOEIC	TOEIC Service International TOEIC Testing Program Educational Testing Service Rosedale Road Princeton, NJ 08541, USA Phone: +1 (609) 734-1540 Fax: +1 (609) 734 1560	www.toeic.com/index.htm
Cambridge ESOL	University of Cambridge ESOL Examinations 1 Hills Road Cambridge CB1 2EU United Kingdom Phone: +44 (0) 1223 553355 Fax: +44 (0) 1223 460278	www.cambridge-efl.org/index.html
JETRO	2-5, Toranomon 2-chome, Minato-ku, Tokyo 105-8466 Tel: 03-3582-5511 Fax: 03-3587-0219	www.jetro.go.jp/it/e/bj/index.html
Alliance Française Centre international d'études pédagogiques	Alliance Française 101, Bd Raspail 75270 Paris Cedex 06 France Tel.: +33-1-45 44 38 28 Fax: +33-1-45 49 15 82 E-mail: info@paris.alliancefrancaise.fr	www.alliancefr.org/

Organisation	Address	Website
The Goethe-Institut	Goethe-Institut Inter Nationes Helene-Weber-Allee 1 München 80637 Germany Tel +49 89 15921 382 Fax +49 89 15921 608 E-mail bolton@goethe.de	www.goethe.de/dll/prf/pba/pwd/deindex.htm
Università per Stranieri, Perugia	University for Foreigners – Perugia Palazzo Gallenga Piazza Fortebraccio, 4 06122 Perugia – Italy Tel +39/075/5746467 Fax +39/075/5746456 E-mail: certific@unistrapg.it	www.unistrapg.it
Instituto Cervantes and Universidad de Salamanca	Instituto Cervantes Colegio del Rey C/ Libreros, 23 Madrid 28801 Alcalá de Henares Spain Tel +34-91-745 3334 Fax +34-91-745 0058 E-mail: jmartinv@cervantes.es parrondo@cervantes.es	www.cervantes.es

References

Abdul-Raof, A H (2002) *The production of a performance rating scale: An alternative methodology*, Unpublished PhD dissertation, University of Reading.

APA (1999) *The Standards for Educational and Psychological Testing*, Washington DC: American Psychological Association.

Alderson, J C (1998) *DIALANG*, paper presented at the Language Testing Forum, Swansea, November 1998.

Alderson, J C and Urquhart, A H (1984) ESP Tests: The problem of student background discipline, in Culhane, T, Klein-Braley, C and Stevenson, D K (Eds) *Practice and Problems in Language Testing*, Essex: University of Essex, 1–13.

Alderson, J C and Urquhart, A H (1985) The effect of students' academic discipline on their performance in ESP reading tests, *Language Testing* 2 (2), 192–204.

Alderson, J C and Urquhart, A H (1988) This test is unfair: I'm not an economist, in Carrell, P, Devine, J and Eskey, D (Eds) *Interactive Approaches to Second Language Reading,* Cambridge: Cambridge University Press, 168–182.

Alwright, J and Alwright, R (1977) An approach to the teaching of medical English, in Holden, S (Ed.) *English for Specific Purposes*, Modern English Publications, 58–62.

Anastasi, A (1988) *Psychological Testing*, New York: Macmillan.

Ashton, M (2003) The change process at the paper level. Paper 1, Reading in Weir, C J and Milanovic, M (2002) (Eds) *Continuity and Innovation: Revising the Cambridge Proficiency in English Examination 1913–2002*, Cambridge: University of Cambridge Local Examinations Syndicate and Cambridge University Press, 121–174.

Bachman, L (1990) *Fundamental Considerations in Language Testing*, Oxford: Oxford University Press.

Bachman, L and Palmer, A (1996) *Language testing in practice*, New York: Oxford University Press.

Bachman, L F, Lynch, B and Mason, M (1995) Investigating Variability in Tasks and Rater Judgements in a Performance Test of Foreign Language Speaking, *Language Testing* 12 (2), 238–257.

Bachman, L F, Davidson, F, Ryan, K and Choi, I–C (1995) *An investigation into the comparability of two tests of English as a Foreign Language: The Cambridge–TOEFL comparability study*, Cambridge: University of Cambridge Local Examinations Syndicate and Cambridge University Press.

Ball, F (2002) Developing wordlists for BEC, *Research Notes* 8, 10–13.

Barber, C L (1962) Some Measurable Characteristics of Modern Scientific Prose, reprinted in Swales, J (Ed.) 1988 *Episodes in ESP*, New York: Prentice Hall, 1–16.

Barratt, N (2003) The change process at the paper level. Paper 3, Use of English, in Weir, C J and Milanovic, M (2002) (Eds) *Continuity and Innovation: Revising the Cambridge Proficiency in English Examination 1913–2002*, Cambridge: University of Cambridge Local Examinations Syndicate and Cambridge University Press, 237–314.

Beeching, K (1997) French for specific purposes: the case for spoken corpora, *Applied Linguistics* 18 (3), 374–394.

Berry, V (1996) *Ethical considerations when assessing oral proficiency in pairs*, paper presented at the Language Testing Research Colloquium, Tampere, Finland.

Berry, V (1997) *Gender and personality as factors of interlocutor variability in oral performance tests*, paper presented at the Language Testing Research Colloquium, Orlando, Florida, USA.

Biber, D, Conrad, S and Reppen, R (1998) *Corpus linguistics: investigating language structure and use*, Cambridge: Cambridge University Press.

Bordeaux, D (2002) Communicating for Results, *Motor Age*, 121 (1), 40–42.

Boroughs, R (2003) The change process at the paper level. Paper 4, Listening, in Weir, C J and Milanovic, M (2002) (Eds) *Continuity and Innovation: Revising the Cambridge Proficiency in English Examination 1913–2002*, Cambridge: University of Cambridge Local Examinations Syndicate and Cambridge University Press, 315–364.

Brindley, G (1984) The role of needs analysis in adult ESL programme Design, in Johnson, R K (Ed.) *The Second Language Curriculum*, Cambridge: Cambridge University Press, 63–79.

Brooks, L (2003) *Converting an Observation Checklist for use with the IELTS speaking paper*, Research Notes 11, 20–21, Cambridge ESOL.

Brown, A (1995) The Effect of Rater Variables in the Development of an Occupation Specific Language Performance Test, *Language Testing*, 12 (1), 1–15.

Brown, A (1998) *Interviewer style and candidate performance in the IELTS oral interview*, paper presented at the Language Testing Research Colloquium, Monterey CA.

Brown, A and Lumley, T (1997) Interviewer Variability in Specific-Purpose Language Performance Tests, in Huhta, A Kohonen, V, Kurki-Suonio, L and Luoma, S (Eds) *Current Developments and Alternatives in Language Assessment*, Jyväskylä: University of Jyväskylä and University of Tampere, 137–150.

Brown, J D (1996) *Testing in Language Programs*, Upper Saddle River, NJ: Prentice Hall Regents.

Brown, J D (1997) Computers In Language Testing: Present Research And Some Future Directions, *Language Learning & Technology*, 1 (1), 44–59.

Brown, W M, Palmeta, B and Moore, B (2003) Are there nonverbal cues to commitment? An exploratory study using the zero-acquaintance video presentation paradigm, *Evolutionary Psychology* 1, 42–69.

Buck, G (2001) Assessing Listening, Cambridge: Cambridge University Press.

BULATS (Undated/a) *BULATS Standard Test, EN00*, Cambridge: Cambridge ESOL.

BULATS (Undated/b) *BULATS Speaking Test, EN40*, Cambridge: Cambridge ESOL.

BULATS (Undated/c) *BULATS Writing Test, EN60*, Cambridge: Cambridge ESOL.

Bygate, M (1987) *Speaking*, Oxford: Oxford University Press.

Cambridge ESOL (2002a) *Business English Certificates: BEC Preliminary Examination Report and Past Examination Papers*, Cambridge: Cambridge ESOL Examinations.

Cambridge ESOL (2002b) *Business English Certificates: BEC Vantage Examination Report and Past Examination Papers*, Cambridge: Cambridge ESOL Examinations.

Cambridge ESOL (2002c) *Business English Certificates: BEC Higher Examination Report and Past Examination Papers*, Cambridge: Cambridge ESOL Examinations.

Canale, M and Swain, M (1980) Theoretical Bases of Communicative Approaches to Second Language Teaching and Testing, *Applied Linguistics* 1, 1–47.

Carver, D (1983) Some propositions about ESP, *ESP Journal* 2, 131–137.

Center for Applied Linguistics (2001) *Self-instructional Rater Training Kits for Simulated Oral Proficiency Interviews*, Washington DC: Center for Applied Linguistics.

Chalhoub-Deville, M (Ed.) (1999) *Issues in computer adaptive testing of reading proficiency*, New York: Cambridge University Press.

Chalhoub-Deville, M (2001) Language Testing and Technology: Past And Future, *Language Learning and Technology* 5 (2), 95–98.

Chalhoub-Deville, M (2003) Second language interaction: current perspectives and future trends, *Language Testing* 20 (4), 369–383.

Chapelle, C (1998) Construct definition and validity enquiry in SLA Research, in Bachman, L and Cohen, A (Eds) *Interfaces between second language acquisition and language testing research*, New York: Cambridge University Press, 32–70.

Chia, R C, Allred, L T, Grossnickle, W F and Lee, G W (1998) Effects of attractiveness and gender on the perception of achievement-related variables, *Journal of Social Psychology* 138 (4), 471–477.

CIC (2003a) *Certificazione della conoscenza dell'italiano commerciale: Handbook*, Perugia: Universiti per Stranreiri.

CIC (2003b) *Certificazione della conoscenza dell'italiano commerciale*: http://www.cvcl.it/canale.asp?id=34 (website accessed September 2005).

Clapham, C M (1996) *The Development of IELTS: A Study of the Effect of Background Knowledge on Reading Comprehension*, Cambridge: Cambridge University Press.

Congdon, P J and McQueen, J (2000) The stability of rater severity in large-scale assessment programs, *Journal of Educational Measurement* 37, 163–178.

Coniam, D (2001) The use of audio or video comprehension as an assessment instrument in the certification of English language teachers: A case study, *System* 29, 1–14.

Cumming, A (2001) ESL/EFL instructors' practices for writing assessment: specific purposes or general purposes? *Language Testing* 18 (2), 207–224.

Davies, A (2001) The logic of testing languages for specific purposes, *Language Testing* 18 (2), 133–147.

Dickerson, L (1975) The learner's interlanguage as a system of variable Rules, *TESOL Quarterly* 9 (4), 401–407.

Douglas, D (2000) *Assessing languages for specific purposes*, Cambridge: Cambridge University Press.

Douglas, D (2001) Language for specific purposes assessment criteria: where do they come from? *Language Testing* 18 (2), 171–185.

Dudley-Evans, R and St John, M J (1996) *Report on Business English: A review of research and published teaching materials*, TOEIC Research Report #2, Princeton NJ: Educational Testing Services.

Educational Testing Services (1986) *TOEIC Users Guide*, Princeton NJ: Educational Testing Services.

Educational Testing Services (1998) *TOEIC Technical Manual*, Princeton NJ: Educational Testing Services.

Educational Testing Services (1999) *TOEIC Users Guide*, Princeton NJ: Educational Testing Services.

Educational Testing Services (2002) *TOEIC: Examinees Handboo*k, Princeton: The Chauncey Group International.

Educational Testing Services (2003a) *Test de français international*: TOEIC: www.toeic.-europe.com/pages/eng/tfi.htm

Educational Testing Services (2003b) *Test de français international*: TOEIC–Europe: www.toeic-europe.com/pages/eng/tfi.htm#description

Educational Testing Services (2001) *TSE & SPEAK Score Users Guide: 2001–2002 Edition*, Princeton NJ: Educational Testing Services.

Elder, C (2001) Assessing the language proficiency of teachers: are there any border controls? *Language Testing* 18 (2), 149–170.

Ellis, R (1989) Sources of Intra-Learner Variability in Language, in Gass, S, Madden, C, Preston, D and Selinker, L (Eds) *Variation in Second Language Acquisition, vol. 2: Psycholinguistic Issues*, Clevedon PA: Multilingual Matters, 22–45.

Engelhard, G Jr. (1994) Examining rater error in the assessment of written composition with a many-faceted Rasch model, *Journal of Educational Measurement* 31, 93–112.

Feldt, L S and Brennan, R L (1989) Reliability, in Linn, R L (Ed.) *Educational Measurement*, New York: American Council on Education and Macmillan, 105–146.

ffrench, A (2003) The change process at the paper level, Paper 5, Speaking, in Weir, C J and Milanovic, M (Eds) *Continuity and Innovation: Revising the Cambridge Proficiency in English Examination 1913–2002*, Cambridge: University of Cambridge Local Examinations Syndicate and Cambridge University Press, 367–472.

Field, J (2000) *CPE Revision Paper 4: Listening*, Unpublished internal UCLES report.

Fisher, A G (1994) Development of a functional assessment that adjusts ability measures for task simplicity and rater leniency, in Wilson, M (Ed.) *Objective measurement: Theory into practice*, Vol II. Norwood, New Jersey: Ablex Publishing Corporation, 145–175.

Foot, M C (1999) Relaxing in Pairs, *ELT Journal* 53 (1), 36–41.

Fulcher, G (1996) Testing tasks: issues in task design and the group oral, *Language Testing* 13 (1), 23–51.

Gledhill, C (2000) The Discourse Function of Collocation in Research Article Introductions, *English for Specific Purposes* 19, 115–135.

Gutteridge, M (2003) Assistive technologies for students with special needs, *Research Notes* 12, 15.

Hawkey, R (1978) *English for Special Purposes*, London: British Council English Teaching Centre.

Hawkey, R (1982) *An investigation of inter-relationships between cognitive/affective and social factors and language learning, A longitudinal study of 27 overseas students using English in connection with their training in the United Kingdom*, Unpublished PhD dissertation, Department of English for Speakers of Other Languages, Institute of Education, London.

Hawkey, R (2001) Towards a common scale to describe L2 writing performance, *Research Notes* 5, 9–13.

Hawkey, R (2004) *The development of CELS: A modular approach to testing English Language Skills,* Cambridge: University of Cambridge Local Examinations Syndicate and Cambridge University Press.

Hawkey, R and Barker, F (2004) Developing a common scale for the assessment of writing, *Assessing Writing* 9 (2), 121–159.

Holden, S (Ed.) (1977) *English for Specific Purposes*, Modern English Publications.

Hughes, A (1989) *Language Testing for Teachers*, Cambridge: Cambridge University Press.

Hüllen, W (1981a) Movements on Earth and in the Air: a study of certain verbs occurring in the language of international pilots, *ESP Journal* 1 (2), 141–153.

Hüllen, W (1981b) The teaching of English for special purposes: a linguistic view, in Freudenstein, R et al (Eds) *Language Incorporated: Teaching foreign languages in industry*, Pergamon and Max Hueber Verlag, 57–71.

Hutchinson, T and Walters, A (1987) *English for Specific Purposes: A learning-centred approach*, Cambridge: Cambridge University Press.

Hymes, D H (1972) On Communicative Competence, in Pride, J B and Holmes, J (Eds) *Sociolinguistics: selected readings*, Harmondsworth, Middlesex: Penguin, 269–293.

Jacoby, S and McNamara, T F (1999) Locating competence, *English for Specific Purposes* 18 (3), 213–241.

JETRO (2003a) *The JETRO JRLT, Introduction*, Tokyo: JETRO: www.jetro.go.jp/it/e/bj/guide/index.html

JETRO (2003b) *Sample Questions from the Listening and Reading Comprehension Test*, Tokyo: JETRO: www.jetro.go.jp/it/e/bj/guide/test-sample.html

JETRO (2003c) *The JETRO JOCT, Introductio*n, Tokyo: JETRO: www.jetro.go.jp/it/e/bj/guide/joct.html

Johns, A (1980) Cohesion in written business discourse: some contrasts, *ESP Journal* 1 (1), 35–44.

Jones, N (2000) Background to the revised ALTE 'Can Do' project and the revised Common European Framework, *Research Notes* 2, 11–14.

Jones, N (2001a) *The Can Do Project*, paper presented at the IATEFL Conference, Brighton, April 2001.

Jones, N (2001b) The ALTE 'Can Do' Project and the role of measurement in constructing a proficiency framework, *Research Notes* 5, 5–8.

Just, M A, Carpenter, P A, Keller, T A, Emery, L, Zajac, H and Thulborn K R (2001) Interdependence of Nonoverlapping Cortical Systems in Dual Cognitive Tasks, *NeuroImage* 14 (2), 417–426.

Kennedy, C and Bolitho, R (1984) *English for Specific Purposes*, London: Macmillan Press Ltd.

Kenyon, D (1997) Further research on the efficacy of rater self-training, in Huhta, A, Kohonen, V, Kurki-Suonio, L and Luoma, S (Eds) *Current developments and alternatives in language assessment: Proceedings of LTRC 96*, Jyvaskyla, Finland: University of Jyvaskyla, 257–273.

Labov, W (1963) The social motivation of sound change, *Word* 19, 273–307.

Lackstrom, J, Selinker, L and Trimble, L (1973) Technical rhetorical principles and grammatical choice, *TESOL Quarterly* 7, 127–136.

Lado, R (1961) *Language Testing*, New York: McGraw-Hill.

Lamprianou, I and Pillas, K (2003) *The Effect of Markers and Optional Questions on the Results of High-Stakes Exams*, paper presented at the AERA Conference, Chicago, April 2003.

Lazaraton, A (1992) The structural organisation of a language interview: a conversational analytic perspective, *System* 20 (3), 373–386.

Lazaraton, A (1996) Interlocutor support in Oral Proficiency Interviews: the case of CASE, *Language Testing* 13 (2), 151–172.

Loevinger, J (1954) The attenuation paradox in test theory, *Psychological Bulletin* 51, 493–504.

LCCIEB (1972) *The non-specialist use of foreign languages in industry and commerce*, Sidcup: London Chamber of Commerce and Industry Examinations Board.

LCCIEB (2001a) *English for Business, Level 3: Extended Syllabus*, London: London Chamber of Commerce and Industry Examinations Board.

LCCIEB (2001b) *German for Business, Level 3: Extended Syllabus*, London: London Chamber of Commerce and Industry Examinations Board.

LCCIEB (2001c) *Spanish for Business, Level 3: Extended Syllabus*, London: London Chamber of Commerce and Industry Examinations Board.

LCCIEB (2001d) *French for Business, Level 3: Extended Syllabus*, London: London Chamber of Commerce and Industry Examinations Board.

LCCIEB (Undated) *English for Business, Preliminary Level: Sample Paper*, London: London Chamber of Commerce and Industry Examinations Board, available at www.lccieb.org.uk/lcciebweb/downloads/EFBPrelimSamplePaper.pdf

Longford, N T (1994) Reliability of essay rating and score adjustment, *Journal of Educational and Behavioral Statistics* 19, 171–200.

Lumley, T (1998) Perceptions of language-trained raters and occupational experts in a test of occupational English language proficiency, *English for Specific Purposes* 17 (4), 347–367.

Lumley, T (2000) *The process of the assessment of writing performance: the rater's perspective*, Unpublished PhD dissertation, The University of Melbourne, Australia.

Lumley, T and McNamara, T F (1995) Rater characteristics and rater bias: implications for training, *Language Testing* 12 (1), 54–71.

Lumley, T and O'Sullivan, B (2001) The Effect of Test-Taker Sex, Audience and Topic on Task Performance in Tape-Mediated Assessment of Speaking, *Melbourne Papers in Language Testing* 9 (1), 34–55.

Lumley, T, Lynch, B K and McNamara, T F (1994) A new approach to standard-setting in language assessment, *Melbourne Papers in Language Testing* 3, 19–40.

Lunz, M E and Stahl, J A (1990) Judge consistency and severity across grading periods, *Evaluation and the Health Professions* 13, 425–444.

Lunz, M E, Wright, B D and Linacre, J M (1990) Measuring the impact of judge severity on examination scores, *Applied Measurement in Education* 3, 331–345.

Luoma, S (2004) *Assessing Speaking*, Cambridge: Cambridge University Press.

McNamara T F (1997) 'Interaction' in second language performance assessment: whose performance, *Applied linguistics* 18, 446–466.

McNamara, T F (1996) *Measuring Second Language Performance*, London: Longman.

McNamara, T F and Lumley, T (1997) The effect of interlocutor and assessment mode variables in offshore assessments of speaking skills in occupational settings, *Language Testing* 14 (2), 140–156.

McNeil, L and Valenzuela, A (2000) The Harmful Impact of the TAAS System of Testing in Texas: Beneath the Accountability Rhetoric, in Orfield, G and Kornhaber, M L (Eds) *Raising Standards or Raising Barriers?* New York: The Century Press Foundation.

Milanovic, M and Saville, S (Eds) (1996) *Performance Testing, Cognition and Assessment: selected papers from the 15th Language Testing Research Colloquium, Cambridge and Arnhem*, Cambridge: University of Cambridge Local Examinations Syndicate and Cambridge University Press.

Munby, J (1978) *Communicative Syllabus Design*, Cambridge: Cambridge University Press.

Myford, C M and Wolfe, E W (2000) *Strengthening the Ties that Bind: Improving the Linking Network in Sparsely Connected Rating Designs*, TOEFL Technical Report 15, Princeton NJ: Educational Testing Services.

Myford, C M and Wolfe, E W (2002) When raters disagree, then what: examining a third-rating discrepancy resolution procedure and its utility for identifying unusual patterns of ratings, *Journal of Applied Measurement* 3, 300–324.

Norris, J, Brown, J D, Hudson, T and Yoshioka, J (1998) *Designing Second Language Performance Assessments*, Technical Report #18, Hawai'i: University of Hawai'i Press.

North, B and Schneider, G (1998) Scaling Descriptors for Language Proficiency Scales, *Language Testing* 15, 217–262.

North, B (1996) *The development of a common framework scale of descriptors of language proficiency based on a theory of measurement*, Unpublished PhD dissertation, Thames Valley University.

O'Sullivan, B (1995) *Oral Language Testing: Does the Age of the Interlocutor make a Difference?* Unpublished MA Dissertation. UK: University of Reading.

References

O'Sullivan, B (1999) *Revision of the Test of English for Educational Purposes*, project funded by the Centre for Applied Language Studies, UK: University of Reading.

O'Sullivan, B (2000a) *Towards a Model of Performance in Oral Language Testing*, Unpublished PhD Thesis, UK: University of Reading.

O'Sullivan, B (2000b) Exploring Gender and Oral Proficiency Interview Performance, *System*, 28 (3) 2000:373–386.

O'Sullivan, B (2002a) Learner Acquaintanceship and Oral Proficiency Test Pair-Task Performance, *Language Testing*, 19 (3):277–295.

O'Sullivan, B (2002b) *Defining the Test Taker: Theoretical and Practical Implications*, plenary address at the CTELT 2002, Dubai.

O'Sullivan, B (2003) Computers in Language Testing: A Negative Perspective, Pre-conference Event – *Debate: Computers in Language Testing*, IATEFL Conference, Brighton, April 2003.

O'Sullivan, B and Lu, Y (2003) *An empirical study on examiner deviation from the set interlocutor frame in the IELTS speaking paper*, Research project funded by IELTS/British Council.

O'Sullivan, B and Rignall, M (2001) *A longitudinal analysis of the effect of feedback on rater performance on the IELTS General Training writing module*, Research project funded by IELTS/British Council.

O'Sullivan, B and Rignall, M (2002) *Assessing the value of multi-faceted Rasch bias analysis based feedback to raters for the IELTS writing module*, Research project funded by IELTS/British Council.

O'Sullivan, B and Weir, C (2002) *Research Issues in Speaking Assessment*, Cambridge: UCLES internal report.

O'Sullivan, B and Weir, C (2000) *Issues in Task Difficulty*, Paper presented at the Language Testing Forum, University of Bristol, November 2000.

O'Sullivan, B and Weir, C (2003) *Does the computer make a difference? Reactions of candidates to a computer delivered versus traditional hand written academic forms of the IELTS writing component*, Research project funded by IELTS/British Council.

O'Sullivan, B, Weir, C and Saville, N (2002) Using observation checklists to validate speaking-test tasks, *Language Testing*, 19 (1), 33–56

Oller, J (1979) *Language Tests at School*, New York: Longman.

Pitman Qualifications (2000) *Examinations Report*, London: City & Guilds.

Pitman Qualifications (2002) *Examinations Report*, London: City & Guilds.

Pitman Qualifications (2003) Centre Handbook, London: City & Guilds.

Pitman Qualifications (Undated) *English for Business Communications, Level 1: Past Paper*, London: City & Guilds.

Pitman Qualifications (Undated) *English for Business Communications, Level 2: Past Paper*, London: City & Guilds.

Pitman Qualifications (Undated) *English for Business Communications, Level 3: Past Paper*, London: City & Guilds.

Pollitt, A and Ahmed, A (1999) *A New Model of the Question Answering Process*, Paper presented to the International Association for Educational Assessment in Bled, Slovenia, May 1999. Available at: www.ucles-red.cam.ac.uk/conferencepapers/IAEA1999APAA.pdf

Porter, D (1991a) Affective Factors in Language Testing, in Alderson, J C and North, B (Eds) *Language Testing in the 1990s*, London: Macmillan (Modern English Publications in association with The British Council), 32–40.

Porter, D (1991b) Affective Factors in the Assessment of Oral Interaction: Gender and Status, in Sarinee Arnivan (Ed.) *Current Developments in Language Testing*, Singapore: SEAMEO Regional Language Centre, Anthology Series 25, 92–102.

Porter, D and O'Sullivan, B (1999) The Effect of Audience Age on Measured Written Performance, *System* 27 (1), 65–77.

Porter, D and Shen Shu Hung (1991) Gender, Status and Style in the Interview, *The Dolphin* 21, Aarhus University Press, 117–128.

Rethinasamey, S (in progress) *The effects on rating performance of different training interventions*, PhD research project, Roehampton, UK: Roehampton University.

Robinson, P C (1980) *English for Specific Purposes*, Oxford: Pergamon.

Robinson, P C (1985) *Needs Analysis: From Product to Process*, paper presented at the 5th Annual ESP Symposium, Leuven, Belgium, August 1985.

Royal Society of Arts (1987) *Report of the pilot scheme for the Certificate in EFL for Secretaries*, London: RSA.

Rubinstein, J S, Meyer, D E and Evans, J E (2001) Executive Control of Cognitive Processes in Task Switching, *Journal of Experimental Psychology: Human Perception and Performance* 27 (4), 763–797.

Saville, N (2003) The process of test development and revision within UCLES EFL, in Weir, C J and Milanovic, M (2002) (Eds) *Continuity and Innovation: Revising the Cambridge Proficiency in English Examination 1913–2002*, Cambridge: University of Cambridge Local Examinations Syndicate and Cambridge University Press, 57–120.

Saville, N and Hargreaves P (1999) Assessing speaking in the revised FCE, *ELT Journal* 53 (1), 42–51.

Schmidt, M (1980) Coordinate structures and language universals in Interlanguage, *Language Learning* 30, 397.

Schröder, K (1981) Methods of exploring language needs in industry, in Freudenstein, R et al (Eds) *Language Incorporated: Teaching foreign languages in industry*, Pergamon & Max Hueber Verlag, 43–54.

Selinker, L and Douglas, D (1985) Wrestling with 'Context' in Interlanguage Theory, *Applied Linguistics* 6 (2), 190–204.

Skehan, P (1998) *A Cognitive Approach to Language Learning*, Oxford: Oxford University Press.

Smith, J (1989) Topic and Variation in ITA Oral Proficiency, *English for Specific Purposes* 8, 155–168.

Spolsky, B (1995) *Measured Words*, Oxford: Oxford University Press.

Sprouse, J L and Webb, J E (1994) *The Pygmalion Effect and Its Influence on the Grading and Gender Assignment on Spelling and Essay Assessments*, Unpublished Master's Thesis, University of Virginia. ERIC_NO: ED374096.

Steffensen, M S and Joag-Dev, C (1984) Cultural knowledge and reading in Alderson, J C and Urquhart, A H (Eds) *Reading in a Foreign Language*, London: Longman.

Straus, G S, Miles, A J, Levesque, L L (2001) The effects of videoconference, telephone, and face-to-face media on interviewer and judgments in employment interviews, *Journal of Management* 27 (3), 363–381.

Swales, J (1971) *Writing Scientific English*, London: Thomas Nelson.

Swales, J (1984) ESP comes of age? – 21 years after 'Some Measurable Characteristics of Modern Scientific Prose', *UNESCO Alsed – LSP Newsletter* 7, 2 (19), 9–20.

Sweedler-Brown, C O (1992) The Effect of Training on the Appearance Bias of Holistic Essay Graders, *Journal of Research and Development in Education* 26 (1), 24–29.

Tarone, E (1985) Variability in Interlanguage use: A study of style shifting in morphology and syntax, *Language Learning* 35 (3), 373–404.

Tarone, E (1988) *Variation in Interlanguage*, London: Edward Arnold.

Taylor, L (2000) Investigating the paired speaking format, *Research Notes* 2, 14–15.

Taylor, L and Gutteridge, M (2003) Responding to diversity: providing tests for language learners with disabilities, *Research Notes* 11, 2–4.

Teasdale, A (1994) Authenticity, validity, and task design for tests of well defined LSP domains, in Khoo, R (Ed.) *LSP Problems & Prospects*, Singapore: SEAMEO RELC, 230–242.

Thurstun, J and Candlin, C (1998) Concordancing and the teaching of the vocabulary of Academic English, *English for Specific Purposes* 17 (3), 267–280.

University of Cambridge Local Examinations Syndicate (1994) *CEIBT Review: March–May 1994*, Unpublished internal document.

University of Cambridge Local Examinations Syndicate (1999) *Minimum Professional Requirements*, Unpublished internal document.

University of Cambridge Local Examinations Syndicate (2000a) EFL Research at UCLES, *Research Notes* 1, 2–4.

University of Cambridge Local Examinations Syndicate (2000b) *BEC Handbook*, Cambridge: University of Cambridge Local Examinations Syndicate.

University of Oxford Delegacy of Local Examinations (1990) *Oxford International Business English Certificate*, Oxford: UODLE.

Vargo, S (1994) *Attention to Nonverbal Cues: A View Through the Perceptual Lens of Gender Schema*, Unpublished PhD, Indiana University.

Weighill, B and Shaw, S (2003) The change process at the paper level, Paper 2, Writing, in Weir, C J and Milanovic, M (2002) (Eds) *Continuity and Innovation: Revising the Cambridge Proficiency in English Examination 1913–2002*, Cambridge: University of Cambridge Local Examinations Syndicate and Cambridge University Press, 175–236.

Weigle, S C (1994) Effects of training on raters of ESL compositions, *Language Testing* 11 (2), 197–223.

Weigle, S C (1998) Using FACETS to model rater training effects, *Language Testing* 15 (2), 264–288.

Weir, C J (1983) *Identifying the language needs of overseas students in tertiary education in the United Kingdom*, Unpublished PhD dissertation, UK: University of London.

Weir, C J (1993) *Understanding and Developing Language Tests*, London: Longman.

Weir, C J (2002) *The History of the CPE, 1913–2013*, paper presented at the IATEFL Conference, York April 2002.

Weir, C J (2003a) A Survey of the history of the Certificate of English (CPE) in the twentieth century, in Weir and Milanovic (Eds) *Continuity and Innovation: Revising the Cambridge Proficiency in English Examination 1913–2002*, Cambridge: University of Cambridge Local Examinations Syndicate and Cambridge University Press, 1–56.

Weir, C J (2003b) Conclusions and Recommendations, in Weir and Milanovic (Eds) *Continuity and Innovation: Revising the Cambridge Proficiency in English Examination 1913–2002*, Cambridge: University of Cambridge Local Examinations Syndicate and Cambridge University Press, 473–478.

Weir, C J (2004) *Language Testing and Validity Evidence*, Oxford: Palgrave.

Weir, C J and Milanovic, M (Eds) (2003) *Continuity and Innovation: Revising the Cambridge Proficiency in English Examination 1913–2002*, Cambridge: University of Cambridge Local Examinations Syndicate and Cambridge University Press.

West, R (1994) Needs analysis in language teaching, *Language Teaching* 27 (1), 1–16.

Wilds, C P (1975) The oral interview test, in Jones, R L and Spolsky, B (Eds) *Testing Language Proficiency*, Arlington: Center for Applied Linguistics, 29–44.

Wilson, K M (1989) *Enhancing the interpretation of a norm-referenced second-language test through criterion referencing: A research assessment of experience in the TOEIC testing context*, TOEIC Research Reports #1, Princeton NJ: Educational Testing Services.

Woodford, P E (1982) *An introduction to TOEIC: The initial validity study*, TOEIC Research Summary – Introduction, Princeton NJ: Educational Testing Services.

Index